The Educator's
Encyclopedia
of School Law

Daniel J. Gatti
Richard D. Gatti

PRENTICE HALL
Englewood Cliffs, New Jersey 07632

Prentice-Hall International (UK) Limited, *London*
Prentice-Hall of Australia Pty. Limited, *Sydney*
Prentice-Hall Canada, Inc., *Toronto*
Prentice-Hall Hispanoamericana, S.A., *Mexico*
Prentice-Hall of India Private Limited, *New Delhi*
Prentice-Hall of Japan, Inc., *Tokyo*
Simon & Schuster Asia Pte. Ltd., *Singapore*
Editora Prentice-Hall do Brasil, Ltda., *Rio de Janeiro*

10 9 8 7 6 5 4 3 2 1

This publication is designed to provide accurate and authoritative information in
regard to the subject matter covered. It is sold with the understanding that the
publisher is not engaged in rendering legal, accounting, or other professional
service. If legal advice or other expert assistance is required, the services of a
competent professional person should be sought.
...From the Declaration of Principles jointly adopted by a Committee of the
American Bar Association and a Committee of Publishers and Associations.

Library of Congress Cataloging-in-Publication Data

Gatti, Daniel Jon, 1946–
    The educator's encyclopedia of school law / Daniel J. Gatti
Richard D. Gatti.
      p. cm.
    Includes index.
    ISBN 0-13-237892-2
    1. Educational law and legislation—United States—Encyclopedias.
I. Gatti, Richard DeY, 1947— . II. Title.
KF4114.5.G37 1990
344.73'07'03—dc20   90-7500
[347.304703]   CIP

ISBN 0-13-237892-2

PRENTICE HALL
BUSINESS & PROFESSIONAL DIVISION
A division of Simon & Schuster
Englewood Cliffs, New Jersey 07632

Printed in the United States of America

About the Authors

Daniel and Richard Gatti are both attorneys in private practice in Salem, Oregon. They received their J.D. degrees from Willamette University College of Law, and their B.S. degrees in secondary education and English at Oregon College of Education. The brothers have taught in public schools; Daniel in grades 1 through 10 and Richard at the high school level. Daniel has worked as an education law specialist for the Oregon State Board of Education. Richard worked with the Governor's Task Force on Public Employee Collective Bargaining and was a legal counsel to the Oregon Legislature's House and Senate education committees. Both Richard and Daniel have handled numerous cases involving teachers' and administrators' legal rights and liabilities. They are the authors of *The Teacher and the Law* and *New Encyclopedic Dictionary of School Law,* published by Parker Publishing Company.

with love to
Dan's wife, Donna Jeane Gatti
and
Richard's wife, Deborah Gatti

About This Resource

The Educator's Encyclopedia of School Law provides you with an easy-to-use, easy-to-understand, thoroughly updated guide to the sometimes bewildering array of legal issues that affect you in your job as teacher, administrator, or school board member. While there is no substitute for the advice of a lawyer—especially since state laws can vary—*The Encyclopedia* will provide you with invaluable background and suggest practical guidelines in important areas, including:

- constitutional rights of administrators, teachers, and students
- liability of educators for student injuries
- contract rights and termination procedures
- collective bargaining and employee organizations
- private school aid, prayer, and religion
- tenure laws and hearing procedures
- expulsion procedures and grounds for suspension
- compulsory attendance laws
- the rights of handicapped individuals
- anti-discrimination legislation

In all, there are over two hundred and thirty entries at your fingertips.

Topics are in alphabetical order, with cross-references and a complete index. There is also a Categorical Index that makes looking up any topic a simple matter. You can follow the cross-references to gain a broad understanding of particular areas of the law; you can also use the Categorical Index as a study to major areas, such as equal protection and due process or school board powers and liabilities.

With *The Educator's Encyclopedia of School Law*, you will be armed with practical knowledge about your rights—everything from freedom of speech in the classroom to maternity leave—and your responsibilities, including your risk of personal liability. You will know how courts have been handling current issues such as AIDS, homosexuality, special education, bilingual education, drug testing, homeless students, and more. And you will find all of this written in plain English for educators, not lawyers.

This book should serve to inform you about the basic laws that affect you in your professional duties on a day-to-day basis. Like the law itself, *The Educator's Encyclopedia of School Law* has been designed to provide administrators, teachers, school board members, and students with the safeguards necessary to make the educational system a safe, enjoyable, and exciting place in which to work or study.

A special thank you is in order for the legal research and writing that was so valuable in the final preparation of this manuscript by Ms. Mary E. Broadhurst and Ms. Sample Brown.

Daniel Jon Gatti
Richard DeY Gatti

Categorical Index

ADMINISTRATION OF SCHOOLS AND SCHOOL PERSONNEL

Accountability

Administrative Agencies

Arbitrary, Capricious or Discriminatory Action

Automobiles

Bilingual/Bicultural

Bus Drivers

Chief State School Officer

Civil Rights Act of 1871

Civil Rights Act of 1964

Commissioner of Education

Competency Testing

Contracts

Curriculum

Debts

Demotions

Discrimination

Education for All Handicapped Children Act of 1975

Elementary and Secondary Education Act of 1965

Equal Access Act of 1984

Financing, Schools

Governmental Immunity

Kindergartens

Labor Unions

Lease of School Property

Liability

Music

Nonresidents

Personnel Records

Police

Principal

Private Schools

Protests

Rehabilitation Act of 1973

Removal from Office

Residence—Students

Residence—Teachers

Reorganization

Safe Place Statutes

School Boards

School Calendar

School Closures

School District Organization

School Funds

Smoking

Special Education

Strikes

Structure of School System

Superintendent

Suspension, Teachers/Students (*see also* Due Process; Expulsion of Students)

Textbooks, Fee

Transfers

Transportation

Tuition

Union Security

Unions

Vice Principals

Vouchers

Workshops

CHURCH AND STATE RELATIONSHIPS

Anti-evolution Statutes

Bible Reading

Child-Benefit Theory

Censorship

Compulsory Education

Constitutional Amendments

Constitutional Law

Evolution

Equal Access Act of 1984

External Benefit Theory

Flag Salute

Fundamental Interest Theory

God, Act of

Loyalty Oaths

Pledge of Allegiance

Prayers

Private and Parochial School Aid

Private Schools

Released Time

Religion

Sex Education

Shared Time

Textbooks

Vaccination

Vouchers

COLLECTIVE BARGAINING AND SCHOOL NEGOTIATIONS

Agency Shop

Annual or Long-Term Contracts

Arbitration

Assembly, Right of

Bargaining Laws

Closed Shop

Collective Bargaining

Contracts

Discrimination

Dues Checkoff

Employee Organizations

Executive Sessions

Factfinding

Grievances

Mediation

Meet and Confer Bargaining Laws

Negotiations

Nonrenewals

Renewals

Reorganization

Sanctions

Scope of Bargaining

Strikes

Union Security

Unions

CONSTITUTIONAL RIGHTS OF SCHOOL PERSONNEL (*see also* Contract Duties and Protections)

Academic Freedom

Anti-evolution Statutes

Antisubversive Laws

Appearance

Arbitrary, Capricious or Discriminatory Action

Assembly, Right of

Association, Freedom of

Beards (*see* Appearance)

Censorship

Civil Rights Act of 1871

Civil Rights Act of 1964

Constitutional Amendments

Constitutional Law

Curriculum

Discrimination

Dress (*see* Appearance)

Due Process

Equal Pay Act

Equal Access Act of 1984

Equal Pay Act

Fifth Amendment

First Amendment

Flag Salute

Fourteenth Amendment

Free Speech

Hair (*see* Appearance)

Homosexuality

Immorality

Loyalty Oaths

Moral Turpitude

Obscenity

Outside Employment

Pledge of Allegiance

Prayers

Privacy

Protests

Religion

Self-Incrimination

Silent, Right to Remain

Speech

CONSTITUTIONAL RIGHTS OF STUDENTS

Abortion

Appearance

Arbitrary, Capricious or
   Discriminatory Action

Assembly, Student Right of

Association

Athletics

Beards (*see* Appearance)

Bible Reading

Censorship

Civil Rights Act of 1871

Civil Rights Act of 1964

Commencement Exercises

Conscientious Objectors

Constitutional Amendments

Constitutional Law

Curriculum

Diplomas

Discrimination

Dress (*see* Appearance)

Drug Testing

Due Process

Equal Access Act of 1984

Equal Protection

Expulsion of Students

Fifth Amendment

First Amendment

Flag Salute

Fourteenth Amendment

Free Speech

Immorality

Library Censorship

Loyalty Oaths

Married Students

Moral Turpitude

Newspapers (*see* Publications)

Obscenity

Pledge of Allegiance

Prayers

Pregnant Students

Protests

Records

Religion

School Publications

Search and Seizure, Unreasonable

Secret Societies

Self-incrimination

Silent, Right to Remain

Speech

Underground Newspapers (*see* School
   Publications)

CONTRACT DUTIES AND PROTECTIONS
(*see also* Constitutional Law)

Abolition of Positions

Absence from Class

Accountability

Agreement

Annual Contracts

Assignments

Arbitrary, Capricious or
  Discriminatory Action

Association

Authority, Teachers

Capacity

Certification

Collective Bargaining

Constitutional Law

Continuing Contracts

Contracts

Damages

Due Process

Equal Pay Act

Equal Protection

Evaluation (*see* Accountability)

Express Authority

Free Speech (*see* Academic freedom)

Grievances

Implied Authority

Implied Contract

Instruction

Insubordination (*see* Contracts; Due
  Process; Tenure)

Labor Unions

Leaves of Absence

Liability

Mass Resignation

Maternity Leave

Merit Pay

Military Leave

Moral Turpitude

Nonrenewal

Notice

Offer

Outside Employment

Paternity Leave

Peace Corps

Renewals

Sabbatical Leave

Salary Schedules

Severance Payments

Sick Leave

Shared Time

Tenure

Unions

DISCIPLINE AND CONTROL OF STUDENTS (*see also* Constitutional Law; Injuries to Students and Staff)

Absence

Academic Freedom

Academic Penalties

Accidents (*see* Negligence)

Activity Funds

Assembly, Student Right of

Assignments

Attendance of Pupils

Automobiles

Battery

Child Abuse

Constitutional Amendments

Constitutional Law

Corporal Punishment

Detention

Discipline

Drug Testing

Due Process

Express Authority

Expulsion of Students

Extracurricular Activities

Field Trips

Free Speech (*see* Academic Freedom)

Implied Authority

In loco parentis

Lockers (*see* Search and Seizure)

Married Students

Negligence

Newspapers (*see* School Publications)

Obscenity

Parental Authority

Parental Liability

Playgrounds

Police

Rules

School Publications

Search and Seizure, Unreasonable

Secret Societies

Sexual Abuse

Student Records (*see also* Defamation)

Supervision

Underground Newspapers (*see* Academic Freedom; School Publications)

DISMISSALS, GRIEVANCES, AND TENURE

Abolition of Positions

Accountability

Annual or Long-Term Contracts

Arbitrary, Capricious or Discriminatory Action

Arbitration

Collective Bargaining

Constitutional Amendments

Constitutional Law

Contracts

Damages

Decertification

Demotions

Due Process

Evaluation (*see* Accountability)

Grievances

Mediation

Meet and Confer Bargaining Laws

Nonrenewal

Offer, Contract

Privacy

Probationary Teachers

Reinstatement

Renewal

Reorganization

Salary Schedules

Sanctions

Scope of Bargaining

Severance Payments

Shared Time

Strikes

Tenure

Testing

Transfers

Union Security

Unions

Witnesses

EQUAL PROTECTION AND DUE PROCESS

Abolition of Positions

Academic Freedom

Accountability

Achievement Tests

Arbitrary, Capricious or
  Discriminatory Action

Assignments

Athletics

Civil Rights Act of 1871

Civil Rights Act of 1964

Constitutional Amendments

Constitutional Law

Contracts

Cross-examination

Decertification

Discipline

Discrimination

Drug Testing

Due Process

Education for All Handicapped
  Children Act of 1975

Elementary and Secondary Education
  Act of 1965

Equal Access Act of 1984

Equal Pay Act

Equal Protection

Evaluation (*see* Accountability)

Explusion of Students

Fifth Amendment (*see* Constitutional
  Amendments; Constutitional Law)

Fourteenth Amendment (*see*
  Constitutional Amendments;
  Constitutional Law)

Grievances

Intelligence Testing

Liability

Mental Examinations

Nonrenewals

Police

Pregnancy Discrimination Act

Privacy

Rehabilitation Act of 1973

Removal from Office

Renewals

School Board Policies

Search and Seizure, Unreasonable

Search Warrant

Self-incrimination

Transfers of Teachers

INJURIES TO STUDENTS AND STAFF

Abortion

Absence from Class

AIDS (*see* Communicable Diseases)

Agent

Assault

Assumption of Risk

Athletics

Authority, Teachers and Students

Automobiles

Battery

Burden of Proof

Bus Drivers

Child Abuse

Communicable Diseases

Comparative Negligence

Contributory Negligence

Corporal Punishment

Damages

Defamation

Detenton

Discipline (*see* Academic Penalties;
    Expulsion of Students; Negligence;
    Supervision)

Extracurricular Activities

False Imprisonment

Field Trips

Foreseeability

God, Act of

Governmental Immunity

Imputed Negligence

Intentional Tort

Liability

Malpractice (*see* Accountability)

Medical Services

Medication

Mental Distress

Negligence

Omissions

Parental Liability

Playgrounds

Reasonable and Prudent

Rules

Slander

Supervision

Trespass to Personal Property

Vocational Programs

JUDICIAL CONSIDERATION

Burden of Proof

Certiorari, Writ of

Common Law

Contempt of Court

Courts, Organization

Cross-examination

Damages

Defendant

Enjoin

Exhibits

Express Authority

Felony

Hearsay

Implied Authority

In loco parentis

Injunction

Malice

Mandamus

Mechanic's Lien

Misdemeanor

Plaintiff

Police

Preponderance of Evidence

Presumptions

Question of Fact

Question of Law

Quo Warranto

Search Warrant

Self-defense

Stare decisis

Statute of Limitations

Statutes

Subpoena

Substantive Law

Torts

Waiver

Witnesses

SCHOOL ORGANIZATIONS, PROPERTY, FUNDS AND FINANCING

Activity Funds

Athletics

Bonds

Buildings

Common Schools

Construction

Curriculum

Debts (*see* Bonds)

Donations

Equal Access Act of 1984

Equality of Educational Opportunity

Federal Aid to Education

Fees

Financing, Schools

Funds, School

Mergers (*see* Reorganization)

Property

Reorganization

School Closures

Shared Time

Structure of School System

Tuition

SCHOOL BOARD POWERS AND LIABILITIES

Administrative Agencies

Authority (*see* School Boards)

Boards of Education

Conflict of Interest

Discretionary Acts

Donations, Acceptance of

Express Authority

Funds

Governmental Immunity

Liability (*see* Governmental Immunity)

Malpractice

Ministerial Acts

Minutes (*see* School Boards, meetings)

Municipal Corporation

Open Hearing

Quorum

Ratification

Records (*see* School Boards, Meetings)

Removal from Office

Reorganization

Save-Harmless Statutes

School Boards

Structure of School System

Comprehensive Table of Topics

A

Ability Grouping, 1

Abolition of Positions, 1

Abortion, 3

Absence, 4

Absence from Class, Liability, 5

Academic Freedom, 6

Academic Penalties, Students, 9

Accidents (*See* Negligence; Torts)

Achievement Testing (*See* Competency Testing, Students)

Accountability, 11

Acquisition of Property (*See* Buildings; Property)

Activity Funds, 11

Administrative Agencies, 11

Administrators (*See* Constitutional Law; Principal; Superintendent; Vice-Principal)

Agency Shop, 13

Agent, 14

Aides, Teacher (*See* Teacher Aides)

AIDS (*See* Communicable Diseases)

Annual or Long-Term Contracts, 14

Anti-Evolution Statutes, 15

Antisubversive Laws, 16

Appearance, Administrators and Teachers, 17

Appearance, Students, 19

Arbitrary, Capricious, or Discriminatory Action, 22

Arbitration, 25

Assault, 26

Assembly, Student Right of, 28

Assignment to Grade and School, Students, 32

Assignments, Nonclassroom, 33

Association, Freedom of, 35

Assumption of Risk, 40

Athletics, Funds (*See* Activity Funds; Funds)

Athletics, Participation Requirements, 41

Athletics, Sex Discrimination in, 42

Attendance of Pupils (*See* Compulsory Education)

Authority, Parents (*See* Parental Authority)

Authority, School Board (*See* School Boards)

Authority, Teachers, (*See* In Loco Parentis; Rules)

Automobiles, 45

B

Bargaining (*See* Collective Bargaining; Meet and Confer Bargaining Laws)

Battery, 47

Beards (*See* Appearance; Constitutional Law)

Bible Reading, 49

Bids (*See* Buildings, Construction)

Bilingual/Bicultural, 51

Boards of Education, 52

Bonds, 53

Borrowing (*See* Bonds)

Boundaries (*See* Reorganization)

Budgets (*See* Funds)

Buildings, 54

Burden of Proof, 58

Bus Drivers, 59

Busing, 59

C

Capacity, 61

Censorship (*See* Academic Freedom; Constitutional Law; Library Censorship; Obscenity; School Publications)

Certification, 62

Ceriorari, Writ of, 64

Chief State School Officer, 65

Child Abuse, 65

Child-Benefit Theory, 66

Church-State Relations (*See* Bible Reading; Prayers; Private and Parochial School Aid; Religion; Shared Time)

Civil Rights Act of 1871, 68

Civil Rights Act of 1964, 69

Closed Shop (*See* Union Security)

Collective Bargaining, 71

Commencement Exercises, 76

Commissioner of Education, 77

Common Law, 78

Common Schools, 78

Communicable Diseases, 79

Comparative Negligence, 81

Competency Testing, Students, 81

Competency Testing, Teachers (*See* Certification)

Compulsory Education, 82

Conflict of Interest, 84

Consolidation (*See* Reorganization)

Constitutional Amendments of the United States, 85

Constitutional Law—Students, 88

Constitutional Law—Teachers and Administrators, 91

Construction (*See* Buildings)

Contempt of Court, 93

Continuing Contracts, 93

Contracts, 94

Contracts, Construction (*See* Buildings)

Contributory Negligence, 103

Controversial Matters, Right to Teach, 103

Corporal Punishment, 104

Court Organization—Federal, 105

Court Organization—State, 105

Cross-Examination, 109

Curriculum, 109

D

Damages, Contracts, 113

Damages, Torts, 115

Debts, Authority of School to Incur (*See* Bonds)

Decertification, 115

Defamation, 116

Defendant, 118

Demotions, 119

Detention, 120

Diplomas, 120

Discharge of Teachers (*See* Due Process; Privacy; Tenure)

Discipline, Students, 121

Discretionary Act, 122

Discrimination, 122

District Reorganization (*See* Reorganization)

Donation, Acceptance of, 124

Dress, Manner of (*See* Appearance; Constitutional Law)

Drug Testing, 124

Drugs (*See* Drug Testing; Search and Seizure)

Dual Enrollment (*See* Shared Time) 125

Due Process, 125

Dues Checkoff, 132

Duties of Teachers (*See* Contracts; Negligence)

E

Education for All Handicapped Children Act of 1975, 133

Elementary and Secondary Education Act of 1965, 143

Emancipated Students, 143

Emotional Distress (*See* Intentional Infliction of Emotional Distress)

Employee Organizations, Right to Join (*See* Assembly; Collective Bargaining; Constitutional Law)

Enjoin, 144

Equal Access Act of 1984, 144

Equal Employment Opportunity Commission (*See* Civil Rights Act of 1964; Discrimination; Equal Protection)

Equal Pay Act, 145

Equal Protection, 146

Equipment, 149

Evaluation, 150

Evolution (*See* Academic Freedom; Anti-Evolution Statutes; Religion)

Executive Sessions, School Board (*See* School Boards)

Exhibits, 152

Express Authority, 152

Expulsion of Students, 152

Extracurricular Activities (*See* Assignments, Nonclassroom; Athletics; Constitutional Law; Funds; Married Students; Negligence)

F

Factfinding, 159

False Imprisonment, 159

Federal Aid to Education (*See* Civil Rights Act of 1964; Constitutional Law; Education for all Handicapped Children Act of 1975; Elementary and Secondary Education Act of 1965; Private and Parochial School Aid)

Federal Courts (*See* Court Organization—Federal)

Fees, 161

Felony, 162

Field Trips (*See* Governmental Immunity; Negligence Rules)

Fifth Amendment (*See* Constitutional Amendments; Self-incrimination; Silent, Right to Remain)

Financing, Schools, 162

First Aid (*See* Medical Services)

First Amendment (*See* Academic Freedom; Assembly; Constitutional Amendments; Constitutional Law; Religion)

Flag Salute, 163

Foreseeability, 165

Fourteenth Amendment (*See* Constitutional Amendments; Constitutional Law; Due Process; Equal Protection; Expulsion of Students)

Fraternities (*See* Assembly, Student Right of; Association, Freedom of; Constitutional Law; Religion; Secret Societies)

Free Speech (*See* Academic Freedom; Assembly, Student Right of; Bible Reading; Constitutional Amendments; Constitutional Law; Obscenity; Prayers)

Fundamental Interest Theory, 167

Funds, 167

G

Gifts, Acceptance of (*See* Donations)

God, Act of, 171

Governmental Immunity, 172

Graduation Requirements (*See* Curriculum; Diplomas)

Grievances, 175

H

Handicapped Students (*See* Education for All Handicapped Children Act of 1975; Rehabilitation Act of 1973)

Health Programs (*See* Abortion; Athletics; Funds; Medical Services; Sex Education; Vaccination)

Hearings (*See* Constitutional Law; Due Process; Expulsion of Students; Open Hearings; School Boards)

Hearsay, 179

Home Instruction (*See* Compulsory Education; Private Schools)

Homeless Students (*See* Resident—Students)

Homework, 180

Homosexuality, 180

I

Immorality (*See* Constitutional Law; Contracts; Due Process; Homosexuality; Privacy)

Immunity (*See* Governmental Immunity)

Immunizations (*See* Vaccination)

Implied Authority, 185

Implied Contract, 186

Indebtedness (*See* Bonds)

Injunction, 186

Injuries (*See* Corporal Punishment; Governmental Immunity; Torts; Negligence)

In Loco Parentis, 187

Innoculation (*See* Vaccination)

Instruction, 187

Insubordination (*See* Arbitrary, Capricious, or Discriminatory Action; Contracts; Due Process; Privacy)

Insurance (*See* Funds; Governmental Immunity)

Integration (*See* Busing; Discrimination)

Intelligence Testing, 188

Intentional Infliction of Emotional Distress, 190

Intentional Tort, 191

K

Kindergartens, 193

L

Labor Unions (*See* Agency Shop; Assembly; Collective Bargaining; Constitutional Law; Union Security)

Lease of School Property (*See* Buildings; Property)

Leaves of Absence, 195

Letters of Intent (*See* Contracts; Nonrenewal; Renewals)

Liability, 196

Libel (*See* Academic, Freedom; Constitutional Law; Defamation; School Publications)

Library Censorship, 197

Lockers, Searches (*See* Constitutional Law; Search and Seizure)

Loyalty, Oaths, 199

M

Maintenance of Property (*See* Buildings, Maintenance)

Malice, 201

Malpractice, 201

Mandamus, 202

Mandatory Education (*See* Compulsory Education)

Marriage (*See* Married Students; Maternity Leave)

Married Students, 203

Mass Resignation, 206

Maternity Leave, 206

Mechanics Lien, 208

Mediation, 209

Medical Services, 209

Medication, 211

Meet and Confer Bargaining Laws, 212

Meetings, 213

Mental and Physical Examinations, 213

Mental Distress, Infliction of (*See* Intentional Infliction of Emotional Distress)

Mergers (*See* Reorganization)

Merit Pay, 214

Methods, 215

Military Leave, 215

Ministerial Acts, 216

Minutes, School Board (*See* School Boards)

Misdemeanor, 216

Mitigation (*See* Contracts; Damages)

Money (*See* Activity Funds; Bonds; Fees; Funds)

Moral Turpitude, 217

Municipal Corporations, 217

Music, 217

N

Negligence, 219

Negotiable Issues (*See* Collective Bargaining; Scope of Bargaining)

Negotiations (*See* Collective Bargaining; Meet and Confer Bargaining; Scope of Bargaining)

Newspapers (*See* Academic Freedom, Constitutional Law; Obscenity; School Publications)

Nonpublic Schools (*See* Private and Parochial School Aid; Private Schools)

Nonrenewal, 222

Notice (*See* Due Process; Nonrenewal; Renewals)

Nurses (*See* Medical Services)

O

Oaths (*See* Loyalty Oaths)

Obscene Literature (*See* Academic Freedom; Constitutional Law; Library Censorship; Obscenity; School Publications)

Obscenity, 225

Offer, Contract, 228

Officers (*See* Principal; School Boards; Superintendent; Vice-Principal)

Omission, 228

Open Hearing, 229

Oral Contract (*See* Contracts)

Outside Employment, 230

P

Parental Authority, 231

Parental Liability, 232

Parochial Schools (*See* Private and Parochial School Aid; Private Schools)

Paternity Leave, 232

Peace Corps Leaves, 233

Performance Bonds (*See* Buildings)

Permission Slips (*See* Assumption of Risk; Detention; Negligence; Parental Authority; Parental Liability; Supervision)

Personal Property (*See* Trespass to Personal Property)

Personnel Records, 234

Petitions (*See* Grievance)

Physical Education (*See* Athletics; Curriculum; Negligence)

Physical Examinations (*See* Compulsory Education; Medical Services; Vaccination)

Picketing (*See* Strikes)

Plaintiff, 235

Playgrounds, 236

Pledge of Allegiance, 236

Police, 237

Policies, School Board (*See* School Boards)

Political Activities (*See* Antisubversive Laws; Association, Freedom of;
    Constitutional Law)

Prayers, 238

Pregnant Students, 241

Preponderance of Evidence, 243

Press, Freedom of (*See* Academic Freedom; Constitutional Law; Library
    Censorship; School Publications)

Presumption, 244

Principal, 244

Privacy, 245

Private and Parochial School Aid, 251

Private Schools, 257

Probationary Teachers, 258

Profanity, 260

Property, 261

Protests (*See* Assembly, Right of; Association, Right of; Constitutional Law)

Provisional Certification (*See* Certification; Decertification)

Proximate cause (*See* Negligence)

Public Office (*See* Conflict of Interest)

Publications (*See* Constitutional Law; Library Censorship; Obscenity; School
    Publications)

Punishment (*See* Categorical Index; Discipline)

Q

Qualified Privilege (*See* Defamation)

Question of Fact, 265

Question of Law, 266

Quo Warranto, 266

Quorum, 267

R

Race Relations (*See* Discrimination)

Ratification, 269

Released Time, 270

Reasonable and Prudent, 271

Records (*See* Defamation; Personnel Records; Student Records)

Rehabilitation Act of 1973, 272

Reinstatement, 274

Related Services, 275

Religion, 275

Remedies (*See* Damages; Reinstatement)

Removal from Office, 278

Renewals, Contract, 279

Reorganization, 281

Recission (*See* Contracts)

Residence, Students, 283

Residence, Teachers, 285

Rules, 285

S

Sabbatical Leave, 289

Safe Place Statutes, 289

Salary Schedules, 290

Sanctions, 291

Save-Harmless Statutes, 291

School Boards, 291

School Buildings (*See* Bonds; Buildings; Property)

School Calendar, 299

School Closures, 300

School Funds (*See* Funds)

School Publications, 300

Scope of Procedure, 302

Search and Seizure, Unreasonable, 304

Search Warrant, 306

Secret Societies, 306

Segregation (*See* Discrimination)

Self-Defense, 307

Self-Incrimination, Students, 307

Severance Payments, 308

Sex, Discrimination Based on (*See* Athletics; Civil Rights Act of 1964; Constitutional Law; Discrimination; Equal Protection; Maternity Leave; Paternity Leave; Pregnancy Discrimination Act; Pregnant Students)

Sex Education, 310

Sexual Abuse, 311

Shared Time, 312

Shop Classes (*See* Vocational Programs)

Sick Leave, 313

Silent, Right to Remain, 314

Slander (*See* Defamation)

Smoking, 315

Sororities (*See* Secret Societies)

Sovereign Immunity (*See* Governmental Immunity)

Special Education, 317

Special Meetings, School Board (*See* School Boards, Meetings)

Speech, Freedom of (*See* Academic Freedom; Constitutional Law; Pledge of Allegiance; Self-Incrimination; Silent, Right to Remain)

Sports (*See* Athletics; Curriculum; Married Students; Negligence; Sports-Related Injuries; Supervision)

Sports-Related Injuries, 317

Spring Notification (*See* Annual or Long-Term Contracts; Contracts; Renewal; Tenure)

Stare Decisis, 318

State Board of Education (*See* Structure of the School System)

State Commissioner of Public Instruction (*See* Chief State School Officer)

State Superintendent of Public Instruction (*See* Chief State School Officer)

Statute of Limitations, 319

Statutes, 320

Strikes, 320

Structure of the School System, 324

Student Liability, 326

Student Records, 327

Student Rights (*See* Categorical Index regarding Constitutional Rights of Students and Discipline and Control of Students)

Subpoena, 330

Substantive Law, 330

Subversive Organizations (*See* Antisubversive Laws; Assembly; Constitutional Law; Loyalty Oaths)

Summer School, 330

Superintendent, 331

Superintendent of Public Instruction (*See* Chief State School Officer; Superintendent)

Supervision, 334

Supplemental Contract (*See* Contracts)

Suspension of Students (*See* Expulsion of Students)

Suspension of Teachers (*See* Categorial Index regarding Dismissals, Grievances, and Tenure)

T

Talented and Gifted Students, 337

Teacher Aide, 337

Tenure, 338

Testing, Student, 342

Testing, Teacher (*See* Mental and Physical Examination; Merit Pay)

Textbooks, Adoption of (*See* Anti-Evolution Statutes; Curriculum; Religion; School Boards)

Textbooks, Free, 343

Threats (*See* Assault; Battery)

Tort, 344

Tracking of Students (*See* Ability Grouping)

Transfers of Students, 344

Transfers of Teachers, 345

Transportation, 346

Trespass to Personal Property, 348

Tuition, 349

U

Underground Newspapers (*See* Academic Freedom; Constitutional Law; Library Censorship; Obscenity; School Publications)

Uniforms (*See* Appearance; Curriculum; Rules)

Union Security, 353

Unions (*See* Assembly; Collective Bargaining; Union Security)

V

Vaccination, 355
Vice-Principals, 356
Vocational Programs, 356
Vouchers, 357

W

Waiver, 361
Witnesses, 361
Workshops, 362

ABILITY GROUPING

Many school districts group students into various "tracks" or ability groups. These groupings are often made based upon INTELLIGENCE TESTING and have come under attack due to the way the groupings are determined and/or the end result of the tracking. The Eleventh Circuit Court of Appeals has held that ability grouping will be prohibited only if it is found to be a ploy to resegregate students on the basis of race.[1] In addition, the same court has upheld the use of ability grouping based upon evidence that ability grouping provides better educational opportunities for minority students.[2]

For a discussion of the challenges made regarding the use of intelligence tests for placement purposes, see INTELLIGENCE TESTING.

ABOLITION OF POSITIONS

As the population growth rate decreases and as school districts consolidate in an effort to provide greater services at less expense, the termination of teachers, tenured or not, for reasons unrelated to their behavior or character will undoubtedly increase. This is a foreseeable trend due to

---

[1]*Bester v. Tuscaloosa City Board of Educ.,* 722 F.2d 1514 (11th Cir. 1984).

[2]*Georgia State Conference of Branches of NAACP v. State of Georgia,* 775 F.2d 1403 (11th Cir. 1985).

declining student enrollment, a greater unwillingness by weak teachers to resign when pressured to do so, changes in program formats, reduced school budgets, reduction in tax revenues, and the reduction or elimination of federal funding.

As a general rule, a teacher or administrator has no legal property right to a position which is being abolished for bona fide reasons. Again, this is true even if the teacher or administrator is tenured and even though the applicable state STATUTES make no reference to abolition of position as a grounds for dismissal. Such action is often characterized with the abbreviation, RIF—"reduction in force."

To avoid the appearance that the action might be arbitrary, capricious, or unreasonable, the SCHOOL BOARD must establish three factors:

1. That the reason for abolition was bona fide.
2. That the position was actually abolished.
3. That no discrimination was involved.

If any one of these factors is not established, the teacher or administrator has a right to retain his or her position. For example, in two cases, the COURTS held that a school district's decision to reduce its staff was based on insufficient justification of its need to do so.[3] When a guidance counselor "got crossways politically" with the board and superintendent by campaigning against them, the board and superintendent claimed a RIF and dismissed the teacher although no evidence suggested the need for elimination of the position. The court saw this as a violation of the teacher's FIRST AMENDMENT right of free speech and struck down the dismissal as punitive.[4] When fiscal insolvency is claimed, the board must substantiate actions with empirical evidence of budgetary constraints.[5] In another case, a statute authorized the dismissal of tenured teachers of woodworking and drafting courses where the entire course offerings in these areas were eliminated due to a decrease in enrollment. The court held that the dismissal would be reversed where a school district failed to prove that the district had made every reasonable effort to transfer the teachers to other teaching positions for which they were qualified if there were other teaching positions that were not being discontinued.[6]

The school district may not dismiss a tenured teacher whose position is abolished and retain a nontenured teacher in a similar position by making

---

[3]*Altoona Area Vocational Technical School v. Pollard,* 520 A.2d 99 (Pa. 1987); *Schnabel v. Alcester School District No. 61-1,* 295 N.W.2d 340 (S.D. 1980).

[4]*Clairborne Co. Bd. of Educ. v. Martin,* 500 So. 2d 981 (Miss. 1986).

[5]*Trolson v. Bd. of Educ.* 424 N.W.2d 881 (Neb. 1988).

[6]*Cooper v. Fair Dismissal Appeals Board,* 570 P.2d 1005 (Or. App. 1977).

a minor curriculum change.[7] Also, several cases have held that when two or more districts are consolidated, teachers who had TENURE in the old districts retain their tenure status in the new district. However, several cases have resulted in a contrary decision and hold that the school board of the consolidated district must remain free to exercise discretion in the initial staffing of the new district and, therefore, the tenure rights do not continue. This split of authority remains unresolved and dependent upon the individual state courts' decisions, statutes, and appropriate COLLECTIVE BARGAINING agreements.

Sometimes, there is one new school constructed to replace two older schools; and, at times, there are two persons who have approximately equal rights to a new position which is being created to replace the two other positions. There are no easy general rules which apply to this situation, but several applicable cases provide an insight into the kinds of factors the courts are likely to consider in deciding who is entitled to the new position. In one case, where budget cuts forced the relocation of a PRINCIPAL to teach a fifth grade class, the court held that the reorganization and subsequent reassignment of school faculty to a lesser position was a valid action.[8] However, the transfer from principal of a junior high school to assistant principal of a high school was considered a demotion, which conduct required a hearing.[9] In an earlier case involving REORGANIZATION, two principals were involved. The board decided to have one principal for grades 7 to 12 and abolished the junior high school principalship. The junior high school principal initiated a court case to compel the board to grant him the "new" principalship instead of the high school principal. The court ruled in favor of the junior high school principal because the two principals were equally qualified, but the plaintiff had seniority as well as a secondary school principal's certificate.[10] Boards must carefully consider nondiscriminatory criteria, document the particular choices, and follow applicable procedures.[11]

See also DUE PROCESS; TENURE.

ABORTION

In 1989, an Alabama student was allowed to sue her school counselor and VICE PRINCIPAL for allegedly coercing the student and her boyfriend into

---

[7]*Hein v. Bd. of Educ.,* 733 P.2d 1270 (Kan. App. 1987).

[8]*Brown v. School District of Cheltenham Township,* 417 A.2d 1337 (Pa. 1980).

[9]*Walsh v. Sto-Rox School District,* 532 A.2d 547 (Pa. 1987).

[10]*Jadick v. Board of Education of the City School District of Beacon,* 204 N.E.2d 202 (N.Y. 1964).

[11]*Taborn v. Hammonds,* 350 S.E.2d 880 (N.C. App. 1986).

terminating the girl's pregnancy.[12] This highly volatile issue involves rights protected under Section 1983 of the CIVIL RIGHTS ACT OF 1871, freedom of RELIGION, and FIRST AMENDMENT considerations protected through CONSTITUTIONAL LAW. In this case, the vice principal and counselor paid the student mother and father money to perform "menial tasks" so that funds could be raised to pay for the procedure. The court indicated that the minor child still in school had the constitutional right to choose whether to abort or bear her child. In addition to allowing the students to sue the district, the court allowed the parents of both the boy and the girl to file separate claims for interfering with PARENTAL AUTHORITY to consult with and raise their children. While the counselor did not have the duty to notify the parents of the student's pregnancy, that same counselor could not prevent the student from seeking parental guidance which in turn would violate "parental freedom to inculcate one's children with values and standards" held by the parents.

ABSENCE

There are COMPULSORY EDUCATION laws governing students in nearly all states, and these laws must be followed. In order to enforce the law, it is reasonable for the district to require a note from the student's parent or, in cases of long illnesses, a note from a doctor. Requiring certification of a child's illness (which is serious enough to make the student unable to attend school) from a physician is a valid exercise of state authority.[13] Excused absences include those which are caused by illness, bereavement, family emergency, or situations beyond the student's control.

One court upheld the EXPULSION for absenteeism of a student who, although on the school grounds, cut classes to watch football practice.[14] If vacations are taken by the child's family during the middle of the school year, advance notice should be given to the school and arrangements should be made for the student to do the necessary assignments and to make up any important lessons which are missed. Parents can be penalized if the student is declared a habitual or chronic truant under criminal codes of most states. In addition, it is appropriate for local districts to enact reasonable rules which may penalize students for unexcused absences by taking away credits for a quarter or even a semester, as long as the students have notice and proper procedures are followed.

See also ABSENCE FROM CLASS, Liability.

---

[12]*Arnold v. Board of Education of Escambia County,* 880 F.2d 305 (11th Cir. 1989).

[13]*People v. Berger,* 441 N.E.2d 915 (Ill. 1982).

[14]*Williams v. Board of Education,* 626 S.W.2d 361 (Ark. 1982).

ABSENCE FROM CLASS, Liability

Although districts are not automatically responsible for every student injury which occurs, liability may exist for injuries resulting from negligent SUPERVISION. NEGLIGENCE is a QUESTION OF FACT which is determined by looking at all of the facts and circumstances surrounding an absence. Four elements must always be present before an injured party can secure monetary DAMAGES for negligence: (1) duty, (2) violation of duty, (3) the violation must cause the injury, and (4) an actual injury.

School authorities, first, have the duty to provide a safe environment for their students. The second element, violation of duty, occurs whenever a school employee fails to use reasonable care which a REASONABLE AND PRUDENT school employee would use in the same or similar circumstances. For example, teachers in a normal education class would ordinarily be able to leave their class of well-behaved fifth graders unsupervised for ten minutes and be reasonable and prudent. However, those same teachers might be deemed negligent if they were to leave a classroom unsupervised when there were known behavior-disordered students in the classroom. As a result, whether the teacher acted in a reasonable and prudent manner is examined with the following considerations:

1. The purpose for the absence;
2. The age and maturity of the students;
3. The activities being conducted in the classroom at the time of the absence;
4. The likelihood of an injury to occur;
5. The length of the absence;
6. Whether the students were aware of the rules governing their conduct while the teacher was absent; and
7. The precautions taken by the teacher.

A high school physical education teacher in Michigan was found negligent when a high school student was injured during a touch football game in gym class. The teacher had left the field and was reading a newspaper when the student was tackled and thrown to the ground. The court held that the teacher had a duty to adequately supervise his class.[15]

In a New York case, a court held that the teacher was not liable for a student injury because of the purpose of the absence from the classroom.[16]

---

[15]*Hyman v. Green,* 403 N.W.2d 597 (Mich. App. 1987).

[16]*Rock v. Central Square School Dist.,* 494 N.Y.S.2d 579 (N.Y. 1985).

The teacher was not supervising the classroom but instead was standing in the doorway supervising students passing in the hallway when an eighth-grade student in the classroom was struck in the eye by an eraser from a pen.

See also NEGLIGENCE; SUPERVISION.

ACADEMIC FREEDOM

The protections of freedom of speech within the classroom stem from the concept of academic freedom. Academic freedom, as applied to teachers, is a substantive right of the teacher to determine the subject matter and methods which serve an educationally defensible purpose without undue interference or restraints from school administrators or government. A second dimension of academic freedom protects a teacher from dismissal or reprimand for exercising this freedom unless the teacher has violated a rightful policy or law duly enacted. Through this doctrine of academic freedom and the FIRST AMENDMENT of the Constitution, the classroom is recognized as a marketplace of ideas—a place where old and new concepts may be questioned and examined. Society is best served when there is a wide exposure to truths and an unlimited exchange of ideas so long as undue disruptions do not occur. Challenging students to think on their own and to question their beliefs is bound to lead to some unpleasantness or discomfort. The COURTS recognize this, and the Supreme Court of the United States has said:

> Any word spoken, in class, in the lunchroom, or on the campus, that deviates from the views of another person may start an argument or cause a disturbance. But our Constitution says we must take this risk....
>
> In order for ... school officials to justify prohibition of a particular expression ... [they] must be able to show that [their] action was caused by something more than a mere desire to avoid the discomfort and unpleasantness that always accompany an unpopular viewpoint.[17]

The United States Supreme Court has provided the test for determining whether or not justification exists for school officials to prohibit particular kinds of expression within the classroom:

> *Freedom of speech may be restricted only where it materially and substantially interferes with the requirements of mainte-*

---

[17]*Tinker v. Des Moines Independent Community School District,* 393 U.S. 503 (1969).

nance of order and appropriate discipline in the operation of the school or the furtherance of the educational process through balanced and relevant presentations.

However, the above does not confer upon a teacher the authority to say whatever one wishes or to use any materials the teacher alone deems desirable. The teacher must be able to show that the statements or materials serve a valid educational purpose, which purpose is supported by a substantial segment of the teaching profession. Local school authorities have the general power to establish CURRICULUM, select textbooks, and prescribe course contents. The English triangular definition of "curriculum" is the primary basis of most court analysis and decisions. One side of the triangle is the scope and sequence of instructional objectives. The second boundary is what is taught and how it is taught. The third is the what and how of testing. The unclear boundaries of some of these areas have resulted in frequent litigation over curriculum content or methods used. Many cases have tested the constitutionality of using the classroom as a forum for criticizing the administration or airing political views.[18] Cases have been fought over the use of sexually explicit language or films in class[19] or using socially sensitive simulations or surveys.[20] Generally, teachers may decide what subjects to incorporate into a syllabus and are allowed to respond to subjects that arise spontaneously.

Statements made or materials used must be relevant to the topic being taught in order for them to serve an educational purpose. If the teacher attempts to use the classroom as a place to express his or her personal political views, which views are completely irrelevant to the topic being taught, he or she may be disciplined. For example, school officials may require and expect teachers of mathematics to confine their classroom teaching to topics relevant to that subject. If the teacher desires to discuss race relations, politics, or sex, he or she should seek employment as a social science teacher or a similar position which lends itself to discussions of a more controversial nature.

On the other hand, teachers have a right to present what some might consider controversial material in their classes. The age, intelligence, and experience of the students will be important considerations in determining the appropriateness of the material. However, censorship of materials based merely on the fact that some parents are offended should not be allowed, because parental views are not the only measure for determining what is proper education. Parties who find materials offensive may seek "administrative remedies through the board of education proceedings or

---

[18]*Moore v. School Board of Gulf County Florida,* 364 F. Supp. 355 (N.D. Fla. 1973).

[19]*Fowler v. Board of Education,* 819 F.2d 657 (6th Cir. 1987).

[20]*Kingsville Independent School District v. Cooper,* 611 F.2d 1109 (5th Cir. 1980).

ultimately at the polls on election day." Exposure to diverse ideas does not constitute promotion of particular religious or philosophical perspective.[21]

As previously suggested, a teacher's authority to discuss controversial topics may depend on the nature of the subject being taught. In one case, a high school civics teacher who had taught a six-day unit on race relations and who, in response to a student's question, replied that he was not personally opposed to interracial marriage, became the object of disgruntled parents' demands for his removal. In the case initiated to compel reinstatement, the court held that the teacher should be reinstated because the teacher had treated both sides of the topic fairly and the administration was aware of what was being taught.[22]

In another case, an English teacher used the word *fuck* in a lecture concerning taboo and socially acceptable words. The court reinstated the teacher but said that school officials who wish to forbid certain types of classroom discussions or teaching methods, such as this one, will be upheld if the teachers have clear and specific guidelines showing what types of classroom discussions or assignments are prohibited.[23] Whether the teacher's right of free speech is unconstitutionally infringed upon can only be determined by a case-by-case inquiry. Teachers who go beyond the bounds using offensive language are not protected under academic freedom. Conduct which is "both offensive and unnecessary to the accomplishment of educational objectives" is not protected.[24]

Teachers cannot be forced to subscribe to a certain idea which conflicts with their freedom of speech. On this basis, teachers may not be required to lead the PLEDGE OF ALLEGIANCE or engage in a FLAG SALUTE. However, the teacher is obligated to remain sitting or standing respectfully and may be required to make arrangements to have a student or another teacher lead such exercises.

However, a teacher may not refuse to abide by [prescribed curriculum] when such a refusal severely deprives students of an education.[25] Academic freedom does not include the right to disregard the school

---

[21]*Mozert v. Hawkins County Board of Education,* 827 F.2d 1058 (6th Cir. 1987). *See also, Stachura v. Truszkowski,* 763 F.2d 211 (6th Cir. 1985) (the teacher sued the parents who initiated the protests).

[22]*Sterzing v. Ft. Bend Independent School District,* 376 F. Supp. 657 (S.D. Tex. 1972), *vacated,* 496 F.2d 92 (5th Cir. 1974).

[23]*Mailloux v. Kiley,* 448 F.2d 1242 (1st Cir. 1971).

[24]*Brubaker v. Board of Education, School District 149,* 502 F.2d 973 (7th Cir. 1974).

[25]*Palmer v. Board of Education of City of Chicago,* 603 F.2d 1271 (7th Cir. 1979), *cert. denied,* 444 U.S. 1026 (1980).

boards' valid instructional directives regarding the use of instructional materials.[26]

Since the 1970s, a substantial body of federal case law regarding content and methods of instruction has emerged. While there is no firm consensus on the limits of academic freedom, the United States Supreme Court seems deeply committed to safeguarding the freedom to act as true educators without preconceived limitations on speech and without unharnessed censorship.

See also CONSTITUTIONAL LAW; FIRST AMENDMENT; OBSCENITY; SCHOOL PUBLICATIONS.

ACADEMIC PENALTIES, Students

Academic penalties encompass all forms of academic sanctions that penalize, restrict, or otherwise prevent a student from successfully completing his or her school's academic program. In most cases, academic penalties take the form of grade reductions, denial of credit, academic probation, and retention. While the legality of the use of academic penalties for poor academic performance is indisputable, its legality when used to solve discipline and attendance problems is less clear.

In one Pennsylvania case, an eleventh grade student, while on a field trip, ordered and drank a glass of wine. The student was suspended for five days, and her grades were reduced two percentage points in each class for each day missed due to the suspension. Relying on state law, the court held that SCHOOL BOARDS may not impose a grade reduction for infractions which are not related to grading.[27] The court commented that they would have allowed a reduction of grades for cheating.

In another case, a New York student was expelled from a special high school aimed at academic excellence due to her poor grades. The mother contested the expulsion, claiming that it deprived her daughter of a free public education. The court upheld the expulsion, observing that the girl could attend a regular local high school.[28] The court also commented that courts should give considerable deference to school officials' professional opinions.

---

[26]*Fisher v. Fairbanks North Star Borough School District,* 704 P.2d 213 (Alaska 1985).

[27]*Katzman v. Cumberland Valley School Dist.,* 479 A.2d 671 (Pa. 1984).

[28]*Spencer v. New York City Board of Higher Educ.,* 502 N.Y.S.2d 358 (N.Y. 1986).

When deciding cases involving academic penalties, courts look at state laws and regulations. Where school boards carry out policies which are beyond the scope of the authority granted to them by statutes or regulations, courts will strike down the policies.

See also DISCIPLINE.

ACCIDENTS

See NEGLIGENCE; TORTS.

ACHIEVEMENT TESTING

See COMPETENCY TESTING, Students.

ACCOUNTABILITY

Accountability and assessment laws were first introduced and enacted in a few states in the 1960s. Now, nearly every state has examined, evaluated, or enacted some form of accountability legislation. The contents of such laws are as widely different as the number of laws enacted.

Accountability legislation is basically aimed at seeking a method to (1) evaluate professional employees, (2) assess the achievement of students, and (3) evaluate and assess management methods.

One must realize that accountability extends beyond the students and what they are taught; it addresses the process of teaching itself. State statutes often prescribe specific requirements for public school teachers. To examine each law individually would not be practical in this work. However, by examining the structure of the teacher TENURE, CERTIFICATION, and COLLECTIVE BARGAINING laws, one should be able to locate and generally grasp the rules and criteria which govern. One can expect that the criteria governing teacher certification will interrelate with the EVALUATION and tenure laws. Mostly, one will find categories covering when and where evaluations are conducted, who will conduct them, how they are conducted, and what the scope of the evaluation will be.

Evalutions are important. However, some courts may not give evaluations a great deal of weight. For example, in New Jersey, a nontenured teacher's claim of entitlement to a contract renewal was rejected despite the local board's failure to conduct the three required evaluations.[29] This flexibility is contrasted with a harsh result in a case where the court upheld the dismissal of a principal based on the principal's failure to complete the evaluations of all the teachers under his supervision.[30]

Perhaps the most noted case on this issue was handed down by the Eighth Circuit Court of Appeals in 1973.[31] The court held that the students' performance on achievement tests could not be the basis for a teacher's dismissal. The important fact was that the court deferred totally to the board's discretion when dealing with standards, such as teacher competence, which are the most appropriate for local administration.

See also EVALUATION; MALPRACTICE; MERIT PAY.

ACQUISITION OF PROPERTY

See BUILDINGS; PROPERTY.

ACTIVITY FUNDS

Income received from student activities, such as athletic events and school plays, are legally considered to be school FUNDS, subject to the control and under the responsibility of the administration. As a result, activity funds are subject to audit and disposal in the same manner as other school funds. The authority to administer and dispose of school funds is governed by the state STATUTES, and local school officials must comply.

ADMINISTRATIVE AGENCIES

State and federal governments create administrative agencies to carry out the laws, policies, and provisions enacted by the legislative branch of

---

[29]*Foleno v. Board of Education,* decision of N.J. Commissioners of Education (1978).

[30]*Schneider v. McLaughlin Independent School District No. 21,* 241 N.W.2d 574 (S.D. 1976).

[31]*Scheelhaase v. Woodbury Central Community School District,* 488 F.2d 237 (8th Cir. 1973).

government. State and local educational agencies are among these administrative agencies. In addition, many states organize intermediate education agencies, particularly in sparsely populated areas. The legislature must prescribe standards for the agency; it must prescribe what is to be done and by whom; and it must specify the scope of authority which is granted.

Legal problems may arise in this area because the United States Constitution requires a separation of executive, legislative, and judicial powers. The legislature cannot delegate legislative powers to an administrative agency like the state board or local boards of education. However, the COURTS will allow some delegation of authority where the legislature has specified required guidelines or standards which act as checks or balances on the administrative agency's actions. There are instances where the legislature may not delegate certain powers. On the other hand, where the legislature has delegated to a specified agency the responsibility for administering certain actions, that agency may not have the authority to delegate its responsibility to still another agency or person. For example, in most states only the local school board has the authority to expel students. If the local board were to attempt to grant that power to the superintendent, the district's individual principals, or even to individual members of the board, it would amount to an unauthorized delegation of powers and any action taken would be improper. For example, one lawsuit was initiated in a case where the Illinois legislature delegated to the state superintendent the power to specify minimum standards for the protection of the health and safety of students. The court found that such a delegation was not unconstitutional because the legislature had supplied guidelines as to the kinds of standards to be formulated—such as those concerning heating, seating, plumbing, and other specified items related to protecting the health and safety of students. However, in this case, although the delegation of authority was upheld, the superintendent had gone beyond the powers granted to him and had set standards far more stringent than those "minimum" standards necessary to assure protection of the students.[32]

The courts will not generally substitute the courts' judgment for a decision which is made within an agency's designated authority and which is in compliance with proper procedures. The wisdom or merit of the agency's act is not usually the subject for judicial inquiry. However, if the agency acts in an arbitrary, capricious, or unreasonable manner, or if the actions are in violation of an individual's constitutional rights, the court will not uphold the agency's acts. The extent of judicial review can be explained in the words of the Supreme Court of Wisconsin:

> ...[A] court in reviewing the action of an administrative board or
> agency ... will go no further than to determine: (1) whether the board

---

[32]*Board of Education of the City of Rockford v. Page,* 211 N.E.2d 361 (Ill. 1965).

kept within its jurisdiction, (2) whether it acted according to law, (3) whether its action was arbitrary, oppressive or unreasonable and represented its will and not its judgment, and (4) whether the evidence was such that it might reasonably make the order or determination in question.[33]

ADMINISTRATORS

See CONSTITUTIONAL LAW; PRINCIPAL; SUPERINTENDENT; VICE-PRINCIPAL.

AGENCY SHOP

An agency shop is an arrangement whereby all employees must either belong to the employee organization or must pay a fixed monthly sum, usually the equivalent of the employee organization's dues and fees, as a condition of employment, to help defray the organization's expenses in acting as bargaining agent for the group. Some arrangements provide that payment may be allocated to the organization's welfare fund or to charity rather than to the organization's treasury. Agency shop agreements may violate a public employee's constitutional rights. In addition, state statutes generally prescribe the grounds for dismissal of a teacher; and no state statutes include refusal to join a labor organization or refusal to grant authority for DUES CHECKOFF as a lawful grounds for dismissal. (See DUE PROCESS.)

Service charges, when used to finance expenditures by the union for COLLECTIVE BARGAINING, CONTRACT administration, and GRIEVANCE adjustment purposes, are all considered valid under the agency shop clause. However, charging dues or using union expenditures for ideological causes not germane to the union's duties as a collective bargaining representative is not a proper utilization of charges or assessments unless the employees do not object to advancing such causes and are not forced into doing so against their will.[34]

See also CLOSED SHOP; COLLECTIVE BARGAINING; UNION SECURITY.

---

[33]*State v. Board of School Directors of Milwaukee,* 111 N.W.2d 198 (Wis. 1961).

[34]*Abood v. Detroit Board of Education,* 431 U.S. 209 (1977).

AGENT

An agent is a person who acts on behalf of another, often termed a "principal" (not to be confused with a "school principal"). The principal is a person with the authority to control the action of the agent. Because of agents' special relationship to their principal, the NEGLIGENCE of an agent may be charged to the principal so long as the agent was acting within the scope of his or her employment.

AIDES, Teacher

See TEACHER AIDES.

AIDS (Acquired Immune Deficiency Syndrome)

See COMMUNICABLE DISEASES.

ANNUAL OR LONG-TERM CONTRACTS

In several states that do not have TENURE laws, annual or long-term contracts are authorized. The fundamental requirements of a CONTRACT (offer, acceptance, consideration, legality, and capacity of the parties) must be met. Most states also have statutory requirements that the contract be written.

These annual or long-term contracts specify the permissible length of the contract period which may be entered into between the school board and the teacher. Term contracts are issued for a set period of time (for example, one or two years). Neither the teacher nor the school board can unilaterally cancel or breach the contract during its term. All parties are bound to the specifics of the contract. Teachers are subject to breach of contract lawsuits and possible loss of certification if they abandon or resign their contracts early without board acceptance. The school board is likewise liable if it changes any contract terms after signing. One school district, for example, delayed the beginning of the school year and was later held responsible for paying teachers for five lost days of salaries.[35]

See also CONTINUING CONTRACT LAWS; CONTRACTS, Teachers.

ANTI-EVOLUTION STATUTES

The theory of EVOLUTION, Darwinism, was the subject of several legal suits in the 1900s. Anti-evolution statutes were enacted to prohibit teaching in the public schools of the theory of evolution, which denies the story of the divine creation of man as taught in the Bible and teaches instead that man evolved from a lower order of animals. These statutes, frequently called "monkey laws," were upheld in the celebrated 1927 case involving John Scopes.[36] However, by 1968, only two states still had "monkey laws" forbidding the teaching of evolution. One such law, in Arkansas, was challenged by a young biology teacher. In that case, the Supreme Court declared anti-evolution statutes to be unconstitutional and said that the state has the right to prescribe CURRICULUM but does not have the right to prohibit the teaching of a scientific theory or doctrine where such a prohibition is in violation of freedoms of speech and RELIGION.[37]

In line with this logic, a subsequent Arkansas statute introduced into its state legislature a compromise evolution statute. The bill, not actually an anti-evolution statute, would require balanced treatment of "evolution science" and a "creation science" taught in public school. The terms "scientific creationism" or "creation science" refer to a biblical account of humankind's origins and its relation to the universe adopted by fundamentalist religious groups. These groups argued that the Biblical theory was scientific and that Darwin's Theory was a kind of religion they call "secular humanism."

The statute required balanced treatment of the two theories in library materials and in any other instructional materials dealing with the origin of humans, life, the earth, or the universe. The federal court in *McLean v. Arkansas Board of Education* declared "creation science" a violation of the establishment clause of the FIRST AMENDMENT.[38] The fact

---

[35]*Monroe City Common Schools v. Frohliger,* 434 N.E.2d 93 (Ind. 1982).

[36]*Scopes v. State,* 289 S.W. 363 (Tenn. 1927).

[37]*Epperson v. Arkansas,* 393 U.S. 97 (1968).

[38]*McLean v. Arkansas Board of Education,* 529 F. Supp. 1255 (E.D. Ark. 1982).

that creation science is inspired by the Book of Genesis makes it a religious doctrine designed to advance and impose particular religious beliefs on youths by state law and is, therefore, unconstitutional. The court's decision was not appealed.

In 1987, the United States Supreme Court analyzed statutes requiring balanced treatment of creation science and evolution science mandated under a Louisiana Act.[39] The court applied the three-pronged *Lemon test.*[40] The justices concluded that laws limiting schools to only two views of creation inhibited teachers' ACADEMIC FREEDOM to lead classroom discussions on controversial topics, including "creation science." However, when teachers are acting in their capacity as classroom instructors, they are state employees.[41] As state actors, the teachers' intent and purpose must be secular and not entangle church and state. Since creation science is too dependent on its religious basis to be separated from that basis, it is impossible to avoid advancing religion. Therefore, statutes requiring the teaching of creation science are invalidated.

See also ACADEMIC FREEDOM; BIBLE READING; CONSTITUTIONAL LAW; RELIGION.

ANTISUBVERSIVE LAWS

Antisubversive laws were enacted during World War II in an effort to prevent infiltration of communists and other persons who advocated the unlawful overthrow of the government by force and violence. New York's Feinberg Law received the most attention. This law was designed to rid the school system of "subversive teachers." The Board of Regents, which controlled the New York schools, was given the power to designate which groups were subversive and to provide that membership in such organizations constituted prima facie evidence for disqualification for a position in the school system. This law was upheld in 1952, but it was challenged again in 1967.

Three instructors from the State University of New York refused to sign a LOYALTY OATH, saying that they were not communists or that, if they had ever been communists, they had communicated that fact to the president of the University. New York's Feinberg Law was used as a basis for not renewing the contract of one of these instructors, Harry Keyishian. Keyishian appealed to the courts; and, in 1967, the Supreme Court of the

---

[39]*Edwards v. Aguillard,* 482 U.S. 578 (1987).

[40]*Lemon v. Kurtzman,* 403 U.S. 602 (1971).

[41]*Breen v. Runkel,* 614 F. Supp. 355 (D.C. Mich. 1985).

United States invalidated the part of the law which provided for removal of any teacher who belonged to any organization which advocated unlawful overthrow of the government. The court said that mere membership in a subversive organization is insufficient to justify dismissal of a teacher. However, if the teacher can be shown to have the intent to bring about the illegal objectives of the organization, he or she may be removed from the public schools.[42] In other words, the Court is saying that "guilt by association" will not be allowed. Subversive teachers and administrators may be removed from their public school positions, but persons are to be considered subversive only if they can be shown to have the intent to further the unlawful aims of the organization of which they are members. Teachers and students may exercise the basic right of freedom of association without fear of reprisals.

Whether a teacher may refuse to answer questions concerning his or her membership or activities in an alleged subversive organization is controlled by the courts' interpretation of the teachers' right to freedom from SELF-INCRIMINATION. Although membership per se is protected, a teacher must respond to queries related to impact of association on classroom performance.[43] Statutes specifically imposing restrictions or sanctions on public employees based on membership in controversial or subversive organizations are clearly unconstitutional.

See also: ASSOCIATION, Right of; CONSTITUTIONAL LAW; STRIKES.

APPEARANCE, Administrators and Teachers

What is "acceptable" in a manner of APPEARANCE changes with the facts and the tenor of the times. There always seem to be people whose appearance attracts attention. Whether the person's manner of dress is several years behind or ahead of the times is not always readily ascertainable; but one thing is certain—school is not always the safest place for fashion trend-setters.

The school system has traditionally attempted to prevent persons from appearing in a manner which is contrary to the accepted norm. Howard Beale wrote a book in 1936[44] in which he related that in 1924 a Santa Paula, California, teacher was dismissed for bobbing her hair. In 1928,

---

[42]*Keyishian v. Board of Regents,* 385 U.S. 589 (1967).

[43]*Beilan v. Board of Public Education, School District of Philadelphia,* 357 U.S. 399 (1958).

[44]H. K. Beale, *Are American Teachers Free?* (New York: Charles Scribner's Sons, 1936), pp. 390–391.

some teachers in West Virginia were forced to sign contracts in which they promised to "fasten their galoshes up all the way." In still another instance, a teacher was dismissed because the wives of some of the more affluent citizens in the town objected to the poor quality of dresses the teacher purchased with her forty dollars a month salary. And, in 1915, some teaching contracts prohibited teachers from wearing "bright colors," required the wearing of two petticoats, and prohibited teachers from wearing dresses which were more than two inches above the ankle.

In the 1970s, the schools found their dress codes and appearance regulations being challenged from every direction—principals, teachers, and students—as abridgements of their protected rights of privacy, liberty, and free expression. By 1975, the majority rule was clearly established that school RULES regulating appearance can only be justified by a showing of reasonableness. Rules which prohibit appearance that causes an actual substantial disruption of the educational process or rules which are necessary for health, safety, or "morals" will be upheld. Rules going beyond these bounds will not be deemed a legitimate state interest justifying grooming policies.

A SCHOOL BOARD's authority to regulate appearance is not supported if the restrictions are void of a legitimate, rationally based educational concern or if the attempt to regulate is arbitrary. For example, the Seventh Circuit reinstated a bus driver who was suspended for wearing a mustache. The court found no valid school purpose for the regulation since the mustache in no way affected the driver's ability to perform his job.[45] However, COURTS have upheld prohibitions against beards in the "interest of teaching hygiene, instilling discipline, asserting authority, and compelling uniformity."[46] These rules are considered to be, at best, a "relatively minor deprivation of protected rights."

Rules regulating the length of a person's hair present stronger liberty interest arguments because such rules control a person's appearance twenty-four hours a day, seven days a week, whereas the person is within the school not more than eight hours a day. When a person's appearance is an expression of his or her heritage, race, or culture and when the appearance does not impair the educational process, such appearance can warrant some protection under the Constitution.[47]

Besides the many cases involving hair, rules prohibiting certain forms of dress have also been challenged. Rules prohibiting the wearing of pantsuits by women have been struck down as being unreasonable when evidence was presented showing that such dress can even aid a teacher,

---

[45]*Pence v. Rosenquist,* 573 F.2d 395 (7th Cir. 1978).

[46]*Domico v. Rapides Parish School Board,* 675 F.2d 100 (5th Cir. 1982).

[47]*Braxton v. Board of Public Instruction of Duval County, Florida,* 303 F. Supp. 958 (M.D. Fla. 1969).

particularly in the elementary grades.[48] A Connecticut school board was held justified in requiring all male teachers to wear ties as a rational means of promoting respect for authority and traditional values.[49] The teacher has the burden of demonstrating that the dress code is "so irrational that it may be branded arbitrary" or the regulation will stand since personal appearance interests are less weighty than other liberty rights on the constitutional scales.[50]

School boards generally may prohibit the frequent wearing of religious apparel (as opposed to a small cross of Star of David) as a symbol of the teacher's dedication to religion as a violation of the establishment clause. An Oregon court upheld the validity of a prohibition of "any religious dress" when it allowed the dismissal of a teacher who converted to the Sikh religion and insisted on wearing a white turban and clothing regularly.[51]

It is clear that all courts recognize that educators should be free from unreasonable rules regulating their appearance. However, the answer to what is unreasonable varies to some extent from state to state and with changing times. As a result, it must be suggested that persons within school confines who are asked to shave, cut their hair, or otherwise conform to appearance regulations should consult an attorney for advice on the position the courts of that state take with regard to a person's freedom of appearance.

See also CONSTITUTIONAL LAW.

APPEARANCE, Students

School authorities may enact reasonable appearance rules concerning student dress and hair styles. RULES are justified if the rules are designed to prevent undue disruptions in the learning environment, to assure health and safety standards, or to maintain discipline. The validity of appearance restrictions depends on the circumstances and the tenor of the times.

Student resistance to dress codes is not new. In fact, in 1923, one 18-year-old high school girl lost in her challenge of a school rule which

[48]*In re School District of Kingley and Kingley Education Association,* 56 Lab. Arb. 1138 (1971).

[49]*East Hartford Education Association v. Board of Education of the Town of East Hartford,* 562 F.2d 838 (2d Cir. 1977).

[50]*Kelley v. Johnson,* 425 U.S. 238 (1976).

[51]*Cooper v. Eugene School District No. 4J,* 723 P.2d 298 (Or. 1986).

prohibited the wearing of "transparent hosiery," "low-necked dresses," and "face paint or cosmetics."[52]

The 1960s and 1970s saw the emergence of new judicial standards regarding student appearances. A long line of cases ruled that:

1. Students have constitutional rights. (See Categorical Index.)
2. School officials have the power and the duty to enact reasonable rules, but authorities must be able to demonstrate reasonableness and that the rules are not arbitrary or capricious.
3. The students' rights of expression and privacy must be weighed against the compelling reasons necessitating the school rules.

Several legal theories have been advanced in order to secure the freedom to govern one's own personal appearance as a fundamental right protected under the United States Constitution. Official restraints on dress and hair should have a rational basis or nexus to the educational interests that are potentially disrupted or the educational purposes to be served. Numerous regulations have fallen because they were ruled unconstitutionally vague or discriminatory or because the rules were applied arbitrarily.

There is a division among the federal circuit courts as to whether appearance regulations infringe on substantial constitutional liberties of students. The First, Fourth, Seventh, and Eighth Circuit Courts uphold students' constitutional rights based on the FIRST AMENDMENT freedom of symbolic expression, the FOURTEENTH AMENDMENT right to personal liberty, and the right to privacy. In contrast, the Third, Fifth, Sixth, Ninth, and Tenth Circuits generally uphold school grooming policies, concluding that no fundamental freedom is implicated. The United States Supreme Court has declined to sort out the different standards which have resulted as a consequence of these cases. (See COURT ORGANIZATION.)

When we consider the continuous flow of changing hairstyles, it seems strange to read about substantial litigation focusing on rules prohibiting male students from having hair extending beyond the collar of their shirts or below the ear. The burden is on the school to present evidence of why the hairstyle creates disruption or causes health or safety hazards. This BURDEN OF PROOF is balanced with the student's showing that a code is vague, not well known, discriminatory, or arbitrarily enforced. School "image" reasons for barring long hair and beards for vocational students and athletes have been upheld as necessary to health, safety, and job recruitment enhancement,[53] but not allowed just to enhance esprit de corps or conformity.

---

[52]*Pugsley v. Sellmeyer,* 250 S.W. 538 (Ark. 1923).

[53]*Menora v. Illinois High School Association,* 683 F.2d 1030 (1982); *Davenport v. Randolph County Board of Education,* 730 F.2d 1395 (11th Cir. 1984).

Unlike hair, clothes can be easily changed after school. Therefore, regulations governing attire can reasonably be imposed if the clothing is immodest, unsanitary, and/or disruptive. Dress codes may not force a student in co-ed classes to wear gym clothes students consider sinful and which abridge their religious conscience.[54]

The following guide rules demonstrate certain restrictions on student appearance, which restrictions have been found reasonable by all courts:

1. Rules *necessary to protect the safety* of the students are uniformly upheld. Examples: prohibiting the wearing of long hair near machinery in "shop"; requiring hairnets for food servers in the cafeteria; prohibiting clothing which will interfere with or make dangerous playground or athletic activities.

2. Rules *necessary to protect the health* of the students are upheld. Example: requirement that students keep their hair reasonably clean. In the 1973 school year, the superintendent of the Montoursville, Pennsylvania, school district was forced to order the district's three schools closed so the 2,800 pupils could get their heads checked by doctors. Lice had been found on some pupils before school opened. A program screening pupils with dirty or lice-infested hair was started, and the superintendent's conduct was certainly reasonable.

3. Appearance which *does not conform with basic rudiments of fundamental* decency may be regulated. For example, "halter tops" or "short shorts" may be regulated as may other garments with vulgar or obscene slogans or symbols embroidered upon them.

4. Appearance which *causes a material and substantial disruption* may be restricted. For example, turbans, hats, or berets may make it difficult for students seated behind these headpieces to see. Where this is the case, the student wearing the disruptive attire could be required to sit nearer to the back of the room or to remove the headgear.

As stated, it is possible that certain athletic or special classroom activities may present special safety hazards. If this is the case, reasonable appearance rules may be enacted to help protect student safety. However, rules going beyond the demands of the activity are subject to question. The courts will balance the individual's personal freedom interests against the school's interest to maintain a proper learning environment. The key to defending an appearance regulation lies in establishing a concise, reason-

---

[54]*Moody v. Cronin,* 484 F. Supp. 270 (C.D. Ill. 1979).

able rule that has a direct bearing on the activities covered and the educational purpose being served when balanced with the student's right to freely express oneself and other constitutionally protected liberties.

A rule requiring uniforms or governing dress enacted for public safety, student safety, or for an otherwise valid educational purpose may be reasonable so long as the rule does not substantially interfere with constitutionally protected guarantees. Each state and possibly even districts within a state may differ, and legal advice should be obtained before uniforms are required in the public schools. Private schools may require uniforms.

ARBITRARY, CAPRICIOUS, OR DISCRIMINATORY ACTION

Educators have many rights that are not always granted to private-sector employees. Public employees are protected from state action which (1) is patently arbitrary or capricious; or (2) is discriminatory.

Today, while outside of the school building, educators should feel free to discuss topics which are of interest and concern to them as individuals. This has not always been so. In the past, statements which had no relationship to the employee's fitness to perform his or her duties were frequently used as a basis for that person's dismissal. As stated by Howard Beale:

> In theory ... [a teacher] is freer to advocate unpopular causes outside class than inside, but in practice the advocacy of unpopular causes in the community gets him into trouble more quickly than doing so in school."[55]

In a 1944 case, a Florida court upheld the dismissal of a teacher whose sole indiscretion had been his statement that he was a conscientious objector and that he would not aid the United States in either a combat or a noncombat status.[56] In another World War II case, a female teacher wrote a letter to a former student who had refused to register for the draft. In the letter, she congratulated him on his "courageous and idealistic stand," and she stated that "you and the others who take the same stand are the hope of America." The court upheld the dismissal.[57]

---

[55]H. K. Beale, *Are American Teachers Free?* (New York: Charles Scribner's Sons, 1936), p. 237.

[56]*State v. Turner,* 19 So. 2d 832 (Fla. 1944).

[57]*Joyce v. Board of Education,* 60 N.E.2d 431 (Ill. 1945), *cert. denied,* 327 U.S. 786 (1946).

Such cases were based on the premise that the public must be protected from unfit teachers. This concept remains unquestioned; but can it be said that a person who is conscientious, experienced, well-qualified, and performs the teaching duties in a capable, competent manner is unfit because he or she challenges accepted opinions? The answer, as of 1990, is "no." In addition, the early cases failed to recognize that the public also has a strong interest in encouraging free and unhindered debate on issues of public importance. The individual's freedom of speech must be protected in order for such open debate to flourish.

In 1968, the Supreme Court of the United States rendered a decision in a case called *Pickering v. Board of Education.*[58] In this case, Pickering, a teacher, was dismissed for writing a letter to a local newspaper which the SCHOOL BOARD believed was detrimental to the efficient operation of the schools. In this letter, Pickering stated, among other things, that (1) the school board had misinformed the public about allocation of finances in a proposed school bond issue; and (2) the superintendent had threatened to discipline any teacher who refused to support the school bond. Although some of Pickering's statements proved to be untrue, the Supreme Court held that teachers have constitutional rights and that Pickering had been denied his FIRST AMENDMENT right of free speech. In considering the fact that several of Pickering's statements were incorrect, the Supreme Court said:

> Absent proof of false statements knowingly or recklessly made by him, a teacher's exercise of his right to speak on issues of public importance may not furnish the basis for his dismissal from public employment.[59]

For school employees' constitutional rights, this was a giant step forward. Prior to this time, educators could be fairly certain to find themselves seeking new employment if they publicly criticized local businesses or offended certain mores of the community. It was out of the question to even consider criticizing the school system.

The United States Supreme Court stated that, before an educator's freedom of speech may be restricted, there must be a showing that the statements (1) harm a substantial public interest or (2) render the person unfit to teach. The problem arises in trying to determine what is a "substantial public interest." In the Pickering case, the Supreme Court provided guidelines to be considered when determining whether a substantial public interest has been harmed. These guidelines are:

1. Disruption of superior-subordinate relationships;
2. Breach of loyalty or confidentiality;

---

[58]*Pickering v. Board of Education,* 391 U.S. 563 (1968).
[59]*Ibid.*

3. General disruption of the public service;

4. Indication of unfitness from content of the statement; and

5. Failure to comply with established GRIEVANCE procedures.

What the United States Supreme Court has said is that educators have a right of free speech; but, where statements harm a substantial public interest, the speaker may be disciplined. In determining whether or not a substantial public interest has been harmed, the above guidelines must be considered. The extent of the harm must also be considered. To help point out how these guidelines are applied, consider the following situation.

Can a teacher be disciplined if he or she publicly criticizes school officials and the school system? The answer is not always yes or always no; the answer will depend on whether a substantial public interest has been harmed. Did the statements substantially disrupt superior-subordinate relationships or have the statements disrupted the public service? Superior-subordinate relationships are those close-working relationships which are necessary to enable the educator to fully perform required duties. This is meant to mean those relationships in which the persons frequently meet and work together. In most schools, teachers are in a superior-subordinate relationship with the PRINCIPAL; but no close-working relationship exists between the SUPERINTENDENT or the SCHOOL BOARD and the teachers. On the other hand, a close-working relationship generally exists between the superintendent and the school principals.

Disruption of the public service occurs when the statements materially and substantially interfere with the order and efficiency in the operation of the school. Some minor disruption frequently will occur, but this disruption must be tolerated. The educator's criticisms need not be couched in mild, ineffective terms; and the use of PROFANITY is not always fatal.

When the educator's comments are related to issues of public importance, these comments enjoy even stronger protections than statements related to the internal operation of the school. Although such comments may at times call into question the employee's fitness to perform, generally, the statements alone may not constitute an independent basis for dismissal. The statements may be used as evidence of general unfitness, but the school board would be forced to demonstrate how the statements have in actuality rendered the employee unfit to continue working in the district.

Where criticisms relating to the internal operation of the school are concerned, the educator may be required to exhaust the school's established internal grievance procedures prior to making the grievance public. However, this is true only when the grievance procedures are capable of providing a solution to the alleged problem. For example, if the criticism is related to TEXTBOOK selection, unsafe facilities or EQUIPMENT, or selection of field trips, potential solutions are available within school channels; and the complaint should first be handled within them. Where established grievance procedures do not exist or are not made known to the employees, the employees are not required to comply.

As in *Pickering,* another case also listed factors to be aware of when considering an educator's comments regarding the operation of public schools:[60]

1. The impact on the harmony, personal loyalty, and confidence among co-workers;

2. The degree of falsity of the statements;

3. The place where the speech or distribution of material occurred;

4. The impact on the staff, faculty and students; and

5. The degree to which the educator's conduct lacked professionalism.

See also CIVIL RIGHTS ACT OF 1871; CIVIL RIGHTS ACT OF 1964; DISCRIMINATION; EQUAL PROTECTION; RENEWAL.

ARBITRATION

Arbitration is a method of settling disputes using an impartial third party or panel whose decision is usually final and binding. Advisory arbitration is sometimes utilized, but the arbitrator's decision is not binding; therefore, this method of resolving disputes is more akin to FACTFINDING or MEDIATION.

"Binding interest arbitration" refers to the formation of contract terms or memorandums of understanding, as distinguished from "GRIEV-ANCE arbitration" which interprets rights under the existing contract. There is widespread support for arbitration as a viable alternative in resolving deadlocks.

Binding arbitration as a means of settling disputes over the provisions of a new contract (sometimes termed "contract arbitration") is not widely accepted because public sector employers view the process as an illegal delegation of government authority over public schools. Arbitration is voluntary when both parties, of their own volition, agree to submit a disputed issue to arbitration. In many states, interest arbitration is compulsory for designated employees, such as in police or fire departments, in

---

[60]*Gilbertson v. McAlister,* 403 F. Supp. 1 (D. Conn. 1975).

order to prevent work stoppages. Several states have authorized voluntary arbitration of new contract provisions as a part of the COLLECTIVE BARGAINING rights of public school employees. In addition, a few states have taken the initiative and mandated grievance arbitration of teachers' CONTRACT disputes, making the process compulsory and binding by law.

Compulsory binding arbitration may be an adequate substitute for the right to STRIKE. Nevertheless, many critics argue that:

1. When the arbitrator settles the dispute, the SCHOOL BOARD is not making the final decision and public sovereignty is infringed upon.
2. Genuine collective bargaining is discouraged.
3. Strikes are not completely eliminated.
4. Arbitrators sometimes ignore or do not adequately understand municipal fiscal difficulties.

There may be some validity to the above arguments; however, even if all of the arguments are well-founded, binding arbitration may have desirable aspects which outweigh the objections. Binding arbitration is gaining acceptance. This is particularly true when binding arbitration is used as a means of settling disputes which do not involve the expenditure of money.

The arbitrator is generally chosen in one of three ways:

1. The school board and the employees each pick a representative and a neutral third representative is chosen.
2. A professional arbitrator is chosen by agreement.
3. An outside body selects the arbitrator.

The arbitrator or panel holds meetings or hearings and takes evidence. Sometimes the arbitrator conducts an independent investigation. After completion of the hearing and/or the investigation, the arbitrator makes a decision as to how the dispute should be settled. This decision is binding on both the school board and the employees. So long as the labor arbitrator's interpretation of the collective bargaining agreement is reasonable, a reviewing court will not overturn a decision.[61]

ASSAULT

An assault is an INTENTIONAL TORT, and it can also constitute a criminal act. *Assault* is defined as (1) an offer to use force, causing the (2)

---

[61]*Mifflinburg Area Educ. Assoc. v. School Dist.,* 545 A.2d 419 (Pa. 1988).

apprehension of (3) immediate, (4) harmful or offensive (5) bodily contact. A person has been assaulted when he or she is put in fear for his or her immediate personal well-being. No physical contact is necessary. If there is physical contact, then a BATTERY has been committed in addition to assault. As with all TORTS, each of the elements in the definition must exist before the tort has been committed.

The first element, the offer to use force, can be verbal or displayed through actions. The second element is the element of fear. If one intentionally threatens immediate harm or acts in a menacing manner, an assault has occurred only if fear is a reasonable result of the act. If a person being assaulted is overly paranoid and if the offer to use force would not put a reasonable person in fear, then no assault has occurred. For example, if a third-grade student threatened to strike his six-foot-tall teacher, there probably would be no assault because the student's offer to use force would not ordinarily cause apprehension.

The third element necessary is immediacy. There must be apprehension of immediate harmful or offensive physical contact. This means that, if a student threatens to "get you" the next time you do something or threatens harm "after school," no assault has been committed. Certainly, the teacher can discipline the student for the threat alone; however, the tort of assault has not yet occurred.

In addition, the offer to use force must be directed toward one's person. A threat to slash the tires on a car or to ransack a house is not an assault. Thus, in establishing that an assault has occurred, one must show the offer to use force, the reasonableness of the apprehension, the fact that the fear was immediate, and that the offer to use force was directed toward one's person.

Threats and assaults are commonplace within the schools. Educators should clearly understand that it is their duty to prevent an assault or battery where either is reasonably foreseeable. (See FORESEEABILITY.) Charges of assault and battery can also be made against educators and other school employees. The use of CORPORAL PUNISHMENT sometimes leads to charges of assault and battery. So long as the corporal punishment is allowed by law and is used in accordance with the law, reasonably and without malice, suits alleging assault and battery will fail. However, if corporal punishment is not allowed and there is no justification, such as self-defense, suits for assault and battery may be successful where students are hit by school employees.

In New York City, where corporal punishment has been banned, a school bus monitor slapped a student in the face. The court held that any person who hits a child for any reason other than self-defense or defense of others is liable to the child for monetary DAMAGES for the tort of battery.[62]

---

[62]*Rodriguez v. Johnson,* 504 N.Y.S.2d 379 (N.Y. 1986).

ASSEMBLY, Student Right of

The right to freedom of speech derives from the FIRST AMENDMENT, which provides in part: "Congress shall make no law...abridging the freedom of speech, or of the press...." In the late 1960s, several students chose to express their opposition to the war in Vietnam by wearing black armbands to school. When the school officials heard of the proposed protest, they quickly enacted a RULE prohibiting the wearing of armbands. This rule was announced at a school assembly, and students were told that any student refusing to remove his or her armband would be suspended from school. The protest took place as planned. A boy named Tinker and two others were suspended. These students sued the school district and asked the court to grant an INJUNCTION prohibiting the school from punishing the students for exercising a protected right of free speech.

The Tinker case was finally ended by the Supreme Court of the United States. For the first time in history, the Supreme Court established that the protections of the First Amendment were available to students. The court stressed the fact that the state has the right to regulate the school's CURRICULUM, but said:

> School officials do not possess absolute authority over their students. Students in school as well as out of school are "persons" under our Constitution. They are possessed of fundamental rights which the State must respect....In our system, students may not be regarded as closed-circuit recipients of only that which the State chooses to communicate. They may not be confined to the expression of those sentiments that are officially approved. In the absence of a specific showing of constitutionally valid reasons to regulate their speech, students are entitled to freedom of expression of their views.[63]

The United States Supreme Court set forth the test to be used in determining whether the reasons for regulating students' speech are "constitutionally valid":

> The student's right of free speech may be restricted where it can be demonstrated that the speech "materially and substantially interfere[s] with the requirements of appropriate discipline in the operation of the school."[64]

---

[63](Emphasis added) *Tinker v. Des Moines Independent Community School District,* 393 U.S. 503 (1969).

[64]*Ibid.* at 512.

Some disturbance is to be expected any time a person challenges someone else's preconceived ideas or seeks acceptance of an opposing viewpoint. The United States Supreme Court states that this minor disruption must be tolerated. It is only when school officials can show that the speech has caused, or in all likelihood will cause, a material and substantial disruption that they may lawfully restrict student speech.

It is most often "controversial" speech that is prohibited by school officials. The Vietnam War was at the top of the list of controversial topics during the Tinker case. Today, HOMOSEXUALITY is one of many controversial topics to which many school officials object. However, the courts have applied the same reasoning as was applied in the Tinker decision. As regards homosexuality, COURTS have held that homosexuals have a constitutional right to symbolically express their views by such activities as forming homosexual student groups in college[65] or by attending high school proms with dates of one's same gender.[66]

From the abovementioned cases and many others which have not been mentioned, guide rules for specific situations have evolved:

1. If the students' speech collides with substantial rights of others, it may be restricted.

2. Unpopular language may be allowed, but "fighting words" and obscene language are not.

3. If the student shows gross disrespect for the principal or the teacher, it is not protected speech.

4. Discussion of all ideas relevant to the material being presented is permitted in the classroom, but this is subject to the teacher's responsibility to maintain order and the right to guide the discussion.

5. Symbolic speech which is not materially disruptive must be allowed, but the equivalent spoken idea in the middle of an unrelated class discussion need not be tolerated.

6. Any speech, including spoken words, armbands, or buttons, which mock, ridicule, or are intended to disrupt the educational process because of race, religion, or national origin, are not permissible.

7. Distribution of armbands, buttons, etc. in halls or classrooms during class may be prohibited.

8. The classroom is not a political forum. The teacher is responsible and accountable for providing students with suitable instruction. There-

---

[65]*Gay Students Services v. Texas A & M Univ.,* 737 F.2d 1317 (5th Cir. 1984), *cert. denied,* 105 S. Ct. 1860 (1985); *Gay Lib v. University of Missouri,* 558 F.2d 848 (8th Cir. 1977).

[66]*Fricke v. Lynch,* 491 F. Supp. 381 (D.R.I. 1980).

fore, control of the order and direction of the class and the scope and manner of treatment of the subject matter rests with the teacher, who has a right to be free of distraction and disruption by dissident students. As a result, disruption of the classroom and insubordination may be forbidden. There ideally should exist a procedure whereby students can present their grievances about an instructor in a proper format and at an appropriate time.

The age, intelligence, and experience of the students are relevant to the consideration of when the speech will create a material and substantial disruption. The students are accountable for speech which is in fact disruptive and may be punished accordingly. In addition, the students are obligated to respect the right of other students to pursue their studies in a relatively tranquil atmosphere.

Although the rules applying to symbolic speech and spoken words are applicable to speech in the form of demonstrations and picketing, school publications and "underground" NEWSPAPERS present special problems. With each form of speech, there are legal issues and rules to be considered.

Demonstrations, Sit-Ins, and Picketing

Demonstrations, sit-ins, and picketing are, in essence, speech in the form of "idea/action." Student activism in the 1980s became much more passive than the militant civil disobedience which struck the nation's colleges and universities in the late 1960s. As a result, most schools have been spared the difficult decisions and problems which are inherent in "idea/action" type of speech. Not all schools have been exempt, however. In one case, a group of black students conducted a library sit-in. The students were seeking integration of the faculty. This case went to the United States Supreme Court, where the court held that:

> [The rights of free speech and assembly] are not confined to verbal expression. They embrace appropriate types of action which certainly include the right in a peaceable and orderly manner to protest by silent and reproachful presence, in a place where the protestant has every right to be.[67]

This case established the rule that peaceful demonstrations may not be totally prohibited on school premises. The students have a right to present their grievances before the school. However, school officials have a right and a duty to protect all students within the school, to prevent disruption of the educational process, and to protect the school PROPERTY. As a

---

[67]*Brown v. Louisiana,* 383 U.S. 131 (1966).

result, the courts have ruled that school officials may enact regulations governing the time, place, and manner of conducting demonstrations and sit-ins. These are "conditions," not "prohibitions," on the speech. These regulations will be found legally reasonable when they are necessary to protect the safety of the students in the school or to protect school property or the normal operations of the school. Besides setting aside a time and place for demonstrations, the school may enforce the following guide rules:

1. Students engaging in demonstrations may not prohibit others from moving freely in the school hallways or other areas of the building.

2. Students may not engage in destruction of property, riotous action, or other unlawful acts.

3. Demonstrations which deprive others of the right to pursue their studies in a relatively tranquil atmosphere are not permitted, and persons who do engage in such action may be punished.

4. All students have the right to be interviewed on campus by military recruiters or by representatives of other legal organizations which are invited by the school. Any student or group may protest against the organization but may not interfere with the other students' right to be interviewed.

Demonstrations which violate the school's reasonable rules are not protected by the First Amendment, and the demonstrators may be punished. Although some of the demonstrators may not have directly participated in the disruptive conduct, they are equally responsible for the actions of the splintered voices of their group.

School officials should be careful to determine the cause of any disruption which occurs. Students engaging in a peaceful demonstration have a right to be protected from the harassment and disruptive conduct of other students who do not agree with the demonstrators' views. Unless the demonstration was calculated to cause disruptive confrontations with other students or such disruption could reasonably have been foreseen, the demonstrators are not responsible for the unforeseen reaction of their fellow students.

School authorities are not obligated to create an open forum for student meetings during noninstructional times. Organizations that are an extension of curriculum generally have access to the public school facilities. However, under the EQUAL ACCESS ACT, when noncurriculum groups are created and the school gives them access to a limited forum, the school must not discriminate against selected groups (with the possible exception of religious groups) because of the content of their meetings.

See also ASSOCIATION, Freedom of; CONSTITUTIONAL LAW.

ASSIGNMENT TO GRADE AND SCHOOL, Students

The grade level to which a student is assigned is within the discretion of the local school board. In assigning a student to a grade, the board must consider his or her age, intelligence, ability, and training. Once the grade level is determined using these considerations, the parent generally has no grounds upon which to object. The courts will most likely refuse to substitute judicial judgment for that of the administration or SCHOOL BOARD. For example, a court refused to intervene when a district failed to promote 22 out of 23 second-grade students who had not passed a reading test.[68] It is permissible for the board to assign students to special classes when it is necessary. The parent cannot preclude the child's attendance without being guilty of failing to allow the child to attend school.

In addition to grade assignment, the school board has wide discretion in determining what school the child shall attend. The school that is nearest the child's home is not necessarily the school that he or she has the right to attend. If that school is overcrowded or if there is some other valid reason for a student to transfer, the courts will not substitute the court's opinion for that of the board. This is true save in exceptional cases. As one text states:

> Because school boards have the authority to assign pupils, and because no pupil has a vested right to attend a particular school, it does not follow that in all circumstances the assignment of a particular pupil to a particular school will not be examined by the courts. An example from North Carolina is illustrative. There a school board attempted to transfer a high school girl who had taken Latin during her freshman year, was a member of the school band, and generally received high grades. Her parents desired that she continue to have the competition and challenge offered by the expanded curriculum, particularly in foreign languages, at the school to which she had been assigned. It was shown that she planned to enter the field of medicine and that additional foreign language study would be helpful to her. She expected to go to a college which required for entrance a minimum of two units in two foreign languages or three units in Latin. The school to which the girl was assigned for her sophomore year had no course in Latin, nor did it have a band....When the Board, after [a] hearing refused to reassign the girl to the original school, the parents sought relief in the courts. The Supreme Court of North Carolina, emphasizing that the statute placed all emphasis on the welfare of the child and the effect upon the school to which reassignment was requested, ordered

---

[68]*Sandlin v. Johnson,* 643 F.2d 1027 (4th Cir. 1981).

her reassigned.[69] It was the judgment of the court that under the facts such reassignment was [not] warranted.[70]

See also DEMOTIONS; RESIDENCE.

ASSIGNMENTS, Nonclassroom

Assignment of teaching duties outside the classroom has been the subject of dissatisfaction and often litigation, particularly when no additional compensation is paid for performance of the "extra" duties. In most jurisdictions, a school board may require reasonable extracurricular activities by the teacher if the tasks are justified as an educational objective or a related school program. The question of whether or not a teacher may legally refuse to perform these extra duties depends on the "reasonableness" of the requirement.

For determining the reasonableness of extra duty assignments, the following guide rules should be considered:

1. A teacher may be required to take over a study hall.
2. A teacher may be expected to supervise student organizations in the area of his or her teaching field or expertise.
3. English and social science teachers may be requested to coach or supervise plays.
4. Physical education teachers may be expected to coach intramurals.
5. Teachers may be required to supervise field trips.[71]

Even in considering the above suggested guidelines, legal issues still arise and must be considered on a case-by-case basis:

1. Is an excessive number of hours involved in the assignments?
2. Are the students benefited?
3. Are the extra assignments distributed evenly among the teachers, i.e. is DISCRIMINATION involved?
4. Are the assignments professional in nature?

---

[69]*In Re Reassignment of Hayes,* 135 S.E.2d 645 (N.C. 1964).

[70]Reutter and Hamilton, *The Law of Public Education,* Foundation Press, Mineola, New York, 1970, pp. 117–118.

[71]*Parrish v. Moss,* 106 N.Y.S.2d 577 (N.Y. 1951).

5. Do the assignments relate to the teacher's field of CERTIFICATION and interest?

A few cases may help to point out how the courts look at challenges to schools' extracurricular duties based on the above questions. For example, question 4 asks if the assignment is professional in nature. This is important because teachers may not be required to perform menial tasks such as janitorial services, police (traffic) service, or bus driving because these are not reasonably related to the job performance of teachers.

Following this reasoning, at least one court has held that a teacher could not be forced to collect tickets at a football game because that was a task that any adult could perform and was not professional in nature.[72] The court added that the administration's requirement that the teachers collect tickets was not intended to benefit the students but rather was motivated primarily by a desire to cut expenses.

In spite of the case just referred to, it is important to remember that classroom duties are not the only duties a teacher may be required to perform. The following cases show that extracurricular assignments will generally be upheld by the courts when they are "fair and reasonable and related to school programs."

In a 1975 case, a teacher challenged the validity of a school policy that required teachers to attend or supervise certain nonacademic school activities, such as football and basketball games, pep rallies, and music programs, which were held on weekday evenings and Saturdays. The court found that, even though the teacher's CONTRACT did not mention such extra assignments, the teacher could be required to attend and supervise such activities because they were reasonably related to the teacher's teaching duties.[73] Other courts have held that boards can make reasonable and appropriate assignments of noninstructional duties without providing additional pay.[74]

Refusal to accept assigned duties can result in dismissal.[75] Courts have decided that refusing to perform extracurricular duties constitutes an illegal strike. In so doing, a New Jersey court reasoned that: "Extracurricular activities are a fundamental part of a child's education, making the

---

[72]*Todd Coronway v. Lansdowne School District No. 785,* Ct. of Common Pleas of **Dela**ware County (Pa. 1961).

[73]*District 300 Education Association v. Board of Education of Dundee Community Unit School District No. 300 of Kane, et al., Counties,* 334 N.E.2d 165 (Ill. 1975).

[74]*Ballard v. Board of Education of Goshen,* 469 N.E.2d 951 (Ohio App. 1984).

[75]*Howell v. Alabama State Tenure Commission,* 402 So. 2d 1041 (Ala. 1981). *See also Jones v. Alabama State Tenure Commission,* 408 So. 2d 145 (Ala. 1981) (counselor refused to supervise students before school hours).

supervision of such activities an integral part of a teacher's duty toward his or her students."[76]

The North Dakota Supreme Court held that a teacher who turned down a coaching position for a girls' high school basketball team, although she was well qualified, could be terminated. The court reasoned in this case that programs aimed at expanding women's physical education were reasonably related to a legitimate educational purpose.[77]

Teachers' dismissals for insubordination over extra duties have been upheld in cases where (1) a teacher (claiming a right to free speech) refused to take part in hall duty,[78] (2) an instructor refused to produce required reports for the administration,[79] and (3) a teacher refused to submit typed copies of examinations for duplication.[80]

If one is questioning an assignment to extra duties, it is advisable to consult state law or administrative rules in order to determine the scope and nature of the school's authority in this area. Such laws or rules may also indicate whether compensation will be paid for the performance of these duties. Of course, COLLECTIVE BARGAINING agreements or teacher CONTRACTS may also spell out duties; if so, these assignments are binding.

ASSOCIATION, FREEDOM OF

Students

The right to freedom of association is implicitly found within the FIRST AMENDMENT, which states in part: "Congress shall make no law…abridging…the right of the people to peaceably assemble." This is also part of the basis for protecting a person's right to demonstrate. Politically instigated walkouts, boycotting, silent sit-ins, or occupations of reserved school areas do not qualify as protected association rights.[81]

---

[76]*Board of Education of City of Asbury Park v. Asbury Park Education Association,* 368 A.2d 396 (N.J. 1976).

[77]*Enstad v. North Central Barnes Public School District No. 65,* 268 N.W.2d 126 (N.D. 1978).

[78]*Lockhart v. Arapahoe County School District No. 6,* 735 P.2d 913 (Colo. 1986).

[79]*Weaver v. Board of Education,* 514 N.Y.S.2d 473 (N.Y. 1987).

[80]*Thomas v. Board of Education of Community Unit School District,* 453 N.E.2d 150 (Ill. 1983).

[81]*Tate v. Board of Education,* 453 F.2d 975 (8th Cir. 1972); *Washington v. State,* 190 S.E.2d 138 (Ga. 1972); *Sapp v. Renfroe,* 511 F.2d 172 (5th Cir. 1975).

Students and educators should be free to organize and participate in voluntary associations of their own choosing, but this right is subject to school regulations assuring that such associations are neither discriminatory nor operated in a manner which is disruptive or interferes with the rights of others. Under this substantial disruptive test, state STATUTES and school RULES may lawfully prohibit students from joining fraternities, sororities, or SECRET SOCIETIES or prohibit school athletes from competing on nonschool sports teams during the season.[82] With rational, compelling state interest reasons, school officials may control rights of ASSEMBLY/ association by not extending assistance (e.g., facilities, communication channels, supervision) to the group's efforts to disseminate the group's views.

Some groups are condoned and encouraged by the schools. If the school aids in the financial support of the group, the school may reasonably require an accounting procedure and a list of officers or other persons responsible for the overall conduct of the association.

The 1984 federal EQUAL ACCESS ACT[83] requires schools "having a limited open forum" to make space available to citizens for meetings without regard to the program content. Numerous litigations have followed this Act, all debating the definition of "public forum." One such case involving a teacher, but which would be analogous for students, defined three categories of forums—public, limited, and nonpublic.[84] The ability of a school to regulate assembly in some forums is limited. Students organizing a "Peace Fair" or peace activities or participating in "career day" have been allowed the equal right of association and assembly if the students follow reasonable time, place, and manner regulations promulgated by the district.[85] If a limited forum for any noncurriculum group is created, all meetings, with the possible exception of religious groups, must have access on equal terms.

See also ACADEMIC FREEDOM; ASSEMBLY, Student Rights of; CONSTITUTIONAL AMENDMENTS; CONSTITUTIONAL LAW.

Teachers

The FIRST AMENDMENT of the United States Constitution provides that individuals have the right to peacefully assemble and petition. Within this guarantee of a "right of ASSEMBLY" is freedom of association. This means

---

[82]*Zuments v. Colorado High School Activities Ass'n.*, 737 P.2d 1113 (Colo. 1987).

[83]20 U.S.C. 4071.

[84]*Perry Education Assoc. v. Perry Local Educator's Assoc.*, 460 U.S. 37 (1983).

[85]*Student Coalition for Peace v. Lower Merion School District*, 633 F. Supp. 1040 (E.D. Pa. 1986); *Searcey v. Crim*, 642 F. Supp. 313 (N.D. Ga. 1986).

that people have a right to associate without fear of punishment with the people or groups of their choice. However, the freedom to associate was not always a protected right of educators. In the early 1900s, white teachers in some towns were not allowed to have or to entertain black friends. On the other hand, in many parts of the South, it could be fatal for black teachers to have white friends. At one time, being a member of the Ku Klux Klan was grounds for dismissal in some communities, while refusing to join was grounds for removal in some others.[86]

Employee Organization Activity

In the past, participation in any form of labor activity, especially attempts to organize a labor organization, was particularly frowned upon. As one writer relates: "In Cleveland there was a fight in 1914 over the teachers' attempt to organize a union. The teachers were beaten, forced to disband the union and sign a "yellow-dog" clause in their new contracts promising not to join."[87] As late as 1920, St. Louis ordered that any teacher who joined a union was to be dismissed. "Little Hatch Acts" restricting educators blossomed throughout various states until those laws were weeded out by more enlightened courts.

Now, the courts clearly hold that teachers and administrators are free to join an employee organization. Educators may assume leadership roles, actively attempt to increase membership, negotiate with the school board on behalf of the organization, and advocate the organization's viewpoints. The educator may not be punished for engaging in such activities even though such activity may become quite vigorous. However, should the educator's activities cause material and substantial harm to the educational process, the First Amendment protections may be overshadowed. In addition, mere membership in an organization which conducts unlawful STRIKES is not grounds for dismissal. The employee must be shown to have the intent to bring about the illegal objectives of the organization, and the educator may be disciplined if he or she incites others to disobey lawful school orders or takes time off to pursue an illegal strike.

See also COLLECTIVE BARGAINING.

Political Activity

Teachers and other public employees have the right to vote, run for office, participate in political campaigns, speak out on public issues, and engage in various forms of political activity. However, state statutes and local school

---

[86] H. K. Beale, *Are American Teachers Free?* (New York: Charles Scribner's Sons, 1936), p. 402.

[87] *Ibid.*

board policies may restrict some of these activities if the activities are clearly disruptive to the integrity of the learning process. Adverse employment actions as the result of an educator's active political participation, a federally protected right, are actionable.[88] Court cases have clearly established that educators cannot be punished for engaging in peaceful civil rights activities during nonschool hours. In addition, it has been established that other forms of political activity can be restricted only where a countervailing state interest exists. For example, a federal court reinstated a Kentucky teacher who had been dismissed after supporting a rival school board candidate.[89]

Under this "countervailing state interest test," laws which attempt to ban public employees from engaging in all types of political activities have been found unconstitutional. Similarly, nonpartisan political activity which does not affect the teacher's fitness or classroom performance may not be prohibited.[90] However, a teacher or administrator is expected not to use his or her position or classroom for political purposes or as a political forum.

Where partisan activity is concerned, the courts are divided, with some holding that partisan political activity could be curtailed and some holding that it could not. Under federal law, the United States Supreme Court held in 1973 that federal and state governments may bar public employees from engaging in partisan political campaigns. Justice White suggested that the reasoning behind this ruling was the belief that:

> [I]t is in the best interest of the country, indeed essential, that federal service should depend on meritorious service rather than political service, and that the political influence of federal employees on others and the electoral process should be limited.[91]

The United States Supreme Court's decision means that laws are constitutional which prohibit state employees in the classified service from:

1. Directly soliciting or receiving funds for a partisan political purpose;
2. Being a member of a political party committee;
3. Being a candidate for any political office; or
4. Actively managing a campaign.

---

[88]*Kercado Melondez v. Aponte Rogue,* 641 F. Supp. 1326 (N.D. Ill. 1986).

[89]*Banks v. Burkich,* 788 F.2d 1161 (6th Cir. 1986).

[90]*Hatcher v. Board of Public Education,* 809 F.2d 1546 (11th Cir. 1987).

[91]*United States Civil Service Commission v. National Association of Letter Carriers,* 413 U.S. 548 (1973).

However, keep in mind that, while the United States Supreme Court said that the state may prohibit its employees from engaging in the previously mentioned partisan political activities, the state is not forced to do so. In addition, state constitutions also need to be addressed. In other words, while partisan political activity may not be protected under federal law, that same activity may be protected under state law.

Although some state laws require the teacher to resign if he or she is a candidate for public office, some states have special laws which specifically allow teachers to run for the legislature or hold other public offices. Some laws also allow a teacher to be a candidate but require that he or she take a LEAVE OF ABSENCE without pay during the campaign, and some require the teacher to resign if elected.

In addition, although some state laws may not specifically provide that teachers are prohibited from engaging in various political activities, certain legal principles would form a sufficient basis for upholding reasonable restrictions. For example, depending on the state's constitution and the nature of the position, a teacher elected to certain public offices may be required to relinquish his or her teaching position when the two positions threaten to present a CONFLICT OF INTEREST. Also, in campaigning for or against school board members or superintendents, the teacher may lawfully be subjected to restrictions which are necessary to prevent a material and substantial disruption in the order and efficiency of the school system.

Subversive Organizations

"Guilt by association" is not allowed under the United States Constitution. Therefore, the Supreme Court of the United States has ruled that mere membership in a subversive organization is not enough to justify dismissal or noncriminal sanctions. The educator must be shown to have the intent to bring about the illegal objectives of the organization before he or she may be punished. The Supreme Court stated that the reasoning behind such a ruling is that:

> Those who join an organization but do not share its unlawful purposes and who do not participate in its unlawful activities surely pose no threat, either as citizens or as public employees. Laws…which are not restricted in scope to those who join with the "specific intent" to further illegal action impose, in effect, a conclusive presumption that the member shares the unlawful aims of the organization.[92]

Where there exists a compelling state interest, teachers can be

---

[92]*Elfbrandt v. Russell*, 384 U.S. 11 (1966).

required to disclose membership in various organizations, but absent such an interest, the teacher has a protected right of PRIVACY.

See also ANTISUBVERSIVE LAWS; ASSEMBLY; CONSTITUTIONAL LAW; FLAG SALUTE; LOYALTY OATHS; PLEDGE OF ALLEGIANCE.

ASSUMPTION OF RISK

Assumption of risk is often used as a defense against claims of NEGLIGENCE. Three elements must be present in order for this defense to apply.

1. The PLAINTIFF must know that the activity or condition is dangerous.
2. The plaintiff must understand and appreciate the risk involved.
3. The plaintiff must voluntarily participate in the activity leading to the injury.

When a person knows of a dangerous condition or activity and understands the inherent risk but voluntarily ignores the danger, he or she is said to assume the risk of any injury which results. If a court finds that the plaintiff voluntarily assumed the risk, the plaintiff will be barred from recovering any DAMAGES.

In the educational setting, assumption of risk has been used particularly for sports-related injuries. While inherent risks are associated with athletics, courts may hold that students did not understand and appreciate the risks. However, this defense has been used successfully against claims brought by teachers and adult spectators at sporting events.

Assumption of risk prevented a teacher's aide from recovering damages for an injury received when a volleyball struck her in the head during a game of "warball" which she was watching. The aide had been in the gym before and knew how the game was played. A student player threw the ball which missed the intended target and hit the aide. The aide sued the student's homeowner's insurer. The court ruled that a participant has no duty to refrain from accidentally injuring a spectator who is fully aware of the risks involved.[93]

Factors which courts consider in determining if participants understand and appreciate the risks include age, intelligence, experience, and the presence of warnings explaining the risks. It should be noted that in order for one to assume a risk he or she must know of the specific risk. In other words, a person only assumes the risk of dangers which are

---

[93]*Melder v. State Farm Fire & Casualty Co.,* 498 So. 2d 1095 (La. App. 1986).

reasonably expected to be inherent in the activity. For example, in baseball, one would assume the risk of injury inherent in sliding or being hit by a baseball once he or she had been instructed how to play the game. On the other hand, if, for example, the teacher does not instruct the students how to hold the bat properly and if, as a result, a student hits the ball and lets the bat fly, thereby injuring the pitcher, the teacher could be held negligent. The pitcher did not assume the risk of being injured by the bat, because the risk is not an inherent danger of the game once the students have been properly instructed. Therefore, it is absolutely necessary for school districts to be certain that coaches and teachers issue sufficient warnings and properly instruct students on how to play the sports and use the equipment.

Many districts use permission slips or release forms in which parents waive the student's right to sue for negligence. While such permission slips indicate that the students assume the normal risks associated with the activity, students do not assume all risks. Even though the permission slip might state that the school will not be held liable for injuries due to the activity itself, such permission slips would not preclude liability if the student were subjected to unreasonable risk of harm or if the district or supervisor was negligent. For example, students in one district were prohibited from participating in interscholastic sports unless parents signed a release form in which the district exempted itself from liability for negligence. Upon hearing the case, a court held that the release form was not valid for public policy reasons.[94] One cannot contract away a duty to be REASONABLE AND PRUDENT in order to avoid liability for negligence.

ATHLETICS, Funds

See ACTIVITY FUNDS; FUNDS.

ATHLETICS, Participation Requirements

Many states have enacted laws requiring students to maintain certain grade point averages in order to participate in school athletics or other extracurricular activities. These laws have been upheld by the courts. In 1986, the

---

[94]*Wagenblast v. Odessa School Dist.,* 758 P.2d 968 (Wash. 1988).

United States Supreme Court dismissed an appeal in which the Texas Supreme Court upheld a state law requiring students, except students with mental retardation and those in honors or advanced classes, to maintain a 70 percent average in all classes in order to be eligible for extracurricular participation.[95] The court held that there is no absolute right to participate in extracurricular activities. The court concluded that the minimum grade point requirement was rationally related to the legitimate state interest of providing a quality education to students.

Courts have also allowed school authorities to attach other conditions such as physical fitness, skill criteria, residency rules, and attendance and training regulations. Educators can avoid problems in this area by assuring that all policies pertaining to extracurricular activities are reasonable, related to an educational purpose, clearly stated and publicized to students and parents, and applied in a nondiscriminatory manner.

Though students can be required to have physical examinations and to be physically fit in order to participate on athletic teams, restrictions which affect students with handicaps have not fared very well. For example, a court held that a school district could not bar a student with only one kidney from playing on the high school football team.[96] The court held that to bar the student from playing would be a violation of the REHABILITATION ACT OF 1973 which prohibits the discrimination of individuals on the basis of handicaps.

See also ASSUMPTION OF RISK; CURRICULUM; DRUG TESTING; FEES; FUNDS; MARRIED STUDENTS; NEGLIGENCE; SUPERVISION.

ATHLETICS, Sex Discrimination in

The denial of sports opportunities for female students and sex segregation on interscholastic teams are two issues which receive much publicity. There are two bases for cases in the area: EQUAL PROTECTION and Title IX of the Educational Amendment Act of 1972. Since the early 1970s, most courts have decided that districts may not deny a female student the opportunity to play in school-sponsored athletics unless the denial serves an important state interest. While the protection of students' health and safety are important state interests, most courts hold that denying a female student the opportunity of participating on the basis of gender alone is a denial of the student's rights to equal protection. If, however, an individual

---

[95]*Spring Branch Independent School District v. Stamos*, 695 S.W.2d 556 (Tex. 1985); *appeal dismissed*, 475 U.S. 1001 (1986).

[96]*Grube v. Bethlehem Area School Dist.*, 550 F. Supp. 418 (E.D. Pa. 1982).

female is too weak, injury-prone, or unskilled, she may be excluded from competition on that basis.

In one case, a sixteen-year-old female was prevented from trying out for the junior varsity football team by a state regulation which prohibited mixed competition in basketball, boxing, football, ice hockey, rugby, and wrestling. The student sued, and the court held that the regulation denied females equal protection of the law since the law assumed that all females were physically incapable of competing safely with males in contact sports.[97] The regulation was struck down because the rule did not sufficiently relate to the state's objective of ensuring safe competition.

In another case, a district rule prohibited girls from wrestling on the all-boy team. At trial, the district introduced evidence that girls are not as fast or strong as boys and that girls' muscle power output was less than that of boys and, thus, that girls were far more likely to be injured than boys. The court held for the girl and stated that no evidence had been put forth regarding the strength, speed, or muscle power of the girl in this case.[98]

In the cases above, the schools had no female football or wrestling teams. It is conceivable that the cases would have been decided differently if there were equivalent teams for girls. For example, an equal protection argument failed when a talented eleven-year-old girl sued a district that denied her a tryout for the boys' basketball team. The district argued that so long as there was a comparable girls' team, there was no violation of equal protection. The court agreed and held that the district's reasoning for separate teams was reasonably related to the legitimate state goal of providing equal athletic opportunities to all students.[99]

There are three possible ways in which school administrators can meet the demands of equal protection with regard to sports programs which include sports offered for boys only:

1. Eliminate the team.
2. Establish a comparable girls' team with funding, coaching, officiating, and an opportunity to play.
3. Open tryouts to all interested students regardless of gender and do not use gender as a basis for team selection.

In the *O'Connor* case, the girl also argued that there was a Title IX violation of the Educational Amendment Act of 1972. However, Title IX allows for separate teams when the activity involved is a contact sport. Title IX, which applies to all districts receiving federal funds, states in part

---

[97]*Lantz v. Ambach,* 620 F. Supp. 663 (S.D.N.Y. 1985).

[98]*Saint v. Nebraska School Activities Ass'n,* 684 F. Supp. 626 (D. Neb. 1988).

[99]*O'Connor v. Board of Educ.,* 545 F. Supp. 376 (N.D. Ill. 1982).

that districts may operate separate teams where selection of such teams is based upon competitive skill or where the activity involved is a contact sport. Contact sports include boxing, wrestling, rugby, ice hockey, football, basketball, and other sports which involve bodily contact. Of course, as mentioned above, girls have won the right to participate on boys' contact sports teams when they have argued equal protection.

In terms of equal opportunity, under Title IX the following factors, laid out in the Title's regulations, are considered:

1. Whether the selection of sports and levels of competition effectively accommodate the interests and abilities of members of both sexes

2. Provisions for equipment and supplies

3. Scheduling of games and practice times

4. Travel and per diem allowance

5. Opportunity to receive coaching and academic tutoring

6. Assignment and compensation of coaches and tutors

7. Provisions for locker rooms and competitive facilities

8. Provisions for medical and training facilities and services

9. Provisions for housing and dining facilities

10. Publicity

A court interpreting Title IX has held that equal opportunity requirements do not mandate the placement of girls' basketball and volleyball seasons in alignment with the national norms.[100] However, the court held that schools must provide equal access to prime practice times, equal access to desirable facilities, and equal team support. The court also held that the schools should increase the amount of sports offered to girls to bring the total number of girl participants in line with the total number of boy participants.

Sex segregation challenges have also come from males who desire to play on girls' teams. In one case, a male student sought to play on the girls' team, but a state law prohibited participation of males on the girls' team. The boy challenged the law arguing that his equal protection rights and Title IX were being violated. The court held that there was no denial of equal protection since the state's law was reasonably related to the legitimate state goal of providing equal opportunity for females.[101] The court reasoned that the law prevents the takeover of all-girl teams by males

---

[100]*Ridgeway v. Montana High School Assoc.*, 858 F.2d 579 (9th Cir. 1988).

[101]*Forte v. Board of Educ.*, 431 N.Y.S.2d 321 (N.Y. 1980).

who already have a disproportionate advantage in overall athletic opportunities. Furthermore, the court ruled that there was no Title IX violation since Title IX prohibits only the exclusion of an athlete where overall athletic opportunities for members of that athlete's gender have been limited in the past.

ATTENDANCE OF PUPILS

See COMPULSORY EDUCATION.

AUTHORITY, Parents

See PARENTAL AUTHORITY.

AUTHORITY, School Board

See SCHOOL BOARDS.

AUTHORITY, Teachers

See IN LOCO PARENTIS; RULES.

AUTOMOBILES

School districts may expend money for the purpose of building parking lots for student vehicles; students may drive their automobiles to school. But, once the auto is on school premises, it is proper for the school to make RULES regarding its use or disuse during the school day. It is reasonable to stipulate that students may not loiter in the student parking lot, that students park only in designated areas, and that automobiles are to be driven at a slow rate of speed. It is also proper to enforce the rules by taking away the privilege of using the parking lot. Reasonable school rules regarding student use of automobiles will be upheld, particularly where the rules are necessary to protect the safety of the students.

B

BARGAINING

See COLLECTIVE BARGAINING; MEET AND CONFER BARGAINING LAWS.

BATTERY

Battery can be both an INTENTIONAL TORT and a criminal act. Battery is defined as the (1) unpermitted, (2) unprivileged (3) physical contact with another (4) in a rude or angry manner. The absence of "hostile" intent or the intent does not preclude a battery. Pranks, practical jokes, and intended horseplay where there is unpermitted, unprivileged contact in a rude or angry manner are all batteries. In one case, a student pulled a chair out from under a teacher as the teacher was sitting. The teacher was injured, and the student committed battery even though the act was meant as a joke.[1]

ASSAULT and battery are often tied together as one crime, but in civil cases, assault is a tort which is distinct and separate from a battery. In the educational setting, battery cases usually arise in one of the following situations: acts committed by students against teachers, by students against other students, and by teachers or administrators against students. There are also times when teachers or administrators are liable for batteries committed by one student upon another. This LIABILITY can be imposed when there is improper SUPERVISION or when it is foreseeable that a

---

[1]*Ghassemieh v. Schafer*, 447 A.2d 84 (Md. 1982).

student is about to injure another and the educator does nothing to prevent the battery. Some students are more dangerous than others; if such a student is identified, he or she must be supervised carefully and possibly be removed if he or she poses a threat to others. Administrators should remember that, if the student is identified as handicapped, the district must follow special procedures in order to remove the student for a period of more than ten days.

As a general rule, there is no duty to come to the defense of another person unless there is a special relationship between the parties which imposes such a duty. In other words, if a stranger saw another person being beaten, he or she would not be obligated to attempt a rescue. On the other hand, a teacher who witnesses an attack on a student has a duty to come to the student's rescue because of the special relationship between the teacher and the student. Teachers are not obligated to subject themselves to grave personal danger but must render possible aid. For example, if a physically small teacher observed two large students battling it out, the teacher would not be obligated to throw himself or herself between the students. However, the teacher would have an obligation to tell the students to stop fighting and to seek other help, if necessary, to force the students to stop.

As with all TORTS, each element of the definition of a battery must be met before liability can be imposed. First of all, the contact must be unpermitted. If two students voluntarily agree to enter into a fight, permission for contact is granted. In other words, one student would generally not be liable to the other for battery. Nevertheless, teachers and administrators may be liable for NEGLIGENCE if they fail to stop the fight.

In addition to the lack of permission, the contact must be unprivileged. Simply put, there are times when one person will have a legal "privilege" to batter another. For example, one may reasonably defend one's self or another without being liable for battery. However, this self-defense or rescue privilege is limited by the rule that a person may only use the kind of force required to repel the attack. Once the attack has been sufficiently stopped, one cannot continue battering the assailant. Naturally, if the assailant does not use force likely to result in permanent or fatal bodily injury, deadly force in self-defense exceeds the privilege.

Teachers and administrators have certain privileges that students do not. As a general rule, in many districts, teachers and administrators have a privilege to use CORPORAL PUNISHMENT. However, in districts which do not allow corporal punishment, school personnel may be liable for battery. For example, in New York City where corporal punishment is banned, a school bus monitor slapped a student in the face. The court held that any person who hits a child for any reason other than self-defense or defense of others is liable to the child for monetary DAMAGES for the tort of battery.[2]

---

[2]*Rodriguez v. Johnson*, 504 N.Y.S.2d 379 (N.Y. 1986).

The third element necessary for battery is contact. The contact can also be with what the person is wearing or carrying. For example, if a shirt is torn off a person's back, a battery has occurred. (See TRESPASS TO PERSONAL PROPERTY.)

In addition, the contact must be in an intentionally rude or angry manner. If a student is running down the hall and accidentally knocks someone over, the student is liable for negligence and probably not battery. On the other hand, if the student decided to sneak a kiss or grab or touch another person unexpectedly, that action can constitute a battery even if there is no serious injury.

Intent can also be transferred. For example, if a student throws a rock at one student and misses but hits another student, he or she could not defend on the grounds that there was no intent to injure the victim. The intent to injure the first student is "transferred," and thus liability can be imposed for battery.

In summary, batteries can be very serious. A battery can be both a crime and a tort at the same time. The fact that a student is criminally punished by the state for committing a battery does not prevent the school from punishing the student. Furthermore, criminal punishment or educational sanctions do not prevent civil liability from being imposed.

BEARDS

See APPEARANCE; CONSTITUTIONAL LAW.

BIBLE READING

The United States Supreme Court has consistently held that Bible reading, unrelated to academic studies, is a violation of the no-aid principle of the Establishment Clause requiring separation of church and state. In one case, a Pennsylvania statute required the reading of Bible verses at the opening of school. Several members of the Unitarian faith brought suit to enjoin enforcement of the statute because specific verses were contrary to the Unitarians' religious beliefs. The district court ruled against the statute; thereafter, the Pennsylvania legislature amended the law to allow any child to be excused upon written request. This amendment was not enough for the PLAINTIFFs, and the case was appealed to the United States Supreme Court. Justice Clark wrote:

It is no defense to urge that the religious practices here may be relatively minor encroachments on the First Amendment. The breach of neutrality that is today a trickling stream may all too soon become a raging torrent and, in the words of Madison, "it is proper to take alarm at the first experiment on our liberties."[3]

As a result of this decision and several subsequent cases, the rule has been firmly established that state laws or local school or school board policies prescribing Bible reading are unconstitutional and in violation of the FIRST and FOURTEENTH AMENDMENTS to the Constitution. Bible reading is prohibited even if students are allowed to be excused during the time the verses are read.

Even when the Bible reading is not mandated by law but is introduced on the initiative of a student or teacher, the courts have held that the Constitution's curtailment of intermingling church and state prohibits such readings. In a 1978 case, the court decided that, even where university students were given the option of leaving the classroom while the instructor read aloud from the Bible, such readings could not be permitted. The court stated:

The alternative afforded [the students] of absenting themselves from the classroom was not sufficient protection to their own constitutional rights in light of the supervisory position of control occupied by the teacher over student grading and conduct, coupled with peer pressure and disapproval which we feel would have a "chilling" effect at best and, more likely, a coercive impact on the students' free exercise of their religious right.[4]

Until 1990, the United States Supreme Court has rejected all attempts to defy or subtly skirt the Court's rulings.[5] Congress expressly refused to adopt proposed constitutional amendments to allow Bible reading activities.[6] However, under the Equal Access Act, 20 USC 4071–4074, the United States Supreme Court in 1990 ruled that a student Bible study group that wished to engage in religious activities could not be denied access to public schools, and that the religious activities did not violate constitutional restrictions against separation of church and state.[7] Schools, under the federal Constitution, cannot discriminate on the basis of religion

---

[3]*School District of Abington v. Schempp*, 374 U.S. 203, 225 (S.D. 1963).

[4]*Lynch v. Indiana State University Board of Trustees*, 378 N.E.2d 900, 903, *cert. denied*, 441 U.S. 946 (1978).

[5]*Alabama Civil Liberties Union v. Wallace*, 456 F.2d 1069 (5th Cir. 1972); *Meltzer v. Board of Public Instruction*, 439 U.S. 1089 (1979).

[6]Senate Bill 1742, 97th Congress, 1st Session (1981).

[7]*Board of Education of the Westside Community Schools v. Mergens*, 58 L.W. 4720 (1990).

during noninstructional time. State constitutional restrictions could vary this result, depending on state interpretations of local constitutions.

It should be noted that the academic study of the Bible, when presented objectively, can be part of a secular program on history, ethics, comparative religions, or civilizations. The Bible may be used neutrally if no student is required to participate directly or indirectly in the activity.[8]

In 1987, a Washington State high school Bible study group was denied permission to meet at the school. The federal district court upheld this ban on the grounds that Bible study group meetings would appear to create an atmosphere of religious partisanship.[9] A Nebraska school's denial of school ground access to a student religious club was upheld, and this denial did not violate the EQUAL ACCESS ACT because the religious club was a noncurriculum club unlike other student clubs (including a chess and photography club).[10]

See also ANTI-EVOLUTION STATUTES; CONSTITUTIONAL LAW; RELIGION; PRAYER.

BIDS

See BUILDINGS; CONSTRUCTION.

BILINGUAL/BICULTURAL

While the fundamental power to select the method of instruction and the courses of study to be pursued in the public schools lies with state legislatures, under Title VI of the CIVIL RIGHTS ACT OF 1964, all districts receiving federal financial assistance must provide English language instruction to students who do not speak English. However, many educators are unsure what school districts must do to meet this requirement. The reason for the uncertainty is clear: Congress, the Department of Education, and the courts continue to hedge on exact requirements.

There are several types of bilingual education programs. The most common type is transitional bilingual education in which students are educated in their native languages and then transferred to an all-English CURRICULUM as soon as they are able to compete with classmates. An alternative to true bilingual education is an English-as-a-second-language

---

[8]*Wiley v. Franklin*, 497 F. Supp. 390 (E.D. Tenn. 1980); *Crockett v. Sorenson*, 568 F. Supp. 1422 (W.D. Va. 1983).

[9]*Garnett v. Renton School District No. 403*, 675 F. Supp. 1268 (W.D. Wash. 1987).

[10]*Mergens v. Board of Education of the Westside Comm. Schools*, CV 85-0-426 (Neb. 1988).

(ESL) program. Under this program, students take a special English class in addition to regular classes. Another type of bilingual education is considered bilingual/bicultural. In this model, students are taught English and integrated in the bilingual program. However, the program seeks to maintain proficiency in the students' native language.

The United States Supreme Court has interpreted federal law to mean that, at a minimum, students are entitled to receive instruction to assist them in learning English.[11] School districts must take affirmative steps to rectify students' language deficiencies.

The Fifth Circuit Court of Appeals used a three-part test when deciding if a remediation program meets federal standards:

1. Is the district's program based upon recognized, sound educational theory or principles?
2. Is the school system's program designed to implement the adopted theory?
3. Has the program produced satisfactory results?[12]

This test has since been used by other courts.[13] Until there are more exact federal guidelines in this area, districts should make sure that their programs meet this test.

BOARDS OF EDUCATION

It should be understood that the duties of boards of education vary from state to state. A state board of education is either created by the legislature or is a constitutional body. Board members are either elected on a partisan or nonpartisan basis or appointed by the state governor with advice and consent from the state senate. Because jurisdictions between state boards and local boards of education often overlap, litigation may result. It is well settled that local SCHOOL BOARDS have only those powers expressly granted to them by the legislature, the constitution, or state boards of education or powers reasonably inferred therefrom. Often local boards, in the absence of direct power grants, will exercise their discretionary authority. Discretionary power is interpreted broadly, and a successful challenge can only be made if the DISCRETIONARY ACT is clearly unreasonable, illegal, arbitrary, or capricious.

---

[11]*Lau v. Nichols*, 414 U.S. 563 (1974).

[12]*Castaneda v. Pickard*, 648 F.2d 989 (5th Cir. 1981); *Castaneda v. Pickard*, 781 F.2d 456 (5th Cir. 1986) (affirmed district court's decision on remand).

[13]*Keyes v. School Dist. No. 1*, 576 F. Supp. 1503 (D. Colo. 1983).

BONDS

School districts sometimes are forced to go into debt in order to finance capital construction or to provide for the day-to-day operation of its schools. The authority of local SCHOOL BOARDS to incur debt is governed by state STATUTES and state constitutions. If no EXPRESS AUTHORITY exists in the state statutes, the board is generally not authorized to incur any indebtedness. However, in all states, authority to incur some debt is expressly granted by state statutes. The extent of such authority varies greatly from state to state; and, since the state statutes will be strictly construed, members of school boards should learn exactly what is required under state law with respect to:

1. The *purpose* for which indebtedness may be incurred;
2. The *procedures* which must be followed; and
3. The maximum *amount* of allowable indebtedness. (The maximum amount is generally based on a percentage of taxable property in the district.)

Most school indebtedness is incurred through the issuance of bonds. Express authority is required before a district may issue bonds. If the bonds are issued without authority or for an unauthorized purpose, the bonds are void. Since powers of the school board are matters of public record, persons dealing with the board are deemed to be on notice of the board's restrictions. Therefore, innocent purchasers of void bonds or bonds which prove to be invalid have only two methods of recourse:

1. *Recovery of money given for the bonds.* This method of recourse is available only if the money has not been spent and is identifiable.
2. *Recovery of property purchased with the proceeds of the invalid bonds.* This recourse is available only if the property will not be harmed and the district will not be hurt.

Some states require that the question of whether bonds shall be issued must be submitted to the voters. Unless limited by statute, the board may repeatedly submit the bond question to the voters. Where voter approval is given, the bonds may be issued only for the purpose or purposes for which they were voted.

Defects in bonds due to failure of the board to follow the required proper procedures may sometimes be cured by ratification or legislative action.

Short-term loans for emergency or day-to-day operation of the district, until tax levy proceeds are obtained, may be negotiated only where there exists express or implied legislative authority. If no such authority exists, any notes issued are void or voidable. (See BUILDINGS.)

BORROWING

See BONDS.

BOUNDARIES

See REORGANIZATION.

BUDGETS

See FUNDS.

BUILDINGS

Construction

Construction of school buildings is governed by state STATUTES. Where the state statute grants construction authority, local boards have the EXPRESS AUTHORITY to exercise discretion and may construct buildings which are deemed necessary or beneficial to any education program. SCHOOL BOARDS also have the IMPLIED AUTHORITY to employ architects to design the buildings.

Some statutes require the local board to employ contractors on the basis of competitive bidding. If this is the case, these statutes must be complied with on a strict basis. If the board does not comply with the law, any contract entered into will be void. Where bidding is not required by statute, the board has discretionary authority and may or may not choose to contract by submitting the construction contract to competitive bidding.

Where bidding is required by statute or voluntarily agreed to by the board, bidders must be given sufficient data to allow the bidder to ascertain a fairly precise estimate of the cost. Construction bids are accompanied by a bond; and, if the contractors fail to enter into the contract after the bid is accepted, the board will be entitled to the value of the bond plus interest *or* the amount of the difference between that bid and the next lowest. Correction of a bid is allowed if the correction is done prior to opening of the bids and, in a few special instances, where the mistake is extremely large or obvious. If not prohibited by statute, the board may reject all bids. In all other instances, if the board is required to accept one of the bids, the board generally must give the contract to the lowest *responsible* bidder. The board is allowed to consider the bidder's reputation and financial stability in order to determine the bidder's responsibility.

The contractor will be liable for poor workmanship and defects in the building and for a reasonable penalty for delays in completion where such a penalty is specified in the contract. An architect's certificate is generally required to be given upon satisfactory completion of the work.

Various performance and payment BONDS are often required by statute to be obtained from the contractor. Since a lien is not usually allowed by law to attach to school property, the contractor's employees have only the payment bond as protection if the contractor goes bankrupt or fails to pay. Consequently, some cases have held that, when a payment bond is required by the contractor and if the school board is negligent in failing to obtain such a bond, the board members may be personally liable for any loss. This is particularly true in those states in which the statutes specifically provide for such liability.

Use

School buildings are generally the PROPERTY of the state, and the state legislature has the power to control the use of school facilities. However, for the most part, state statutes usually do not make mention of the possible uses of the property; therefore, use is generally within the discretion of the local school boards.

Four main rules control the use of school property for activities which are not school functions:

1. Neither the state nor local school boards may authorize the use of school facilities for any purpose which is in violation of the state or federal constitution.
2. The use cannot interfere with the school program.
3. Uses which could foreseeably result in damage to school property cannot be allowed.

4. Under the EQUAL ACCESS ACT of 1984, if a school opens part of the campus to expressive activities for certain groups, the school district must allow equal access to other groups of similar character.

Subject to these four rules, the school board generally is granted the discretionary authority to allow the use of school property for other than educational purposes.

In the absence of a contrary law, the local board may not be compelled to open school buildings for use by the public for meetings or entertainment. However, where the board decides to open school buildings for public use, the board cannot exercise its discretion in an arbitrary or discriminatory fashion. Many cases in the area of school use arise as the result of "career day" activities.

For example, in one case, a group of peace activists were excluded from participation in "Career Days." The group wanted to present information to students on career and educational opportunities relating to peace. A court determined that the school board's decision to deny access was a violation of the group's FIRST AMENDMENT rights.[14]

School boards may not discriminate even where the board's purpose is to prevent discrimination. For example, the Ku Klux Klan brought suit against a school board which denied the group access to school facilities. The board's policy was to deny access to groups advocating racial discrimination. The court held that to have the state pick and choose which groups may use the facilities, even in the name of civil rights, is not constitutionally sound.[15]

Generally, the local board may allow the school building to be used for any activity which does not interfere with the educational program. The local board may charge an admission or use fee. However, the board cannot allow the use of school buildings for religious services or religious instruction. Furthermore, the board may deny a particular group's use of facilities if the board can show that a clear and present danger for substantial disruption exists and/or possible damage to the facility will result if the use is allowed.

Maintenance

School districts have a duty to provide reasonable maintenance of facilities though there is no obligation to anticipate every possible danger. The courts will consider whether a school employee had knowledge of, or should have had knowledge of, the dangerous condition.

---

[14]*Searcey v. Crim*, 815 F.2d 1389 (11th Cir. 1987).

[15]*Knights of the Ku Klux Klan v. East Baton Rouge Parish School Bd.*, 643 F.2d 1034 (5th Cir. 1981).

In one case, a student recovered DAMAGES when the student permanently injured his hand while attempting to open a door by pushing on the door's glass panel. The ordinary window glass broke causing permanent injury to the student's hand. The 1986 jury heard evidence that the glass used in the door had been regarded as dangerous since the 1960s in areas where children had played. The court held that wired or tempered glass should have been used.[16] However, wired glass alone will not always protect school districts.

In a different district, a Connecticut student recovered damages for injuries suffered when she permanently injured her hand. In this case, the door was equipped with wired glass but had no crash bar or warnings despite the fact that within the previous three months students had twice broken similar glass panels at the school.[17] (See NEGLIGENCE.)

School districts also have a duty to maintain grounds owned by the district. (See PROPERTY.) School districts can be held liable for damages even in cases where employees do not know of the dangerous condition. There is a duty to inspect premises and to maintain facilities so that they may be used without them.

Disposal

The public owns the school property. Therefore, disposition of such property is controlled by state statutes. Local school officials must comply with these statutory requirements in disposing of school property, or the conveyance will be declared invalid. Local school officials have no authority to sell school property unless the authority is specifically granted under the law. Where such authority is not granted, the legislature has complete control of disposal. When the power to dispose is granted, the disposal is subject to the three following rules:

1. The disposal must be for the benefit of the district;
2. School property generally may not be given away; and
3. School property must be sold for the fair market value and not sold for a nominal or token consideration.

A split of authority exists as to whether school property may be leased. A majority of COURTS hold that school property may be leased for a reasonable period of time when the use is not entirely foreign to public policy. However, if the period of the lease is for an excessively long time, the majority of courts will not allow it.

---

[16]*Johnson v. City of Boston*, 490 N.E.2d 1204 (Mass. App. 1986).

[17]*Bielaska v. Town of Waterford*, 491 A.2d 1071 (Conn. 1985).

If the school district ceases to use school property for school purposes, there is a possibility that the land may, in some cases, revert to the original owner. However, the property will not revert if there have been no provisions for reversion made in a deed granting the property to the school. In such cases, the board may dispose of the property in the manner authorized by statute.

BURDEN OF PROOF

Burden of proof means having the duty to go forward with the evidence to prove disputed facts. In a trial or administrative hearing, each side has certain things that must be proven. If the initial burden of proof is met, the other side has the burden of rebutting the other party's evidence. In a lawsuit, the PLAINTIFF has the burden of showing a prima facie case. The plaintiff must prove all of the elements of his or her cause of action sufficient to justify an inference of liability. If the plaintiff proves the necessary elements, the burden of proof shifts and it becomes the DEFENDANT's duty to rebut the plaintiff's prima facie evidence. If one side does not meet its burden, the other side should automatically prevail. On the other hand, if one side proves its prima facie case but the other side presents reliable evidence to dispute that case, then it is for the jury or hearing panel or referee to weigh the evidence and reach a decision.

In order to go forward with a case, the burden of proof requires a fact to be established at one of three progressively more difficult levels: (1) by a PREPONDERANCE OF THE EVIDENCE; (2) by clear and convincing evidence; or (3) by proof beyond a reasonable doubt.

In a criminal case, the prosecutor must prove the prima facie elements of a crime and the fact that the defendant committed that crime "beyond a reasonable doubt," otherwise defined as "a moral certainty." This is the heaviest burden in our court system.

In many other types of cases, the burden of proof must be "clear and convincing." This burden is somewhat less than "beyond a reasonable doubt" and easier to meet, but nevertheless it is still a heavy burden. "Clear and convincing" evidence is sometimes the burden needed for a teacher's dismissal.

In most civil cases, the plaintiff is only required to prove his or her case by a "preponderance of the evidence." This means that, if there is a 51 percent chance versus a 49 percent chance, then he or she has met the burden. In other words, "it is more likely than not." This is the burden used to justify most disciplinary acts of teachers or administrators.

BUS DRIVERS

In addition to federal law, state STATUTES generally set forth the minimum requirements for school bus drivers and frequently include standards of character, physical condition, and special licensing. Minimum and maximum ages are prescribed, and some states require school bus drivers to have had first-aid training.

Suspending students from TRANSPORTATION is not generally within the scope of bus drivers' employment. For example, in one case a bus driver suspended an elementary student from transportation services for a day. District policy was that discipline of this sort was usually handled by the school principal and included a call to the student's parents. The driver did not notify the school or the boy's parents of the suspension. The student did not tell his parents of the suspension and instead rode a bike to school. On the way, he swerved into a truck and was severely injured. The court found the bus driver liable for the injuries.[18] (See NEGLIGENCE; SUPERVISION.)

BUSING

Besides its obvious utility in transporting students who live a great distance from school, busing is identified as an affirmative attempt to rectify some of the inequities caused by past racial discrimination. Many school districts have implemented programs requiring the transportation of students away from the neighborhood schools to schools located in other areas. The purpose of busing programs is to create equal opportunities in education for all children, regardless of their racial or socioeconomic backgrounds.

However, busing programs have been objected to by parents who view busing as a threat to the neighborhood school system and as a hardship for children. Efforts have been made in several states and cities to pass laws or ordinances designed to prohibit busing. Parents who object to busing often remove their children from the public school system either by enrolling the children in private academies or by moving to suburbs not affected by the busing plan. In a Virginia district, school board consultants concluded that, if busing were to continue, the district would become

---

[18]*Toeller v. Mutual Service Casualty Ins. Co.*, 340 N.W.2d 923 (Wis. App. 1983).

segregated due to the "white flight." The school board abolished busing and adjusted neighborhood boundaries to achieve racial integration. However, some schools were 100 percent black and others as little as 16 percent black. In this case, the court held that preventing "white flight" was a valid school objective and upheld the plan.[19]

In a similar case, a second court held just the opposite.[20] The United States Supreme Court has refused to consider appeals in both of these cases. Therefore, state law will be controlling until the Supreme Court addresses this difficult issue.

See also CHILD BENEFIT THEORY; DISCRIMINATION; FUNDS; TRANSPORTATION.

---

[19]*Riddick v. School Board or Norfolk*, 784 F.2d 521 (4th Cir. 1986); *cert. denied*, 479 U.S. 938 (1986).

[20]*Board of Educ. of Oklahoma City Pub. Schools v. Dowell*, 795 F.2d 1516 (10th Cir. 1986); *cert. denied*, 479 U.S. 938 (1986).

C

CAPACITY

Capacity as used in this context is intended to mean the "legal ability" to enter into CONTRACTS. Mentally incompetent persons and minors are examples of those persons who do not have the legal ability to enter into a contract and make it binding.

SCHOOL BOARDS and educators must have the capacity to enter into a contract with each other. In order for a school board to have capacity, its members must be acting in a properly convened MEETING and have contracts approved by a majority of the board. Since the board has the exclusive authority to contract with school personnel, individual board members lack the legal capacity to enter into a contract on behalf of the entire board.[1] This means that a teacher's or administrator's contract should be signed while the board is in session; and, if it is not, it must at least have been agreed to in a proper session. If a contract with the board has not gone through the statutorily mandated procedures, it is void or voidable.

The teacher or administrator also must have legal capacity to enter into an agreement. This means that the teacher or administrator must have a valid state certificate or else he or she is not a competent party to be paid under the contract.[2] Some states say that there must be legal capacity (certificate) at the time of entering into the contract; other states say that there must be legal capacity before one commences his or her duties. Either way, there must be capacity before one can demand payment for the services he or she performs. For example, if one teaches without a proper

---

[1] *Minor v. Sully Buttes School District*, 345 N.W.2d 48 (S.D. 1984).
[2] *See Nelson v. Doland Board of Education*, 380 N.W.2d 665 (S.D. 1986).

61

certificate but later obtains one, he or she generally will only be able to obtain payment for those days in which he or she had the required legal capacity to teach.

See also CERTIFICATION.

CENSORSHIP

See ACADEMIC FREEDOM; CONSTITUTIONAL LAW; LIBRARY CENSORSHIP; OBSCENITY; SCHOOL PUBLICATIONS.

CERTIFICATION

An educator's certificate is a document which specifies that the named individual has fulfilled the legal requirements of the particular state to be a teacher, to be an administrator, or to be a specialist or be qualified to perform specific duties or job functions in that state. The certificate is a license, not a contract, and does not confer any right to employment or a specific position.[3] A certificate is required before a person can enter into a valid contract. Without a certificate, a person performing teaching, administrative, or other services is deemed to be a volunteer and, as such, is not entitled to payment for services performed. Furthermore, many states have laws which forbid school boards from employing persons to perform duties who do not have valid teaching certificates. The penalty for violation is generally a loss of the state funds which are normally contributed to help finance the costs of the particular teaching position.

States are divided as to just when an educator must possess the certificate. Some states say that the educator must have the certificate when the contract is signed or else the CONTRACT is void. The majority of states say that professional school personnel must have the certificate before any duties are performed. Without this license, the employee generally lacks legal CAPACITY to enter a contract. For example, an Alabama court upheld the dismissal of a teacher for failure to acquire valid certification. The court declared there was "good and just" cause for his discharge when the teacher did not meet the certification requirements for driver education instruction.[4] Similarly, the Supreme Court of New York

---

[3]*Lombard v. Board of Education*, 645 F. Supp. 1574 (E.D.N.Y. 1986).

[4]*Rogers v. Ala. State Tenure Comm'n.*, 372 So. 2d 1313 (Ala. App. 1979).

sustained the dismissal of a teacher for "incompetency" because the teacher failed to qualify for permanent certification during an alloted six-year period.[5]

Legislative STATUTES and administrative qualifications for certificates vary among the individual states. Most states require that the person complete a prescribed course of training at an approved educational institution and that the person meet various character standards.

Generally, the minimum personal and professional requirements needed to obtain certification include:

1. The necessary college preparation;

2. Physical capability; and

3. Moral character.

Approval of the course of study and of the institutions' programs is generally within the power of the state board of education. The state board is also generally granted the power to set the minimum standards required for approval. A state can reasonably change certificate requirements and require all currently certified employees to pass a competency examination to retain their credentials.[6]

Local SCHOOL BOARDS are frequently allowed to prescribe standards and qualifications for employment which go beyond the minimum state requirements for certification; these additional requirements are upheld unless they are unreasonable, arbitrary, or capricious. For example, one school board policy required that, in order to be employed, teachers must achieve a minimum score on the Graduate Records Examination (GRE) or fulfill one of several various other alternatives. This policy had the effect of disqualifying a disproportionate number of black teachers, nine of whom sued on the alleged grounds of denial of EQUAL PROTECTION and DISCRIMINATION. The court did not rule on the discrimination issue. The court held, however, that the GRE requirement was arbitrary because such a test was not designed to, nor could it, adequately measure teacher competency. The rule eliminated good teachers and had no reasonable relation to the purpose for which it was designed. However, the court suggested that the alternative requirements that teachers have an AA Teaching Certificate or Master's Degree could perhaps be justified.[7] Another example is where a local board has the right to require continuing

---

[5]*Linton v. Board of Education of Yonkers City School Dist.*, 417 N.Y.S.2d (N.Y. 246 1979).

[6]*State v. Project Principle, Inc.*, 724 S.W.2d 387 (Tex. 1987).

[7]*Armstead v. Starkville Municipal Separate School District*, 461 F.2d 276 (5th Cir. 1972).

education requirements from its staff.[8] Competency testing for educators is allowed if the testing is related to a proper educational purpose and is not discriminatory in nature.

A state board of education has the right to certify professional school personnel; and obviously the board has the authority to suspend, deny, or revoke certificates for just cause. There must be statutory standards and requisite DUE PROCESS procedures. For example, if the board is trying to determine moral character, the board must have basic guidelines which are capable of objective scrutiny. The primary inquiry into a person's moral character must be related to his or her fitness to perform a particular certifiable position and to the protection of students. This means that the measures and standards must be relevant and appropriate to the educator-pupil relationship. If the criteria are not relevant and a person is denied a certificate as a result, the denial would be deemed arbitrary and capricious and the license would be granted.

Acts which have resulted in the denial or revocation of a certificate include:

1. Commission of a FELONY
2. Conviction of a crime involving MORAL TURPITUDE
3. Repetitive patterns of committing MISDEMEANORS
4. Fraud in obtaining the certificate.

There are other acts which would constitute grounds for denial of a certificate. Nevertheless, these grounds must relate to the position being sought and cannot violate the applicant's constitutional rights or be arbitrarily or discriminatorily enforced.

See also CONSTITUTIONAL LAW; DECERTIFICATION.

CERTIORARI, Writ of

A writ of certiorari is an original writ commanding judges or officers of inferior COURTS to produce a certified record of case proceedings for judicial review. Frequently, a party wishing to appeal a case to the United States Supreme Court will request the Supreme Court to issue a writ of certiorari to inspect the record for irregularities. The decision of the reviewing court on certiorari is controlling. Thus, a denial of certiorari to review an issue or issues involved in such proceedings makes the lower court's ruling final.

---

[8]*Harrah Independent School Dist. v. Martin*, 440 U.S. 194 (1979).

CHIEF STATE SCHOOL OFFICER

The chief state school officer's title varies from state to state: State Commissioner of Education, State Superintendent of Public Instruction, or the State Superintendent of Public Schools. The chief state school officer's relationship to the State Board of Education depends upon the board's policies and RULES. The title used to describe this relationship also varies: Executive Secretary to the Board, Chief Administrative Officer, and others.

In nearly one-half of the states, the chief state school officer is selected by the State Board of Education. This is often felt to be the superior method of selection because it helps to prevent politicians who have little or no experience in education from becoming the chief officer. In most of the remaining states, selection is by popular vote.

Few qualifications, and in many states no qualifications, are required by the state STATUTES for the person who will be selected as the chief officer. In the states which do prescribe qualifications, the most common is that the chief officer must be able to qualify for a teaching certificate.

The term of office varies. Almost one-third of the states have no specific term specified, and most of these provide that the superintendent remains in office at the pleasure of the board. Most of the other states prescribe a specific number of years, the most common being four-year terms.

See also COMMISSIONER OF EDUCATION; STRUCTURE OF THE SCHOOL SYSTEM.

CHILD ABUSE

The United States Department of Health and Human Services' National Center on Child Abuse and Neglect reports indicate that nearly one million children each year are abused or neglected. Because many of these children are of school age, many states have enacted STATUTES which impose a duty on school employees to report children who they have reason to believe have been abused or neglected. Thus, whenever a school employee has reasonable cause to believe that any child with whom he or she comes into contact in his or her official capacity has suffered abuse or neglect or that any adult with whom he or she has had official contact has abused or neglected a child, he or she must report the abuse.

Failure to report may subject the school employee to liability for the foreseeable injuries caused by further abuse. Furthermore, many states' statutes impose criminal liability for failure to report. Penalties include fines ranging from $500 to $1,000, prison terms of up to one year, or both. School employees may also face disciplinary actions by SCHOOL BOARDS. In a case involving a school psychologist who delayed reporting information about alleged sexual activity between a teacher and a student, a federal court of appeals found that disciplinary action taken by the school board was appropriate.[9]

All states grant immunity from civil and criminal liability to individuals if reports are made in good faith. In a case where parents sued a teacher who reported suspected child abuse that was later unsubstantiated, a court held that the teacher was immune because the teacher acted in good faith and on reasonable grounds pursuant to a statutory duty.[10]

Sometimes, the use of CORPORAL PUNISHMENT leads to the accusation of abuse against school employees. However, under the doctrine of IN LOCO PARENTIS, school officials generally have the right to use corporal punishment in districts where this form of punishment is not banned as a means of maintaining discipline. When the punishment becomes excessive or abusive, the teacher or administrator may be liable for ASSAULT, BATTERY, or both. (See SAVE-HARMLESS STATUTES.)

School districts may be liable in cases where districts hire or retain educators who the district knows or should know have abused children. For example, in a case where a teacher molested a number of his fourth-grade female students, a court found that the school had a duty to protect its students and, if the school was aware of the teacher's previous molestations, then it must be held responsible for the foreseeable consequences of not preventing the teacher from harming the students involved in the case.[11]

See also SEXUAL ABUSE; SUPERVISION.

CHILD-BENEFIT THEORY

The child-benefit theory is occasionally applied by the COURTS to uphold certain uses of public money directly or indirectly in support of children attending private or parochial schools. This theory originated out of a case involving a Louisiana STATUTE which provided for free TEXTBOOKS to all

---

[9]*Pesce v. J. Sterling Morton High School, District 201, Cook Co., Ill.*, 830 F.2d 789 (7th Cir. 1987).

[10]*McDonald v. State of Oregon*, 694 P.2d 569 (Or. App. 1985); *rev. denied*, 698 P.2d 964 (Or. 1985).

[11]*Doe v. Durtschi*, 716 P.2d 1238 (Idaho 1986).

students, even if the students attended PRIVATE SCHOOLS. The court upheld the law by saying that the statute provided free books for the children and was enacted for the children's benefit and not for the benefit of the church. The aid to the private schools was seen as being merely incidental.[12] The Supreme Court again ruled in 1975 that textbook loans at no cost to children in both public and private schools neither advanced nor inhibited religion.

Under the child-benefit theory, use of public funds for busing children to nonpublic schools within the district boundaries was also held not to violate the United States Constitution Establishment Clause since child safety and welfare were at issue.[14] However, the concept of child benefit does not extend to the use of tax funds to pay teachers in nonpublic schools.

There is a strong possibility that the child-benefit theory could violate individual state constitutions; and, if so, the theory would be invalid under state rather than federal law.

The child-benefit theory depends on a two-part test:

1. What is legislative intent, and

2. Who receives the aid—the school, or the parent and child?

The child-benefit theory has lost much of its past support. More often than not, state courts have (contrary to United States Supreme Court) ruled against using tax funds for children in parochial schools.[15]

See also FUNDAMENTAL INTEREST THEORY; PRIVATE AND PAROCHIAL SCHOOL AID; RELIGION.

CHURCH-STATE RELATIONS

See BIBLE READING; PRAYERS; PRIVATE AND PAROCHIAL SCHOOL AID; RELIGION; SHARED-TIME.

---

[12]*Cochran v. Louisiana State Board of Education*, 281 U.S. 370 (1930).

[13]*Meek v. Pittinger*, 421 U.S. 349; *reh'g. denied*, 422 U.S. 1049 (1975).

[14]*Everson v. Board of Education of the Township of Ewing*, 330 U.S. 1 (1947).

[15]*Paster v. Tussey*, 512 S.W.2d 97 (Mo. 1974); *Gaffney v. State Board of Education*, 220 N.W.2d 550 (Neb. 1974); *Bloom v. School Comm.*, 379 N.E.2d 578 (Mass. 1978); *California Teachers Ass'n. v. Riles*, 632 P.2d 953 (Cal. 1981).

CIVIL RIGHTS ACT OF 1871

A federal STATUTE enacted in 1871 is frequently used as the legal basis for seeking DAMAGES or other remedies for infringement on individuals' basic personal rights guaranteed by the Constitution. This statute reads as follows:

> Every person who, under color of any statute, ordinance, regulation, custom or usage, of any State or Territory, subjects, or causes to be subjected, any citizen of the United States or other person within the jurisdiction thereof to the deprivation of any rights, privileges, or immunities secured by the Constitution and laws, shall be liable to the party injured in an action at law, suit in equity, or other proper proceeding for redress. (R.S. § 1983).[16]

DISCRIMINATION based on race, color, age or religion is prohibited in school policies and practices. This act makes school personnel liable to persons suing for injunctive relief and damages for violation of constitutional rights that accompany citizenship. When suing on the basis of this federal act, reinstatement, back pay, compensation for financial loss, damages for loss of promotion in career, damages for loss of reputation and professional status, damages for physical or mental suffering, and even punitive damages have been found to be available as remedies in appropriate instances.

In 1978, the United States Supreme Court decided that boards of education can be sued as "persons" and are not immune from liability under 42 U.S.C. Section 1983.[17] In 1982, the United States Supreme Court again addressed the immunity issue and stated that government officials performing discretionary functions generally are shielded from liability for civil damages insofar as their conduct does not violate clearly established statutory or constitutional rights of which a reasonable person would have known.[18] While public officials are not expected to predict the future course of constitutional law, they are expected to adhere to principles of law that are well established.[19]

---

[16]42 U.S.C. Section 1983 (Act April 20, 1871, Chap. 22, Section 1, 17 Stat. 13), Section 1983, Civil action for deprivation of rights.

[17]*Monell v. Department of Social Services of the City of New York*, 436 U.S. 658 (1978).

[18]*Harlow v. Fitzgerald*, 457 U.S. 800 (1982).

[19]*Davis v. Scherer* 468 U.S. 183 (1984).

An educator whose employment has been terminated or who has been disciplined in violation of constitutional rights may bring suit in federal court under the Civil Rights Act of 1871 (42 U.S.C. Section 1983) for monetary or injunctive relief even before exhausting state administrative remedies.[20] However, the Supreme Court has rejected the use of Section 1983 as a fountain of federal tort law, making it clear that the protections of the DUE PROCESS clause are "not triggered by a lack of due care by state officials."[21] The alleged TORT must be egregious enough to be a systematic abuse or arbitrary exercise of government power.[22]

See also CONSTITUTIONAL LAW.

CIVIL RIGHTS ACT OF 1964

Although education is primarily a state function, the federal government may impose various restrictions on state action by conferring federal grants with prescribed conditions. The Civil Rights Act of 1964 was designed to provide federal financial aid for various educational programs in such a manner as to insure individuals' freedoms and equal opportunity.

Initially, no guidelines for implementation or interpretation of this act were published; however, several sets of guidelines have since been issued by the Equal Employment Opportunity Commission (EEOC). Some of the interpretive guidelines were necessary to clarify Section 601 of Title VI, which provides that:

> No person in the United States shall, on the ground of race, color, or national origin, be excluded from participation in, be denied the benefits of, or be subjected to discrimination under any program or activity receiving federal financial assistance.

As a result, the following discriminatory practices are prohibited: SEGREGATION; DISCRIMINATION in quality, quantity, or manner of benefit given; discriminatory requirements for participation; discrimination in employment; and discrimination on the basis of sex.

If a person believes he or she has been discriminated against, the person may file a complaint with the chairperson of the EEOC in Washington, D.C., or consult an attorney. In some instances, violations of

---

[20]*Patsy v. Board of Regents of State of Florida*, 457 U.S. 456 (1982).

[21]*Paul v. Davis*, 424 U.S. 693 (1976).

[22]*Daniels v. Williams*, 474 U.S. 327 (1986).

the provisions of the Civil Rights Act will not necessarily amount to a violation under the EQUAL PROTECTION clause of the Constitution.

Complaints registered with the EEOC have involved PATERNITY LEAVES, sex discrimination in ATHLETICS, and equal access to facilities. In one example, an Ohio court held that the district could not provide male teachers with locker room facilities including self-contained offices, private toilets and showers, while at the same time the female teachers' facilities consisted only of a small area separated from the student facilities by a partition. The court ruled that this was unequal treatment based on sex and violated Title VII.[23]

The ELEMENTARY AND SECONDARY EDUCATION ACT OF 1965 provides federal aid to schools and is, therefore, also subject to the Civil Rights Act of 1964. In addition, cases involving pregnant teachers have at times been brought under this act.

However, the Pregnancy Discrimination Act has amended Title VII of the Civil Rights Act of 1964; and it provides that women affected by pregnancy, childbirth, or related medical conditions shall be treated the same for all employment-related purposes, including the receipt of benefits and fringe benefit programs, as other persons not so affected but similar in their ability or inability to work.[24] Therefore, a woman unable to work for pregnancy-related reasons is entitled to disability benefits on the same basis as employees unable to work for other medical reasons.[25]

Title VII of the Civil Rights Act of 1964 prohibits an employer from discriminating against any individual with regard to compensation, as well as terms, conditions, or privileges of employment because of race, color, religion, sex, or national origin.[26]

Similar to the Equal Pay Act, Title VII allows compensation differentials based on bona fide seniority or merit systems or production-measuring systems. Unlike the Equal Pay Act, however, Title VII specifically disallows compensation differentials if they are "the result of an intention to discriminate" and which contain a specific exception allowing an employer to act upon the results of a professionally given aptitude test.

Under Title VII, employment decisions, including matters of compensation, cannot be predicated upon mere stereotyped impressions about a woman's inability to perform certain kinds of work. There are no acceptable reasons for refusing to employ qualified female individuals nor for paying them less.

Moreover, Title VII's prohibition of gender-based wage discrimination is not restricted to claims of equal pay for equal work. The Supreme Court

---

[23]*Harrington v. Vandalia-Butler Board of Education*, 585 F.2d 192 (6th Cir. 1978).

[24]U.S.C. Section 2000 e(k).

[25]29 C.F.R. Section 1604.

[26]42 U.S.C. Section 2000 e-2(a)(1).

has held that claims of intentional sex wage discrimination may be brought under Title VII even if a violation of the equal work standard is not asserted. Plaintiffs may not recover under Title VII for such discrimination where such practices are specifically authorized by the Equal Pay Act—that is, where such payment is made pursuant to (1) a seniority system, (2) a merit system, (3) a system which measures earning by quantity or quality of production, or (4) a differential based on any factor other than sex.[27]

See also EQUAL PAY ACT; MATERNITY LEAVE.

CLOSED SHOP

See UNION SECURITY.

COLLECTIVE BARGAINING

Prior to the Civil War, STRIKES for higher wages were treated as criminal conspiracies; but, in the following fifty years, the United States witnessed a tremendous growth in industry and a consequent growth in the organization of laborers. By 1900, labor organizations were not considered criminal; but many organization activities, including strikes and picketing, were prohibited by law. With the aid of various federal acts, many restrictions against UNIONS gradually were removed. Enacted in 1935, the National Labor Relations Act (NLRA) became the major piece of legislation which formed the basis for authorizing bargaining and strike rights of private employees. The Taft Hartley Act, in 1947, amended the NLRA by regulating abusive union practices. The individual employee has greater freedom of choice in bargaining when employer and union interference is controlled under federal legislation.

The organization rights of public employees lagged far behind their counterparts in the private business sector. However, in the mid 1900s, the ranks of public employees began to swell as the public demanded more and more services. On the education side of public employment, teachers were in great demand as the "baby boom" subsequent to World War II necessitated more schools and more educators. In addition, the 1950s and 1960s were times that witnessed a large increase in the number of men joining the teaching profession.

---

[27]*County of Washington v. Gunther*, 452 U.S. 161 (1981).

As the number of public employees began to grow, so did the desire for greater bargaining rights. These employees wanted to form employee organizations to bargain over wages, hours, and other employment conditions. Public employees patterned bargaining plans after those in the private sector and demanded equal rights.

The legislatures of many states made efforts to pacify public employees by granting them some employment rights; and the COURTS also were called upon to define the bargaining rights to which public employees were entitled. It is now clearly recognized that public employees have the right to organize and to be represented by an employee organization. Bargaining laws range from the minimal right to bargain to comprehensive regulations over negotiation rights. Wisconsin, in 1949, was the first state to enact a special law designed to guarantee bargaining rights to public employees. Since then, more than two-thirds of the states have enacted laws granting collective bargaining rights to the public sector. The scope of negotiable issues, the use of binding ARBITRATION, and the right to strike are all issues which have not been uniformly resolved. However, bargaining rights have been expanding; it appears that this trend will continue, and public employees, including public school educators, will have greater bargaining rights in future years.

Currently, the most comprehensive and protective bargaining laws (from an employee's standpoint) have been enacted in the midwestern and eastern states. These states, long experienced with private industrial unionism, were the most receptive to public employee unionism. Conversely, the southern and southwestern states, without the history of industrial union activities, have been slower to enact laws granting bargaining rights to public employees. However, the trend is for more states to provide for some form of bargaining procedure.

All contracts entered into by employee associations and public employers are invalid without enabling legislation. In the absence of a federal law covering public school employees, it is advisable to be familiar with the collective bargaining laws in your state because there is great diversity among the states' bargaining practices and labor laws. At present, the basic form of collective bargaining laws and the procedures utilized in bargaining and settling labor disputes is controlled by individual state statutes and court rulings. Congress may again consider uniform collective bargaining legislation since the 1985 Supreme Court ruling in *Garcia v. San Antonio Metropolitan Transit Authority* that ordered municipal governments to comply with Fair Labor Standards Act requirements of minimum wage and overtime.[28]

Collective bargaining is a method of determining conditions of employment through bilateral negotiations between representatives of the

---

[28]*Garcia v. San Antonio Metropolitan Transit Authority*, 469 U.S. 528 (1985).

employer and the certified employee organization. These parties are required by law to reach a settlement which is mutually binding. This settlement is then set forth in a written agreement. Collective bargaining, as defined by the National Labor Relations Act and several state laws, is:

> ...The performance of the mutual obligation of the employer and the representative of the employees to meet at reasonable times and confer in good faith with respect to wages, hours and other terms and conditions of employment, of the negotiation of an agreement or any question arising thereunder, and the execution of a written contract incorporating any agreement reached if requested by either party, but such obligation does not compel either party to agree to a proposal or require the making of a concession...

Note that the parties meet as equals and determinations are made pursuant to bilateral negotiations. This differs considerably from pure "MEET AND CONFER" statutes in which the employees are given the right to discuss employment relations, but management retains the right to act unilaterally. Also, meet and confer statutes are distinguishable in the range of legally permissible topics about which the parties may "confer" as opposed to "negotiate." Under collective bargaining, the SCOPE OF BARGAINING is considerably more extensive.

Collective bargaining laws do not compel the public employer to give up its sovereign authority to make decisions. Once a SCHOOL BOARD enters into the negotiating process, the parties are subject to established judicial principles and legal constraints. These laws require the parties to follow certain bargaining procedures which must be followed. The requirements are that the employer must bargain in good faith and in so doing must negotiate with the recognized bargaining agents. After a reasonable period of good faith bargaining, if a settlement has not been reached, the board cannot unilaterally formulate the bargaining agreement. The parties can each make a final offer which, if not accepted, will then move the process to impasse.

An impasse occurs when the parties are unable to reach an agreement. Impasse machinery is designed to help the parties reach a settlement on their own. MEDIATION and FACTFINDING are found in nearly all collective bargaining laws, and these are utilized to aid the parties in resolving the dispute. If mediation and/or factfinding are unsuccessful, some laws provide for a third party to settle the dispute through what is known as binding ARBITRATION. A few laws allow the public employees to STRIKE at this point in the impasse.

In order for collective bargaining to work effectively, there must exist impasse machinery which provides both parties with equal bargaining power if the dispute is submitted to impasse. In this way, the parties will theoretically bargain in good faith during the earlier stages of the

COLLECTIVE BARGAINING

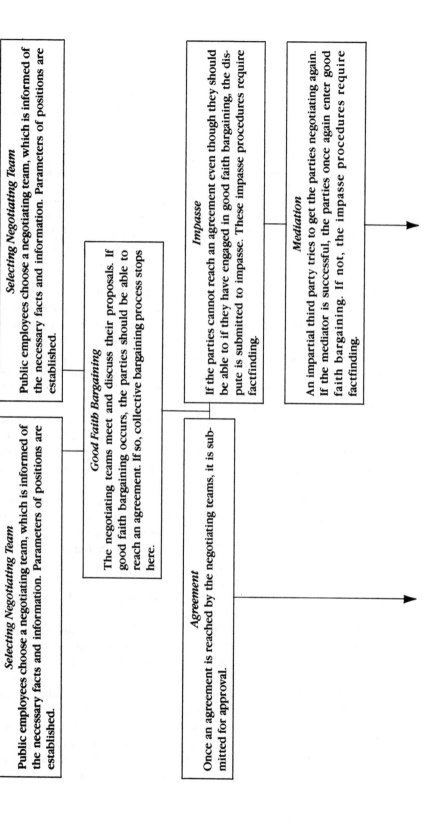

Selecting Negotiating Team
Public employees choose a negotiating team, which is informed of the necessary facts and information. Parameters of positions are established.

Selecting Negotiating Team
Public employees choose a negotiating team, which is informed of the necessary facts and information. Parameters of positions are established.

Good Faith Bargaining
The negotiating teams meet and discuss their proposals. If good faith bargaining occurs, the parties should be able to reach an agreement. If so, collective bargaining process stops here.

Agreement
Once an agreement is reached by the negotiating teams, it is submitted for approval.

Impasse
If the parties cannot reach an agreement even though they should be able to if they have engaged in good faith bargaining, the dispute is submitted to impasse. These impasse procedures require factfinding.

Mediation
An impartial third party tries to get the parties negotiating again. If the mediator is successful, the parties once again enter good faith bargaining. If not, the impasse procedures require factfinding.

COLLECTIVE BARGAINING (*Cont'd*)

Employee Organization Approval

The public employees vote as to whether or not the agreement is acceptable to them. If not, the parties are forced into negotiations again.

Voter Approval

If the agreement reached involves the expenditure of money, voter approval is generally required in order to obtain the necessary funds. If the required approval is not granted, the agreement is broken and the negotiations begin again.

Factfinding

A factfinder listens to both sides of the dispute, makes findings of facts and recommends a solution. If the parties accept the recommendations, agreement is reached. If not, the factfinder's findings and recommendations are made public.

If factfinding fails to encourage the parties to reach an agreement, the laws vary in their approaches to the final step on impasse. The most common approach is arbitration, but strikes are allowed in some states.

Strike

Several states authorize public employees to strike at this point. Strikes generally will get the negotiations started again. Most laws provide that injunctive relief is available in the event that the strike creates a clear and present danger to the public health, safety or welfare.

Binding Arbitration

A third party holds a hearing, listens to both sides of the dispute, investigates the facts, and recommends a solution. The arbitrator's recommendations are binding.

Advisory Arbitration

This process is much like that used in binding arbitration but the arbitrator's recommendations are advisory and not binding. As a result, this step is closer akin to factfinding and it is an added expense. Therefore, it is not widely adopted.

negotiations. Binding arbitration provides the parties with an equal chance of obtaining a favorable settlement in the event of an impasse. Many states have recognized the alternative of binding arbitration, and the trend is toward greater utilization of binding arbitration in settling public employee labor and contract disputes.

Even where collective bargaining for teachers has been recognized, problems still arise. Foremost among these problems is the question of who should be allowed to unite in bargaining units. In a series of decisions, the National Labor Relations Board has held that ROTC officers, teacher support personnel, part-time teachers, and retired teachers may not join professional teacher collective bargaining units. Courts have held that employees with supervisory or managerial status, such as principals, cannot be represented by the same union as teachers in light of potential conflicts of interest.[29] On the other hand, librarians and athletic coaches have been allowed to join the bargaining unit of professional teachers. To determine whether different employees may join together in one bargaining unit the following guide rules may be considered:

1. Do the employees seeking representation comprise a homogeneous, identifiable, and distinct group?
2. Is there a recognizable community of interest sufficiently distinct from other employees in terms of skills and working conditions so as to warrant their inclusion in a single unit?

To keep school officials from infringing on protected rights of ASSOCIATION and participation in union activities by SANCTIONS of loss of benefits, the courts' decisions have consistently supported educators. For example, the courts have overturned suspensions, dismissals, and assignments of teachers when the sanction was seen as a hostile action in retaliation for union membership or activities.[30]

COMMENCEMENT EXERCISES

SCHOOL BOARDS have the authority to enact reasonable RULES governing student conduct and the operation of schools. Requiring that students who wish to participate in commencement exercises wear caps and gowns has been held to be a reasonable rule.[31] This requirement would seem to be

---

[29]*In Re Manchester Bd. of School Comm.*, 523 A.2d 114 (N.H. 1987).

[30]*Gavrilles v. O'Connor*, 611 F. Supp. 210 (D. Mass. 1985).

[31]*Valentine v. Independent School District of Casey*, 183 N.W. 434 (Iowa 1921).

unreasonable, however, if no provision were made for providing caps and gowns to students who could not afford them. In such cases, it would seem that the school would either have to provide the caps and gowns or would have to allow the students to participate without them.

Requiring a certain style of clothing under the cap and gown has also been deemed to be a reasonable rule. In 1979, the appeals court in North Carolina decided that a school administrator's decision to exclude a boy from the high school graduation ceremony was permissible because the dress code called for "dress pants" to be worn and the boy wore brushed denim jeans. The court ruled that local school boards and officials have the IMPLIED AUTHORITY to define the type of clothing to be worn in a high school graduation as a matter of decorum.[32]

Religious elements included in graduation exercises, activities that the courts have consistently not allowed in the classroom, have been permitted if what is done is considered ceremonial and of a minimal nature.[33] The courts have deemed rules allowing prayers to be reasonable under these limited circumstances.

The school may not condition granting of the DIPLOMA upon participation in the commencement exercises. Such a rule would be arbitrary, because the rule is not reasonably related to the educational process. However, one court concluded that, although a student suspended for fighting had a property right to his diploma, he had no property right to attend graduation exercises.[34]

COMMISSIONER OF EDUCATION

This designated superintendent of public instruction functions in an executive capacity over the policy-making state board's professional staff. In general, state education authorities are allowed wide discretion in the formulation and enforcement of rules. (For an explanation of the commissioner's legal status, qualifications, etc., see CHIEF STATE SCHOOL OFFICER.)

Most states authorize the Commissioner of Education to adjudicate school disputes. Commissioners traditionally have extensive authority to render binding decisions which will not be overruled by a court unless they are arbitrary or lack a rational basis.[35]

---

[32]*Fowler v. Williamson*, 251 S.E.2d 889 (N.C. App. 1979).

[33]*Wiest v. Mt. Lebanon School District*, 320 A.2d 362 (Pa. 1974).

[34]*Mifflin Co. School District v. Stewart*, 503 A.2d 1012 (Pa. 1986).

[35]*Gundrum v. Ambach*, 433 N.E.2d 531 (N.Y. 1982).

COMMON LAW

Common law is the general universal law of the land. This law is not derived from state STATUTES enacted by legislatures but is developed by usage, customs, and principles of antiquity and through court decisions over hundreds of years. Common law prevails in England and the United States and is the controlling law unless modified by state or federal statutes, by a constitutional amendment or by a decision of a higher court which adjudicates a constitutional issue.

For example, NEGLIGENCE involves the elements of (1) duty, (2) breach of duty, (3) cause, and (4) injury. This concept is not generally defined by statute but has developed through the years with court decisions. It is because of the "common law" that one can generalize about the law all over the United States without having to specifically research each state's statutes. Only where states modify or abolish the common law is it necessary to look at individual states specifically. For example, most states have statutes changing the common law status of TENURE or GOVERNMENTAL IMMUNITY; and, yet, the common law concept of IN LOCO PARENTIS still prevails in the majority of states, limited and defined by the court decisions and not by state statutes.

See also COURTS; STARE DECISIS.

COMMON SCHOOLS

Many state constitutions and STATUTES provide that the state shall establish and maintain common schools. Common schools are schools which may be attended by any school-age child residing within designated boundaries. Such schools are supported by public FUNDS and must be provided free of charge to any attending students.

The extent of education required by local districts depends upon the wording of applicable state constitutions and statutes. High schools, junior high schools, and elementary schools are common schools.

However, in some states KINDERGARTENS are not considered to be common schools which the legislature must establish. Schools for adults and community or junior colleges are also not required. These additional education programs may be established by the legislature, but common school funds may not be expended on them without the necessary constitutional or statutory amendments.

COMMUNICABLE DISEASES

Historically, the courts assumed that, if a child were infected with a communicable disease, the local school authorities could exclude the student from public schools until the child was no longer a danger to the other students. School employees who had contracted communicable diseases were also excluded from the schools either by termination or indefinite leaves of absences. Most state laws still allow SCHOOL BOARDS the power to exclude students and employees who are infectious.

The question of whether students and employees with acquired immune deficiency syndrome (AIDS) should be permitted in schools has been at the center of many emotional battles. AIDS is the clinical manifestation of a dysfunction of the human immune system caused by a virus that is transmitted by infected blood and semen. To date, there is no vaccine or cure. The courts have held in several instances that school authorities cannot automatically exclude students or employees who have AIDS.

Using the test adopted by the United States Supreme Court in an earlier case involving a teacher with tuberculosis, a federal district court held that a teacher with AIDS was handicapped under the REHABILITA-TION ACT OF 1973 and was otherwise qualified to teach.[36] In the tuberculosis case, the court found that the disease was a handicapping condition under the Rehabilitation Act and held that the district could not dismiss the teacher if the teacher were "otherwise qualified to teach."[37] To determine if a person is otherwise qualified when a person is handicapped with a contagious disease, the court held that there must be an individual inquiry based on reasonable medical judgments which consider the following:

1. The nature of the risk (how the disease is transmitted);
2. The duration of the risk (how long the carrier is infectious);
3. The severity of the risk (what is the potential harm to third parties); and
4. The probabilities the disease will be transmitted.

Reasonable accommodations, those which do not impose undue

---

[36]*Chalk v. United States District Court of Central Dist. of Ca.*, 840 F.2d 701 (9th Cir. 1988).

[37]*School Bd. of Nassau County v. Arline*, 480 U.S. 273 (1987).

financial or administrative burdens on the employer, must be made if the accommodations would lessen the risks and make the person otherwise qualified. In other words, if a district can diminish the risk to third parties in an inexpensive and nonproblematic way, then the district must make the accommodation. However, if, after reasonable accommodation is considered, a significant risk of transmission still exists, the person is not otherwise qualified and may be excluded.

Regarding students, a court held in 1989 that an incontinent, drooling, developmentally disabled child with AIDS could not be excluded from the classroom.[38] The court applied the same test used in the tuberculosis case. Regarding the severity of the harm, they found that the disease was most likely fatal. The duration of the risk was found to be nonchanging during the course of the disease. However, the court found that the nature of the transmission of the disease was such that there was very little risk to third persons. To reach this conclusion, the court relied on findings of the Center for Disease Control which showed that the risk of transmission of AIDS from bodily fluids and material other than blood or semen is extremely low or nonexistent. The court held that the probability of transmission was only a remote theoretical probability. Indeed, to date, there are no known or suspected cases of children being infected by AIDS in schools. Thus, the court held that the school could not exclude the student.

A student with AIDS may also be considered handicapped and eligible for special education services under the EDUCATION FOR ALL HANDICAPPED CHILDREN ACT OF 1975 if the student has limited strength, vitality, or alertness due to disease and if the disease's effect adversely affect the student's educational performance.

COMPARATIVE NEGLIGENCE

Comparative negligence is a refinement of the doctrine of CONTRIBUTORY NEGLIGENCE. While contributory negligence bars recovery of DAMAGES, comparative negligence allows the amount of NEGLIGENCE between the parties to be allocated comparatively on the basis of degrees of fault. For example, a jury may find that a student who, while running in the hall, tripped over a mop handle which was lying on the floor 40 percent negligent and the school's agent, the custodian, 60 percent negligent. Under contributory negligence, the student would be unable to recover any damages. In states using comparative negligence, if the

---

[37]*Martinez v. The School Bd. of Hillsborough County*, 711 F. Supp. 1066 (M.D. Fla. 1989).

student's damages amounted to $10,000, the student would be entitled to recover $6,000, or 60 percent, from the district. In some comparative negligence states, PLAINTIFFS may not recover if their negligence is the same or greater than the DEFENDANT's negligence.

COMPETENCY TESTING, Students

In response to the growing number of illiterate high school graduates, many states have enacted STATUTES requiring that students be administered and pass minimum competency or achievement tests prior to advancing in school or receiving a high school DIPLOMA. Again, as with INTELLIGENCE TESTING, the main criticism of this type of testing has been that the tests are culturally discriminatory.

Courts have upheld the use of competency tests as a graduation requirement. In one case, when a large portion of minority students failed the test, the students' parents brought suit against a district. The court found that the results of tests punished victims of earlier racial segregation and held that the tests were unconstitutional.[39] The court went on to state that, had the repercussions of a segregated system not been present, graduation requirements based on the test would be permitted. In fact, years later, upon rehearing the issue, it was held that the results of past intentional segregation did not cause the exam's disproportionate impact on blacks. Thus, the court found the test constitutional.[40]

Challenges to competency-based tests which are used to retain students have also been unsuccessful. A highly publicized case involved twenty-two second-grade students who were not promoted to the third grade after failing to pass a competency test in reading. All but one student in the class failed the test. The court held that the district could retain the students in the second grade.[41]

See also ACCOUNTABILITY; INTELLIGENCE TESTING.

COMPETENCY TESTING, Teachers

See CERTIFICATION.

---

[39]*Debra P. v. Turlington,* 474 F. Supp. 244 (M.D. Fla. 1979).

[40]*Debra P. v. Turlington,* 730 F.2d 1405 (11th Cir. 1984).

[41]*Sandlin v. Johnson,* 643 F.2d 1027 (4th Cir. 1981).

COMPULSORY EDUCATION

For the most part, compulsory education laws were enacted in the years 1852–1918 in an effort to protect children from widespread labor abuses and to ensure that the enormous number of immigrants who had come to America would learn the English language and American customs.

The common law doctrine of *parens patriae* means the state in its guardian role has the authority to enact laws with respect to the protection and education of children within the state's jurisdiction. The valid power of the state to compel school attendance is the best interest of society, and this best interest overrides the custodial authority of the parent over the child. Every state has statutes compelling attendance of children from age 6 to age 18 at a qualified school or alternative educational program.. Offending parents or truant students are penalized for noncompliance.[42]

Many state laws provide that particular individuals are declared exempt from compulsory attendance, for example, severely physically or mentally HANDICAPPED STUDENTS. Also, MARRIED STUDENTS are emancipated from being compelled to attend school against their will. However, the school may not deny a married minor the right to attend school because of pregnancy or marriage.

There are prerogatives of home instruction or attendance at private, profit, nonprofit, sectarian, or secular schools. A child may also be exempt from required attendance because of physical or mental incapacity (with valid medical proof), distance of travel, or other substantial reasons.

In 1972, the Supreme Court of the United States stated, "However strong the state's interest in universal compulsory education, it is by no means absolute to the exclusion or subordination of all other interests."[43] This landmark case involved a challenge to Wisconsin's compulsory education statute which required children between the ages of seven and sixteen years to attend school regularly. The parents of one such school-age child who was not yet sixteen years old refused to send the child to school after the eighth grade. The parents felt that continued education violated the tenets of the Amish religion. The parents were convicted of violating the Wisconsin compulsory education statute. The parents appealed the conviction saying that the compulsory education statute infringed upon their free exercise of RELIGION and was, therefore, unconstitutional.

---

[42]*In re Jeanette L.*, 523 A.2d 1048 (Md. 1987); *Trower v. Maple* 774 F.2d 673 (5th Cir. 1985); *In the Interest of C. S.*, 382 N.W.2d 381 (N.D. 1986); *Commonwealth v. Hall*, 455 A.2d 674 (Pa. 1983).

[43]*Wisconsin v. Yoder*, 406 U.S. 205 (1972).

The Wisconsin Supreme Court agreed with the parents' argument. The United States Supreme Court affirmed this decision and held that the establishment of the religion clause of the FIRST AMENDMENT, made applicable to the states through the FOURTEENTH AMENDMENT, prohibits state action which needlessly interferes with a parent's right to control the religious training of his or her children.

The above case does not invalidate laws requiring students to attend school beyond the eighth grade. This case merely suggests that, although minimum literacy is a compelling state interest, high school education may not be. Nevertheless, only those students having a unique self-supporting community life, such as the recognized Amish religious beliefs against higher education, are allowed freedom from compulsory attendance beyond the eighth grade. Generally, the courts consistently refuse to abrogate states' compulsory attendance laws because of religious beliefs. In two cases concerning Pentecostal Christians and Bible Baptists, one court recognized the sincerity of the beliefs but found that compliance with state regulations to prepare children to be self-sufficient participants in society outweighed the significant burdens on their rights of free expression of religion.[44] While it is possible that some modification of compulsory attendance is in order, the states' commitment to education will continue to be protected.

To comply with compulsory attendance laws, parents or guardians may elect to send their children to the assigned public school or to a private school of their choice so long as such schools meet the requirements of the state education CERTIFICATION law. The minimum regulatory standards for such PRIVATE SCHOOLS vary from state to state. Courts have been striking down restrictive statutes that impose an undue burden on the free exercise of RELIGION or requirements that make private schools indistinguishable from public schools.[45]

The minimum standards for "home schools" vary depending upon the individual state's compulsory education law or the court decisions interpreting the law. Several states do allow "equivalent education." The minimum instructional programs, i.e., number of days, hours, courses, etc., are most often prescribed by the state laws or State Board of Education rules, and these minimum requirements must be met by the home school. However, before compulsory attendance can be upheld, it is the burden of the state to establish that the minimum requirements have not been met by the home school. Thus, as a typical example, where the state failed to show

---

[44]*Duro v. District Attorney*, 712 F.2d 96 (4th Cir. 1983); *State v. Shaver*, 294 N.W.2d 883 (N.D. 1980).

[45]*Kentucky State Board v. Rudasill*, 589 S.W.2d 877 (Ky. 1979); *State v. Whisner*, 351 N.E.2d 750 (Ohio 1976).

that the parents did not provide their child with proper instruction, a Missouri appellate court held that compulsory school attendance would not be enforced.[46] The state's compelling interest in education does allow reasonable state supervision of parental decisions for home education.[47]

CONFLICT OF INTEREST

Teachers and other school officials are government employees; as a result, the separation of powers doctrine generally prevents these educators from holding additional public offices. "Conflict of interest" agreements have prevented teachers and other school officials from being state legislators. Several states, however, have amended their constitutions to specifically allow teachers to serve in the legislature.

In addition, many state constitutions have a conflict of interest provision which prevents legislators and other government officials from holding certain other offices or positions. For example, some local SCHOOL BOARD members cannot hold other public offices which may present conflicts of interest with their positions on the board. Thus, if a board member accepts the position of city mayor, the member automatically vacates his or her school board position.

Other typical conflicts of interest arise when a member of a school board has a contract with that same school board to provide services or materials. Generally, this is not allowed. It is certainly not allowed without full disclosure of the agreement and a disclosure of the potential conflict of interest. Conflict of interest provisions may also prevent school board members from being employed as teachers or administrators in the same district.

CONSOLIDATION

See REORGANIZATION.

---

[46]*State v. David*, 598 S.W.2d 189 (Mo. App. 1980).

[47]*Murphy v. State of Arkansas*, 852 F.2d 1039 (8th Cir. 1988).

CONSTITUTIONAL AMENDMENTS OF THE UNITED STATES

Amendment I

Freedom of religion, speech, and press; right to assemble and petition

Congress shall make no law respecting an establishment of religion, or prohibiting the free exercise thereof; or abridging the freedom of speech, or of the press; or the right of the people peaceably to assemble, and to petition the Government for a redress of grievances.

Amendment II

Right to bear arms

A well regulated Militia, being necessary to the security of a free State, the right of the people to keep and bear Arms, shall not be infringed.

Amendment III

Quartering soldiers in private homes

No Soldier shall, in time of peace, be quartered in any house, without the consent of the Owner, nor in time of war, but in a manner to be prescribed by law.

Amendment IV

Security from unreasonable searches and seizures.

The right of the people to be secure in their persons, houses, papers, and effects, against unreasonable searches and seizures, shall not be violated, and no Warrants shall issue, but upon probable cause, supported by Oath or affirmation, and particularly describing the place to be searched, and the persons or things to be seized.

Amendment V

When prosecution to be by presentment or indictment; double jeopardy; self-incrimination; due process; compensation for property taken for public use.

No person shall be held to answer for a capital or otherwise infamous crime, unless on a presentment or indictment of a Grand Jury, except in cases arising in the land or naval forces, or in the Militia, when in actual service in time of War or public danger; nor shall any person be subject for the same offence to be twice put in jeopardy of life or limb; nor shall be compelled in any criminal case to be a witness against himself, nor be deprived of life, liberty, or property, without due process of law; nor shall private property be taken for public use, without just compensation.

Amendment VI

Rights of accused in criminal prosecutions

In all criminal prosecutions, the accused shall enjoy the right to a speedy and public trial, by an impartial jury of the State and district wherein the crime shall have been committed, which district shall have been previously ascertained by law, and to be informed of the nature and cause of the accusation; to be confronted with the witnesses against him; to have compulsory process for obtaining witnesses in his favor, and to have the Assistance of Counsel for his defense.

Amendment VII

Trial by jury in civil cases

In Suits at common law, where the value in controversy shall exceed twenty dollars, the right of trial by jury shall be preserved, and no fact tried by a jury, shall be otherwise re-examined in any Court of the United States, than according to the rules of the common law.

Amendment VIII

Bail, fines, and punishments

Excessive bail shall not be required, nor excessive fines imposed, nor cruel and unusual punishment inflicted.

Amendment IX

Rights retained by people

The enumeration in the Constitution, of certain rights, shall not be construed to deny or disparage others retained by the people.

Amendment X

Powers reserved to states or people

The powers not delegated to the United States by the Constitution, nor prohibited by it to the States, are reserved to the States respectively, or to the people.

Amendment XI

Judicial power not to extend to certain suits against states

The Judicial power of the United States shall not be construed to extend to any suit in law or equity, commenced or prosecuted against one of the United States by Citizens of another State, or by Citizens or Subjects of any Foreign State.

Amendment XII

Election of President and Vice President

The Electors shall meet in their respective states and vote by ballot for President and Vice-President, one of whom, at least, shall not be an inhabitant of the same state with themselves; they shall name in their ballots the person voted for as President, and in distinct ballots the person voted for as Vice-President, and they shall make distinct lists of all persons voted for as President, and of all persons voted for as Vice-President, and of the number of votes for each, which lists they shall sign and certify, and transmit sealed to the seat of the government of the United States, directed to the President of the Senate;—The President of the Senate shall, in the presence of the Senate and the House of Representatives, open all the certificates and the votes shall then be counted;—The person having the greatest number of votes for President, shall be the President, if such number be a majority of the whole number of Electors appointed; and if no person have such a majority, then from the persons having the highest numbers not exceeding three on the list of those voted for a President, the House of Representatives shall choose immediately, by ballot, the President. But in choosing the President, the votes shall be taken by states, the representation from each state having one vote; a quorum for this purpose shall consist of a member or members from two-thirds of the states, and a majority of all the states shall be necessary to a choice. And if the House of Representatives shall not choose a President whenever the right of choice shall devolve upon them, before the fourth day of March next following, then the Vice-President shall act as President, as in the case of the death or other constitutional disability of the President.—The person having the greatest number of votes as Vice-President, shall be the Vice-President, if such number be a majority of the whole number of Electors appointed, and if no person have a majority, then from the two highest numbers on the list, the Senate shall choose the Vice-President; a quorum for the purpose shall consist of two-thirds of the whole number of Senators, and a majority of the whole number shall be necessary to a choice. But no person constitutionally ineligible to the office of President shall be eligible to that of Vice-President of the United States.

Amendment XIII

Section 1. Slavery and involuntary servitude abolished

Neither slavery nor involuntary servitude, except as a punishment for crime whereof the party shall have been duly convicted, shall exist within the United States, or any place subject to their jurisdiction.

Section 2. Enforcement

Congress shall have power to enforce this article by appropriate legislation.

Amendment XIV

Section 1. Citizenship; privileges and immunities; due process; equal protection

All persons born or naturalized in the United States, and subject to the jurisdiction thereof, are citizens of the United States and of the State wherein they reside. No State shall make or enforce any law which shall abridge the privileges or immunities of citizens of the United States; nor shall any State deprive any person of life, liberty, or property, without due process of law; nor deny to any person within its jurisdiction the equal protection of the laws.

CONSTITUTIONAL LAW–Students

In 1967, the Supreme Court of the United States was called upon to hear a case involving a fifteen-year-old boy who had been committed to the state reform school for a period of up to six years. The boy had been convicted of making an obscene phone call to a neighbor. Had the boy been an adult, the maximum punishment he could have received for having committed such an offense would have been a $50 fine and two months in jail. Also, among other things, the boy had been denied a lawyer and the right to confront and cross-examine his accuser. The United States Supreme Court set aside the boy's conviction and ruled that, when a substantial punishment is involved, a juvenile is entitled to DUE PROCESS of law.[48] As a result, in 1967, for the first time, it was clearly and firmly established that the Bill of Rights is not for adults alone; juveniles also have some constitutional rights.

Whether a juvenile retained his or her constitutional rights when in school remained an open question. In the 1960s and 1970s, school officials were bombarded with lawsuits and demonstrations challenging school RULES involving everything from restrictions on content of school NEWSPAPERS to dress codes. The COURTS were divided as to whether students had constitutional rights. Finally, the Supreme Court of the United States settled the issue. During its 1968 term, the Supreme Court, for the first time in twenty-five years, reviewed a case involving students' rights to freedom of expression. In this case, several students were disciplined for wearing armbands protesting the Vietnam War. In holding that students do have constitutional rights, the Supreme Court in *Tinker* said:

> First Amendment rights applied in light of the special characteristics of the school environment are available to teachers and students. It can hardly be argued that neither students nor teachers shed their constitutional rights to freedom of speech or expression at the schoolhouse gate.[49]

The Supreme Court said that students have some constitutional rights. However, these rights are not absolute. The school has the power and the duty to make rules governing student conduct and to enforce such rules. School officials' rights to enact rules are recognized by all courts, for as one court explains:

> It cannot be seriously disputed that the interest of the State in maintaining an educational system is of such importance that the State is in fact charged with the duty to further and protect the public school system. Nor can it be denied that rules and regulations governing student conduct are required to maintain an orderly educational program. School officials of necessity have thus been given a

---

[48]*In re Gault*, 387 U.S. 1 (1967).

[49]*Tinker v. Des Moines Independent Community School District*, 393 U.S. 503, 506 (1969).

wide latitude of discretion in formulating rules and regulations to prescribe and control student conduct within the school.[50]

Schools have the authority to prescribe rules, but the rules must be reasonable and must be weighed against the students' rights.

Early case law held that the school had authority to enact rules and discipline students, and the courts would not interfere with the wide discretion granted the school authorities. Now, the courts are saying that school officials' rules must be reasonable and school officials have the burden of articulating facts sufficient to demonstrate reasonableness. How the courts will handle cases involving student rights versus school rules or punishment is explained by a federal circuit court:

> It is always within the province of school authorities to provide by regulation the prohibition and punishment of acts calculated to undermine the school routine. This is not only proper in our opinion but it is necessary.
>
> Cases...which involve regulations limiting freedom of expression and the communication of an idea which are protected by the First Amendment, present serious constitutional questions. A valuable constitutional right is involved and decisions must be made on a case by case basis, keeping in mind always the fundamental constitutional rights of those being affected. Courts are required to "weigh the circumstances" and "appraise the substantiality of the reasons advanced" which are asserted to have given rise to the regulations in the first instance....The constitutional guarantee of freedom of speech "does not confer an absolute right to speak" and the law recognizes that there can be an abuse of such freedom. The Constitution does not confer "unrestricted and unbridled license" giving immunity for every possible use of language and preventing the punishment of those who abuse this freedom....In each case [courts] must ask whether the gravity of the "evil," discounted by its improbability, justifies such invasion of free speech as is necessary to avoid the danger....In *West Virginia State Board of Education v. Barnette,*...involving a school board regulation requiring a "salute to the flag" and a pledge of allegiance, the Court was careful to note that the refusal of the students to participate in the ceremony did not interfere with or deny rights of others to do so and the behavior involved was "peaceable and orderly."[51]

Since the *Tinker* decision, the United States Supreme Court has had several opportunities to refine its holding. In one case, the court upheld the disciplining of a high school student who, while delivering a nomina-

---

[50]*Sims v. Colfax Community School District*, 307 F. Supp. 485, 487 (S.D. Iowa 1970).

[51]*Blackwell v. Issaquena County Board of Education*, 363 F.2d 749, 753–4 (5th Cir. 1966).

tion speech to the student body, referred to his candidate in terms of elaborate, graphic, and explicit sexual metaphor.[52] The court distinguished between the political "message" of the armbands in *Tinker* and offensive and obscene language. The court stated that the freedom to advocate unpopular and controversial views in schools must be balanced against society's countervailing interest in teaching students the boundaries of socially appropriate behavior.

In a second case limiting the *Tinker* decision, the court held that the opinion issued in *Tinker* did not apply to school-sponsored expressive activities.[53] The *Hazelwood* case involved a high school principal who deleted two pages of a student newspaper because they contained articles he felt were not suitable for publication. The articles addressed divorce and teenage pregnancy.

The court said that, while personal speech was still protected, school officials can exercise editorial control over the style and content of student speech in school-sponsored activities so long as their actions are reasonably related to legitimate educational concerns.

While the courts recognize student rights, those same courts will allow reasonable rules to incidentally infringe on these rights. What is reasonable will depend on the facts. In addition, different judges may tend to see or give greater weight to various facts and judicial distinctions. However, there are certain judicial criteria which all judges are forced to consider; and there are certain legal standards and rules which have been clearly established for cases involving student rights. For a discussion involving specific rights, please refer to the CATEGORICAL INDEX of this text under CONSTITUTIONAL RIGHTS OF STUDENTS.

CONSTITUTIONAL LAW—Teachers and Administrators

Laws governing employees of the public school system come from three major sources:

1. COMMON LAW;

2. State constitutions and STATUTES; and

3. The United States Constitution.

The FOURTEENTH AMENDMENT of the United States Constitution

---

[52]*Bethel School Dist. v. Fraser*, 478 U.S. 675 (1986).

[53]*Hazelwood School Dist. v. Kuhlmeier*, 484 U.S. 260 (1988).

provides in part that "no state shall make or enforce any law which shall abridge the privileges or immunities of citizens of the United States." In the Bill of Rights, the Constitution specifically states that individual citizens have certain fundamental rights and freedoms. Through the Fourteenth Amendment, the Supreme Court of the United States has ruled that the rights and freedoms as enumerated in the Bill of Rights are protected against infringement by the state.

States have the responsibility to establish and maintain the public schools. Even though local SCHOOL BOARDS do the actual hiring, the state is the employer of public school teachers and administrators. The school board acts as an agent of the state, as do the school district employees when they are performing their governmental duties. As the United States Supreme Court has said, the state may not enact any laws or engage in any activities which are in violation of an individual's constitutional rights. It follows, therefore, that local school boards and school officials are also prohibited from enacting any RULES or regulations which substantially infringe on an individual's constitutional rights.

This means that teachers and administrators have certain constitutional protections assuring them of such liberties as:

1. Freedom of speech outside the school environment
2. Freedom of speech within the classroom (See ACADEMIC FREEDOM.)
3. Freedom from undue restrictions on personal APPEARANCE
4. Freedom to lead their lives in PRIVACY
5. Freedom of ASSOCIATION
6. Freedom of RELIGION
7. Protection from ARBITRARY, CAPRICIOUS, OR DISCRIMINATORY ACTIONS or dismissals on the part of the local board
8. DUE PROCESS

The above protections are substantial. Nevertheless, it must be stressed that these rights are not absolute. Reasonable restrictions may be placed upon one's constitutional rights because the COURTS must weigh constitutional rights against the need for effective school management and operation. Therefore, certain restrictions may incidentally curtail the teacher's or administrator's constitutional rights. That is, restrictions will be upheld if these restrictions are necessary to promote compelling interests of the school and if the restrictions outweigh the rights protected on the other hand. The courts will use a balancing test—a balancing which is not always easy or predictable. The problem lies in weighing or balancing the teacher's or administrator's protected rights against the state's right to maintain the schools free from actions or persons which pose a material and substantial threat to the order and efficiency of the school system.

The United States' system of democracy is built upon a foundation which stresses the importance of freedom and openness. Certain rights, such as freedom of speech, necessitate close protection because threat of dismissal from employment clearly has a chilling effect on free speech. The public has an interest in protecting all individuals' rights, and this interest must be considered in the balancing process.

For a discussion involving specific rights, please refer to CATEGORICAL INDEX of this text under CONSTITUTIONAL RIGHTS OF SCHOOL PERSONNEL and CONTRACT DUTIES AND PROTECTIONS.

CONSTRUCTION

See BUILDINGS, Construction.

CONTEMPT OF COURT

Contempt of court is any act which is calculated to embarrass, hinder, or obstruct a court in the administration of justice or is calculated to lessen its authority or dignity. "Direct" contempt of court is misbehavior committed in the immediate presence of the court, such as violent acts or insulting language. "Indirect" (constructive) contempt of court occurs when a person fails or refuses to obey a lawful order. Every court has the inherent discretionary power to punish willful disrespect by fine or imprisonment.

CONTINUING CONTRACTS

Continuing CONTRACTS call for periodic performance over a specific space of time. Continuing contract law generally provides for "spring notification," requiring that the teacher be given notice of NONRENEWAL prior to the expiration of the contract. Generally, notification laws do not require a statement of the reasons for nonrenewal unless a reason is statutorily mandated. Only when the current contract has been fulfilled and the board follows contract renewal provisions regarding notice of nonrenewal is the teacher's continuing contract officially terminated.

Guide Rule

Under continuing contract law, unless the school board *properly notifies* the teacher of nonrenewal by the date specified in the law, the teacher's contract is deemed to be automatically renewed for the succeeding school year.

If proper notice has not been given by the specified date, the educator should communicate in writing within a reasonably short period of time (10–15 days) his or her acceptance of the "new" contract.

In one case, it was decided that a teacher waived his continuing contract rights when the teacher failed to sign and return his employment contract for the next year. The court ruled that the failure to sign and return the contract was a valid waiver because there had been express written and personal notice that such conduct could result in the school board's rejection of the board's employment offer.[54] If the SCHOOL BOARD refuses to issue the contract to the teacher with a clear legal right to RENEWAL, the teacher can bring an action in MANDAMUS which will compel the board to perform its duty imposed by the law.

In a New York case, the board's termination of a probationary teacher was procedurally defective. Proper procedures must be carefully followed. Therefore, the probationary teacher's contract was enforceable and the teacher was reinstated with back pay, benefits, and seniority credits.[55]

A basic difference between this "continuing contract law" and the TENURE law is the absence of protective provisions requiring a statement of the charges, clear and convincing proof of the charges, and "just" procedural DUE PROCESS, coupled with a right to a hearing before the teacher's employment can be terminated.

See also CONTRACTS; DUE PROCESS; RENEWALS.

CONTRACTS

A contract is a mutual agreement to definite terms that is supported by consideration. Both parties must have the capacity to sign, and the contract must be lawful in its purpose or it is not binding.

All the legal rights of employment are derived from the educator's

---

[54]*Corcoran v. Lyle School District No. 406*, 581 P.2d 185 (Wash. 1978).

[55]*Frasier v. Board of Education*, 516 N.Y.S.2d 44 (N.Y. 1987).

contract and any COLLECTIVE BARGAINING agreements in effect at the time. The express duties and responsibilities should be outlined in the contract in a clear and comprehensive manner.

Making up a contract is like making up a law. In other words, even though the statutory law might not say an educator has the right to an OPEN HEARING at any dismissal, that same right can be agreed to and, therefore, granted by contract. If the law does not mention GRIEVANCE procedures, grievance procedures can be adopted pursuant to a binding agreement. If teachers or administrators do not have TENURE rights, those rights can be granted through a contract. The contract is the most important thing under which an educator works. Unfortunately, contracts are often far too ambiguous and fail to clearly outline rights and responsibilities.

In all contracts, there are terms. Generally, for example, the contract will state that the teacher is to teach in the school system at the elementary or secondary level. It is possible for teachers to negotiate that the contract will specify the school and grade level. Otherwise, a TRANSFER could be made without the teacher's approval. For example, teachers generally talk with their principal or superintendent and the parties agree at what school and at what grade the teacher will teach. However, the contract that is signed is generally silent as to that outside agreement. When the school year begins, it is, therefore, possible for the teacher to be assigned to a different school or a different grade level than actually agreed upon as long as it is consistent with the limits of CERTIFICATION and the terms of the contract. When teachers were transferred to various school sites throughout a district as part of a complex desegregation plan, the teachers' contracts were not breached.[56]

"Implied terms" under which the teacher works are not always in the signed agreement itself. There are outside terms that are often incorporated or "read into" the teacher's contract by reference. Somewhere in the contract one will almost always find a statement like: "This agreement is subject to the laws of this state and the duly adopted rules and regulations of the State Board of Education and of the district; and, by this reference, said laws, rules and regulations are made a part of this agreement as if fully set forth herein." This sentence carries with it important implications to the teaching agreement. Under this agreement, the educator is put under constructive notice of all RULES and regulations of the state and local boards. Those rules and regulations are a part of the contract. The rules bind the parties; if one violates the rules or regulations, he or she is breaching the contract. A breach of contract is generally grounds for dismissal.

The contract also binds the SCHOOL BOARD. Therefore, if the local

---

[56]*United States v. Lawrence Co. School Dist.*, 799 F.2d 1031 (5th Cir. 1986).

board adopts policies regarding board members' duties, administrators' duties, and various procedures for such things as EVALUATIONS, dismissals, grievances, and RENEWALS, the board is bound by these policies. If the board does not follow its own policies, the board would be in breach of contract. Negotiating committees should seek to have the board outline administrators' duties in relation to teachers and the board, together with delineating the duties of the school board. The negotiating committee would be well advised to seek a written policy providing that educators will be afforded DUE PROCESS and fundamental fairness in cases of dismissal or NONRENEWAL of contracts and in all matters relating to the teacher's duties of instruction, SUPERVISION, and safety toward students. Once the policies are adopted, the parties are protected by their contract. Sometimes contracts offer far better protection to the teachers and administrators than the state STATUTES provide.

Elements of a Contract

The basic requirements of a binding contract are (1) offer, (2) acceptance, (3) consideration, (4) legality and (5) legal capacity of the parties. First of all, a contract is an agreement. Two parties agree to bind themselves to certain terms. Oral contracts can be just as binding as written contracts. However, a COMMON LAW called the Statute of Frauds does require that employment contracts lasting over a year, contracts for the sale of goods over $500, and contracts for the sale of real PROPERTY all have to be in writing. There are a few other types of contracts that have to be in writing; but, in general, all other contracts are binding even though oral.

In addition to the agreement, there must be consideration. Consideration, for our purposes, is something of value given or promised for some act or promise by the other person. The teacher promises to teach. The administrator promises to administrate. The board promises to pay for services rendered. The promises and the performance of those promises constitute valuable consideration, and, therefore, the promises are binding.

Consideration given does not have to be of equal value. One can promise to give something or perform services which are of more value than what is promised in return, or vice versa; but the contract will be binding nevertheless. The contract can still be valid even if the salary is unfair or inadequate.

In addition to agreement and consideration, all parties to a contract must have the CAPACITY to enter into the contract or the contract is not binding or may be voidable. For example, a minor lacks the capacity to enter into a binding contract, and his or her agreements are voidable. Educators, in order to effect a binding agreement, must have proper legal capacity. In order for a teacher or administrator to have the capacity to enter into a contract, the party must have proper CERTIFICATION or the contract is not enforceable.[57] In some states, teachers must be certified prior to beginning the performance of his or her duties. Teachers who are not properly certified cannot force payment for teaching services. This is important to note because many certificates expire during the summer and are sometimes forgotten until the school year begins.

The school board, as well as the educator, must have the legal capacity to enter into a contract. (See SCHOOL BOARDS.) Only the board acting as a whole in a properly called meeting has the capacity to enter into contracts. The superintendent or individual board members all lack capacity in and of themselves to sign an agreement and bind the school district.[58] Realistically, the superintendent makes the contract offer; but that offer is later ratified by the board and only then becomes binding.

In discussing contracts, it is necessary to mention the terms "offer" and "acceptance." A contract, though offered, becomes binding only upon acceptance.

An offer must meet certain legal requirements. Generally, the offer must state:

1. The services the parties are to render;
2. The compensation to be paid;
3. The time for the services to begin; and
4. The time for the services to end.

Furthermore, the offer must be made with the *present* intent to enter into the contract and to bind oneself. *Future* intent to enter into a future contract does not constitute a binding offer.

Some difficulty can arise when districts do not come out with contract proposals regarding dollars until after budgets and negotiations are settled. Therefore, in such cases, deadlines for renewal are passed and "letters of intent" are sent. These letters constitute binding offers even though the letters do not offer concrete proposals. The letters state that the board intends to hire the employee and asks if the teacher or administrator intends to accept. The board's offer is binding if the educator accepts the letter of intent. If the deadline for nonrenewal notice has passed, the board is required to renew the educators' contracts in most states. If the deadline for nonrenewal notice has not passed, the letter of intent is still a binding offer, subject to completing the agreement regarding monetary matters in the future. However, the educator's acceptance of a future contract is not necessarily binding on the educator even though the board may be bound.

---

[57]*Nelson v. Doland Board of Education*, 380 N.W.2d 665 (S.D. 1986).
[58]*Minor v. Sully Buttes School Dist.*, 345 N.W.2d 48 (S.D. 1984).

The board knows what the educator has to offer, and the educator's terms are not going to change. The teacher or administrator, on the other hand, does not know the essential ingredients of the board's terms and so accepts, "subject to" a final acceptance at a later date.

Once an offer is made, it must be accepted in order for a binding contract to come into existence. The acceptance must be clear and unequivocal and with the present intent to bind oneself. Furthermore, there are generally laws or procedures that have been adopted regarding proper acceptance. If the law says that the parties must accept in writing, oral acceptance would generally not be sufficient. If the law says that the parties must accept within a certain period of time, then that time limit must be met. Time limits and procedures are extremely important, and the parties are under constructive notice of those regulations.

In addition to offer and acceptance, one might need to consider "counteroffers" and "rejections." Counteroffers and rejections can play important roles in determining whether a contract exists. If an offer is made and it is not accepted but the party makes a counteroffer, the original offer dies and cannot be later accepted. For example, if the school board offered a teacher a position at $17,000 and the teacher wrote back and said he or she would take the job if they offered $20,000, the teacher has made a counteroffer. If the board rejects the counteroffer, the teacher cannot say, "Okay, I'll accept the job at $17,000." Before the teacher can accept the original offer, the board must reoffer the position or there is no offer on the table that is subject to acceptance.

A rejection has the same legal effect as a counteroffer. If the board makes an offer and an administrator says he or she will not accept, that administrator cannot later change his or her mind and bind the board without another offer being made. It works both ways. An offer, once accepted, cannot be unilaterally rescinded. DAMAGES can be awarded according to the terms of the contract if one of the parties breaches the agreement.

Services Required Under Teaching Contracts

Problems frequently arise in the interpretation of teachers' contracts. The terms of a teacher's contract are not necessarily confined to the provisions in a written contract but rather include any pertinent statutory provisions in effect at the time the agreement was entered into. Moreover, the terms of the teacher's contract also include the rules and regulations of the school district. The school board has the right to impose certain implied duties on teachers. This right, however, is limited.[59]

---

[59]*Haverland v. Tempe Elementary School District No. 3*, 595 P.2d 1032 (Ariz. App. 1979).

In the past, teachers were expected to wash the floors of their classrooms, to act as custodians after the children left, to participate in certain community activities, and to follow without question the instructions of the local board. Today, it is clear that the teacher has no duty to do menial, janitorial, or police services. However, a teacher may be required to supervise a study hall or the cafeteria. The teacher could be required to attend faculty meetings or open house or even go to a football game as a supervisor. Nevertheless, the nonclassroom assignments and duties that are imposed on the teacher must be reasonable, and the assignments must generally relate to the teacher's classroom position or to collateral activities stemming from the classroom. The duties may not violate the teacher's constitutional rights and in no way may the duty be punitive or discriminatory. All duties must be distributed impartially; they must be reasonable in time and number; and all teachers should have to take their share of the duty.

Supplemental Contracts

Supplemental contracts are frequently entered into when one is hired to teach or administrate and is also hired to coach, direct plays, direct a musical band, or is otherwise required to perform extra services that require a substantial amount of extra time. In some districts, the primary contract is agreed upon and signed and a separate, supplemental contract covering the extra services is agreed upon and signed. Problems are created when questions are raised as to whether both contracts have to be offered and/or whether breach of one contract constitutes breach of the other. The answer to these questions depends upon the facts and circumstances under which one was hired. For example, if it was written or orally agreed upon that the teacher would teach English and also coach the baseball team, the teacher would have to do both. In other words, if the two contracts are really meant as one and the coaching requirement was a major consideration made in hiring the teacher, breach of one contract is a breach of the other. On the other hand, if the teacher was teaching math and the board asked him or her to coach baseball and the teacher did so, the teacher could not generally be forced to continue coaching in subsequent years because the coaching position was not contingent or dependent upon the teaching position. Therefore, the question is whether the coaching duties go to the essence of the teaching position. If they do, the two positions and the two contracts would legally be treated as one.

The reverse of the above is also true. The school board could not take the coaching position away from the teacher without complying with the state's dismissal law or other due process procedures if the teacher was hired for the purpose of teaching and coaching. This can be a very tricky area. In most instances, the supplemental contract is not a tenured type of right. Although the educator may be tenured, seldom does he or she have tenure as a coach unless hired that way in the original contract. Non-renewal of the supplemental contract without reason is generally allowed unless the teacher or administrator can show that the position goes to the very essence of the main agreement. Nevertheless, if the party can show that the supplemental contract, though not part of the main agreement, was not renewed for reasons that are in violation of CONSTITUTIONAL LAW, he or she would be entitled to have the contract renewed and the courts would do so. Many potential problems could be solved by including the duty of coaching in the main contract or by establishing written procedures for termination of supplemental contracts.

A school district may not avoid the protections granted under continuing contract laws by issuing "supplemental contracts" for the basic school year curriculum.[60]

Termination of Contracts

There are times when, after a contract has been signed, a party wants to be released from the obligation. Performance can be excused without liability in certain instances. An "act of God," death, fraud, duress, impossibility of performance, and prolonged illness are examples where one can be excused without liability. However, transfer of a teacher's spouse will not excuse performance, without permission.

One may also be excused for performance without liability where there is a mutual rescission. This means that, where both parties agree to rescind their mutual obligations, they may do so without liability. Of course, this is true only where fraud or undue influence is not exerted. The rescission must come voluntarily or there is no mutual agreement.

In addition to the aforementioned possibilities for excuse of performance, there are many state statutes which give reasons or excuses to rescind without liability. In many states, a teacher or administrator may rescind without liability from 60 to 90 days prior to school beginning. If this recision is allowed by law, there can be no liability even though the school board does not have the same right of rescission.

Performance is also not required under certain conditions where the contract is "void" or "voidable." A void contract is one that is unenforceable at its inception and forever. It simply does not exist. A voidable contract is a valid contract that has the possibility of becoming permanently void. In fact, a voidable contract may be valid in its inception. The voidable contract has all of the elements, but there is something wrong with the contract that makes it possible for one of the parties to set it aside. Examples would be where the contract is signed by the superintendent

---

[60]*Kelso Educ. Ass'n. v. Kelso School District No. 453*, 740 P.2d 889 (Wash. App. 1987).

under the superintendent's apparent authority (not actual authority) or a contract that is signed at an improperly called board meeting. These contracts could be set aside and declared void by the school board. If the contracts are voided, the contracts would not become binding. However, once the voidable element of the contract is eliminated (such as later adopting the contract at a proper meeting), the contract becomes enforceable for all parties.

As one can see, there are times when contracts can be terminated without liability. However, without lawful excuse, if one party wrongfully fails or refuses to perform his or her duties under a contract, he or she is said to have "breached" the contract. For wrongful breach of contract, DAMAGES may be assessed against the breaching party. However, if no injury occurs as a result of the breach, there will be no grounds for assessment of damages unless the state sets up certain penalties. For example, if a teacher walked out of the school building improperly and refused to return to his or her teaching duties, that teacher would be in breach of contract. If the school district were able to find a substitute teacher of the same general caliber and for the same amount of money, there would be little financial loss, if any, to the district; and, therefore, the amount of damages to be assessed would be negligible. Because of this, some states have enacted laws providing for financial penalties for wrongful breach of contract (for example, unlawful STRIKES); and many state laws provide that, if a teacher or administrator improperly resigns, his or her certificate may be revoked for a certain period of time. Also, some statutes have declared that, if a teacher or administrator has a contract with one district, any contract made with another district covering that same period of time is automatically void. This type of statute acts as a deterrent against improper breaches of contract on the part of educators. These deterrent laws work to some extent. However, one should note that the local school district does not have the power to revoke certificates. The power to revoke lies only with the state board of education which is the grantor of the certificate. The local board may only initiate a complaint and recommend that the certificate be revoked. Without the recommendation, no revocation will be made; and, even with a recommendation, the ultimate decision rests with the state board.

If the local board improperly breaches a contract, damages are not automatic. In other words, there is a duty on the part of the educator to mitigate or lessen the damages as much as possible. For example, assume that a teacher is hired for one year at $16,000 and, after three months, the local board improperly terminates the position. The teacher has been paid $4,000 and has $12,000 coming on the contract. In addition to other possible damages, one would ordinarily expect to receive the remaining $12,000. However, it is the teacher's duty, even though he or she is not the wrongdoer, to go out and try to find another teaching job. The teacher must try to lessen the school board's damages. If another teaching job is (1) available, (2) within a reasonable distance of the old position, and (3) is of the same general status and pay, the teacher is generally obligated to make reasonable attempts to obtain the position. On the other hand, if the position is inferior or too far away or if the position is not available, the teacher would not normally be expected to take a job outside of the teaching profession.

If the teacher takes another position, even an inferior position, the money earned will be subtracted from the original damages. As stated previously, if an equal position was available, the teacher had to take it or the money he or she "would have" earned would be deducted. Where there is an inferior position available, the teacher is not obligated to accept; but, if he or she does, the money will be subtracted.

The money the teacher earned is not subtracted automatically. If the position the teacher accepted could have been performed while teaching at the old position, that money will not be subtracted. For example, if the teacher secured an evening sales position, that money would not be subtracted from the $12,000 because the teacher could have held down the sale position while teaching at the same time.

"Substitute teaching" is not considered to be of an equal status to a regular teaching position. If the school board wrongfully dismisses a teacher, that teacher should try to mitigate damages; but, since substitute teaching is not of the same status, the teacher is not obligated to do this kind of work. However, if the teacher does accept substitute teaching employment, the amount of money earned may be used to mitigate damages because the teacher could not have earned this money had he or she been employed under the original contract.

It is also important to realize that, if a tenured teacher or administrator refuses to agree to a new contract provision, that refusal does not permit the board to summarily declare that the teacher or administrator has resigned or that the teaching or administrative position was vacated.[61]

For further discussion regarding dismissal of teachers under contract, see DUE PROCESS.

CONTRACTS, Construction

See BUILDINGS.

---

[61]*Haas v. Madison County Board of Education*, 380 So. 2d 873 (Ala. 1980).

CONTRIBUTORY NEGLIGENCE

Contributory negligence is a defense alleging that the PLAINTIFF's own NEGLIGENCE contributed to the plaintiff's injuries and, therefore, the plaintiff cannot hold the DEFENDANT liable. Contributory negligence is conduct on the part of the plaintiff which falls below the standard to which the plaintiff should conform to protect his or her own person. If a court or jury finds the plaintiff contributorily negligent, the plaintiff may be completely barred from recovering DAMAGES. In some states, contributory negligence may bar partial recovery. Other states use a COMPARATIVE NEGLIGENCE test to determine whether a recovery for damages may be reduced. One needs to check local laws to see what test will be applied if negligence is alleged. In assessing whether contributory negligence exists, students are held to a standard of care which is REASONABLE AND PRUDENT for a student of a similar age in similar circumstances taking into account experience, training, education and maturity.

Contributory negligence was successfully used as a defense by a vocational education teacher against a fourteen-year-old boy who was injured while using a power saw. The teacher stated that each student had received twenty minutes of instruction on the proper use of the power saw immediately prior to the accident. The court ruled that the teacher had acted reasonably under the circumstances and that the boy's injuries were the result of his own contributory negligence.[62]

Contributory negligence was found where a twelve-year-old student died after receiving head injuries when he leaned out a school bus window and struck a guide wire supporting a utility pole. The court found that the student's actions were the proximate cause of the injury and constituted contributory negligence since the student was a bright, alert, and intelligent student who had heard school monitors often warn students not to have any part of their bodies outside the bus windows.[63]

CONTROVERSIAL MATTERS, Right to Teach

Generally, see ACADEMIC FREEDOM; CONSTITUTIONAL LAW; CURRICULUM.

---

[62]*Izard v. Hickory City Schools Bd. of Educ.*, 315 S.E.2d 756 (N.C. App. 1984).

[63]*Arnold v. Hayslett*, 655 S.W.2d 941 (Tenn. 1983).

CORPORAL PUNISHMENT

Corporal punishment constitutes the use of physical force for the purpose of causing physical pain or discomfort as a disciplinary measure. Historically, corporal punishment has been one of the most frequently challenged forms of student punishment. Courts often cite the doctrine of IN LOCO PARENTIS as grounds for allowing corporal punishment.

The United States Supreme Court in 1975 held that school authorities had the duty to maintain discipline in the schools and that corporal punishment could be used as a method of discipline even where parents specifically forbid the schools from using corporal punishment on their child.[64] The court held that students must be informed beforehand that specific conduct could lead to corporal punishment. The court also held that a second school official must be present while the student is being corporally punished. Furthermore, the court held that corporal punishment should never be used as a first line of punishment.

Corporal punishment has also withstood a constitutional challenge claiming that corporal punishment was cruel and unusual punishment. In this case, the United States Supreme Court held that the cruel and unusual provision of the constitution applies only to situations involving criminal punishments.[65] While recognizing that corporal punishment implicates students' constitutionally protected liberty interests, the court held that DUE PROCESS was afforded to students in the form of available remedies, such as suits for ASSAULT and/or BATTERY, when the punishment is excessive or arbitrary.

Although the United States Supreme Court allows the use of corporal punishment, several states and many cities and SCHOOL BOARDS specifically ban its use. Other states, cities, and school boards have set up specific guidelines which must be followed whenever corporal punishment is to be used. These guidelines must be followed very carefully if one wishes to escape liability from the student or disciplinary measures from supervisors or the board. Where corporal punishment is authorized, one must be certain that the action is reasonable, prudent and necessary under the circumstances. Generally, it is reasonable and prudent to use corporal punishment if:

1. The punishment is administered for correction purposes and without malice;
2. The student knows why he or she is being punished;

---

[64]*Baker v. Owen*, 395 F. Supp. 294 (M.D.N.C. 1975); *aff'd without written opinion*, 423 U.S. 907 (1975).

[65]*Ingraham v. Wright*, 430 U.S. 651 (1977).

3. The punishment is not excessive and is in consideration of the student's age, size, and physical and emotional frailty; and

4. The punishment is administered in the teacher-student relationship.[66]

COURT ORGANIZATION–Federal

Article III, Section I, of the Constitution of the United States provides that "the judicial power of the United States shall be vested in one Supreme Court, and in such inferior Courts as the Congress may from time to time ordain and establish." The Supreme Court of the United States is, therefore, the highest court in the land and its decisions form the law of the land.

The United States Courts of Appeals are directly under the United States Supreme Court. These courts are divided into "circuits." In the United States, there are eleven circuits encompassing various states, together with the District of Columbia circuit. There is one Court of Appeals in each circuit to review the decisions of the district courts.

Below the United States Courts of Appeals are the United States District Courts. These are trial courts for cases under federal jurisdiction. Except for a few special kinds of cases, decisions of the district courts may be appealed to the Court of Appeals.

The United States Supreme Court, if it wishes, may review all lower federal court decisions and any cases in state courts which involve questions concerning federal statutes or the United States Constitution. There are two methods through which cases are brought before the Supreme Court: (1) by writ of CERTIORARI or (2) by appeal. The United States Supreme Court is not required to review a case and render an opinion; but, again, if the Supreme Court does render an opinion, then that opinion becomes the law that must be followed in all lower federal courts and state courts interpreting federal law. This power, however, does not extend to state courts interpreting individual state laws or state constitutions. Because of this limitation, state laws may vary unless those laws are in direct conflict with minimum guarantees protected under federal law.

See also COURT ORGANIZATION–State.

COURT ORGANIZATION–State

As a check upon the legislative and executive branches of government, the judicial branch was established to ensure impartial justice. The state

---

[66]*See also Garcia v. Miera*, 817 F.2d 650 (10th Cir. 1987).

FEDERAL JUDICIAL SYSTEM

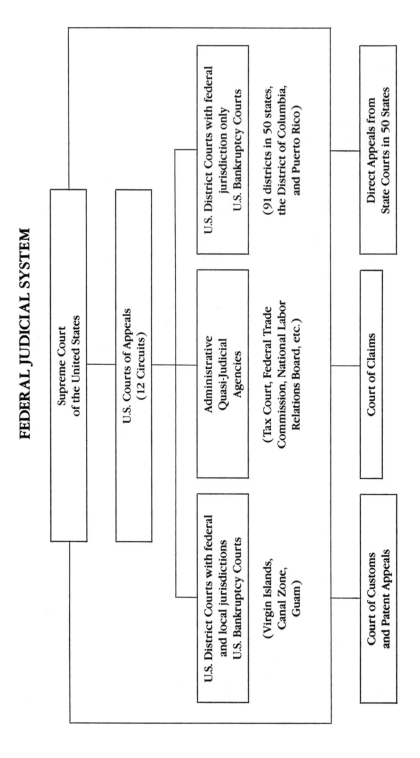

Supreme Court
of the United States

U.S. Courts of Appeals
(12 Circuits)

U.S. District Courts with federal
jurisdiction only
U.S. Bankruptcy Courts

(91 districts in 50 states,
the District of Columbia,
and Puerto Rico)

Direct Appeals from
State Courts in 50 States

Administrative
Quasi-Judicial
Agencies

(Tax Court, Federal Trade
Commission, National Labor
Relations Board, etc.)

Court of Claims

U.S. District Courts with federal
and local jurisdictions
U.S. Bankruptcy Courts

(Virgin Islands,
Canal Zone,
Guam)

Court of Customs
and Patent Appeals

The Twelve Federal Judicial Circuits
See 28 U.S.C.A. § 41

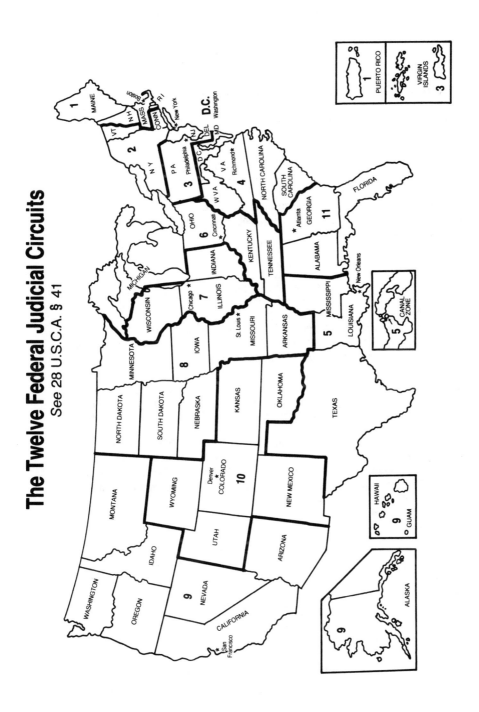

FEDERAL JUDICIAL SYSTEM

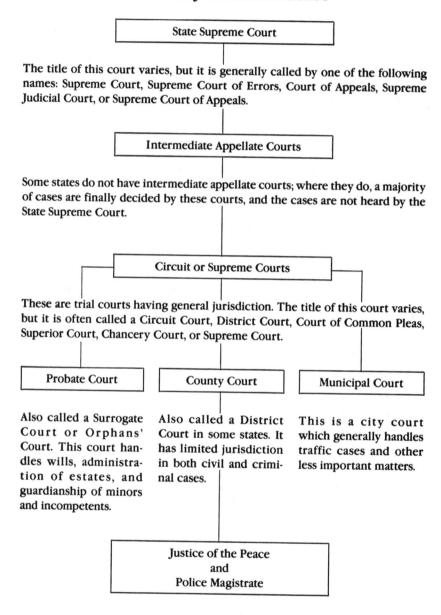

State Supreme Court

The title of this court varies, but it is generally called by one of the following names: Supreme Court, Supreme Court of Errors, Court of Appeals, Supreme Judicial Court, or Supreme Court of Appeals.

Intermediate Appellate Courts

Some states do not have intermediate appellate courts; where they do, a majority of cases are finally decided by these courts, and the cases are not heard by the State Supreme Court.

Circuit or Supreme Courts

These are trial courts having general jurisdiction. The title of this court varies, but it is often called a Circuit Court, District Court, Court of Common Pleas, Superior Court, Chancery Court, or Supreme Court.

Probate Court

Also called a Surrogate Court or Orphans' Court. This court handles wills, administration of estates, and guardianship of minors and incompetents.

County Court

Also called a District Court in some states. It has limited jurisdiction in both civil and criminal cases.

Municipal Court

This is a city court which generally handles traffic cases and other less important matters.

Justice of the Peace
and
Police Magistrate

These courts have very limited jurisdiction in both civil and criminal cases.

judicial power is frequently vested in one state supreme court, together with an intermediate court of appeals, followed by the trial courts and other courts which the state legislatures establish.

In addition to the regular court system and in order to ease the burden on courts and to alleviate excessive costs and delay, several states have vested certain ADMINISTRATIVE AGENCIES with the power to settle GRIEVANCES in the educational system. (See COMMISSIONER OF EDUCATION.)

The courts, to a large extent, exercise a policy of noninterference with school administration. Since the individual state legislatures have the responsibility for determining educational policy, the courts will rule on the legality of school RULES and action on an infrequent basis.

The courts usually follow precedent in making rulings, but the courts are not forced to do so. Facts and circumstances often vary, and important factors may change due to changing times or attitudes. However, as United States Supreme Court Justice Holmes once stated, "The life of law has not been logic; it has been experience."

See also COURT ORGANIZATION–Federal; STARE DECISIS.

CROSS-EXAMINATION

Cross-examination is the questioning of a witness in a trial or hearing or in the taking of a deposition by the party opposed to the one who produced the witness. The scope of examination is generally limited to matters covered on direct examination. Direct examination is the questioning of a witness by the person who produces that witness.

See also DUE PROCESS; WITNESSES.

CURRICULUM

The legislature of each individual state has the power to prescribe the curriculum the schools shall or shall not offer and the manner in which the curriculum shall be offered. This is true as long as the curriculum does not conflict with the state's constitution or the Constitution of the United States.

Some states legislate that certain subjects must be included in the school's curriculum, including instruction with reference to the United

States Constitution, civics, American history, and citizenship. In addition, some states specify that instruction is to be given in the English language. Nevertheless, in states or districts where there are many students who speak a foreign language and do not speak English very well, instruction by teachers trained in the additional languages may be required.

For the most part, state legislatures only prescribe broad general guidelines and delegate the authority to prescribe the specifics of the curriculum to the state board of education and local SCHOOL BOARDS. As a general rule, with the notable exception of curriculum of a sectarian nature, the COURTS have been reluctant to interfere with school board authority in prescribing curriculum. There are some cases providing certain legal principles to be noted.

The courts have upheld the right of the school board to include language arts, music, art, math, science, dance, and physical education in its curriculum. However, the board cannot require students to engage in BIBLE READING, FLAG SALUTES, the PLEDGE OF ALLEGIANCE, or PRAYERS.

If the school has RULES requiring students to take certain prescribed courses, the question often arises as to what action should be taken if a parent refuses to allow a child, or the child himself refuses, to take a certain course. One early case established the rule that, if a student refuses to take a required course, the proper administrative action is suspension or EXPULSION and not physical punishment of the child. In this case, the child had refused to take an algebra class because her father had instructed her not to do so because of her rather frail physical condition.[67] School officials had decided to punish the child by whipping her.

If the student's objection to certain subjects is based on religious or constitutional grounds, the school may have no power to force the student to take the objectionable course. The school would have to make reasonable allowances for the child and would have no right to punish the student for refusing to take the course. For example, in a 1962 Alabama case, a high school girl contended that she could not be required to participate in a physical education class because the costume was immodest and sinful; and, even if she were allowed to dress in a costume which she personally did not find immodest, she could not be forced to remain in the presence of other girls who were dressed in an immodest and sinful manner. The student also objected to some of the kinds of required exercises. School officials, when confronted with the girl's religious objections to the course, reacted very responsibly. The officials proposed that the girl could wear clothing that she herself considered to be suitable and that the girl would not be required to perform exercises which she considered immodest. The

---

[67]*State v. Mizner*, 50 Iowa 145 (Iowa 1878).

girl and her parents still objected and sued the school. The court held that the school's concessions were sufficient to overcome the girl's religious objections to the manner of dress and that there was no violation of the student's constitutional rights by requiring her to be in the same class with girls who were dressed in a manner which the student considered immodest and who performed exercises to which she objected.[68]

The school has the authority to prescribe that certain courses be offered but cannot require students having valid religious objections to participate. This rule frequently arises in cases involving such courses as dancing and SEX EDUCATION.

See also TEXTBOOKS, Selection.

---

[68]*Mitchell v. McCall*, 143 So. 2d 629 (Ala. 1962).

D

DAMAGES, Contracts

Damages in the form of money may be recovered in the courts by any person who has suffered a loss or injury to his or her person, property, or rights through the wrongful conduct of another.

Damages may be recovered if the SCHOOL BOARD has breached its CONTRACT with a teacher or administrator or if the board has dimissed or failed to renew a teacher's or administrator's contract for wrongful reasons or through inappropriate procedures.

Compensatory damages are meant to "make whole" a person who has been wronged. Damages may include the following items:

1. Back pay. Loss of salary is recoverable. However, if the person accepts or is offered employment of the same general status, pay, and location, part of the salary received or available from the offered employment may be used to mitigate or lower the amount of damages. (See CONTRACTS.)

2. The difference between one salary and the possible earnings from the former position. Consideration will be made for the increments the person would have received.

3. Losses or costs incurred in attempting to find new employment. These costs include such items as résumé or printing costs, placement services costs, postage, telephone, travel expenses, or costs incurred in obtaining additional training.

4. Costs involved in selling an old residence and moving to a new place of residence. These costs may include real estate broker

fees, travel costs, costs of motels and meals while seeking or waiting for a new home, and closing fees involved in the purchase of a new home.

5. Losses caused by the withdrawal from a state or local retirement system if the new position does not provide the same or an equivalent system.

6. Medical or dental expenses incurred which would have been covered under the school district coverage, and fringe benefits or medical expenses incurred from injuries resulting from intentional TORTS or NEGLIGENCE.

7. Medical or dental insurance costs incurred to obtain coverage equivalent to the employer's policies.

8. Costs of transportation to a school which is further from the old school.

9. Damages for noneconomic losses, such as emotional or physical pain and suffering, or losses resulting from an interference with normal and usual activities in personal injury cases.

10. Attorney's fees in some cases if authorized by contract or by state or federal law.

Monetary damages may be recovered by students or educators for violations of their constitutional rights. Under the CIVIL RIGHTS ACT OF 1871, Section 1983, both school boards and school officials are liable for payments of monetary damages. However, the United States Supreme Court emphasizes that full compensation should be provided for a person's actual losses rather than a jury's perception of the value of a right impaired.[1] The court also held that punitive awards—damages awarded to deter officials and others from committing similar offenses in the future—are not to be assessed against governmental bodies such as school boards.[2]

Illustrative of circumstances that can result in an award of damages is the case where a principal and superintendent wrongfully harassed and terminated a teacher for exercising her federally protected speech rights; the administrators were ordered to pay the teacher $26,000 and $39,000 respectively.[3] In another case, a principal who was not provided procedural DUE PROCESS before termination was compensated $51,000 for loss of salary, physical and mental stress, out of pocket costs, and damage to his reputation.[4]

See also DAMAGES, Torts.

---

[1]*Memphis Community School District v. Stachuras,* 477 U.S. 312 (1986).

[2]*City of Newport v. Facts Concerts,* 453 U.S. 247 (1981).

[3]*Fishman v. Clancy,* 763 F.2d 485 (1st Cir. 1985).

[4]*Schreffler v. Bd. of Educ. of Delmar School Dist.,* 506 F. Supp. 1300 (D. Del. 1981).

DAMAGES, Torts

In TORTS, whether intentional or negligent, there are basically three types of damages that are awarded. First, there are *compensatory damages.* Compensatory damages are awarded in order to make an injured party "whole." If a student breaks a leg as a result of someone else's NEGLI-GENCE, he or she has to be made whole again. One cannot give back an unbroken leg, so a price tag is put on the suffering. That is, the jury decides how much the broken leg is worth and grants the injured party a judgment for that amount. Included in compensatory damages is the value for anything the injured party lost. Doctor bills, lost wages, pain and suffering, and property damages are all included. The court attempts to put the injured party back into the position he or she was in prior to the injury or would have been in had the injury not occurred.

In addition to compensatory damages, there are *punitive damages.* Rather than making one whole, punitive damages are awarded for the purpose of deterring further acts of the kind which caused the injury. Punitive damages are meant to punish the wrongdoer. For ordinary negligence, punitive damages are not allowed. Punitive damages are generally allowed only for gross acts which shock the public conscience. If the jury finds that the DEFENDANT acted with "willful and wanton" disregard, there is a possibility that punitive damages will be allowed. Also, punitive damages may be awarded when intentional TORTS are committed.

The third type of damages awarded are *nominal damages.* These damages are awarded when there is really no injury or the injury is only slight. The amount of money awarded is nominal; but, in some cases, punitive damages of a more significant sum may accompany the nominal award.

See also DAMAGES, Contracts.

DEBTS, Authority of School to Incur

See BONDS.

DECERTIFICATION

In cases of decertification of teachers or administrators, the requirements of DUE PROCESS must be stringently followed. The grounds for decertification should relate to the person's ability or fitness as a teacher or as an administrator.

Grounds for decertification are specified in state STATUTES. The statutes differ somewhat, but the laws frequently specify that grounds for decertification may exist when the person:

1. Has been convicted of a crime involving MORAL TURPITUDE;

2. Has been convicted of a crime involving various sexual offenses;

3. Knowingly made any false statement in applying for a certificate; or

4. Has been guilty of gross neglect of duty or any gross unfitness.

Certificates may be revoked by the state for unprofessional conduct in the classroom and sometimes for conduct involving outside activities. The state bears the BURDEN OF PROOF; the proponent of decertification must, therefore, prove all of the elements in the case with substantiated, competent evidence which clearly and convincingly establishes just cause for revocation.[5]

See also CERTIFICATION, Teachers.

DEFAMATION

Defamation is that which tends to injure "reputation" in the popular sense; to diminish the esteem, respect, goodwill, or confidence in which the PLAINTIFF is held; or to incite adverse, derogatory or unpleasant feelings or opinions against that person. Slander and libel are the two forms in which defamation takes place. Slander is an oral expression; libel is a written expression. Defamation is an intentional TORT. Liability for defamation comes from the legal principle that, except where certain "necessary privileges" are granted for special statements, people have a right to enjoy their reputation free from false or disparaging remarks.

Much has been written about defamation, and teachers and administrators must be aware of the liability that can be imposed for committing this intentional tort. By "intent," we do not mean to say that the teacher or administrator "intends" the injury. In torts, the law provides that, where a person intends to do an act, he or she is deemed to have intended all of the consequences which reasonably may result from that act.

Defamation may be established by evidence that discloses:

1. Previous ill will;

---

[5]*Fields v. Turlington,* 481 So. 2d 960 (Fla. App. 1986).

2. Hostility;

3. Threats;

4. Rivalry;

5. Former libel and slanders; or by the

6. Violence of the speaker's language (i.e., the mode and extent of the defamatory words).[6]

Unfortunately, faculty rooms are sometimes hotspots for rumors about students, teachers, and administrators. While people generally do not have the right to cast untrue aspersions on others, there are times when it is necessary to make disparaging comments simply because the comments are required for reports and files. This raises the question of when a teacher or administrator may make untrue statements without being subject to liability.

The law gives protection for certain "privileged" communications; and, when such protection is granted, liability will not be imposed even though the statements made are false. Statements made at school board MEETINGS are often *statutorily privileged.* For example, a teacher sued a Minnesota school board as the result of untrue allegations brought and discussed before the board.[7] The trial court and the court of appeals found that the SCHOOL BOARD had an absolute privilege since the allegations were discussed according to statute.

Another privilege is the *qualified privilege.* This means that, although certain statements are privileged, the privilege is qualified by requirements of "good faith" and "statements made within the scope of one's duty." In other words, the person making the statement should be acting in good faith and the statement must be based upon reasonable grounds. Furthermore, even if there is good faith, the statement must be made within the scope of the teacher's or administrator's duty. This qualified privilege protects educators with reference to maintaining student records. A New York court emphasized the "good faith" requirement of the qualified privilege. The court stated that, absent evidence that certain statements are actuated solely by personal spite or ill will or by culpable recklessness or NEGLIGENCE, there can be no recovery for slander or libel even though the statements may be false.[8]

It should be noted that those statements protected under the qualified privilege can subsequently be held *absolutely privileged* when, for example, a teacher requests that the reasons for his or her dismissal be

---

[6]*Fulton v. Advertiser Company,* 388 So. 2d 533 (Ala. 1980).

[7]*Grossman v. School Bd. of I.S.D. No. 640,* 389 N.W.2d 532 (Minn. App. 1986).

[8]*Kilcoin v. Wolansky,* 428 N.Y.S.2d 272 (N.Y. 1980).

made public. In one case, an Oregon teacher demanded the school board to furnish, upon request of the teacher, reasons for NONRENEWAL of the teacher's CONTRACT and to publish those reasons in the record.[9] Had the teacher not solicited the derogatory comments, those comments would not have been made public. Once the demand was made, the board had the "absolute" privilege to respond.

In addition to circumstances·which grant the right to make privileged communications without liability, there are other defenses which may cloak one from exposure. It has been said that truth is *always* a defense. This statement is not exactly true. Truth is a defense, but only so long as there is no malice involved. If one person knows of something another person did in the past, he or she cannot go spreading it around with the intent to maliciously injure that person. On the other hand, if the person merely comments on the defamatory fact without any malice intended, then truth will be a defense.

Many times, an educator is asked to evaluate and make comments about a person's personality. Conclusions about a person's psychological state should be left out of an opinion unless the person making the statement is qualified to make a psychological diagnosis. Allegations of schizophrenia or manic depression, for example, may not only be erroneous but subject to a lawsuit. Even though one acts in good faith, that person must be competent to make the conclusion a part of the record. Remember, always, that student records and PERSONNEL RECORDS are protected records, and the contents of these records may not be disclosed unless the laws and board policies are strictly followed.

See also ACADEMIC FREEDOM; SCHOOL PUBLICATIONS.

DEFENDANT

The defendant is the person accused of wrongdoing or the party being sued. In a criminal case, the accused is the defendant who is being sued by the State for wrongdoing committed against the State. In a civil case, the defendant is the party being sued for wrongdoing allegedly committed against another.

See also PLAINTIFF.

---

[9]*Christensen v. Marvin,* 539 P.2d 1082 (Or. 1975).

DEMOTIONS

While the SCHOOL BOARD has the authority to transfer or reassign teachers within the district, the new position must be one of EQUAL PAY and status or the reassignment may be considered tantamount to a demotion. If the action is in fact a demotion, a teacher would be entitled to his or her procedural DUE PROCESS rights, and good cause is generally required for a demotion to be allowed without liability for DAMAGES. All reassignments must use objective, reasonable, and nondiscriminatory criteria.

In considering whether a reassignment is a demotion, COURTS look at factors such as reduction in salary, responsibility, and stature of position.[10] In Alabama, the only factor in determining status is TENURE status. Therefore, a principal's transfer to a position paying $4,000 less was not a demotion.[11]

Sometimes it is difficult to determine which positions have equal status. Reassignment of an assistant principal to a classroom teaching position would be considered a demotion. However, it has been held that it is not a demotion to reassign a ninth-grade teacher to teach the sixth grade where the sixth-grade teaching assignment is at a similar rank and equal salary. The court reasoned that:

> There is no less importance, dignity, responsibility, authority, prestige, or compensation in the elementary grades than in the secondary. Here, the young student is still pliant, still susceptible, still in the formative stage, receives his earlier impression, his inspiration, his direction.... To be charged with the responsibility for children in this critical time of their lives is no demotion.[12]

The reassignment must be to a position in which the teacher is certified. If the teacher is forced to incur new training at his or her own expense to become certified for the new position, the reassignment would be tantamount to a demotion.

---

[10]*Jett v. Dallas Independent School Dist.,* 798 F.2d 748 (5th Cir. 1986).

[11]*Alabama State Tenure Comm'n. v. Shelby Co. Bd. of Educ.,* 474 So. 2d 723 (Ala. App. 1985).

[12]*In re Santee's Appeal,* 156 A.2d 830, 832 (Pa. 1959). *See also, Hood v. Alabama State Tenure Comm'n,* 418 So. 2d 131 (Ala. App. 1982).

The BURDEN OF PROOF is on the teacher or administrator to establish that the reassignment is less than his or her former position in terms of importance, responsibility, authority, or prestige. The educator must be aware that, with budget cuts removing many positions from the faculty schedules, necessary REORGANIZATION and subsequent reassignments to lesser positions will not be considered arbitrary demotion.

This approach was evidenced in a case where budget cuts forced the relocation of a principal. Although the principal was reassigned to teach a fifth-grade class, the court held that, under the circumstances, this was not a demotion.[13] A school board's decision to change a music teacher's duties to that of permanent substitute was also not a sufficient demonstration of demotion or constructive discharge.[14]

DETENTION

After-school detention of a student is reasonable either as a form of punishment or to enable the student to make up or catch up on required school assignments. The detention must be for a reasonable length of time and for a valid purpose. The detention should take into consideration a student's age and intelligence and the availability of TRANSPORTATION home. Reasonable supervision is required, and parents should probably be notified in advance of the detention which is to take place. Of course, no notification would be required for detention during school hours.

In many districts, parents are notified prior to the detention; at the same time, parents are given the choice of either picking the student up from school or granting permission in writing to allow the student to walk home in the event a bus is usually used by the child. If the parent neither grants permission for the student to walk home due to age or distance nor provides for alternative means of supervision or travel, then the school would be best advised not to use detention and to seek other means of accomplishing the intended goal.

See also FALSE IMPRISONMENT; NEGLIGENCE; SUPERVISION.

DIPLOMAS

A diploma is a document issued to an individual to certify the satisfactory completion of a prescribed course of study. Academic standards required

---

[13]*Brown v. School District of Cheltenham Township,* 417 A.2d 1337 (Comm. Pa. 1980). *See also, Rossi v. Bd. of Educ.,* 465 N.Y.S.2d 630 N.Y. 1983).

[14]*Christie v. San Miguel Co. School Dist.,* 759 P.2d 779 (Colo. App. 1988).

to receive a diploma are established by the local SCHOOL BOARD within the board's delegated powers from the state education department. Courts will not intervene or evaluate established requirements as long as the requirements are reasonable and not arbitrary or applied in bad faith.

Many states use standardized COMPETENCY TESTS as a minimal criterion to obtain a diploma. Those who do not pass the test may receive only a certificate of program completion. Competency tests of functional literacy as a prerequisite to graduation from public school is within the education authority's powers provided that the students have a fair opportunity to learn the materials on the test.[15]

Legal questions occasionally arise as to when and for what reasons the school district may withhold a diploma. School officials have the quasi-judicial authority to make the final determination as to whether a student has completed the required courses or passed the competency tests necessary for his or her degree. If the student has not done so, the diploma may be withheld. In one case, a court ruled that the SCHOOL BOARD could not deny a diploma to a student who was expelled after passing final exams.[16] A diploma may not be withheld if a student refuses or fails to participate in a COMMENCEMENT EXERCISE or fails to wear the "proper" attire to the ceremony. The reason for this is that the actual granting of the diploma is merely a MINISTERIAL ACT involving no DISCRETIONARY ACT or authority. Therefore, if the student has successfully completed the necessary requirements, school officials are obligated to grant the student his or her diploma as a property interest which cannot be arbitrarily taken away.

See also CURRICULUM; TESTING, Student.

DISCHARGE OF TEACHERS

See DUE PROCESS; PRIVACY; TENURE.

DISCIPLINE, Students

The right to control the conduct and behavior of students in school has been established under the COMMON LAW doctrine of IN LOCO PAR-

---

[15]*Debra P. v. Turlington*, 730 F.2d 1405 (11th Cir. 1984).

[16].*Shuman v. Cumberland Valley School Dist.*, 536 A.2d 490 (Pa. 1988).

ENTIS, meaning "in the place of the parent." Districts utilize several methods to maintain order in the schools, including the use of EXPULSIONS, suspensions, student TRANSFERS, CORPORAL PUNISHMENT, DETENTION, and ACADEMIC PENALTIES. (See RULES.)

Limitations regarding the discipline of students with handicaps may be different in some situations. (See EDUCATION OF ALL HANDICAPPED CHILDREN ACT OF 1975.)

DISCRETIONARY ACT

A discretionary act is the action or inaction school officials choose whenever the effective limits on their power leaves them free to make a choice among possible courses of action or inaction. (See GOVERNMENTAL IMMUNITY.)

See also CONSTITUTIONAL LAW; DUE PROCESS; PRIVACY; TENURE.

DISCRIMINATION

Discrimination, unfair treatment, or the denial of normal privileges on the basis of race, national origin, handicaps, sex, age, or RELIGION is prohibited by the Constitution of the United States and by various federal and state laws. Some of the federal STATUTES which prohibit discrimination are: Title VII of the CIVIL RIGHTS ACT OF 1964, Age Discrimination in Employment Act (ADEA), EQUAL PAY ACT, and Pregnancy Discrimination Act. These laws and others protect against bias in hiring, promotion, compensation, and other employment practices. What this means to each particular school district, student, or educator cannot be simplified into concrete tests or categories. Each case must be considered separately, giving due weight to the types of discrimination alleged and all of the varying facts and circumstances. However, there are certain questions which frequently arise; the COURTS have provided answers to these questions as well as to problems which are similar in nature. The Constitution guarantees each person EQUAL PROTECTION of the laws. Action that discriminates against individuals on the basis of a suspect classification, such as race or national origin, cannot be justified unless the discrimination passes the rational basis test of serving a compelling state interest or goal.

Race or sex may be considered in making certain discriminations where there is strong public policy supporting such considerations. For example, it is permissible to take race into account in order to remedy the effects of past racial discrimination. Granting blacks the first opportunity to apply for positions or hiring a certain quota of minority persons before considering white applicants has, in many cases, been found to be valid and lawful to compensate for past deprivations.

Discrimination on the basis of sex is not allowed unless a showing can be made of an important governmental interest sufficient to uphold the reasonableness of the discrimination. Under this rule, it is allowable to select males to teach wrestling for boys, for example. But, it is not permissible to pay women less for performing the same tasks male teachers perform, and promotions to administrative positions may not be prevented. The Civil Rights Act of 1964 also forbids discrimination in employment practices without a showing of bona fide occupational reasons. (See MATERNITY LEAVE.)

The Age Discrimination in Employment Act and its amendments prohibit employers, employment agencies, and labor unions from discriminating in employment practices and decisions against workers who are between the ages of 40 and 70, on account of age, and also prohibits the placing of help-wanted ads which indicate preference based on age. This act is remedial, humanitarian legislation and should be liberally construed to effectuate the congressional purpose of ending age discrimination in employment. Excluded from the prohibitions of the act are employment decisions and practices, otherwise discriminatory, which are considered justified because they relate to a bona fide occupational qualification or to certain types of employee retirement and benefit systems or which are based on factors other than age.

A worker nearing retirement age is entitled to the same protections as workers with several years of working ahead of them. Thus, a SCHOOL BOARD was required to consider the merits of an employee promotion, regardless of the fact that the worker could hold the position in question for a maximum of one year before retirement.[17]

It is discriminatory to single out one particular group of teachers for special treatment unless there is a reasonable basis for such classicification. A failure to treat all persons equally where no reasonable distinction can be found between those chosen or not chosen is discrimination. Therefore, it is illegal to discipline a group of teachers merely for belonging to a particular civil rights organization or to a certain political party due to the right of freedom of ASSOCIATION.

In addition, although a particular school RULE or policy may be valid, if the rule or policy is intentionally applied in a discriminatory manner, it will be held to violate the requirements of equal protection.

See also ARBITRARY, CAPRICIOUS OR DISCRIMINATORY ACTION; ATHLETICS; CONSTITUTIONAL LAW; RELIGION.

---

[17].*Marshall v. Board of Education,* 15 CCHEPD, Section 8056, 15 VNA, SEP Ca. 5, 368 (Utah 1977).

DISTRICT REORGANIZATION

See REORGANIZATION.

DONATIONS, Acceptance of

School districts may accept donations of PROPERTY to be used for school purposes. However, COURTS will invalidate donations in two circumstances:

1. If the acceptance of the donated property will create a CONFLICT OF INTEREST or undue influence on any school board member; or

2. If the site is improper or unsuitable for school lands. (This restriction is not guaranteed in all states. In addition, if the donated property is readily convertible into funds or other property proper for school purposes, then the restriction may be lifted.)

DRESS, Manner of

See APPEARANCE; CONSTITUTIONAL LAW.

DRUG TESTING

Many courts have held that schools violate students' PRIVACY rights when they require students to submit to blood or urine tests to determine drug use. In a case where a student was required to submit to a urinalysis test, the court held that there were less obtrusive methods for determining RULE infractions.[18] The court stated that the use of the test constituted "an improper attempt by school officials to regulate off-campus conduct."

In another case, a SCHOOL BOARD adopted a policy requiring all students to have annual physical examinations which included urine

---

[18]*Anable v. Ford,* 653 F. Supp. 22 (W.D. Ark. 1985).

samples to detect the presence of controlled substances. When urine tests were positive, the school district notified parents and referred students to rehabilitation programs. The court held that the policy violated the students' constitutional right to be free of unreasonable SEARCH AND SEIZURE.[19]

Drug testing has been allowed when it was limited to participants in extracurricular athletics. An Indiana court allowed the testing after finding that the testing was reasonable.[20] The procedures were mandatory only for those students wishing to participate in athletic competition. The procedures provided for confidentiality and allowed for hearings which protected students' DUE PROCESS rights. Furthermore, the court found the testing to be reasonable in that the most stringent penalty was exclusion from athletic competition.

DRUGS

See DRUG TESTING; SEARCH AND SEIZURE.

DUAL ENROLLMENT

See SHARED-TIME.

DUE PROCESS

Due process of law is a fundamental right guaranteed to citizens of the United States under the FOURTEENTH AMENDMENT of the Constitution. This amendment provides in part: "No state shall...deprive any person of life, liberty, or property, without due process of law;..." Basically, due process is a course of proceedings following established rules which assure enforcement and protection of individual rights. Thus, SCHOOL BOARDS must give people the protection of a fair hearing whenever property or

---

[19]*Odenheim v. Carlstadt-East Rutherford Regional School Dist.,* 510 A.2d 709 (N.J. 1985).

[20]*Schaill v. Tippecanoe County School Corp.,* 579 F. Supp. 883 (N.D. 1988).

liberty interests are involved. To determine if either is present, the following questions should be asked:

1. Is the eduator tenured?
2. Is there a COLLECTIVE BARGAINING agreement?
3. Is there a written CONTRACT which establishes an expectation of continued employment?
4. Is the charge one that would impose a stigma on the educator which would limit future opportunities?

The formality and the extent of the due process requirements depend on the seriousness of the threatened harm to the interests of life, liberty, or property, as well as the procedures outlined in applicable state law. In the states which provide for TENURE by STATUTE, the law also prescribes certain procedures which must be carefully followed in order to lawfully dismiss a tenured educator. If mandated procedures are not followed, the educator will be entitled to DAMAGES and REINSTATEMENT.[21]

Teachers, administrators, and students all have a right to due process of law. This section will discuss when due process is required and will explain the requirements of due process where educators, both teachers and administrators, are concerned. Students' rights to due process are examined in EXPULSION OF STUDENTS.

Substantive protections guaranteed under the United States Constitution are of little benefit if procedural protections do not exist. Without requiring that certain procedures are followed in order to remove or punish educators for alleged wrongdoing, educators are left with only the accuser's honesty and good faith. Due process procedures are necessary in order to assure that the reasons for dismissal, NONRENEWAL, or DEMOTION do, in fact, exist and that these reasons are not based on unsubstantiated rumors, falsehoods, or reasons which are in violation of constitutional rights.

There are two main questions when addressing the issue of due process.

1. Which educators are entitled to due process?
2. If an educator is entitled to due process, how much due process must they receive? Is an explanation sufficient or must there be a hearing?

---

[21]*Irwin v. Board of Education of School District No. 25,* 340 N.W.2d 877 (Neb. 1983).

Educators whose liberty or property interests are involved have the right to due process procedures. The second question, how much due process, depends on the type of action proposed. For example, if a school board wishes to dismiss or nonrenew educators who have property or liberty interests in their position, it is necessary to provide the educators with an opportunity for impartial hearings. On the other hand, if the school board wished to privately reprimand those same educators, no hearing would be necessary.

In January of 1969, David Roth, a nontenured assistant professor at a Wisconsin university, was notified that he would not be rehired at the end of his one-year contract. No reasons were given and no hearing was offered. Mr. Roth sued the Board of Regents claiming, among other things, that failure to advise him of the reasons for nonretention and failure to grant him a hearing violated his right to procedural due process.

In 1969, Robert Sinderman, a member of the faculty at Odessa Junior College in Texas, was notified that his one-year teaching contract was not being renewed. Although he had held his position for approximately fifteen years, no explanation for the action was given and Sinderman was not granted a prior hearing. In his suit seeking reinstatement and damages, Sinderman contended, among other things, that the Regents' failure to provide him with a hearing violated his right to due process.[22]

The *Roth* and *Sinderman* cases were quite similar in the legal issues which they presented. Both cases were appealed through the courts and eventually wound up in the hands of the Supreme Court of the United States. The Supreme Court heard the arguments presented in these cases on the same day and rendered its decisions in the middle of 1972.[23] The Supreme Court held that the requirements of procedural due process apply only where an individual is being deprived of his or her protected interests of "liberty" or "property." When the individual is being deprived of one of these interests, he or she must be granted "some kind of prior hearing." Under this test, Roth lost his case as the court determined he had neither a liberty nor property interest. Specifically, a nontenured position does not give a teacher "expectancy of reemployment," requiring procedural due process in order to dismiss. In *Sinderman,* the court recognized the implementation of the de facto status in Texas and upheld the teacher's protected interests of "liberty" or "property."

The United States Supreme Court pointed out the fact that mere nonrenewal of a nontenured teacher's contract is insufficient to require that a hearing be granted. Nontenured educators' right to a hearing on nonrenewal will depend upon whether the nonrenewal will deprive them

---

[22]*Perry v. Sindermann,* 408 U.S. 593 (1972).
[23]*Board of Regents v. Roth,* 408 U.S. 564 (1972).

of liberty or property. Where either of these interests are implicated, educators have a right to a hearing *prior* to the board making a decision regarding nonrenewal. The question, therefore, is what constitutes an interest in liberty or property?

Property Interests of Educators

Property interests are taken whenever educators are:

1. Dismissed from a tenured position;
2. Dismissed during the term of their contract; or
3. Dismissed when there is a clearly implied promise of continued employment.

Property interests protected under the Fourteenth Amendment have certain attributes:

> To have a property interest in a benefit, a person clearly must have more than an abstract need or desire for it. He must have more than a unilateral expectation of it. He must instead have a legitimate claim of entitlement to it.[24]

This legitimate claim can arise out of state law, a contract, or the rules or understandings of the parties with regard to the rights and benefits the teacher has secured.

Under the United States Supreme Court's "property interest" test, a teacher, for example, would have a legitimate claim or entitlement to his or her position if the district has established a "de facto" tenure policy. This could be done either by written policies or by statements in the district indicating a clear course of conduct giving rise to the conclusion that teachers in the district shall continue in their positions and shall be removed only for cause. Also, some CONTINUING CONTRACT laws are written in such a manner as to arguably amount to a sufficient property interest. In their contract negotiations, teachers can seek to have such a "de facto" tenure policy established.

In an Oklahoma case where the tenure policy was not in question but the school's use of that policy seemed less than fair, it was decided that teachers were not entitled to due process hearings. In this case, the state had a three-year statutory period for refusing to grant tenure and the teachers were given notice of nonrenewal only a short time before they had completed three years of teaching.[25]

---

[24]*Stachura v. Truszkowski*, 763 F.2d 211 (6th Cir. 1985), 477 U.S. 299 (1986).

[25]*Scott v. Oklahoma State Board of Education*, 618 P.2d 410 (Okla. App. 1980).

Liberty Interests of Educators

When considering whether a teacher's nonrenewal or dismisal constitutes deprivation of a liberty interest and thus requires that procedural safeguards be granted, the following guide rules should be observed.

1. The meaning of "liberty" should always be broadly construed.
2. Nonrenewal based on a public charge that might seriously damage a teacher's standing and associations in the community involves a liberty interest.
3. Nonrenewal based on a charge that would impose a stigma or other disability on the teacher, such as to foreclose a range of opportunities, involves a liberty interest.[26]

What Constitutes an Impartial Hearing?

General Nature of the Hearing

A hearing is basically a formal process. Its main purpose is to allow educators to offer evidence and reasons in support of their position that they should not be terminated. The school board must act in good faith in attempting to provide a fair and impartial hearing. The United States Supreme Court held that educators who feel that the school board was not impartial have the burden of proving actual, not merely potential, bias.[27] Many states avoid potential problems by statutorily requiring that hearings be conducted by outside third parties.

The following elements are traditionally required in order to comply with the requirements of due process:

1. Fair and timely notice of the charges
2. An impartial hearing on those charges
3. Fair opportunity to prepare for the hearing
4. The right to present oral and written evidence
5. The right to confront adverse evidence and witnesses
6. The right to be represented by legal counsel

Notice

In order to comply with the requirement of fair and timely notice, the school board must give written notice of intent to dismiss. This notice

---

[26]*Board of Regents v. Roth,* 408 U.S. 564 (1972).

[27]*Hortonville Joint School Dist. No. 1 v. Hortonville Education Association,* 426 U.S. 482 (1976).

must include the reasons for the proposed dismissal, including the testimony and evidence giving rise for dismissal. The notice also must state the date and time that a hearing will be held on the charges.

Right to Counsel

Educators have a right to be represented by an attorney if they desire. In most dismissal cases, the school board is represented by their attorney.

Evidence

Any evidence which the school board has is generally put on file for the educator or his counsel to inspect. All of this evidence may be used at the hearing. Educators have the right to present any evidence which tends to show that the charges against them are not factual. Both sides may only introduce evidence which pertains to the charge of misconduct stated in the notice. Only evidence which is trustworthy should be admitted, but there are few formal rules of evidence. HEARSAY evidence, statements made outside of the hearing usually by third persons, is allowed in many circumstances.

Witnesses

Educators have the right to subpoena any witesses they will need or desire to have at the hearing. All witnesses are sworn and administered an oath. Educators have the right to cross-examine witnesses on any testimony they give at the hearing and on any statement they made in preliminary evidence.

Burden of Proof

The BURDEN OF PROOF is on the school board. They have the burden to prove by a PREPONDERANCE OF THE EVIDENCE that the charges are factual. This burden is met where the evidence is sufficient enough that the alleged facts can be established and reasonable inferences can be drawn from the facts to support the charges.

A great deal of discretion is given to the board. The main limitation is that the board's decision must rest on evidence presented at the hearing, not on the board members' personal knowledge of the case or on suspicion or speculation.

Written Decision

The school board must make a written decision. The decision must state the cause for the dismissal, if that is the result, and the evidence on which the board relied to support its decision. Decision of dismissal must be supported by a vote of at least a majority of the entire board.

Transcript of the Hearing

Most states require that a written record of the hearing be made. This will facilitate the review process.

Review of Dismissal Decision

All states provide for some form of review, but the appeal procedures vary greatly among states. Some states provide for appeal to the state public employee relations board while others provide for an appeal directly to the courts. On appeal, the reviewer will check to see if the proper procedure was followed, if the hearing was fair, and if the decision was supported by evidence.

Suspensions Pending Hearing

Courts have generally approved suspensions pending hearing where a post-suspension hearing was promptly arranged and where the educators would not suffer financial harm and would suffer no harm to their reputation. In exceptional situations, courts have allowed suspensions where the educator suffered financial harm or harm to reputation. For example, one court held that due process procedures were adequate where the board suspended a principal, pending hearing, who was arrested for drug possession even though a hearing was not held for three months.[28] The court held, however, that the suspension must be with pay until the hearing.

In summary, the following general guide rules should be observed.

No educator may be dismissed, suspended, or in any manner substantially punished without a hearing when:

1. The educator is tenured;
2. The educator is under contract; or
3. The reasons for the action would deprive the educator of "liberty" or "property."

Most of the hearings required are formal in nature; but, in some cases involving nonrenewal of nontenured educators, due process may be satisfied by an informal board hearing. In the absence of deprivation of interests of liberty or property, a nontenured educator whose contract is not being renewed is not entitled to hearing or even a statement of the

---

[28]*Summers v. Vermillion Parish School Board,* 493 So. 2d 1258 (La. App. 1986).

reasons unless these rights are granted by local policy or other contract provisions.

See also ARBITRARY, CAPRICIOUS OR DISCIMINATORY ACTION; PRIVACY.

DUES CHECKOFF

When authorized by STATUTE or CONTRACT agreement, dues checkoff permits public employers, on the voluntary written authorization of the public employee, to regularly withhold organizational dues from the employee's wages and to transmit such funds to the designated employee organization. Recognized employee organizations representing a majority of the employees in an appropriate unit are eligible for dues checkoff privileges. Some court decisions rule that minority UNIONS are allowed dues checkoffs as well as to ensure that only fair share expenses are met and dues are not used to increase membership in the majority union.

A public employer has no duty or right to make deductions in salary for union dues unless there is a statutorily mandated COLLECTIVE BARGAINING agreement or employee consent.[29]

The United States Supreme Court has upheld the constitutionality of mandatory payment of agency fees by public employees in order to ensure labor peace and eliminate "free riders." The dues can be prorated to reflect only costs of bargaining and administration of the contract because an employee cannot be compelled "to contribute to the support of an ideological cause he may oppose as a condition of holding a job as a public school teacher."[30] If the fee objection is based upon religious beliefs, an employee may substitute a donation to a charitable organization.[31]

See also AGENCY SHOP; UNION SECURITY.

DUTIES OF TEACHERS

See CONTRACTS; NEGLIGENCE.

---

[29]*Weissenstein v. Burlington Board of School Commissioners,* 543 A.2d 691 (Vt. 1988).

[30]*Abood v. Detroit Board of Education,* 43 U.S. 209 (1977); *see also, Chicago Teachers Union v. Hudson,* 475 U.S. 292 (1986).

[31]*McDaniel v. Essex International, Inc.,* 696 F.2d 34 (6th Cir. 1982).

E

EDUCATION FOR ALL HANDICAPPED CHILDREN ACT OF 1975

The Education for All Handicapped Children Act of 1975 (EHA), sometimes called Public Law 94-142, affects the way in which local school districts educate students with handicaps. The EHA is a funding act which gives federal monies to states which abide by the EHA requirements. The requirements ensure that school authorities provide students with handicaps a free and appropriate public education. This means that special education, as well as any necessary related services, must be provided by the local school district at no cost to the parents. Where local districts cannot afford the costs, the state is responsible.

Though federal monies under the EHA are dwindling as a result of budget cuts and, therefore, provide less incentive for states, the states continue to have an obligation to provide students with handicaps an appropriate education under the REHABILITATION ACT OF 1973, Section 504. The Tenth Circuit Court of Appeals ruled that New Mexico, a state which did not participate in the EHA funding program, was obligated under Section 504 to provide appropriate education programs for students with handicaps.[1] Many courts hold that requirement for a free and appropriate public education are the same under both laws.

In the 1980s, over 60 percent of education cases involved students with handicaps. This statistic could continue into the twenty-first century,

---

[1] *New Mexico Ass'n for Retarded Citizens v. New Mexico*, 678 F.2d 847 (10th Cir. 1982).

133

in part due to the allowance of attorney fees from the local school district whenever parents prevail at hearing or trial. A thorough understanding of the EHA is the best protection local school districts can have against costly special education litigation.

The EHA's purpose is to ensure that all students with handicaps from ages three through twenty-one receive a free and appropriate public education individualized to meet each student's unique educational needs. The term *education* encompasses all of the skills necessary for a person to lead a productive life in society. Skills such as communication and feeding and dressing oneself are just some of the areas encompassed.

Students with certain handicaps who, because of their handicaps, require special education and related services are protected by the EHA. Handicaps covered include mental retardation, hearing losses, deafness, speech or language impairments, visual handicaps, serious emotional disturbances, specific learning disabilities, orthopedic impairments, and other health impairments.

Many of these terms are defined by the EHA. "Special education" is defined as specially–designed instruction, at no cost to the parent, which meets the unique needs of a student with handicaps. However, fees assessed to regular education students, such as physical education towel fees, may also be charged to special education students. Special education includes whatever instruction is necessary to meet the individual needs of the student, such as classroom instruction, instruction in physical education, home instruction, and instruction in hospitals and institutions.

Related services means TRANSPORTATION and developmental, corrective, and other supportive services as are required to assist the student to benefit from special education, including:

1. Speech pathology and audiology

2. Psychological services, including administering and interpreting psychological and educational tests; consulting with staff members in planning school programs to meet the special needs of students as indicated by psychological tests, interviews, and behavioral evaluations; and providing psychological counseling for students and their parents where necessary

3. Physical and occupational therapy, including the improvement, development or restoration of functions impaired or lost through illness, injury, or deprivation

4. Recreational services, including assessment of leisure functions, therapeutic recreation services, recreation programs in school and community, and leisure education

5. Early identification and assessment of the handicap

6. Medical services for diagnostic or evaluation purposes

Seriously emotionally disturbed is defined as a condition exhibiting one or more of the following characteristics which adversely affect educational performance:

1. An inability to learn which cannot be explained by intellectual, sensory, or health factors
2. An inability to build or maintain satisfactory interpersonal relationships with peers and teachers
3. Inappropriate types of behaviors or feelings under normal circumstances
4. A generally pervasive mood of unhappiness or depression
5. A tendency to develop physical symptoms or fears associated with personal or school problems

The above definition is not intended to include students who are socially maladjusted unless they are shown to be clinically seriously emotionally disturbed.

Specific learning disability is a disorder which affects at least one of the basic psychological processes in understanding or in using written or spoken language. The disorder may manifest itself as an imperfect inability to listen, think, speak, read, write, spell, or do mathematical calculations. Such disorders include conditions as perceptual handicaps, brain injury, minimal brain dysfunction dyslexia, and developmental aphasia. The term does not include students who have learning problems which are primarily the result of environmental, cultural, or economic disadvantage.

How the EHA Works

If a student is suspected of having a handicap, an evaluation is conducted at no cost to the parents. The evaluation is based on observations of the student, medical information, information provided by the parents, and nondiscriminatory testing by specialists, which can include assessments of physical and emotional health, vision, intelligence, hearing, and communication. For most students, there is no need for a written report of the evaluation, although one is required where the student is suspected of having a specific learning disability.

Since the evaluation results are part of the student record, parents have the right to see the results. If parents disagree with the results of the evaluation, they are entitled to an independent evaluation at public expense unless the school district can show at an impartial hearing that the school's results are correct.

In order for a student to qualify for special education, the student's handicap must adversely affect the student's educational performance. Education has been interpreted by many courts to include basic self-help skills and social skills. Therefore, just because students have passing grades does not mean that students are not eligible for special education services since the students' handicaps may affect other areas of educational performance.

Once a student is found eligible, an evaluation must be done at least once every three years. Parents, as well as teachers, may request more frequent evaluations.

The next step involves one of the most important procedures of the EHA: the development of the "individualized education program" (IEP) for each student with a handicap. The IEP is a plan, written yearly, which contains specific goals and objectives and includes a basis for measuring the student's progress. The IEP must be in effect before any special education services begin. Once a student is identified as a student with a handicap, an IEP must be formulated by an IEP team within thirty days.

The IEP team includes a district representative who is able to commit the school's resources to the student's program, the student's teacher(s), one or both of the parents, the student (if appropriate), and any other individual the parents or school authorities wish to invite, such as an attorney or someone else familiar with the law, the student, or both. The initial IEP team must also include a person knowledgeable about the procedures and the results of the evaluation which identified the student as handicapped.

Prior to the IEP meeting, the parents must be given appropriate notice. The written notice should include the time, place, and purpose of the meeting. It should also consist of a full explanation of all of the procedural safeguards available to the parents under the EHA. These safeguards include the right to view the student's record, the hearing and review rights of all decisions affecting the provisions of a free and appropriate public education, and the right to keep the student in the current placement until the review procedures have concluded.

If the parents do not respond to the IEP meeting notice, phone calls and personal visits are required. School authorities must keep detailed records of the attempts to convince the parents to attend the IEP meeting.

The IEP must include:

1. A statement of the student's present level of performance;

2. A statement of annual goals and short-term objectives (how much and by when):

goal example: By June 1, Kai will read second-grade material accurately and fluently;
objective example: By February 1, Kai will read aloud second-grade material at an average of 60 words per minute with no more than four errors;

3. A statement of the specific special education and related services to be provided to the student;

4. Appropriate objective criteria and evaluation procedures and schedules for determining whether the objectives are being achieved;

5. A statement of the extent the student will be able to participate in regular educational programs;

6. The date the IEP will take effect and the anticipated duration of the services.

Related services must be afforded to the student if they are necessary to meet the objectives of the IEP.

The IEP team must meet at least once a year to review the IEP and revise it where necessary. Both parents and school authorities have the right to request a new IEP at any time. Parents must be provided with a copy of the IEP.

Once the IEP is developed, a placement decision is made based on the IEP. The placement must address all the needs spelled out in the IEP and is reviewed each time the IEP is changed. Placements can include a regular classroom with support services, a regular classroom supplemented with resource room instruction, self-contained special classes, home instruction, and hospital or institutional instruction.

Changes in placement, defined by the United States Supreme Court as any exclusion from a current placement for more than ten days,[2] may be made more frequently as long as the procedures of the EHA are followed. These procedures include notifying the parents of the intended change, giving both reasons for the proposed change and notice of all the procedural safeguards. A change in placement made without following the EHA procedures was held invalid by the Fourth Circuit Court of Appeals.[3]

Congress provided extensive procedural safeguards to ensure that students with handicaps receive a free and appropriate public education. These safeguards include parental rights which allow the opportunity for meaningful parental input into all decisions affecting their child's education as well as the right to seek review of decisions with which they

[2]*Honig v. Doe,* 484 U.S. 305 (1988).

[3]*Spielberg v. Henrico County Public Schools,* 853 F.2d 256 (4th Cir. 1988).

disagree. Local school authorities have the responsibility under the EHA to inform parents of their rights anytime school authorities propose, or refuse to initiate upon parental request, a change of a provision of the free and appropriate public education.

Significant rights include the parent's right to an impartial hearing and, if desired, a timely review of the hearing officer's decision. The EHA sets up timely administrative review procedures for the parents to use whenever there is a disagreement regarding a student's evaluation, IEP or placement. The law provides for an impartial due process hearing which must be held within forty-five days of the request. The hearing process provides an opportunity for both sides to present their evidence and positions before an impartial hearing officer.

Parties to hearings are entitled to be accompanied and advised by counsel and by individuals with special knowledge or training with respect to the problems of students with handicaps; to present evidence and confront, cross-examine, and compel the attendance of witnesses; to a written or electronic verbatim record of the hearing; and to written findings of fact and decisions. Parties also have the right to exclude the introduction of any evidence that has not been disclosed to them at least five days before the hearing. Parties dissatisfied with the decision of the hearing officer may appeal the decision.

There are two channels of review, and states may adopt either channel. In states using the first channel where the initial hearing is conducted by the local educational agency, an administrative appeal may be made to the state educational agency; and, if a dispute still remains, a civil action appealing the final decision may be brought. In states using the second channel, the first channel, the local educational agency, is bypassed and the initial hearing is conducted by the state educational agency. A civil action to review the hearing officer's decision may then be brought in the proper state or federal court.

The parties to the administrative appeal have the same rights which were accorded to them in the hearing process. The appeal process does not involve a new hearing, but instead it is a review of the hearing officer's decision. The official conducting the review determines if there were any errors made which substantially affect the rights of the parties involved. The reviewer examines the entire hearing record, insures that the lower proceedings were consistent with EHA requirements, seeks additional evidence if necessary, and affords the parties an opportunity for oral or written argument. The official makes an independent decision and gives a copy of written findings and decisions to the parties. The appeal decision must be made within thirty days of the request for an appeal.

Once a party has exhausted its right to administrative appeal, he may seek judicial appeal of the hearing officer's decision. On appeal, the court receives the records from the administrative proceedings, hears additional evidence at the request of a party, and, based on a PREPONDERANCE OF EVIDENCE, grants relief that the court deems appropriate. Where the exhaustion of the administrative review process would be futile or inadequate, the United States Supreme Court has ruled that parties may seek relief from the courts before administrative exhaustion.[4]

To further protect students with handicaps, once parents indicate that the parents have a complaint about the action or inaction of the school authorities, the district cannot change the student's placement unless the parents agree to the change. This provision in the EHA, known as the "stay-put" provision, allows students to continue in their current placement until the review process, including judicial review, if any, has concluded.

The EHA was substantially amended in 1986 to include an attorney fees provision. This provision allows parents to recover attorney fees from the local school district whenever parents prevail at hearing or trial. As a result of potential litigation and high resulting costs for mistakes, school authorities must have a thorough understanding of the obligations required under the EHA.

Courts interpreting the EHA have provided some guidance to school districts and parents. Illustrations follow.

What is "appropriate" education?

The United States Supreme Court has ruled that the appropriate program requirement is met when sufficient special education and support services are provided to allow the student to benefit from that instruction and the procedural requirements of the EHA have been followed.[5] In this case, the student's parents sought an interpreter for their deaf daughter although she was receiving high grades and advancing from grade to grade. The court held that the grading advancement system constitutes an important factor in determining educational benefit and that all the procedural requirements of the EHA had been followed. A federal court of appeals interpreting the United States Supreme Court's decision held that the benefit must be meaningful, not merely trivial.[6]

Several states have laws which specify that sufficient services must be provided to maximize each student's potential. These higher state standards will prevail in these states.[7]

---

[4]*Honig v. Doe*, 484 U.S. 305 (1988).

[5]*Hendrick Hudson Board of Educ. v. Rowley*, 458 U.S. 176 (1982).

[6]*Polk v. Central Susquehanna Intermediate Unit 16*, 853 F2.d 171 (3d Cir. 1988).

[7]*David D. v. Dartmouth School Comm.*, 775 F.2d 411 (1st Cir. 1985).

What is "least restrictive environment"?

The EHA states that "to the maximum extent appropriate, students with handicaps, including students in public or private institutions or other care facilities, are to be educated with students who are not handicapped." This creates a preference in favor of regular school placement. While the least restrictive environment (LRE) is a preference under the EHA, an appropriate placement is mandated by the EHA. Regular classroom placement is not always appropriate.[8] Thus, the question of the LRE should be raised only when there are two or more appropriate placements from which to choose.[9]

When providing related services, what medical services must school districts provide?

First, school districts must provide medical services which are necessary for diagnostic and evaluation purposes. Second, the United States Supreme Court has held that districts must provide medical services which assist a student with handicaps to benefit from special education unless the medical service can only be performed by a licensed physician.[10] This 1984 case involved a student who required clean intermittent catheterization.

Two courts since 1984 have carved further exceptions.[11] The services in question in both cases involved constant monitoring of life-threatening respiratory conditions. The courts held that, where the extensive nursing services to be provided were more in the nature of medical services, the school districts did not have to provide the services.

Must schools provide extended year programs?

In one of the first cases brought under the EHA, the authors of this book filed suit on behalf of a handicapped student who regressed during summer vacation, and the Oregon Court of Appeals ruled that schools are required to provide twelve-month education programs to students with handicaps who would suffer significant setbacks without year-round instruction.[12] This decision has consistently been followed. The fact that a district may have no summer services for the nonhandicapped is irrelevant when determining if a student with handicaps should be provided with

---

[8]*See Hendrick Hudson Central School Dist. v. Rowley,* 458 U.S. 176 (1982).

[9]*DeWalt v. Burkholder,* EHLR 551:550 (Va. 1980).

[10]*Irving Independent School Dist. v. Tatro,* 468 U.S. 883 (1984).

[11]*Detsel v. Auburn Enl. City School Dist. Board of Educ.,* 820 F.2d 587 (2d Cir. 1987); *Bevin v. Wright,* 666 F. Supp. 71 (W.D. Pa. 1987).

[12]*Mahoney v. Administrative School of District #1,* 601 P.2d 826 (Or. App 1979).

summer services. As another court ruled, as long as summer programs are necessary to furnish appropriate education, lack of funds may not limit the availability of summer programs more severely than the lack of funds limits the availability of appropriate educational services to students without handicaps.[13]

Can districts be required to provide educational services to students over twenty-one years old?

When appeals of administrative decisions are made, the EHA states that courts shall receive records of the administrative proceedings, shall hear additional evidence at the request of a party, and shall grant such relief, as the court determines is appropriate. Such relief may be an extension of educational services past the age of twenty-one. For example, the Eleventh Circuit Court of Appeals ordered a district to provide a student with two additional years of education past the student's twenty-first birthday as compensation for the time the district did not comply with the EHA.[14]

When must school districts pay tuition at a private school?

An appropriate education must be provided to every eligible student at public expense. The United States Supreme Court held that, where a school district's offer did not constitute an appropriate education and the parents unilaterally placed the student in a PRIVATE SCHOOL which provided an appropriate education, the school district had to pay retroactive tuition to the date its program offering became appropriate.[15] Alternatively, where the district has an appropriate program available and the parents choose a private school, the parents, not the school district, must pay.

What should school authorities do when they wish to discipline students with handicaps?

The EHA is silent on the discipline of students with handicaps. However, the United States Supreme Court held that an EXPULSION of more than ten days constitutes a change in placement, requiring that the EHA procedures be followed.[16] Time-outs, DETENTION, restrictions of privileges, and suspensions of up to ten days are allowed.

---

[13]*Crawford v. Pittman,* 708 F.2d 1028 (5th Cir. 1983).

[14]*Jefferson County Board of Educ. v. Breen,* 853 F.2d 853 (11th Cir. 1988).

[15]*Burlington School Comm. v. Dept. of Educ.,* 471 U.S. 359 (1985).

[16]*Honig v. Doe,* 484 U.S. 305 (1988).

The United States Supreme Court held that, in situations of extreme need, when parents will not agree to a change in placement, if there exists a likelihood of injury either to the student or to others, the school authorities may bypass the procedures of the EHA and go directly to court for relief in the form of a preliminary INJUNCTION.

When a student's behavior is handicap-related, courts have all agreed that there can be no expulsion. However, the courts have not agreed on what constitutes handicap-related behavior. The Ninth Circuit Court of Appeals held that a behavior is handicap-related only if the handicap significantly impairs the student's behavioral controls.[17] A broader view, which is held by the Fourth, Fifth and Sixth Circuit Courts of Appeals, is that handicap-related behavior is any behavior which can be attributed to the handicap.[18]

One court has also inquired into the appropriateness of the placement before allowing expulsions and ruled that a student who is disruptive due to an improper educational placement could not be expelled.

When behavior is not handicap-related, school authorities may use the same methods of discipline with which they discipline students in the regular education programs. However, if authorities wish to expel the student for more than ten days they must use the change in placement procedures. This means they must send a written notice informing the parents of the intended change in placement and the reason for the change. The notice must include a full explanation of all the procedural safeguards available, including a full description of the hearing and review process, and explanation of the "stay-put" provision.

The issue of whether all educational services may cease when the student has been properly expelled is not resolved. The EHA contemplates only the change in placement and is silent on the elimination of programs. It is difficult to imagine circumstances where a placement team would conclude that an appropriate placement for a student would be no placement at all.

Another issue not resolved is the issue of serial suspension. Serial suspensions (two or more suspensions which together total more than ten days during the school year) may be considered a change in placement. Factors which should be considered are the length of time involved in the service interruption, frequency and number of the interruptions, the nature of the interim services, and the effect on the student's individual needs as stated in the IEP.[19] In-house suspensions lasting over ten days may

---

[17]*Doe v. Maher,* 793 F.2d 1470 (9th Cir. 1986); *aff['d in part, modified in part, Honig v. Doe,* 484 U.S. 305 (1988).

[18]*Kaelin v. Grubbs,* 682 F.2d 595 (6th Cir. 1982); *S-1 v. Turlington,* 635 F.2d 342 (5th Cir. 1981); *School Board of Prince William County, Va., v. Malone,* 762 F.2d 1210 (4th Cir. 1985).

[19]*Van Vleck,* EHLR 305:437 (1986).

also create problems for school districts if the services provided are less than those in the IEP. In those instances, the in-house suspension may be considered a change in placement.

Until there are clearer rules in this area, school authorities should avoid litigation. This avoidance may be accomplished by better-written IEPs which include specific behavior management objectives where there is a likelihood of student misbehavior. The IEP should specify what types of inappropriate behavior might be expected and what steps will be taken to help reduce or prevent the inappropriate behavior. Where individualized discipline methods are spelled out in the IEP, after consideration of the effect of the method on the student's behavior, the school authorities are in effect changing the punishment from a method of discipline to the educational service of behavior management. Students are protected by this approach since their parents have the opportunity to seek review of any portion of the IEP with which they disagree.

ELEMENTARY AND SECONDARY EDUCATION ACT OF 1965

The Elementary and Secondary Education Act of 1965 was directed at student populations who were seen as having educational deficiencies due to their economic environments. The act had many titles which provided for direct financial aid to states. Its main title, Title I, granted federal aid in excess of one and one-half billion dollars for expenditures targeted at low-income families. Title I was superceded by Chapter I of the Education Consolidation and Improvement Act of 1981. The 1981 Act provided for direct reading and math instruction to students who fall behind in class yet who do not qualify as handicapped students under the EDUCATION FOR ALL HANDICAPPED CHILDREN ACT OF 1975. Other titles in the act were consolidated in Chapter II of the Education Consolidation Act of 1981. Federal funding of Chapters I and II is in the form of state-administered block grants.

EMANCIPATED STUDENTS

An emancipated student is one who is free from parental or guardian control. Even though that student might be a minor, it is possible for him or her to become emancipated. When this occurs, the student may choose his or her own RESIDENCE or domicile. This could have some effect on the student's right to attend school within a particular school district without paying nonresident TUITION.

See also COMPULSORY EDUCATION; MARRIED STUDENTS.

EMOTIONAL DISTRESS

See INTENTIONAL INFLICTION OF EMOTIONAL DISTRESS.

EMPLOYEE ORGANIZATIONS, Right to Join

See ASSEMBLY; COLLECTIVE BARGAINING; CONSTITUTIONAL LAW.

ENJOIN

To enjoin means to order a person, by writ of INJUNCTION, to perform, or to abstain or desist from, some act.

See also CONTEMPT OF COURT; STRIKES.

EQUAL ACCESS ACT

The 1984 Equal Access Act provides in operative part: "It shall be unlawful for any public secondary school which receives Federal financial assistance and which has a limited open forum to deny equal access or a fair opportunity to, or discriminate against, any students who wish to conduct a meeting within that limited open forum on the basis of the religious, political, philosophical, or other context of the speech at such mettings."[20]

See also BIBLE READING; BUILDINGS, *Use;* EDUCATION FOR ALL HANDICAPPED CHILDREN ACT OF 1975; PRAYERS.

EQUAL EMPLOYMENT OPPORTUNITY COMMISSION

See CIVIL RIGHTS ACT OF 1964; DISCRIMINATION; EQUAL PROTECTION.

---

[20]EAA § 802(a), 20 U.S.C.A. § 4071(a).

EQUAL PAY ACT

The Equal Pay Act[21] prohibits an employer from discriminating in wage payments on the basis of gender for jobs which require equal skill, effort, and responsibility and which are performed under similar working conditions. The Act will apply unless wage differentials are attributable to a seniority system, a merit system, a system measuring earnings by quantity or quality of production, or differences based on any factor other than gender. For example, a difference in pay between a male teacher and a female teacher assistant may be justified by the difference in skill, effort, and responsibility required by each job.[22] In order for a person to establish a prima facie case of gender-based wage DISCRIMINATION against the district, one must not rely upon a mere showing, for example, that the average male faculty salary is higher than the average salary of female faculty members. Rather, one must break down the comparisons by discipline or by department.[23] Once it has been shown that there is unequal pay for the same work, it is up to the employer to show that the differential pay scale is justified under the Act. In one district, pay differentials based on the sex of the sports participants, rather than on the sex of the coaches, were upheld as a valid basis for disparity in salaries.[24]

The Equal Pay Act does not prohibit an employer from hiring employees purely on the basis of sex,[25] and the Act must be applied on a case-by-case basis to factual situations that are for all practical purposes unique.[26]

It is important to understand that the Equal Pay Act and Title VII of the CIVIL RIGHTS ACT OF 1964 are *in pari material* (of the same structure), construed with reference to each other. Neither STATUTE may be interpreted in a manner which would undermine the other.[27]

See also DISCRIMINATION.

---

[21] 29 U.S.C. § 206(d).

[22] *Katz v. School District,* 411 F. Supp. 1140 (E.D. Mo. 1976).

[23] *Kitchen v. Chippewa Valley Schools,* 825 F.2d 1004 (6th Cir. 1987); *Sweeney v. Board of Trustees,* 569 A.2d 169 (N.H. 1978).

[24] *McCullar v. Human Rights Commission,* 511 N.E.2d 1375 (Ill. App. 1987); *Odomes v. Nucare, Inc,* 653 F.2d 246 (6th Cir. 1987).

[25] *Marshall v. Magnavox Co. of Tennessee,* 494 F. Supp. 1 (E.D. Tenn. 1977).

[26] *Brennan v. Prince William Hospital Corporation,* 503 F.2d 282 (4th Cir. 1974).

[27] *Shultz v. Weaton Glass Co.,* 421 F.2d 259 (3d Cir. 1970)

EQUAL PROTECTION

The FOURTEENTH AMENDMENT to the United States Constitution provides in part that "no state shall...deny to any person within its jurisdiction the equal protection of the law." Through this provision of the Constitution, the COURTS are able to protect DUE PROCESS rights and to protect people against DISCRIMINATION. The schools have been involved in many suits involving the equal protection clause, many of which have involved DESEGREGATION, MARRIED STUDENTS, PREGNANT STUDENTS, and pregnant teachers.

The equal protection clause does not necessarily require that every person must be treated in exactly the same manner. People may be classified in a manner which is relevant to a rule or program where that rule or program is constitutionally permissible. As a result, when a question of equal protection arises, two things will come under close scrutiny by the courts: (1) the purpose of the rule and (2) the classification. The classification will be strictly reviewed by the courts when FUNDAMENTAL INTERESTS of individual liberties are implicated. Classifications based on race, RELIGION, or national origin are presumed invalid because they are almost always irrelevant to a valid purpose of a permissible rule or program.

Fundamental interests include the following:

1. Voting
2. Marriage, procreation, and family-related activities
3. Most travel
4. Privacy
5. All other rights expressly granted in the Constitution, such as speech

When any of these rights are denied or when access to any other benefit or activity is made dependent upon a classification which involves race or religion, the following guide rules must be observed:

1. The classification must serve a compelling state objective.
2. There must be no better alternative means of accomplishing that objective.

Such classifications are rarely upheld. The United States Supreme Court ruled that a discriminatory classification could be upheld only if it furthered a substantial goal of the state. In a United States Supreme Court case, the court reviewed a Texas law that denied alien children public schooling. The public interest of monetary savings was deemed insignificant compared to the discriminatory deprivation of the fundamental right to education of a class of students even though the students were not citizens of this country.[28] However, a number of other "less suspect" classifications may be upheld.

For example, in the past, classifications based on sex were almost always upheld. The courts of the past could rightfully be termed "chauvinistic," since their opinions reflected the view that women were meant to be homemakers. For example, in 1908, the United States Supreme Court upheld maximum working hours for women,[29] and, in 1948, a Michigan law prohibiting women from tending bar was upheld.[30] In 1956, one state court ruled that a law which prohibited women from wrestling was valid.[31] However, women's status in the eyes of the law began to change; by the late 1960s and early 1970s, the courts were willing to scrutinize classifications based on sex. Many laws and rules which singled out women for special treatment were found to be unconstitutional, including those which required unmarried women under the age of twenty-one to live in the dormitory while attending a state college,[32] excluded women from an all-male college in the state university system,[33] and required pregnant women to take mandatory MATERNITY LEAVES.[34]

In a landmark decision, a California court invalidated a prohibition against women tending bar. In doing so, the court said:

> Sex, like race and lineage, is an immutable trait, status into which the class members are locked by accident of birth...[As such, sexual gender] frequently bears no relation to ability to perform or contribute to society.[35]

The court went on to say that a suspect classification like sex tends to impose a "stigma of inferiority and second class citizenship on those persons who are so wrongfully classified."

---

[28]*Plyler v. Doe,* 475 U.S 202 (1982).

[29]*Muller v. Oregon,* 208 U.S. 412 (1908).

[30]*Goesaert v. Cleary,* 335 U.S. 464 (1948).

[31]*State v. Hunter,* 300 P.2d 455 (Or. 1956).

[32]*Mollere v. Southeastern Louisiana College,* 304 F. Supp. 826 (E.D. La. 1969).

[33]*Kirstein v. Rector and Visitors of University of Virginia,* 309 F. Supp. 184 (E.D. Va. 1970).

[34]*Williams v. San Francisco Unified School District,* 340 F. Supp. 438 (N.D. Cal. 1972).

[35]*Sail'er Inn, Inc. v. Kirby,* 485 P.2d 529 (Cal. 1971).

Although California has recognized sex as a suspect classification,[36] most courts, including the United States Supreme Court, have been unwilling to grant this level of protection to individuals asserting claims based on sex discrimination.[37] The United States Supreme Court has opted to classify sex as "quasi suspect."[38] To determine whether a classification based on gender is constitutional, the following criteria must be met:

1. The classification must serve an important state objective.
2. The classification must be substantially related to achievement of that objective.
3. The classification must not depend solely upon administrative ease or convenience for justification.

The United States Supreme Court has considered a number of equal protection cases involving discrimination on the basis of sex. A survey of these cases may be helpful in understanding the nation's courts' treatment of sex discrimination cases. In 1971, the United States Supreme Court held unconstitutional an Idaho statute providing for male preference when both a male and a female were equally entitled to administer a decedent's estate. The court enunciated the following test to be applied in such cases:

> A classification "must be reasonable, not arbitrary, and must rest upon some ground of difference having a fair and substantial relation to the object of the legislation, so that all persons similarly circumstanced shall be treated alike."[39]

One question frequently asked regarding special classifications for women is: "Aren't women more delicate than men?" In a 1972 case, a court answered this question in the following way:

> To anyone who even once has viewed women participating in a roller derby, the argument that all women are the weaker sex, desirous of only the more genteel work, carries little weight. The success of women jockeys is further evidence of which we can take notice. It is no longer possible to state that all women desire or have an "interest" in any one type or classification of work. Some women have the desire, ability and stamina to do any work that men can do.[40]

A Washington State Supreme Court applied the above rationale to a case involving the exclusion of two girls from the "boys'" high school

---

[36]*Frontiero v. Richardson,* 411 U.S. 677 (1973).

[37]*Reed v. Reed,* 404 U.S. 71 (1971).

[38]*Craig v. Boren,* 429 U.S. 190 (1976).

[39]*Reed v. Reed,* 404 U.S. 71 (1971).

[40]*Pittsburgh Press Co. v. Pittsburgh Commission on Human Relations,* 287 A.2d 161 (Pa. Commw. 1972).

football team. This particular case involved two sisters who, at the time they were excluded from competing on the team, were 14 and 16 years old. The sixteen-year-old girl was 5 feet 6 inches and weighed 170 pounds while the fourteen-year-old girl was 5 feet 6 inches and weighed 212 pounds. The court found that, according to their coach, "...both of the girls have been able to hold their own with the boys in practice sessions and would be allowed to play in interscholastic contests were it not for the WIAA regulation [excluding them from the team]."[41] The court held that the regulation denying the girls the opportunity to compete was unconstitutional and stated:

> The notion that girls as a whole are weaker and thus more injury-prone, if they compete with boys, especially in contact sports, cannot justify the [school regulation]. Nor can we consider the argument that boys are generally more skilled. The existence of certain characteristics to a greater degree in one sex does not justify classification by sex rather than by particular characteristics. If any individual girl is too weak, injury-prone, or unskilled, she may, of course, be excluded from competition on that basis but she cannot be excluded solely because of her sex without regard to relevant qualifications.[42]

Opening another legal approach for public employees, the Seventh Circuit Court of Appeals recognized a sexual harassment claim under the Equal Protection clause. The court said, "Forcing women and not men to work in an environment of intentional sexual harassment is no different than forcing women to work in a dirtier or more hazardous environment than men simply because they were women."[43]

Through this line of cases, it is apparent that the equal protection clause prevents discrimination on the basis of sex, as well as on the basis of race, religion, and national origin. School districts' hiring and promotional practices and distribution of benefits are all subject to this provision of the Constitution.

See also ATHLETICS; CIVIL RIGHTS ACT OF 1964; CONSTITUTIONAL LAW.

EQUIPMENT

Equipment must be kept in good working order to prevent suits in NEGLIGENCE. Equipment includes that which is used in ATHLETICS as well as shop equipment. Physical education teachers and coaches should

---

[41]*Darrin v. Gould,* 540 P.2d 882 (Wash. 1975).

[42]Ibid.

[43]*Boben v. City of East Chicago,* 799 F.2d 1180 (7th Cir. 1986).

make sure that sporting equipment is in good condition and that the equipment properly fits the student using it. In a case where a football player suffered injuries related to defective equipment issued to the student by the coach, the court held that the coach was liable for injuries caused by the coach's failure to inspect the equipment.[44]

In a shop-related injury, a court found a teacher negligent when the teacher intentionally removed a safety guard from a power saw.[45] The instructor in this case felt that the guard itself was a hazard and, thus, removed it prior to the student's injury.

See also INSTRUCTION.

EVALUATION

Evaluations are used to judge an educator's effectiveness within that person's job description. Generally, the purposes of an evaluation are to aid the employee in improving his or her methods, to allow for the identification and termination of ineffective employees, or both. The COURTS consistently hold that evaluation content and procedure must not, in fact, be discriminatory on the basis of race, sex, or other unconstitutional discriminatory grounds.

State STATUTES or administrative regulations provide substantive and procedural guidelines for developing equitable evaluation systems. These systems include defining the intent of the evaluation, determining the areas to be assessed, ensuring that evaluation standards are used consistently, proper notification to employees regarding deficiencies, and opportunity and support for improvement of performance. Standardized evaluation forms are recommended, and certain procedural safeguards are necessary. In most states, local school districts are allowed to prescribe their own criteria and procedures for appraisal. Once these procedures are enacted, the procedures must be followed strictly or else the dismissal, DEMOTION, promotion, or TRANSFER is void.[46]

Evaluations are more of an administrative function than a legal one. In other words, most courts are hesitant to interfere with the evaluation process. However, many statutes provide that an educator has a right to a copy of the evaluation, that the person must sign, indicating that the evaluation has been read, and that usually one must be given an oppor-

---

[44]*Thomas v. Chicago Board of Educ.,* 377 N.E.2d 55 (Ill. App. 1978).

[45]*Amon v. New York,* 414 N.Y.S.2d 68 (N.Y. 1979).

[46]*Trimboli v. Board of Education,* 280 S.E.2d 686 (W.Va. 1981).

tunity and space on the evaluation form to rebut anything which has been said. Since the primary purpose of evaluations is generally improvement, evaluations which are shown to be in retaliation for exercising constitutionally protected rights are invalid and subject to judicial review.

Proper procedures identified in statutes, board policies and CONTRACTS must be followed. For example, if the statute says a teacher is to be "observed," a reasonable observation—long enough to determine areas needing improvement—should take place. A documented and honest evaluation must be done, and the teacher must be given an opportunity to see and rebut the remarks or have another person evaluate his or her performance. The standard of competency is not one of perfection but rather one which meets the performance required of others executing the same or similar duties.

In school dismissal proceedings, evaluations play an essential role for documenting evidence. At times, embarrassment may result because proper procedures have not been followed or because the evaluations have not been truly objective. For example, if a teacher is being dismissed for "incompetency," an administrator might, in such a case, be confronted by past evaluations directly to the contrary. Another example might be when a teacher who has been evaluated only once each year suddenly finds that he or she is evaluated several times after becoming president of the local teachers' association. In some of these instances, it may be possible to show that the real purpose of the evaluation was not for improvement of the teaching performance in the classroom but was really intended as a means for obtaining possible grounds for dismissal. The potential for possible prejudice is obvious. It is legally proper to evaluate a teacher more often than is required by statute, but it is not proper to evaluate for wrongful purposes.

Although many courts have determined that the retention or NONRENEWAL of nontenured teachers falls within the exclusive competence of SCHOOL BOARDS, nonetheless, objective criteria and evaluation procedures must be observed. Thus, the Montana Supreme Court indicated that, while decisions regarding the continuation of probationary teachers would not themselves be arbitrable, a claim that the school district failed to comply properly with the specified evaluation or hearing procedures would be subject to ARBITRATION.[47] Courts have overturned discharges where school officials did not strictly adhere to evaluation statutes or afford the teacher an opportunity to improve his or her performance.[48]

Administrative personnel, such as assistant principals, principals, central office staff and superintendents, will often be subject to evaluation

---

[47]*Wilbaux Education Ass'n. v. Wilbaux High School,* 573 P.2d 1162 (Mont. 1978).
[48]*Wren v. McDowell County Board of Education,* 327 S.E.2d 464 (W.Va. 1985).

procedures, and the relevant statutes should be consulted in order to determine proper procedures.

See also CONTRACTS; DEFAMATION; DUE PROCESS; PERSONNEL RECORDS; PRIVACY.

EVOLUTION

See ACADEMIC FREEDOM; ANTI-EVOLUTION STATUTES; RELIGION.

EXECUTIVE SESSIONS, School Board

See SCHOOL BOARDS.

EXHIBITS

An exhibit is a paper, document, or other article which is produced and exhibited to a COURT or an ADMINISTRATIVE AGENCY during a hearing or trial for use as evidence. An exhibit is an item of tangible, physical evidence, connected with the subject matter, which is made part of the case.

EXPRESS AUTHORITY

Express authority is authority which is delegated to an AGENT by words which expressly authorize him or her to do something. The authority may be granted orally. However, some powers must be in writing, such as a power of attorney or authorities covered under state law or CONTRACT.

EXPULSION OF STUDENTS

The distinction between expulsion and suspension of students varies from state to state depending on the definition found in the state's STATUTE or regulation. Suspension refers to the temporary exclusion from the school setting. In-school suspensions may also be imposed which deny the student participation in regular courses and activities. Suspensions usually last anywhere from one to ten days. Expulsion refers to a long-term exclusion from school and often means that the student is prohibited from returning to the school for the duration of the school year and sometimes prevents the student from ever returning. Because of the severity of this form of discipline, most state statutes and district policies provide that only a SCHOOL BOARD has the authority to expel a student.

In the past, school officials were practically free to prescribe any and all RULES governing student conduct, to enforce such rules, and to discipline or expel students in any manner the officials deemed desirable. However, in the 1960s, the courts began to give recognition to the idea that education is a "property right" which cannot be denied without proper grounds and without compliance with procedures designed to assure a student that a proper reason for expulsion does in fact exist. The FOURTEENTH AMENDMENT of the United States Constitution provides in part that neither the state nor any of its employees may deprive "...any person of life, liberty, or property without due process of law." In 1975, in perhaps the most noted case concerning student suspension, the United States Supreme Court concluded that students are entitled to a certain amount of DUE PROCESS. When suspensions under ten days are imposed, *minimum* due process rights include (1) the right to notice of charges, (2) an explanation of the evidence against the student, and (3) an opportunity to present his or her side of the story.[49] The courts emphasize that procedural due process is a flexible standard, and the amount of due process required will be determined based on the severity of the penalty.

Required Expulsion or Suspension Procedures

First, before a student can be suspended or expelled, a valid school rule must have been violated. Second, certain procedures must be followed or the discipline will be in violation of the students' right to due process. In addition to these procedures, in order to expel or suspend students with handicaps, special procedures must be followed so that the EDUCATION FOR ALL HANDICAPPED CHILDREN ACT OF 1975 is not violated.

Minor misconduct which does not call for suspension is not serious enough to require a set procedure; therefore, summary discipline is allowed. The allowed discipline could be in the form of CORPORAL PUNISHMENT (where allowed) or DETENTION. School employees need to be aware that state statutes may require that certain procedures ensuring due process be followed before discipline for minor misconduct is allowed.

---

[49]*Goss v. Lopez,* 419 U.S. 565 (1975).

Again, for suspensions of [less] than ten days, students must be afforded:

1. Written or oral notice of the charges against them;
2. An explanation of the evidence against them; and
3. An opportunity to tell their side of the story.

These procedures are easily met. For example, suppose a custodian reports students for SMOKING in a restroom. The school has a valid rule of which all students are aware: students can be suspended for up to ten days for smoking on school premises. The principal wishes to suspend the students. The principal tells the students they are to be suspended for five days since they have been caught smoking in the restroom. The students must have the opportunity to state their side of the story. This requirement is met as long as the principal allows each student the chance to explain. In this case, all the procedural requirements for due process can be met in a two-minute conversation between the principal and the students.

Where more serious disciplinary punishment is contemplated, there is a need for more procedures to insure that students' due process rights are not violated. A serious disciplinary punishment involves one of the following:

1. A suspension or expulsion for over ten days
2. The withholding of a DIPLOMA
3. A punishment which seriously jeopardizes a student's education or future, for example, certain kinds of entries made on a student's permanent record

Whenever serious disciplinary measures are to be taken against a student, the following procedures must be followed:

1. The student must be given notice of the charges, the nature of the evidence supporting the charges, and the consequences if the charges are proven to be true.
2. The student must be given notice of a right to a hearing at which he or she may respond to the charges.
3. The student must be given a reasonable amount of time to prepare his or her defense before the hearing occurs.
4. The student must be afforded a fair hearing, including the right to present witnesses and evidence.
5. The student must be afforded a fair and impartial decision maker.

The above items constitute the minimum requirements of due process for a significant suspension or long-term expulsion. If the student is not granted a right to these protections, any disciplinary action taken may be invalidated and reversed by the courts. Courts may also award DAMAGES to students whose due process rights are violated.

An informal procedure for expelling or suspending the student is legally permissible when the student has been informed of his or her right to a hearing but voluntarily chooses the informal procedure.

No exact due process measures are mandated by law in most states. The procedures must, therefore, be established by the state board of education or by the local school board. The procedures must be fair and reasonable. The following safeguards specify the requirements of a fair and reasonable due process procedure.

Due Process Procedures for Discipline of Students

1. Written rules specifying the types of behaviors for which disciplinary SANCTIONS may be imposed should be circulated to students and parents.

2. Though only the school board has the power to adopt and promulgate the rules for due process procedures, the rules should be prepared by all persons concerned: students, teachers, administrators, and parents.

3. The due process procedures should be written and circulated to students, teachers, administrators, and the students' parents.

4. The due process procedures should specify that, in cases of minor infractions, discipline may be imposed without the use of any due process procedures.

5. The due process procedures should specify that, in cases of suspensions of less than ten days, students are afforded only minimum due process rights which include the right to notice of the charges against them, an explanation of the evidence, and an opportunity to tell the student's side of the story.

6. The due process procedures should specify that, in cases of serious misconduct for which serious disciplinary sanctions may be imposed, the student is entitled to written notice of the charges; that the written notice of charges must be given to the student and his or her parents; that such notice should include a statement of the evidence against the student as well as the possible punishment; and that the notice should be given early enough to allow the student time to adequately prepare a response to the charges.

7. The due process procedures should specify that, when students request hearings on the charges, the following rights are afforded the students:

a. *Right to inspect evidence.* The student has a right to inspect the evidence against him or her prior to the hearing. Such evidence generally includes summations of the school's witnesses and copies of any statements.

b. *Right to present and refute evidence.* The student has a right to present evidence on his or her own behalf and to refute the evidence presented against the student.

c. *Right to witnesses.* The student has the right to call his or her own WITNESSES.

d. *Right to a decision based on the evidence.* Any disciplinary action taken must be supported by the evidence presented at the hearing. As a general rule, the proof against the student forcing expulsion must be clear and convincing. For a suspension, proof may be a PREPONDERANCE OF THE EVIDENCE in some states or to a lesser extent in other states (that is, in order for the student to be suspended, the educator must merely act in good faith and base the decision on a rational basis).

8. The due process procedures should specify that interim suspensions, pending the hearing, may be imposed if the student's continued presence poses a threat to the safety or well-being of other students or school personnel or would interrupt or threaten the efficient operation of the school. However, an informal preliminary hearing should be held either before or shortly after the interim suspension is imposed.

9. The due process procedures should specify that mass hearings may be used in cases involving large numbers of disruptive demonstrators.

10. The due process procedures should specify that public hearings are not required.

11. The due process procedures should specify who has the authority to expel students and how the decision may be appealed. Various appeals are possible once administrative channels have been exhausted.

12. The due process procedures should specify that an informal procedure for expelling and suspending a student is legally permissible when the student has been informed of his or her right to a hearing but voluntarily chooses the informal procedure.

The main test of a school's expulsion or suspension procedure is one of fairness. If the school board acts fairly and in good faith in expelling a student, its action will probably be upheld by the courts.

Several states have statutes that provide further procedural safeguards for students who are disciplined, such as student GRIEVANCE procedures. When this is the case, the school officials are required to comply strictly with the state's additional safeguards.

EXTRACURRICULAR ACTIVITIES

See ASSIGNMENTS, Nonclassroom; ATHLETICS; CONSTITUTIONAL LAW; FUNDS; MARRIED STUDENTS; NEGLIGENCE. Also see CATEGORICAL INDEX.

FACTFINDING

Factfinding is the investigation of a labor dispute by an individual, a panel, or a board. The factfinder issues a report which describes the issues involved and makes recommendations for settlement of the dispute. The report is frequently made public if the parties fail to resolve their dispute or to accept the recommendations.

Factfinding is relatively formal. Factfinders hold hearings, gather evidence from parties interested in the dispute, and make public recommendations. Theoretically, public opinion on the labor dispute issues will be influenced by the factfinder's recommendations and will pressure the parties into agreeing on a solution to the dispute along the lines of the recommendations. However, the parties are not forced to accept those recommendations.

See also ARBITRATION; COLLECTIVE BARGAINING; MEDIATION.

FALSE IMPRISONMENT

A student is falsely imprisoned when he or she is confined within boundaries stipulated by the teacher or administrator without authority. False imprisonment is an intentional TORT. False imprisonment exists when the teacher or administrator wrongfully detains a student for an unreasonable amount of time or in a wrongful manner.

Teachers and administrators have the authority to detain students from participating in such things as recess, play activities, and field trips.

Educators may also keep a student after school, provided the student has a way of getting home safely. (If teachers or administrators take students home, they have the responsibility of exercising due care or possible liability for NEGLIGENCE may result if students are injured in an automobile accident.)

The DETENTION must be reasonable. Assume, for example, that a teacher believes that a student has possession of illegal or dangerous contraband. Also assume that one may easily dispose of this illegal or dangerous contraband. Under these circumstances, the teacher would have the right to detain the student until a proper search could be conducted. If the educator's belief is based upon probable cause or reasonable grounds, the teacher cannot be held liable for false imprisonment even if it is later found that the student did not in fact possess any illegal or dangerous contraband. However, a teacher could be held liable if the imprisonment is clearly unreasonable. For example, isolating a child in a box or locking a youngster in a closet can be grounds for DAMAGES.

It should also be noted that, even if the detention would normally be considered reasonable, the detention cannot be based on ill will towards the student. In addition, the detention should not be used to enforce an unreasonable RULE, nor should the detention create an unsafe or hazardous situation for the student. Liability for false imprisonment will generally not amount to a great deal in the nature of compensatory damages, but the conduct might result in SANCTIONS from school authorities. Furthermore, if it can be shown that the imprisonment was willful or grossly unreasonable, punitive damages may be assessed against the wrongdoer.

See also INTENTIONAL INFLICTION OF EMOTIONAL DISTRESS.

FEDERAL AID TO EDUCATION

See CIVIL RIGHTS ACT OF 1964; CONSTITUTIONAL LAW; EDUCATION FOR ALL HANDICAPPED CHILDREN ACT OF 1975; ELEMENTARY AND SECONDARY EDUCATION ACT OF 1965; PRIVATE AND PAROCHIAL SCHOOL AID.

FEDERAL COURTS

See COURT ORGANIZATION–Federal.

FEES

Most state constitutions require the state to establish free public schools. Questions frequently arise as to whether such constitutional provisions allow the schools to charge any fees. There are several types of fees including:

1. Incidental fees
2. TEXTBOOK fees
3. TUITION fees
4. Registration fees
5. Extracurricular fees

Incidental fees include such charges as towel and locker fees, course supply fees, fees for driver education courses, class picture fees, and damage deposits. These and other similar fees have been generally allowed by the COURTS. For example, a court upheld a lunchroom supervision fee for students who lived near a school but elected to eat their lunches at the school.[1]

Whether districts may charge tuition or textbooks fees are issues which depend solely on court interpretation of state constitution and STATUTE. Where the law requires that education be provided "without payment of tuition," the courts have generally allowed textbook fees. On the other hand, court decisions have been less uniform when state statutes require "free public schools." Most all of these court decisions hold that states may not charge tuition. Some of these courts allow textbook fees while others hold that textbooks are a necessary part of education and, therefore, fees may not be charged. Note, however, that even in states allowing textbook fees, a waiver is usually provided for students who cannot afford to pay the assessed amount. Registration fees, often equated to tuition by the courts, have been found to be in violation of constitutional provisions requiring free public schools.

Because of budget cuts, many schools are increasingly conditioning participation in extracurricular activities on the payment of fees. Several state Supreme Court decisions in the 1970s found policies charging fees for extracurricular activities to be acceptable. These decisions were based on the premise that extracurricular activities were outside of the regular academic courses or CURRICULUM.

---

[1] *Ambroiggio v. Bd. of Educ. of School Dist. No. 44,* 427 N.E.2d 1027 (Ill. App. 1981).

Additional cases questioning the practice of charging fees continue to come before the courts due to budget restrictions. Courts hearing these cases appear to be split. For example, in 1984, the California Supreme Court held that a district may not charge student fees for participation in dramatic productions, musical performances, and athletic competition.[2] However, the following year, a Michigan court upheld the imposition of fees for participation in athletics.[3] The Michigan court stated that athletics were not an integral part of the educational program. The court also recognized that there was a waiver program for those students who could not afford the fees.

See also TRANSPORTATION.

FELONY

A felony is a serious crime which, under federal law and state law, can lead to imprisonment for a period in excess of one year. There are several classes of felonies (Class A, B, C, etc.) with varying minimum and maximum sentences imposed by STATUTE for each class.

See also MISDEMEANOR.

FIELD TRIPS

See GOVERNMENTAL IMMUNITY; NEGLIGENCE; RULES.

FIFTH AMENDMENT

See CONSTITUTIONAL AMENDMENTS; SELF-INCRIMINATION; SILENT, Right to Remain.

FINANCING, School

Individual state laws and the interpretation of state consitutions will determine how local school districts are funded in the future. A major

---

[2]*Hartzell v. Connell,* 679 P.2d 35 (Cal. 1984).

[3]*Attorney General v. East Jackson Public Schools,* 372 N.W.2d 638 (Mich. App. 1985).

source of litigation in the 1990s will involve school financing and whether or not school districts must spend the same amount of dollars on each student in order to equalize educational opportunities throughout the state. The source of financing and the disparity that may result in different forms of financing will vary from state to state, and this issue does not necessarily involve a federal constitutional question that would clarify how schools are to be financed on the nationwide basis.

An entire text could be written on this financing issue, and the content of that text would change yearly. In a 1990 New Jersey Supreme Court decision, the court ruled that New Jersey must insure that the poorest cities of New Jersey spend as much on their children's education as wealthy suburbs.[4] The court reasoned that education includes not just the basic curriculum but also such programs as music and sports. While the court did not order a ceiling on spending by the wealthy districts, the court did rule that the state must provide enough money for poor districts to compete with wealthy districts and noted that students in the poorest districts "have already waited too long for a remedy, one that will give them the same level of opportunity, the same chance, as their colleagues who are lucky enough to be born in a richer suburban district."

One can only speculate whether the New Jersey decision will be followed by other states. States are wrestling not only with the issues presented by the economic status of a student, but also with whether an equal education should be afforded to nonresident aliens, resident aliens, and/or those who are not fluent in English. Again, individual state interpretations will determine the level of financing and the form of financing that is required as a result of local state control of school financing.

FIRST AID

See MEDICAL SERVICES.

FIRST AMENDMENT

See ACADEMIC FREEDOM; ASSEMBLY; CONSTITUTIONAL AMENDMENTS; CONSTITUTIONAL LAW; RELIGION. Also refer to CATEGORICAL INDEX.

---

[4]*Abbott v. Burke*, 477 A.2d 1278 (N.J. 1990).

FLAG SALUTE

As long ago as 1943, the Supreme Court of the United States held that to compel a student to salute the flag or to say the PLEDGE OF ALLEGIANCE, if such compulsion is contrary to the students' religious or moral beliefs, violated the FIRST AMENDMENT of the United States Constitution. The court said:

> If there is any fixed star in our constitutional constellation, it is that no official, high or petty, can prescribe what shall be orthodox in politics, nationalism, religion, or other matters of opinion, or force citizens to confess by word or act their faith therein.[5]

The court did not rely on the students' religious convictions; instead, the court based its decision on the students' right to free speech. The court explained that:

> To sustain the compulsory flag salute we are required to say that a Bill of Rights which guards the individual's right to speak his own mind, left it open to public authorities to compel him to utter what is not in his mind.[6]

As a result, the court did not sustain the compulsory flag salute. Subsequent courts have followed this decision. All have unanimously held that schools may not compel students to salute the flag.

Educators too may not be forced to salute the flag if this violates the educator's religious beliefs or moral convictions. However, it is clear that, if school policy is to have the students salute the flag or say the pledge of allegiance each morning, the teacher may be required to appoint one of his or her students to lead the exercise and the teacher must sit or stand respectfully during the flag salute or pledge. If an administrator chooses, the teacher may be relieved of a homeroom assignment where the flag salute or pledge takes place so long as this is not meant as a punishment to the teacher.

A teacher may, however, be dismissed for refusing to teach his or her school children about the flag salute and other historical and patriotic subjects. A federal appeals court decided that a probationary kindergarten teacher who was a member of the Jehovah's Witnesses could rightfully be dismissed for failing to adhere to prescribed CURRICULUM. The teacher refused to recite the pledge of allegiance and to teach children patriotic songs and historical facts about national and other holidays (for example,

---

[5]*West Virginia State Board of Education v. Barnett,* 319 U.S. 624 (1943).

Columbus Day, Halloween, Valentine's Day, Lincoln's or Washington's birthdays, Thanksgiving, and Christmas). The teacher also refused to provide bulletin boards instructing about these occasions. In upholding the school's decision to dismiss the teacher, the court stated:

> Plaintiff [teacher] in seeking to conduct herself in accordance with her religious beliefs neglects to consider the impact on her students who are not members of her faith. Because of her religious beliefs, plaintiff [teacher] would deprive her students of an elementary knowledge and appreciation of our national heritage....Plaintiff's right to her own religious views and practices remains unfettered, but she has no constitutional right to require others to submit to her views and to forego a portion of their education they would otherwise be entitled to enjoy.[7]

When students are not adversely influenced or otherwise harmed and no disruption occurs, SCHOOL BOARDS carry a heavy burden to justify any action against a teacher's substantive rights.

See also ACADEMIC FREEDOM; CONSTITUTIONAL AMENDMENTS; CONSTITUTIONAL LAW; PRAYER; RELIGION.

FORESEEABILITY

Foreseeability is a legal term relating to NEGLIGENCE. Whether or not an injury is foreseeable is a QUESTION OF FACT that the jury will decide, and foreseeability will depend on the individual facts and circumstances of every case. It is not necessary that a *specific* type of injury be foreseeable. If a REASONABLE AND PRUDENT person under the same or similar circumstances would have foreseen the injury and the injury occurs, then LIABILITY may be imposed.

When a teacher or administrator foresees or reasonably could foresee that an injury might occur if a particular condition is not corrected or preventive action is not taken, he or she has a duty to do something prior to the injury occurring. If the educator does not respond reasonably, liability may be imposed for negligence. Two indicators of foreseeability are past events, including past behavior patterns of the students, and unreasonably dangerous situations.

There are times when school personnel are obligated to foresee an event occurring. For example, in a case where a young student was seriously burned by a candle on a teacher's desk, the court held that the

---

[7]*Palmer v. Board of Education of City of Chicago,* 603 F.2d 1271 (7th Cir. 1979); *cert. denied,* 444 U.S. 1026 (1980).

injury was foreseeable.[8] The candle had been lit by the teacher, and the court held that the teacher should have foreseen that the mix of a class full of children excitedly dressing for the play and the lit candle was a dangerous combination. In a second case involving a student who was raped on school property, a court held that a school district had an obligation to warn students of possible physical attacks because the act was foreseeable since there had been a similar attack the week before.[9]

Injuries are also foreseeable when a large group of students are gathered and are unsupervised, when a teacher is absent from class for long periods of time, or if there are particularly hazardous activities taking place in shop, science, or physical education classes. When a group of young students has gathered, the reasonable and prudent teacher or administrator would provide supervision or disperse the students. If a teacher is going to be absent from class, he or she must generally provide substitute SUPERVISION and have RULES governing student conduct while he or she is absent. In shop classes and the like, it is imperative that the teachers have rules of safety that are communicated, learned, and enforced. It is also important that teachers adequately instruct students about the proper methods of using power tools or performing athletic endeavors (see INSTRUCTION).

The teacher or administrator has a higher standard of care and should be more able to foresee an accident than the average "man on the street." Sometimes, there are unique situations where a teacher or administrator "knows" there is a hazardous condition, but there does not seem to be anything he or she can do about it. For example, assume that a shop teacher has a class that is overcrowded and, therefore, dangerous because it is difficult to supervise the class properly; or assume that an elementary teacher knows that there is a post sticking out of the playground and that it, therefore, is dangerous; or assume that a principal knows that part of a building is unsafe because of a fire hazard. What can these people do? If someone is injured and that person is in charge, it is very likely that he or she would be named as a DEFENDANT for failure to exercise due care in rectifying the hazardous condition. In order to possibly relieve themselves of liability, the teacher or administrator in each of these instances should notify his or her immediate supervisor in writing. This notification should point out that the condition is dangerous, that an injury is foreseeable, that he or she wants the condition to be corrected, and that there is nothing the teacher or administrator can do about it without help. A copy of the letter should be saved. Then, should an injury occur, the injured party will not be able to hold the teacher or administrator liable for negligence, assuming that person had done all that could be done in order to eliminate the condition. (See GRIEVANCES.)

There are certain supervisory duties which the teacher or admin-

---

[8]*Smith v. Archbishop of St. Louis,* 632 S.W.2d 516 (Mo. App. 1982).

[9]*Fazzolari v. Portland School Dist. No. 1J,* 734 P.2d 1326 (Or. 1987).

istrator is required to perform, and it is the SCHOOL BOARD's duty to provide that teacher or administrator with the equipment, facilities, and staff necessary to carry out these duties properly. If the board does not and the board has notice, there are occasions when the board could be acting in a negligent manner. For example, if there are three hundred young students playing outside and only one teacher is assigned to supervise, the teacher should point out in writing that such circumstances are not safe for students. The teacher must supervise as adequately as he or she can; but, should an injury occur which might otherwise have been prevented if adequate supervisory personnel had been provided, the liability, after having been notified, would rest with the school district and its administrators—not with the individual teacher.

Students, teachers, and administrators have a right to a safe environment. Everybody, including students, teachers, administrators, and the school board, has the duty to provide this safe environment within the limits of his or her capability.

FOURTEENTH AMENDMENT

See CONSTITUTIONAL AMENDMENTS; CONSTITUTIONAL LAW; DUE PROCESS; EQUAL PROTECTION; EXPULSION OF STUDENTS.

FRATERNITIES

See ASSEMBLY, Student Right of; ASSOCIATION, Freedom of; CONSTITUTIONAL LAW; RELIGION; SECRET SOCIETIES.

FREE SPEECH

See ACADEMIC FREEDOM; ASSEMBLY, Student Right of; BIBLE READING; CONSTITUTIONAL AMENDMENTS; CONSTITUTIONAL LAW; OBSCENITY; PRAYERS.

FUNDAMENTAL INTEREST THEORY

The fundamental interest theory is one method or yardstick used to test the validity of aid to parochial schools. Under this theory, education is perceived as being a basic concern for everyone in our society. The benefits derived by granting certain aid to parochial schools in furtherance of this fundamental interest is then balanced against the FIRST AMENDMENT's "Establishment of Religion Clause." If the *main* effect of the aid is furtherance of this fundamental interest in education and the benefit to RELIGION is merely *incidental,* the aid will be upheld. On the other hand, if there is a significant benefit to religion and there exists no overriding benefit to the state's fundamental interest in education, the aid to the religious institution will be judged impermissible. However, the Supreme Court of the United States has held that education is not a "fundamental interest" under the United States Constitution and, therefore, individual state constitutions or court rulings may be controlling.

See also CHILD-BENEFIT THEORY.

FUNDS

Administration

Expenditures of school funds are frequently governed by state STATUTES. As a result, what is a proper expenditure of school funds in one state may be improper in another state. However, as a general rule, the SCHOOL BOARD is granted a great deal of discretion in this area and has the power to make expenditures which are necessary to give effect to the powers, duties, and authority granted to the board. The legislature may designate procedures for expenditure of school funds and may designate who has the authority and responsibility for the funds. If the legislature makes the designation, the provisions must be strictly followed. As a general rule, school funds may be deposited in a bank in order to draw interest income.

Some state statutes appropriate education money for special purposes. The funds established to accomplish these purposes must be administered separately from the general school fund. Also, when school districts receive federal funds, these funds must be spent according to the terms of the grant and in accordance with the rules of administration and expenditure specified by federal regulations. (See EDUCATION FOR ALL HANDICAPPED CHILDREN ACT OF 1975; ELEMENTARY AND SECONDARY EDUCATION ACT OF 1965.)

Authorized Expenditures

Aside from administrative problems, most of the questions concerning school funds deal with the kinds of particular expenditures which the school board may lawfully make. In many states, the laws will expressly state the purposes for which school funds may be spent. Along with the expressly authorized purposes of the expenditure, the board will have the power to spend school funds on certain implied purposes. For example, where the school board is expressly authorized to establish various education programs, the power to make related expenditures is deemed to be implied. An example of a related expense is the expenditure of funds for extracurricular activities and the purchase of athletic facilities and equipment.

A school board may employ doctors, nurses, or dentists to *diagnose* or *inspect* students to see if health regulations have been complied with. However, in the absence of statutory authorization, the board may not employ such persons to *treat* students. This limitation is subject to the rule that the board may, and frequently must, incur the expense of providing first aid services or emergency MEDICAL SERVICES. Also, if a student is injured due to the NEGLIGENCE or willful acts of school personnel, the school may incur liability for medical services. Many statutes specifically authorize school districts to purchase liability insurance for its employees. (See GOVERNMENTAL IMMUNITY.)

By statutory or IMPLIED AUTHORITY school districts are generally deemed to have the power to purchase group medical, dental, disability, and life insurance for its employees. In addition, the school board may employ legal counsel to advise the board members on problems related to the school district.

School districts have the implied power to insure school property but generally must do so by conventional means. Mutual association forms of insurance have been invalidated where the contingent liability of the district was not limited.

The school district may not use school funds for a solely private mercantile purpose which is unrelated to education. The operation of cafeterias is educationally related and is for the benefit of the students. Therefore, this expenditure of school funds is legally permissible. The same rationale has upheld the establishment of school bookstores which sell school books, supplies, stationery, and the like as long as the stores are not operated for a profit and the items are sold at cost plus an amount necessary to cover operating expenses.

Several miscellaneous expenditures have at times been the subject of dispute. Band uniform purchases have been held to be proper expenditures under some state statutes. Expenditure of school funds to cover the costs of board members' attendance at various school-related conventions has also been upheld. The school district may employ architects and pay a commencement speaker's expenses. Whether a school district may purchase campsites for use by students and residences for school personnel has not received a wide acceptance, and COURTS are split on this issue.

The most talked-about expenditure of school funds involves TRANS-

PORTATION. Spending school funds for the transportation of students is allowed under most statutes. Some state statutes require that transportation be furnished to *all* school-age children, including students attending private or religious schools. These statutes have withstood constitutional attack by being recognized as laws which benefit the general public welfare and which are only an incidental benefit to RELIGION. (See BUSING; PRIVATE AND PAROCHIAL SCHOOL AID.)

Most statutes are broad enough to permit school boards to provide transportation to students participating in extracurricular activities. However, the board is not allowed to use school funds to supply transportation to the students' parents or to patrons of such events.

If the school board is in doubt as to what school funds may be spent on, the board should seek out a legal opinion on the scope of authorization granted in the statutes of the state in which the board is located.

Persons Allowed to Authorize Expenditures

Occasionally, questions arise as to who may authorize the expenditures of school funds. A board of education may not delegate its DISCRETIONARY AUTHORITY to make expenditures to employees of the district or to a single member or committee of the board. A few state statutes specifically authorize school boards to delegate some of its purchasing authority; but, in the absence of such authority, the school board may not delegate the authority to purchase goods and services for the school district to the district superintendent, principals, teachers, or other employees. This means that the board of education will not be bound by purchases made by persons other than the board unless the purchases are ratified by the board.

In nearly all districts, school district personnel make purchases for the school. Final approval is left to the board's discretion, however; the board may ratify such purchases by accepting and paying for the goods or by voting to accept a CONTRACT to that effect. If the board does not ratify the purchase, the supplier must try to recover the goods or sue on an unjust enrichment principle.

Most states have statutes requiring an annual reporting and publishing of school district financial reports. These statutes must be followed closely; and, of course, a board of education may employ an accountant to audit the district's financial records.

See also ACTIVITY FUNDS; FEES.

G

GIFTS, Acceptance of

See DONATIONS.

GOD, Act of

There exist certain legal defenses which at times will protect persons from LIABILITY. One such defense is "an act of God." If an injury occurs and it can be shown that the proximate cause of the injury was an act of God, liability will not be imposed. This is true even though the party being sued might have been negligent to a minor degree. For example, assume that the school district erected a flagpole on the playground and that this flagpole was weak and poorly constructed. If the pole broke and a student was injured as a result, liability would be imposed for NEGLIGENCE. However, if a bolt of lightning struck a properly constructed and installed pole, causing it to break, and a student was injured as a result, no liability would be imposed because the proximate cause was an act of God.

Acts of God come in many forms: lightning, hurricanes, floods, blizzards, hail, tornadoes, and other storms. However, if school district personnel reasonably can foresee that "God" is brewing up a storm, they must take reasonable precautions to avoid subjecting students to an unreasonable risk of harm, or liability may be imposed for negligence.

GOVERNMENTAL IMMUNITY

Governmental immunity means that the state or federal government and lower governmental agencies are immune from suit and cannot be held liable for any injuries caused while carrying out governmental functions. In the past, it was a well-accepted rule of law that a person could not sue City Hall. Governmental immunity still exists in some states. The laws with reference to governmental immunity are constantly changing; in order to determine the status of the law in your state, the educator must consult with an attorney or do the necessary research in order to determine LIABILITY in this complicated area.

Governmental immunity has important implications to all educators and school districts in the United States. If a person is injured as a result of an educator's NEGLIGENCE, that injured party may only have recourse against the actual person injuring that party. For example, if a teacher wrongfully batters a student while trying to carry out discipline, that teacher may be liable standing alone unless the student can also name the school district as a party DEFENDANT. The school district is a governmental agency of the state. Therefore, the school district is immune from suit unless the state has given permission for its citizens to sue the state, thus waiving the state's immunity.

To many, it seems strange that a law exists which prevents a person from suing a governmental agency which has wronged that person in some way. In some states, it is felt that the "king can do no wrong." In these states, the laws remain rigid, and legislatures insist that an innocent victim has no recourse against the state or the state's agencies. For example, assume that a person is visiting City Hall and a ceiling tile falls because of loose brackets and a person suffers head injuries. If the injury occurred in a state under complete governmental immunity, there would be no recourse against the City for the injuries sustained. There is a possibility that the injured party could sue the contractor of the building; but, realistically, it is the City which should be responsible for maintaining a safe environment in which people can visit. This example reflects the situation existing within some schools.

Governmental immunity tells an educator how immunity will affect that educator's liability. The school is an arm of the state, and educators are AGENTS of the school. Whether or not the school may exercise the school's right to immunity depends, as earlier stated, on the laws of that particular state. This immunity does not necessarily flow and thus cloak educators. Educators are liable for their own TORTS and cannot defend themselves on the basis of immunity. Insurance might be the only cloak available for protection. Educators may be saved from personal liability only if the state will indemnify and protect the educator from any liability which might be imposed.

The doctrine of governmental immunity can be broken down into four categories with distinctions which must be made within each category. Again, each state's laws should be reviewed so that the educator can determine which category fits that educator's role in that educator's state.

1. There are states which exercise the *complete right to immunity*. This complete right to immunity means, for example, that, if a student is injured by a teacher acting within the scope of that teacher's duty, the student may only have recourse against the teacher, and possibly not even that. In a state with complete right to immunity, the teacher could not look to his or her employer for protection or for indemnification. The teacher would, therefore, have to pay any DAMAGES incurred out of his or her own pocket. Of course, liability insurance would be imperative and certainly reassuring. If the educator falls within the first category of complete right to immunity, then that educator must carry liability insurance through his or her local education association, or other coverage should be purchased if one is to be protected.

2. There are states which distinguish between "governmental acts" and "PROPRIETARY ACTS." A *governmental act* is one which is for the purpose of fulfilling the school's obligation or educational objective. A school district within this category will not be liable for injuries sustained while the school is performing a governmental act. If the school district is involved in an activity that is not in the furtherance of the school's duties as required by law and if the school is involved in an activity which is for the school's own convenience or an activity which could be provided by a private third party or corporation, then the school is involved in a "proprietary act" and can be held liable. It should be noted that most acts in which a school is involved could automatically be deemed governmental acts, depending upon the viewpoint taken; but a helpful test is to ask:

1. Is the activity required by state law? If so, it is governmental.

2. Can the activity be done by a third party, or is the activity for the purpose of saving or raising extra money? If so, the activity is proprietary.

For educators who work within category 2, school district liability will depend upon the nature of the act which causes the injury. For example, if a teacher negligently injures a student while teaching the student swimming (a governmental act), the teacher would be solely liable for any negligence. On the other hand, if the school requested a teacher to transport students to football games in the teacher's private car and if a student was injured when the teacher negligently drove into a ditch, the teacher and the school district would both be liable. Realistically, the school district would be the ultimate bag holder of the debt because the school district has the deeper pocket or assets from which to draw. However, this does not necessarily provide the educator with too much protection. The SCHOOL BOARD could force the teacher to pay his or her share because the teacher is jointly liable with the school district. For this reason, the teacher working within a district in category 2 should also carry liability insurance.

3. In some cases, liability will be dependent upon whether the **school** district purchases liability insurance. In the first two categories, school districts are not generally allowed to buy insurance (with the possible exception of liability insurance in specific areas, such as bus transportation). For those educators within category 3, however, these persons can be saved from liability if the educator acted or omitted to act in an area covered by school district insurance. Educators would include administrators, teachers, school board members, TEACHER AIDES, custodians, cafeteria personnel, and all others who are employed by the school district. Here, school districts have the discretionary power to decide whether to buy insurance (with the possible exception of bus transportation insurance, which is mandatory in some states, and with possible other exceptions). In other words, should the district decide to buy insurance covering the negligence of its employees, an injured party could name the school district as a party defendent along with the employee. Although such action would generally make the school district the ultimate bag holder, there are seldom any clauses barring a later suit for contribution by the employee to the school district. It should also be noted that liability exists only to the extent of the insurance coverage. Therefore, should a judgment be rendered for $300,000 and should the school district be insured for only $100,000, the remaining $200,000 would be on the employee's shoulders. Again, private insurance by the employee or school board member is recommended.

4. There are states which have waived immunity for the negligent acts and sometimes for the intentional TORTS of its employees while the employees are acting within the scope of their employment. Again, this includes school board members as well as others working for the school district. In category 4, the employees will be saved from liability to the extent that the state has waived immunity. For example, if the state has waived immunity up to $200,000, the employee would not have to pay for anything except that which is over the maximum amount. In some states, injured parties can ask for more than the amount covered under governmental immunity states. In other states, the maximum liability would be to the extent waived and no more. There are some states which must defend

and pay the employees' costs for defending a lawsuit, and there are other states where the decision to defend and pay is discretionary. If one is in a discretionary state and should the district choose not to defend the employee, that employee would be left on his or her own. This does not mean that the employee is necessarily helpless. The school district must still pay for the district's own defense and must pay a portion of the judgment. The employee simply has to contribute the employee's own share should that share be divided. The share can, in fact, be substantial; and, should a judgment be rendered for more than what is waived by the state, the excess would be the sole responsibility of the educator.

Governmental immunity protects the state and state agencies while sometimes forcing employees and students to fend for themselves. Every day people are injured on our school grounds, and many of these injuries are very serious in nature. Administrators and teachers are often injured, in addition to injuries to students. Although injuries occur, many states continue to remain immune from suit. Some states have waived immunity to a limited extent. Other states have waived immunity through SAVE-HARMLESS STATUTES to a point where most injuries can be compensated. This area is very complex, and a number of factors are taken into consideration in determining whether an educator will or will not be subject to liability. Many lawyers and judges have great difficulty in distinguishing between proprietary and DISCRETIONARY ACTS. Until "save-harmless statutes" are mandatory in all states, this area of the law will continue to generate litigation. Educators are best advised to carry liability insurance so that the COURTS and lawyers can worry about who pays and the educators can worry about performing appropriate educational objectives.

GRADUATION REQUIREMENTS

See CURRICULUM; DIPLOMAS.

GRIEVANCES

A grievance is a statement of dissatisfaction usually made by an individual but sometimes made by an employee organization or by management concerning interpretation of an agreement or of a work-related matter concerning the internal operations of the school.

The method of dealing with grievances arising out of the interpretation of the terms of a contract agreement are generally specified in the CONTRACT or in a memorandum of understanding. These kinds of grievances are frequently resolved by binding ARBITRATION.

Where the grievance involves a personal complaint of a school district employee regarding the internal operations of the school, most school districts have established their own local grievance procedures. These grievance procedures are extremely important to the district's employees for two reasons:

1. These procedures provide a forum where employees can air their views. Grievance procedures allow school district personnel to resolve quickly and equitably complaints at the lowest possible administrative level. At the same time, the procedures protect the parties to the dispute against undesirable publicity and legal expenses.

2. When a school district employee's grievance involves the internal operations of the school, the employee is not generally allowed to take the complaint to the COURTS or to the public without first proceeding through the grievance procedure process. The process must be followed carefully. If there is a legitimate grievance, start at the beginning of the process and not at the end or in the middle. In other words, if there is a dispute, for example, on whether a certain subject or book may be discussed, the teacher would first be required to go to the immediate supervisor and then on up the ladder. The teacher should not bypass the grievance process and take the issue of ACADEMIC FREEDOM to the local television station. That action might constitute grounds for dismissal based on insubordination for failing to follow proper channels to the detriment of the school.

Local grievance procedures should be used by teachers, administrtors, and other district employees to present complaints regarding everything from textbook selections and personnel policies to personality conflicts and possible unsafe conditions existing on school premises. Courts consistently strike down any policies limiting teachers' direct access to the SCHOOL BOARD as impermissible prior restraint of expression rights.[1]

Grievance procedures are beneficial to the school board and its administrative staff because they are designed to provide a quick and inexpensive solution to possibly serious problems. For example, assume that a physical education instructor believes that the school board's failure to provide padding for a wall which is three feet from the basket presents an unreasonable risk of danger to students engaged in a basketball game.

---

[1]*Anderson v. Central Point School Dist.*, 554 F. Supp. 600 (D. Or. 1982).

Also assume that this teacher puts in a requisition for padding but the school board fails to provide funding in its budget for this EQUIPMENT. The teacher could file a grievance. In this manner, the teacher is able to bring a better understanding of the situation to the school board, and the teacher's actions are likely to protect the teacher from being sued for NEGLILGENCE if a student suffers an injury during a basketball game.

In a significant 1983 decision, the United States Supreme Court narrowed the categories of protected speech for public employees. The threshold question is whether the expression involves matters of public concern or is simply a personal employment grievance. In this case, an employee distributed a questionnaire airing the employee's various grievances. The court upheld the employee's dismissal because personal expressions of dissatisfaction were not constitutionally protected in a public service environment.[2]

Also, the dismissal of an athletic director who made private and public statements criticizing the department deficiencies and improprieties was upheld because the director's manner of grievance airings were outweighed by the school's significant interest in personnel loyalty and proper procedural channels for complaints.[3]

---

[2]*Connick v. Meyers*, 461 U.S. 138 (1983).

[3]*Hall v. Ford*, 856 F.2d 255 (D.C. Cir. 1988).

HANDICAPPED STUDENTS

See EDUCATION FOR ALL HANDICAPPED CHILDREN ACT OF 1975; REHABILITATION ACT OF 1973.

HEALTH PROGRAMS

See ABORTION; ATHLETICS; FUNDS; MEDICAL SERVICES; SEX EDUCATION; VACCINATION.

HEARINGS

See CONSTITUTIONAL LAW; DUE PROCESS; EXPULSION OF STUDENTS; OPEN HEARINGS; SCHOOL BOARDS.

HEARSAY

Hearsay consists of testimony in COURT by a WITNESS about what he or she heard another say out of court. Hearsay statements are not based on the witness's personal observations or knowledge, but the statements rest on the veracity and competency of other persons who are not present to be questioned. When offered to prove the truth of the matter asserted, hearsay is generally excluded or admitted only under specified exceptions.

HOME INSTRUCTION

See COMPULSORY EDUCATION; PRIVATE SCHOOLS.

HOMELESS STUDENTS

See RESIDENCE–Students.

HOMEWORK

Teachers may assign students homework and discipline students who do not satisfactorily complete the assignments. The homework must be reasonable and may not substantially interfere with the student's private life. For example, it would be reasonable to require a two-hour homework assignment; however, it would not be reasonable to require that the assignment be completed only between the hours of 7:00 and 9:00 P.M. every day of the week.

See also DETENTION.

HOMOSEXUALITY

Teachers

Cases dealing with discharge proceedings for HOMOSEXUAL or other unconventional sex acts have some parallel with heterosexual actions but also have many distinctions. The right to privacy for teachers who select a homosexual lifestyle has become increasingly controversial. The COURTS have not clarified a homosexual's scope of constitutional protections. Factors such as the nature of the conduct (public or private), the notoriety surrounding the conduct, and the conduct's effect on teaching fitness are considered on a case-by-case basis.

A widely publicized 1986 United States Supreme Court decision upheld the constitutionality of a Georgia STATUTE that attached criminal penalties to public or private consensual sodomy.[1] The court declared that homosexuals do not have a fundamental constitutional right (under the United States Constitution) to engage in sodomy and that antisodomy legislation reflects the citizenry's views of sodomy as immoral and unacceptable. Although not generally enforced, many other states currently have criminal SANCTIONS for private sodomy; some states might declare penalties for private homosexual acts as unconstitutional under individual state constitutions.

Educators can clearly be dismissed for convictions under state antisodomy laws; but, in the absence of criminal charges, dismissals based solely on an individual's sexual orientation have produced a split of authority in various states. The cases are divided on whether school authorities may lawfully dismiss teachers for pursuing or advocating private consensual homosexual activity.

The Tenth Circuit Court of Appeals ruled that one part of an Oklahoma law that authorized dismissal of teachers who indiscreetly engaged in "public homosexuality" was constitutional. However, the court distinguished another section of the same statute, ruling that dismissal for advocating or promoting homosexual conduct was unconstitutional because the FIRST AMENDMENT allows the freedom to express ideas, no matter how unpopular.[2]

The Supreme Court of California ruled that mere disapproval of private conduct is not adequate grounds for dismissal of a teacher. The California court said that evidence of impaired teaching effectiveness must accompany a teacher's discharge for private homosexuality.[3] Another leading case found that a one-time incident that was not publicized and which was an isolated noncriminal act not likely to be repeated was not grounds to revoke a certificate, and that the license to teach must be restored unless the board could show actual unfitness to be in the classroom.[4] A board of education must demonstrate a rational nexus between the conduct of the teacher and fitness to teach. Potential adverse

---

[1]*Bowers v. Hardwick*, 478 U.S. 186; *rehearing denied*, 478 U.S. 1039 (1986).

[2]*National Gay Task Force v. Board of Education*, 729 F.2d 1270 (10th Cir. 1984), *affirmed by an equally divided Court*, 470 U.S. 903 (1985).

[3]*Board of Education of Long Beach Unified School District v. Jack M.*, 566 P.2d 602 (Cal. 1977).

[4]*Morrison v. State Board of Education*, 461 P.2d 375 (Cal. 1969).

effect on students, controversies anticipated within the community, contextual surroundings, and possible effects on discipline may be used to establish fitness.[5]

The various state courts disagree on the relevance and nexus of homosexual activity to teacher fitness. There is disagreement on the kinds of proof needed to establish a disqualifying connection. Should an educator be held to the "role model" rationale, or must the effect of the conduct be shown by objective evidence and observable events?

In some cases involving the privacy rights of homosexuals, the courts have had little difficulty in establishing the nexus. For example, a California court used the characterization of "seriously defective moral character, normal prudence and good common sense" and upheld the dismissal of a sixth grade nontenured teacher who was discovered in an act of oral copulation with another man in a doorless stall of a public restroom in a downtown department store during store hours.[6]

Some dismissals have been based on the mere knowledge of a teacher's homosexuality. Reasoning that such knowledge was sufficient to show an impairment of teaching effectiveness, the Washington Supreme Court upheld a teacher's dismissal after the teacher admitted to a school administrator that the teacher was a homosexual. The court did not say homosexuality may or may not hamper an educator's effectiveness; however, due to the teacher's continued discussions and public admissions, the court felt that the ability to discharge the teacher's responsibilities when interacting with students, fellow teachers, and school administrators suffered and, therefore, the teacher had to leave.[7] The Sixth Circuit Court of Appeals also upheld the nonrenewal of a guidance counselor who talked about her bisexuality to other school personnel.[8]

Courts have upheld SCHOOL BOARD terminations of "immoral" teachers despite "a blizzard of oral and written communications" in support of the teachers's character[9] and where a public outrage led to a teacher's "resignation" over an alleged homosexual relationship with another teacher.[10]

---

[5]*Burton v. Cascade School District, Union High School No. 5,* 512 F.2d 850 (9th Cir. 1975), *cert. denied,* 423 U.S. 839 (1975).

[6]*Governing Board v. Metcalf,* 111 Cal. Rptr. 724 (Cal. App. 1974).

[7]*Gaylord v. Tacoma School District No. 10,* 559 P.2d 1340 (Wash. 1977).

[8]*Rowland v. Mad River Local School District,* 730 F.2d 444 (6th Cir. 1984), *cert. denied,* 470 U.S. 1009 (1985).

[9]*Melrose Municipal School Board of Education v. New Mexico State Board of Education,* 740 P.2d 123 (N.M. App. 1987).

[10]*Conway v. Hampshire County Board of Education,* 352 S.E.2d 739 (W. Va. 1986).

Since the United States Supreme Court does not recognize a constitutional privacy right to engage in homosexual conduct, lower courts' differing interpretations of homosexual teachers' rights seem likely to continue.

Students

Although many courts have failed to agree on some issues involving homosexual teachers, homosexual students have had their rights much more clearly defined, at least when the students are adults. The majority of the decisions upholding homosexual student activities have been based on the First Amendment free speech guarantee.[11] On the university level, courts have held that gay student organizations may not be denied official campus recognition[12] nor may the group be denied the use of campus meeting facilities.[13] In still another case, a federal court in Rhode Island ordered school officials to allow an eighteen-year-old male homosexual senior high school student to be escorted to the senior prom by his male date. The school had refused the student permission on the basis that it would be dangerous for the boy and his date to attend due to threats from other students. However, the court ruled that the school must provide security protection for the couple and that the students had a constitutionally guaranteed right to attend the dance to make a symbolic statement regarding homosexuality. The court reasoned:

> To rule otherwise would be completely to subvert free speech in the schools by granting other students a "heckler's veto," allowing them to decide—through prohibited and violent methods—what speech will be heard. The First Amendment does not allow mob rule by unruly school children.[14]

See also CONSTITUTIONAL LAW; CONTRACTS.

---

[11]*Tinker v. Des Moines Independent Community School District,* 393 U.S. 503 (1969).

[12]*Gay Student Organization v. Bonner,* 509 F.2d 652 (1st Cir. 1974).

[13]*Student Coalition for Gay Rights v. Austin Peay State University,* 477 F. Supp. 1267 (M.D. Tenn. 1979).

[14]*Fricke v. Lynch,* 491 F. Supp. 381, 387 (D.R.I. 1980).

I

IMMORALITY

See CONSTITUTIONAL LAW; CONTRACTS; DUE PROCESS; HOMOSEXUALITY; PRIVACY.

IMMUNITY

See GOVERNMENTAL IMMUNITY.

IMMUNIZATIONS

See VACCINATION.

IMPLIED AUTHORITY

Implied authority is an indirectly expressed power or right to act. It is reasonably incidental that a granting of certain EXPRESS AUTHORITY necessarily incorporates a granting of implied authority to carry out that which is necessary, usual, and proper to accomplish the delegated task. For example, if a teacher is given the express authority to control student conduct within the classroom, it necessarily follows that the teacher has the implied authority to make and enforce reasonable RULES and regulations governing that conduct.

IMPLIED CONTRACT

An implied contract is a CONTRACT in which the promise by the obligor is not express but is inferred by his or her conduct or is implied in law. Terms are implied where the subject matter is not manifested by explicit and direct words but can be deduced by the general language or circumstances.

See ASSIGNMENTS, Non classroom; CONTRACTS.

INCOMPETENCY

See CATEGORICAL INDEX—Dismissals, Grievances, Tenure.

INDEBTEDNESS

See BONDS.

INJUNCTION

An injunction is an order issued by a COURT which restrains individuals or groups from committing specified acts which, in the court's opinion, would do irreparable harm. A mandatory injunction commands a person to do some positive act, while a prohibitory injunction (sometimes called a restraining order) directs one not to do a certain thing. Failure to comply with the court's injunction order may result in CONTEMPT OF COURT proceedings.

See also STRIKES.

INJURIES

See CORPORAL PUNISHMENT; GOVERNMENTAL IMMUNITY; TORTS; NEGLIGENCE. Also see CATEGORICAL INDEX.

IN LOCO PARENTIS

In loco parentis is a Latin phrase which means "in the place of parents." This legal doctrine was established by the COURTS in order to give school officials the necessary authority to regulate student conduct. In essence, *in loco parentis* means that, when students are within the jurisdiction of the school, school officials may discipline the students as if the students were their own children.

Until the late 1970s, the doctrine of *in loco parentis* was available for use by the school in defending nearly any manner of discipline or punishment. This doctrine also was used as a basis for upholding school RULES. However, since the advent of COMPULSORY EDUCATION laws, the idea that parents voluntarily delegate unrestricted authority to school officials lacks realism. It is now recognized that parents entrust their children to school officials for a specific educational purpose. Therefore school officials have authority over their charges only for the purpose of accomplishing that educational obligation.

INOCULATION

See VACCINATION.

INSTRUCTION

Teachers have a duty to provide students with sufficient and appropriate instruction before allowing students to engage in activities which may present a risk of harm. When teachers fail to instruct properly, they may be liable for injuries which result from NEGLIGENCE.

In a physical education case, a teacher who provided improper instruction for performing a vertical jump in a physical education class was found liable for injuries a student received when the student collided with a wall while attempting a vertical jump.[1] The proper method for a vertical jump is to start with the body parallel to the wall, shoulders perpendicular to the wall, and then crouch and jump with arm extended. The instructor did not demonstrate or teach the proper method, but instead instructed students to take two or three quick steps in the direction of the wall. Testimony at trial revealed that students were standing six to eight feet from the wall and running at the wall before jumping.

See also ACADEMIC FREEDOM.

INSUBORDINATION

See ARBITRARY, CAPRICIOUS, OR DISCRIMINATORY ACTION; CONTRACTS; DUE PROCESS; PRIVACY.

INSURANCE

See FUNDS; GOVERNMENTAL IMMUNITY.

INTEGRATON

See BUSING; DISCRIMINATION.

INTELLIGENCE TESTING

Intelligence, for school purposes regarding CURRICULUM, DIPLOMAS, TRACKING, and the like, is measured for the most part through the use of a standardized intelligence test. The most commonly used tests are the

---

[1]*Dibortolo v. Metropolitan School Dist. of Washington Township, 440 N.E.2d 506 (Ind. App. 1982).*

Stanford-Binet I.Q. Test and the *Wechsler Intelligence Scale for Children.* Many school districts use the results of such tests as a basis for grouping students into various "tracks" or ability groups. Such tests are not always able to measure the innate intellectual ability of youths of varied racial, cultural, or socio-economic backgrounds. The reason is that the standards which are used to validate such tests are usually those of a white, middle-class society, and the questions selected also represent those values.

The educational and psychological effects of grouping based on intelligence tests is being subjected to in-depth studies. The use of intelligence testing continues to foster a number of legal challenges to the tests' application as the basis for assigning students to different CURRICU-LUM levels. The COURTS do not like to interfere with school matters which are discretionary in nature, because the courts realize that educators are far more competent to decide the merits of various school policies than the judges usually are. However, where such policies are discriminatory or are in other ways in violation of constitutional rights, the validity of the testing may become a matter for judicial determination.

Intelligence tests have often been used to group students according to ability. While ABILITY GROUPING is permissible and perhaps desirable in that grouping allows teachers to use curricula that are geared to students with similar needs, some legal challenges have been made due to the use of intelligence testing as a method of determining student placement. One federal district court concluded that intelligence tests were biased against minority students and banned their use in determining placement of students.[2] Because the EDUCATION FOR ALL HANDI-CAPPED CHILDREN ACT OF 1975 specifically states that screening procedures for special education placement must be culturally and racially nondiscriminatory, the court also prohibited intelligence tests from being used as a criterion for placement in special education programs. However, a second court came to the opposite conclusion.[3] Though the second court found some racial and cultural biases, the court held that there was no evidence to show that misassessments occurred as a result of the racial or cultural biases. Thus, the court held that standardized intelligence tests could be used in conjunction with other criteria to determine student placement.

While this issue is not completely resolved, it is apparent that school districts would be wise not to rely solely on standardized intelligence tests in the placement of students. Curriculum-based assessments can provide a reliable assessment of students' abilities.

See also DISCRIMINATION.

---

[2]*Larry P. v. Riles*, 495 F. Supp. 926 (N.D. Cal. 1979); *aff'd*, 793 F.2d 969 (9th Cir. 1984).

[3]*Parents in Action in Special Education v. Hannon*, 506 F. Supp. 831 (N.D. Ill. 1980).

INTENTIONAL INFLICTION OF EMOTIONAL DISTRESS

Intentional infliction of emotional distress is a TORT involving conduct which exceeds all bounds tolerated by a decent society and which conduct is especially calculated to cause and does cause emotional distress of a very serious nature. Not much is heard about emotional distress because it is a realtively unused cause of action. In the past, emotional distress generally had to be accompanied by some sort of physical injury. This was true because proof of mental injury was difficult to achieve; and, without physical injury, fraudulent claims could be asserted. Today, many states have ruled that no physical injury is necessary for *intentional* infliction of emotional distress. However, for *negligent* infliction of emotional distress, a physical injury generally still has to be present.

Teachers and administrators have the right to discipline students, but educators may not discipline students in a manner calculated to cause severe emotional distress. In one instance reported to the authors, a teacher took a "rocket ship" that had been used in a school carnival and hung it from the ceiling of her classroom. Whenever a child got "carried away," the teacher would have the student stand under the rocket ship as she lowered it over the student in front of the class. There, the student would stand in the dark until he or she was ready to fit into the classroom activities.

In another instance, a fifth-grade student was "clowning around." The teacher took her lipstick, painted a clown's face on the child, and told the student to return to the teacher's classroom after school was out in order that the teacher might make certain that the student hadn't removed the mask. The child was obligated to wear the face and take the ridicule of his fellow students the entire school day.

None of these cases ever went to court. In each of these cases, the teacher might have been sued and might well have been liable for any emotional distress the children suffered. These are actions the reasonable teacher or administrator would not tolerate, and they are actions especially calculated to cause severe emotional distress.

This does not mean that a teacher or administrator cannot admonish a student in front of his or her peer group, and isolating a student in a separate part of the classroom or out of the classroom entirely is on many occasions appropriate discipline. However, these things must be done in a reasonable manner. If a teacher or administrator takes action which is calculated to cause or does cause emotional distress of a very serious nature and a student suffers such distress as a result, the teacher or administrator may be held liable.

The following case presents another situation where districts may be liable for infliction of emotional distress. Over a period of four months, an eight-year-old student was sexually assaulted en route to school and on school premises by a thirteen-year-old boy. After four months of assaults, she was raped by the boy. Throughout this time, the girl's teacher, principal, and school psychologist knew of the assaults but failed to inform the girl's mother. The mother claimed that, had the mother been informed of the assaults, the mother could have taken precautionary measures to prevent the rape. As a result of the school's failure to warn the mother of the assaults, the mother claimed to have suffered severe emotional distress. The court, in holding that a special relationship existed between the school and the mother, found that the school had a duty to notify the mother and held that emotional distress was reasonably foreseeable from the school's failure to inform the mother of the events.[4] Of course, the school was also liable to the student for NEGLIGENCE in failing to act in a REASONABLE AND PRUDENT manner under the circumstances existing.

INTENTIONAL TORT

An intentional tort exists when an injury is wrongfully caused and the person causing the injury intended the act. Intentional torts are not NEGLIGENCE. There are several intentional torts of which educators need to be aware, including:

1. ASSAULT
2. BATTERY
3. DEFAMATION
4. FALSE IMPRISONMENT
5. INTENTIONAL INFLICTION OF EMOTIONAL DISTRESS
6. TRESPASS OF PERSONAL PROPERTY

See also GOVERNMENTAL IMMUNITY; SAVE-HARMLESS STATUTES.

---

[4]*Phyllis P. v. Superior Court*, 228 Cal. Rptr. 776 (Cal. 1986).

KINDERGARTENS

Whether a state legislature is forced to establish kindergartens depends upon the wording and intent of the state's constitution. If the necessary language is missing, the legislature is free to determine whether kindergartens will be established.

Most state constitutions do not specify the range of ages of students for which schools must be established. Instead, they have a general provision that the legislature shall establish and maintain a system of free public schools. As a result, if the range of ages is not specified, the legislature makes the determination.

Six years of age is the most common specified minimum in state constitutions. The COURTS have held that the legislature has the authority to go beyond the minimum constitutional requirements. Therefore, where free public education is required by the state constitution to be provided for children between the ages of six and twenty years, the legislature is allowed to establish kindergartens. Where state COMPULSORY EDUCATION law requires children to attend schools between ages six and eighteen, the state cannot require that children attend kindergarten as a prerequisite of first-grade admission.[1]

---

[1]*Morgan v. Board of Education*, 317 N.E. 2d 393 (Ill. App. 1974).

L

LABOR UNIONS

See AGENCY SHOP; ASSEMBLY; COLLECTIVE BARGAINING; CONSTITU-
TIONAL LAW; UNION SECURITY.

LEASE OF SCHOOL PROPERTY

See BUILDINGS; PROPERTY.

LEAVES OF ABSENCE

There are a number of different types of leaves of absence. SABBATICAL
LEAVE, SICK LEAVE, MATERNITY LEAVE, MILITARY LEAVE, PATERNITY
LEAVE, and PEACE CORPS LEAVE are the most common. Contractual leave
provisions are often the topic of COLLECTIVE BARGAINING negotiations.
Some of these leaves are mandatory and must be granted to the teacher or
administrator. Others are left to the discretion of the local SCHOOL
BOARDS. This is possible because the COURTS have recognized that the
continuity of instruction is a significant and legitimate educational goal.
Nonetheless, these rules and regulations should be clearly stated in school
board policies and cannot be arbitrary, in violation of a person's constitutional rights, or violate federal and state antidiscrimination laws.

One should consult the applicable state STATUTE and school board policies to determine whether a leave of absence is granted with or without pay. Specific eligibility criteria for benefits and restrictions may be imposed by a local board.

Although the states specify various employee's rights in regards to leaves of absence, the local board has discretion in determining requirements. For example, if the state says an educator has the right to ten sick leave days a year, there is nothing to prevent the board from adopting a policy of granting eleven days. Also, state statutes may be silent as to "personal" or "professional" leaves of absence. If so, the local board could adopt a policy that each teacher or administrator is entitled to one or two days leave for personal business or professional endeavors. Bereavement leave and family sickness are also examples of leaves commonly granted by local board policy.

Local boards can adopt RULES or regulations governing sick leaves. Typical rules include requiring a doctor's certificate in cases of long absences or requiring the teacher or administrator to make an application for leave within a certain period of time. The rules must generally have an educational purpose and, of course, may not be discriminatory. If all the procedural and statutory requirements are met by the teacher requesting the specific leave, the request cannot be denied by the board.[1]

See also EQUAL PROTECTION.

LETTERS OF INTENT

See CONTRACTS; NONRENEWAL; RENEWALS.

LIABILITY

(See also: Categorical Index)

1. *Contracts*: See BUILDINGS; CONSTRUCTION; CONTRACTS.

2. *Insurance*: See FUNDS; GOVERNMENTAL IMMUNITY.

3. *Parents*: See PARENTAL AUTHORITY; PARENTAL LIABILITY; TEACHER AIDE.

---

[1] *Bristol Township School District v. Karafin*, 478 A.2d 539 (Pa. Commw. 1984); *Collins v. Orleans Parish School Board*, 384 So.2d 336 (La. 1980).

4. *Principals:* See PRINCIPAL; NEGLIGENCE; TORTS.

5. *School boards and school board members:* See GOVERNMENTAL IMMUNITY; SCHOOL BOARDS.

6. *Students:* See STUDENTS, Liability.

7. *Superintendents:* See SUPERINTENDENTS; NEGLIGENCE; TORTS.

8. *Teachers:* See GOVERNMENTAL IMMUNITY; NEGLIGENCE; TORTS.

9. *Teacher Aide:* See TEACHER AIDE.

10. *Volunteers:* See TEACHER AIDE.

See also ALLOCATION OF LIABILITY.

LIBEL

See ACADEMIC FREEDOM; CONSTITUTIONAL LAW; DEFAMATION; SCHOOL PUBLICATIONS.

LIBRARY CENSORSHIP

Partially because of the IN LOCO PARENTIS doctrine and the "indoctrination theory," COURTS have traditionally deferred to local school officials in matters of CURRICULUM and library book selection. Obviously, school officials have a great interest in controlling the materials used in teaching a required course. A growing number of courts have recognized that students also have an interest in and should have some choice in what the students are allowed to read. The school library is a valuable adjunct to the classroom experience. Federal courts have held that students possess a constitutional "right to know," inherent in the freedom of speech. Logistically and economically, a school library must be more selective than a public library and acquire materials appropriate for student use.

Library censorship challenges usually involve a student's claim for access to literature (library materials or instruction books) which have been or which threaten to be removed. In one case, the court reasoned that the SCHOOL BOARD or the state was not compelled to provide a library; but, once a library was created, the school board could not place conditions on library use if the restrictions were based solely on the social or political tastes of the school board members. The court states:

A library is a storehouse of knowledge. When created for a public school it is an important privilege created by the state for the benefit of the students in the school. That privilege is not subject to being withdrawn by succeeding school boards whose members might desire to "winnow" the library for books the content of which occasioned their displeasure or disapproval.[2]

However, in 1982, seven of the nine United States Supreme Court Justices wrote separate opinions regarding the use of school libraries and the propriety of removing books from library shelves.[3] Only three of the justices endorsed the protected right of students to receive information. The right of school boards to remove "pervasively vulgar" or educationally unsuitable material was upheld. The court did note that school boards must not use school board power to "strangle the free mind" or to limit youth in acquiring and evaluating important information which will teach students to become responsible citizens.

School boards and educators should formulate and follow publicized guidelines to reduce the possibility of receiving complaints. Selected committees should identify the educational objectives to be achieved, and unbiased procedures should be developed for inclusion or exclusion of controversial materials. FIRST AMENDMENT rights are breached when school boards arbitrarily censor materials based on personal displeasure without taking into consideration the right of ACADEMIC FREEDOM within public schools.

See also TEXTBOOKS.

LOCAL CONTROL

See SCHOOL BOARDS.

LOCKERS, Searches

See CONSTITUTIONAL LAW; SEARCH AND SEIZURE.

---

[2]*Minarcini v. Strongsville City School District*, 541 F.2d 577, 581 (6th Cir. 1976).

[3]*Board of Education, Island Trees Union Free School District No. 26 v. Pico*, 457 U.S. 853 (1982).

LOYALTY OATHS

In the past, SCHOOL BOARDS have zealously sought to keep subversives from teaching in the public schools. In doing so, many loyalty oaths were enacted which prohibited current or past membership in various organizations and which forbade educators from making certain kinds of statements within and outside the school. Frequently, criminal penalties were included for false swearing.

Loyalty oaths came under fire in the 1950s, and many decisions have been handed down since. In 1952, the Supreme Court of the United States was faced with its first loyalty oath case and held by a unanimous decision that it was unconstitutional to disqualify a person from teaching based on his having been a member of a subversive organization when that person did not know the nature of the organization's activities or its philosophy at the time the teacher had been a member.[4]

Since this 1952 case, the United States Supreme Court has upheld some loyalty oaths and stricken down several others. In 1966, the court set forth the test which must be applied in determining whether an oath is valid. The court said that a person cannot be punished for merely being a member of an organization unless it can be shown that he or she has the intent to further the unlawful aims of the organization or participates in carrying them out. This test was reiterated in a case involving three instructors at the State University of New York who had refused to sign a statement that they were not Communists and that if they had ever been Communists they had communicated that fact to the president of the university. The court explained that "guilt by association" cannot be allowed under the United States Constitution and, therefore, the teachers were reinstated.[5]

This is not to say that all loyalty oaths are invalid. The United States Supreme Court has merely said that educators may be disqualified from public employment only if they can be shown to have the specific intent to further the unlawful objectives of the controversial organization or not be of a "patriotic disposition." Therefore, school employees should be willing to sign a loyalty oath such as the following one which the United States Supreme Court upheld in 1968:

> I do solemnly swear (or affirm) that I will support the constitution of the United States of America and the constitution of the State of New

---

[4]*Wieman v. Updegraff,* 344 U.S. 183 (1952).

[5]*Keyishian v. Board of Regents of the University of the State of New York*, 385 U.S. 589 (1967).

York and that I will faithfully discharge, according to the best of my ability, the duties of the position of _____ to which I am now assigned.[6]

It should also be noted that the membership of the United States Supreme Court changes, and the philosophy of some of the decisions reflects this. A loyalty oath case decided in the early 1970s, although strongly criticized by legal commentators, suggests that the court has taken a new stand on loyalty oaths. The court presumes that such oaths are valid. In a 1972 case, the court went so far as to uphold a Massachusetts loyalty oath for state employees which reads:

I do solemnly swear (or affirm) that I will uphold and defend the Constitution of the United States of America and the Constitution of the Commonwealth of Massachusetts and that I will oppose the overthrow of the government of the United States of America or of this Commonwealth by force, violence or by any illegal or unconstitutional method.[7]

Note that this oath uses the terms "uphold and defend" and "oppose." Public employees should be willing to sign an affirmation of minimal loyalty to the government similar to the above.

Should a teacher encounter a disclaimer provision within a loyalty oath, he or she may object to its inclusion as such provisions have been held unconstitutional. An example of a disclaimer provision within a loyalty oath might be that the teacher swear he or she does *not* believe in the overthrow of the United States government or of the state by force or violence. This second provision falls within those United States Supreme Court decisions which proscribe "summary dismissal from public employment without hearing or inquiry required by due process... That portion of the oath, therefore, cannot stand."[8]

It is clear that school officers and employees may be required to sign a properly worded oath as a condition of employment. It is advisable for school officials to keep oaths simple, straightforward, and unequivocal. Vagueness and overbreadth in oath construction may render the oath unconstitutional.

See also ANTISUBVERSIVE LAWS; ASSEMBLY; CONSTITUTIONAL LAW.

---

[6]*Knight v. Board of Regents*, 269 F. Supp. 339 (S.D.N.Y. 1967), *aff'd*, 390 U.S. 36 (1968).

[7]*Cole v. Richardson*, 405 U.S. 676 (1972).

[8]*Connell v. Higginbotham*, 403 U.S. 207 (1971).

M

MAINTENANCE OF PROPERTY

See BUILDINGS, Maintenance.

MALICE

Malice is an expression of hatred or ill will. Basically, in malice there is an intent to cause injury to another through the use of an express or implied plan. It is a state of mind which is reckless of the legal rights of others and the law.

MALPRACTICE

Malpractice is a term of art for NEGLIGENCE of a professional. PLAINTIFFS who sue for malpractice seek compensation for injuries allegedly resulting from the professional's failure to perform at the level reasonably expected of members of that profession. Educational malpractice suits began to appear in the late 1970s. As a matter of public policy, COURTS do not entertain educational malpractice claims. The main reason cited is that there are no readily acceptable standards of care against which to measure the performance of teachers.[1] Some courts fear that allowing malpractice claims against educators would open the flood gates and that the courts would be burdened with untested litigation. Other courts have fallen back on the tradition of abstaining from review of educational decisions. Courts have also cited the fact that parents have recourse through the administrative process of local SCHOOL BOARDS. If parents are dissatisfied with their children's education, the parents have the right to affect change through administrative channels.

Placement malpractice has had more success than malpractice alleging a student's failure to learn. One court awarded DAMAGES to a deaf individual who was admitted to a state school at the age of two and diagnosed as retarded.[2] The state then failed to reassess the student after it was learned the student was deaf. The court pointed out how, although the failure to properly place the child affected the child's educational performance, the primary cause of the injuries was due to medical malpractice. Holding that the state school was more like a hospital than a school in this case, the court held that damages were appropriate.

In one unsuccessful suit, the Supreme Court of Montana left open some possibility for future successful malpractice suits.[3] The court stated that unintentional acts might result in LIABILITY where districts have violated mandatory STATUTES relating to special education placements such as the EDUCATION FOR ALL HANDICAPPED CHILDREN ACT OF 1975. However, another court held that unintentional acts resulting in the improper placement of children in special education classes could not result in liability since there were appropriate administrative remedies available.[4]

MANDAMUS

Mandamus is a writ which issues from a court having higher authority, directing an official or inferior court to perform a designated official act or legal duty. A writ of mandamus is used, for example, to compel a school district to issue a CONTRACT where it is the district's legal duty to do so. If the deadline for RENEWAL has passed or if there is an improper teacher

---

[1]*Peter W. v. San Francisco Unified School Dist.*, 131 Cal. Rptr. 854 (Cal. App. 1976).

[2]*Snow v. State*, 469 N.Y.S.2d 959 (App. Div. 1983); *aff'd.*, 485 N.Y.S.2d 987 (N.Y. App. 1984).

[3]*B.M. v. State*, 649 P.2d 425 (Mont. 1982).

[4]*Doe v. Board of Educ. of Montgomery County*, 453 A.2d 814 (Md. 1982).

dismissal, the legal course of action is generally through a writ of mandamus. Where the SCHOOL BOARD has a duty imposed by the law and the PLAINTIFF has a clear legal right, the court will order that the writ of mandamus be issued to compel the performance of that duty.

MANDATORY EDUCATION

See COMPULSORY EDUCATION.

MARRIAGE

See MARRIED STUDENTS; MATERNITY LEAVE.

MARRIED STUDENTS

As long ago as 1929, a school board RULE which permanently prohibited a married student from attending a public school was found to be invalid. The court suggested that such a rule would be reasonable only if there was a showing of immorality or misconduct or a deleterious effect on the other students.[5] Some schools attempted to get around this rule by merely "suspending" students for various periods of time rather than forcing the student to permanently withdraw. A clear majority of the COURTS have declared such rules to be unreasonable and arbitrary. For example, a school rule requiring withdrawal from school for a period of one year subsequent to marriage was invalidated,[6] and a rule requiring withdrawal from school after marriage for the remainder of the school year was also invalidated.[7]

In addition, a case involving a sixteen-year-old mother established the rule that a married student has the right to attend school even though she has a child.[8] However, marriage emancipates a minor from COMPULSORY

---

[5]*McLeod v. State,* 122 So. 737 (Miss. 1929).

[6]*Board of Education of Harrodsburg v. Bentley,* 383 S.W.2d 677 (Ky. App. 1964).

[7]*Anderson v. Canyon Independent School District,* 412 S.W.2d 387 (Tex. 1967).

[8]*Alvin Independent School District v. Cooper,* 404 S.W.2d 76 (Tex. 1966).

EDUCATION laws; and, therefore, the courts hold that a married minor cannot be compelled to attend school against his or her will.

In the past, prohibitions on a married student's right to engage in EXTRACURRICULAR ACTIVITIES did not meet with opposition from the courts. Some courts have upheld these rules based on a belief that the rules are reasonable because the school board has an interest in:

1. Discouraging teenage marriages;
2. Preventing students from losing interest in or dropping out of school;
3. Protecting the student's marriage by having the student spend more time at home;
4. Protecting the moral welfare of other students;
5. Maintaining discipline and avoiding disruption.

Most courts, however, reject the validity of the above arguments. This is not to say that school officials are not rightfully concerned about these interests; however, it is doubtful that preventing married students from participating in extracurricular activities does in fact protect any of the above stated objectives. Schools consistently fail to demonstrate that such restrictions on married students are rationally related to or are necessary to promote any legitimate state interest.

Extracurricular activities have often been viewed as special privileges which the board may grant or withhold at its discretion. However, modern judicial reasoning has resulted in tests which suggest that denying such privileges amounts to a denial of EQUAL PROTECTION and DUE PROCESS, and such a denial can only be upheld if there is a valid state purpose and the denial does in fact accomplish such a purpose. It is extremely doubtful that restrictions on married students can be justified under these tests since the restrictions discourage and punish marriages which are perfectly legal and consonant with public policy.

In another case, a high school student was married and a school board policy prohibited her from participating in extracurricular activities because she was married. The purpose of the school board policy was to focus married students on their basic education and their family responsibilities. The problem created for this young woman was that she had played on the girls' basketball team her freshman year in high school and had been described as a "star player." After not playing during her second and third years of high school, she hoped to play on the basketball team during her senior year and had hopes of securing a college scholarship. She challenged the school board and the court invalidated the board's policy, stating:

It is clear that a board policy which discriminates against those who exercise that right (the right to marry) violates the equal protection clause of the Fourteenth Amendment, unless there exists a compelling state interest which justifies that discrimination.[9]

Unfortunately for the student, the season had ended before the court could settle the dispute.

In addition, one court has spoken of marriage as a constitutionally protected right. Infringement on this vital personal right would be permissible only where it is "necessary to promote a compelling state interest."[6] Since education has also been seen as a fundamental right, limiting educational opportunities would infringe on the student's right to marry and right to an education. If such rules are intended to punish a student for exercising this protected right, the rules are in violation of equal protection, deny DUE PROCESS, and are not based on a compelling state interest. Discouraging teenage marriages could perhaps be seen as a compelling state interest, but rules of this type do not accomplish the purpose and, in addition, are often intended more as a means of punishing the student.

In another case, a high school senior honor student married a sixteen-year-old girl who was pregnant. This young man was also an excellent baseball player and was sought by several colleges and major league teams. A district rule prohibited married students from participating in school-sponsored extracurricular activities. Under this rule, the boy was denied the opportunity to play varsity baseball. He sued and the court invalidated the rule and held that such a rule puts an undesirable strain on the student's marriage and constitutes an invasion of marital privacy. The court also stated that:

> [E]xtracurricular activities are, in the best modern thinking, an integral and complementary part of the total school program. The rule which plaintiff attacks cuts him off from a part of the education which under the Ohio statutes he has a right to receive...[7]

These cases suggest that school rules barring married students of both sexes from participating in extracurricular activities will no longer be upheld by the courts. Students of school age possess an entitlement to an education and shall not be denied admission or full participation solely because of their marital status.

See also CONSTITUTIONAL LAW; DISCRIMINATION; EQUAL PROTECTION; PREGNANT STUDENTS.

---

[9]*Beeson v. Kiowa County School District*, 567 P.2d 801 (Col. App. 1977).

[10]*Holt v. Shelton*, 341 F. Supp. 821 (M.D. Tenn. 1972).

[11]*Davis v. Meek*, 344 F. Supp. 298, 301 (N.D. Ohio 1972).

MASS RESIGNATION

Mass resignation involves the simultaneous submission of resignations by a large group of teachers. The purpose of a mass resignation is to force the SCHOOL BOARD to accede to the teachers' demands. Frequently, the teachers' employee organization will hold the resignations and use them as a threat but do not necessarily submit them to the board.

A STRIKE is defined as any concerted refusal to work. Mass resignations are often looked upon by the COURTS as a form of a strike.[12] If seen as being a truly valid resignation of the teachers involved, the teachers have no obligation to return to work and the court will not compel them to do so. On the other hand, if the resignations are treated as being valid, the school board would have no obligation to "rehire" the teachers. Moreover, under a few state STATUTES, TENURE and seniority rights are granted on the basis of continuous service, and an interruption (such as a resignation) might adversely affect these rights.

MATERNITY LEAVE

Maternity leave is a LEAVE OF ABSENCE granted to tenured and non-tenured teachers and administrators due to pregnancy. There was a time when marriage and pregnancy were considered grounds for dismissal. Teachers even signed CONTRACTS which said that they would not be secretly married or date young men "except insofar as it may be necessary to stimulate Sunday School work."[13] Of course, this restriction was only directed towards the female gender of our society who, it was felt, could be adversely affected by "falling in love, becoming engaged, or by tolerating any familiarity on the part of men."[14]

While modern thinking has allowed educators to be married, it took longer to deal with pregnancy. For some, pregnancy verged on immorality and certainly constituted a breach of contract. By STATUTE, most local SCHOOL BOARDS may dismiss teachers only on specific grounds. As a result, one board went so far as to try to dismiss a teacher for giving birth because, the board asserted, the act of getting pregnant constituted an act

---

[12]*Board of Education, City of New York v. Shanker,* 283 N.Y.S.2d (N.Y. 1967).

[13]H.K. Beale, *Are American Teachers Free?*, New York: Charles Scribner's Sons, 1936.

[14]Ibid.

of "NEGLIGENCE." The court refused to uphold the board's reasoning and ordered that the teacher be reinstated.[15]

The EQUAL PROTECTION clause of the FOURTEENTH AMEND-MENT has been used as a basis for striking down arbitrary policies disallowing maternity leave. For example, a school board may not refuse a nontenured teacher a maternity leave, particularly where such a leave is granted to tenured teachers. In addition, the CIVIL RIGHTS ACT OF 1964 makes it clear that a teacher may not be dismissed due to her pregnancy. As a result, the right to be pregnant is assured. In 1979, many questions regarding maternity leave were resolved by Congress when it passed the Pregnancy Discrimination Act which amended Title VII of the Civil Rights Act of 1964. This act provides that women affected by pregnancy, childbirth, or related medical conditions shall be treated the same for all employment-related purposes, including the receipt of fringe benefit programs, as other persons not so affected but similar in their ability or inability to work. Therefore, a woman unable to work for pregnancy-related reasons is entitled to disability benefits on the same basis as employees unable to work for other medical reasons.[16]

In 1974, the Supreme Court of the United States reinforced the maternity leave issue when the court ruled that schools could not force pregnant teachers to take a leave of absence after the fourth or fifth month of pregnancy. Rules requiring teachers to give notice are rationally related to preserving continuity of instruction goals; but arbitrary cutoff dates, when pregnant teachers were forced to stop teaching, were held to be unconstitutional. Cutoff dates violate the DUE PROCESS clause by creating a presumption that all women become physically incompetent at a specified date. Although the court did not close the door on the possibility of mandatory leave during the last few weeks of pregnancy, the basic rule is that an educator must be allowed to remain in her position until she and her doctor determine that her health necessitates taking the leave.[17]

Many school boards have changed policies to conform with these requirements. The state of New York has, for example, a liberal maternity leave policy for state workers to allow pregnant employees to continue working during the pregnancy as long as the employee desires. The law permits payment of accumulated sick leave for the maternity absence and allows unpaid maternity leave for up to two years as with other prolonged disabilities. This type of law complies with the EEOC requirements and guidelines.

---

[15]*In re Leahey*, 43 Lack. Jur. 227 (Pa. Commw. Pleas 1942).

[16]42 U.S.C. Section 2000 e(k).

[17]*Cleveland Board of Education v. LaFleur*, 414 U.S. 632 (1974). *See also, Ponton v. Newport News School Board*, 632 F. Supp. 1056 (E.D. Va. 1986).

Moreover, at least one state court has ruled that requiring teachers to choose between disability leave of absence and maternity leave, but not both, was an unconstitutional DISCRIMINATION on the basis of sex. Under the disability leave of absence, a teacher could receive her accumulated sick leave benefits but was required to return to work as soon as she was able. Under the maternity leave of absence, the teacher could take an extended leave from her teaching duties but had to do so without pay. Furthermore, the board allowed other teachers who were temporarily disabled for reasons other than pregnancy to utilize accumulated sick leave payments. The Superior Court of New Jersey held that the board policy, as it related to pregnant teachers, was invalid. The court ruled that pregnant teachers were entitled to both accumulated sick leave for the time in which they were actually disabled, followed by maternity leave for the purpose of raising the child.[18] Employees retain seniority rights and accumulate credits toward TENURE while on maternity leave.[19]

School boards may, of course, enact reasonable RULES governing the procedures for maternity leave, such as requiring that the educator make a written application for maternity leave at least one month prior to the date the leave is to take affect or submission of a doctor's certificate.

Courts will generally hold that the period of a woman's postdelivery absence, as with her predelivery absence, is up to the teacher and her doctor. If she is physically and mentally able, the teacher or administrator may return immediately. The school board may require a certificate from a doctor as to her physical fitness. In addition, the United States Supreme Court has suggested that a board rule requiring educators to wait for return until the beginning of the following school term might be valid.

In designing personnel regulations, boards should provide leave policies, conditions of employment, and disability benefits which do not disadvantage pregnant employees.

See also CIVIL RIGHTS ACT OF 1964; PATERNITY LEAVE; PRIVACY.

MECHANIC'S LIEN

A mechanic's lien is a statutory claim for payment allowed to a worker for work performed or materials furnished for the CONSTRUCTION or improvement of real property. Generally, a mechanic's lien will not be allowed to a subcontractor for improvements made to school PROPERTY because school property is not owned by the local board but by the state. A

[18]*Farley v. Ocean Township Board of Education*, 416 A.2d 969 (N.J. 1980).

[19]*Daly v. Three Village Central School District*, 486 N.Y.S.2d 286 (N.Y. 1985); *Solomon v. School Comm. of Boston*, 478 N.E.2d 137 (Mass. 1985).

lien can attach to the construction contract itself provided money is owed on that contract. In order to prevent unjust enrichment or inequitable results, STATUTES generally provide that a BOND shall be had prior to construction. This bond is for the purpose of insuring that the subcontractor shall be paid for services or materials rendered.

See also BUILDINGS.

MEDIATION

Mediation is the effort by a third party to reconcile the parties in a dispute so that settlement can be reached. If parties are negotiating CONTRACTS but are unable to reach agreement, COLLECTIVE BARGAINING laws frequently provide that a mediator is to be provided by an impartial state agency which is created to administer the negotiation laws. This mediator tries to get the parties back on the road leading to a solution of the dispute by making suggestions, advising the parties, and trying to get the parties to modify some of their demands. Occasionally, some mediators will recommend terms for a solution, but the mediator has no power to force a solution.

However, a recent trend is to combine the functions of both the mediator and the arbitrator. The effect of this is to force the parties to offer more honest and realistic negotiations at the state of negotiations. This is because the arbitrator not only will suggest ways to keep the parties negotiating constructively, but he or she may at any time declare a final decision as to any particular topic. The use of mediation/ARBITRATION may well serve to reduce time and expense; however, whether an arbitrator has the expertise to effectively serve as a mediator during the majority of grievance disputes is yet to be seen.

In addition to contract disputes, mediation is increasingly being used to settle disputes between parents of children with handicaps and school districts. However, the use of mediation cannot delay the specific hearing timelines mandated by the EDUCATION FOR ALL HANDICAPPED CHILDREN ACT OF 1975.

See also COLLECTIVE BARGAINING; MEET AND CONFER BARGAINING LAWS.

MEDICAL SERVICES

Medical services as used in this context is meant to refer to the medical facilities and diagnostic and first aid treatment which are provided by the school district for students. The SCHOOL BOARD has the authority and the right to hire professional doctors and nurses in order to diagnose and inspect students to see if health regulations have been complied with. These medical services, however, are limited. In the absence of statutory authorization, the school district cannot provide free medical treatment for such things as COMMUNICABLE DISEASES, operations, or dentistry. School districts may be required to provide medical services to students with handicaps. (See EDUCATION FOR ALL HANDICAPPED CHILDREN ACT OF 1975.)

School board authority in this area is limited. Each state has minimum health requirements for students and teachers. Thus, under the guise of its police power, the state may require VACCINATIONS and reasonable physical examinations. In addition, schools have the right to check teeth, eyesight, and hearing in cooperation with the local board of health. Should a student wish to be excluded from the medical examination, he or she would need a doctor's certificate. A question might arise as to whether medical services may be imposed upon a student in violation of his or her constitutional rights. The answer to this would depend on the form of the treatment and the religious convictions or other constitutional provisions asserted by the child. The COURTS would have to balance the constitutional rights with the school's duty to maintain a safe and healthy atmosphere for school attendance. If the circumstances are such that by not allowing oneself to be treated the student would endanger others, the treatment can be a prerequisite to entering school.

Teachers and administrators have a duty to respond to medical emergencies. Emergency treatment must be rendered if the circumstances are such that immediate aid is necessary. Teachers and coaches not taking appropriate measures following an injury may be liable for the additional injuries caused by the failure to act.

In one case, an eleven-year-old student recovered a judgment of $2.5 million for NEGLIGENCE when a teacher failed to provide medical assistance for one full hour and a blood clot the size of a walnut grew to the size of an orange after the initial injury to the student.[20] In this case, the district argued that the district had followed district policy and was not negligent in its care of the boy. The school authorities had called the boy's parent who told the school to take the boy to the hospital which was across the street from the school. The school authorities called 911 for the ambulance service. Employees called a total of three times before the ambulance arrived. A full hour passed before the ambulance arrived during which time the boy was exhibiting signs of severe head injury. The court reasoned that the school authorities should have taken the boy across the street to the hospital.

---

[20]*Barth v. Board of Educ.*, 490 N.E.2d 77 (Ill. App. 1986).

In a 1989 Minnesota case, a court held that a school nurse had to have the competency level of a hospital nurse if students and others relied upon the nurse's ability to assess the need for emergency medical care.[21] In this case, an eighteen-year-old asthmatic student went to the nurse's office complaining of difficulty in breathing. The school nurse sent the student back to class after allowing the student to borrow another student's Albuterol asthma inhaler. When the student's condition worsened, the student was returned to the nurse's office; and the nurse determined that neither an ambulance, a wheelchair, nor oxygen was necessary. The student died within minutes thereafter as a result of respiratory failure, and the school was held responsible.

See also EQUAL ACCESS ACT.

MEDICATION

Generally, school authorities do not dispense medications. However, students may require medications as a result of illness or handicaps; and some giving of medication may be necessary. The Committee on School Health, American Academy of Pediatrics, suggests the following guidelines be used:

1. Written orders from a physician should detail the name of the drug, dosage, time interval that the medication is to be taken, and diagnosis or reason for the medication to be given.

2. Written permission should be provided by the parents or guardian requesting that the school district comply with the physician's order.

3. Medication should be brought to school in a container appropriately labeled by the pharmacy or physician.

4. One member of the staff should be designated to handle this task, ideally health personnel if available.

5. A locked cabinet should be provided for storage of medication.

6. Opportunities should be provided for communication between the parent, school personnel, and physician regarding the efficacy of the medication during school hours.

7. A designated member of the school staff should notify the parent or guardian as quickly as possible in the event of an emergency.

---

[21]*Schluessler v. Independent School Dist. No. 200* (Dakota County District Court, No. 105196, 1989.)

The parent's current telephone number should be available in the student's record specifically for this purpose.

See also MEDICAL SERVICES.

MEET AND CONFER BARGAINING LAWS

Meet and confer laws provide a method of determining wages, hours, and conditions of employment through discussions between the SCHOOL BOARD and the employee organization. In many states, the parties are required to meet and discuss employment relations and are obligated to act in good faith in an effort to reach an agreement.

An exact definition of meet and confer bargaining is difficult due to differences in the wording of individual state laws. Proponents of COLLECTIVE BARGAINING laws criticize meet and confer laws and argue that the meet and confer STATUTES force an employee organization to engage in "collective begging" rather than collective bargaining. There may be some justification for this view; however, most laws do not follow the pure meet and confer concept.

The pure meet and confer concept was founded on the notion of complete sovereign authority. Under this concept, the public employer retains broad managerial discretion subject only to recall. The outcome of employer-employee negotiations is dependent more on school board determinations than on bilateral decisions by equals at the bargaining table. Employees have the right to discuss, but the SCHOOL BOARD retains the right to act unilaterally on any matter pertaining to wages, hours and conditions of employment. The board must consider the presentation made by the employee representative; but, after giving the presentation reasonable consideration, the board may act unilaterally, without being bound by previous negotiations. Only a small number of states have retained the pure meet and confer approach to public employee bargaining.

Other jurisdictions having meet and confer statutes define the meet and confer obligation as "...the process whereby the representatives of a public agency and representatives of recognized employee organizations have the mutual obligation to meet and confer in order to exchange freely information, opinions and proposals to endeavor to reach agreement on conditions of employment." This kind of law requires bargaining with an eye toward reaching agreement. In addition, some of these laws require the parties to "meet and confer in good faith." This is even more explicit in requiring the employee to approach the discussions with an open mind to try and agree. Arguably, although this kind of meet and confer law suggests at first glance that the parties do not meet as equals, in reality, the employees are granted many bargaining rights which are not far from approaching the right to collective negotiations.

Meet and confer laws are continually being exchanged for collective bargaining laws. Each year, more states examine the need for improvement of employer-employee relations in the public sector, and most states are replacing meet and confer language with language that enables each side to bargain on an equal footing.

MEETINGS

School board meetings, student meetings, and teacher meetings are regulated either by state law or by RULES of the local administration or school board. The first of these, school board meetings, is regulated by state law; a thorough discussion of the law and procedures in this matter is found in the section, SCHOOL BOARDS.

Student meetings are not regulated by law but are governed by rules of the local administration and school board. Generally, rooms do not have to be provided for any meetings not approved by the administration or school board. Attendance at student meetings, such as assemblies, may be required. On the other hand, attendance at meetings involving EXTRACURRICULAR ACTIVITIES after school hours cannot be required. Of course, the conduct of the students at any meetings may be regulated by teachers and administrators.

As for teachers' meetings, the school district should provide for these; sometimes, meetings are a topic for "discussion" at the COLLECTIVE BARGAINING table. Board members may attend formal teachers' meetings and may voice opinions on the topics discussed. The school administration may require teacher attendance at regularly scheduled meetings but must allow for absences with valid excuses.

See also EQUAL ACCESS ACT; OPEN HEARINGS.

MENTAL AND PHYSICAL EXAMINATIONS

A teacher or administrator may be required to take a physical or mental examination to determine job-related fitness to perform the required teaching or administrative function. The State Board of Education may also have the power to require a teacher to take an intelligence test to determine minimum levels of competency, although the teacher's certificate is prima facie evidence of competence; individual state laws in this regard must be consulted.

Reasonable health and physical condition requirements must be rationally related to job performance and should not be used to disqualify otherwise competent persons such as the handicapped. These conditional aspects of employment are upheld by the COURTS if the testing is constitutional in its scope and if the testing is applied uniformly and not as a basis for DISCRIMINATION.

MENTAL DISTRESS, Infliction of

See INTENTIONAL INFLICTION OF EMOTIONAL DISTRESS.

MERGERS

See REORGANIZATION.

MERIT PAY

Merit pay is a system by which an educator is or is not promoted to higher pay scales based upon performance or educational achievements. Unfortunately, "merit pay" has become synonymous with such terms as "career ladder." Nevertheless, it is clear that school districts may determine annual increments on the basis of merit. This authority has caused some controversy, but the controversy is generally based upon the evaluations and evaluation procedures. The COURTS have held that local boards have a great deal of DISCRETIONARY AUTHORITY in the area of criteria for merit pay increases.[22] So long as the determination of pay increases is specific and not discriminatory and is based upon relevant criteria, the merit pay schedule will be upheld. Professional growth requirements are examples of proper criteria. The Supreme Court affirmed South Carolina's use of the National Teachers' Examination for CERTIFICATION and salary purposes

---

[22]*Hughes v. Jefferson County Board of Education,* 370 So. 2d 1034 (Ala. 1979).

since the test furthered the purpose of an improved teaching force.[23] Salary schedules pertaining to graduate degrees should apply only to those who earned the credits from accredited institutions.

It is essential that one consult the applicable state STATUTE in force. For example, in Ohio, a statute authorizes a salary schedule credit for military service. In New York, a state statute dictates that, after a substitute teacher teaches more than 135 days for one or more years, he or she must be paid according to the salary schedule for those excess days.[24]

Although a teacher may have met the minimum state requirements for certification, it is within the school board's authority to require further educational qualifications.

METHODS

A teacher's teaching method is within his or her own discretion. This method may be subject to evaluations, and the methods may require changes if changes are necessary for improvement.

See also ACADEMIC FREEDOM.

MILITARY LEAVE

Military leave is leave granted to a teacher or administrator who has been drafted or is required to perform duties for the National Guard or military reserve training. SCHOOL BOARDS establish requirements and procedures for these leaves within the parameters of state law. Most often, military leave must be given if the teacher or administrator has been employed for more than six months. The teacher or administrator is not entitled to his or her salary during the time of the absence but does have the right to the same position upon return. However, there is generally a time limit on the length of time a person can be absent. If that time is surpassed, the board has the right to hire a permanent replacement.

Federal STATUTES allow for the granting or accrual of seniority

---

[23]*National Educ. Ass'n. v. South Carolina,* 434 U.S. 1026 (1978). *See also, Newman v. Crews,* 651 F.2d 222 (4th Cir. 1981).

[24]*Berthiaume v. School Committee of City of Woonsocket,* 397 A.2d 889 (R.I. 1979).

rights for educators while they serve in the armed forces, but the retirement system is not likewise required to grant retirement credits.[25]

See also MERIT PAY; LEAVES OF ABSENCE.

MINISTERIAL ACTS

Local school districts are obligated to perform certain duties. Many of these duties are governmental in nature and cannot be delegated. For example, duties that include the exercise of discretion cannot be delegated. However, duties that are private in nature or that can be carried out by anyone without having to make a decision between various factors are ministerial in nature and can be delegated. For example, the local board has the duty to hire teachers and administrators. That duty involves decisions and the exercise of DISCRETIONARY ACTS. Therefore, this duty cannot be delegated to someone such as the SUPERINTENDENT. The superintendent may make recommendations, but the final decision rests with the SCHOOL BOARD. On the other hand, taking minutes at board meetings or taking a survey to determine how many students are enrolled for the coming year can be done by almost anyone. These acts are, therefore, ministerial and can be delegated. (See GOVERNMENTAL IMMUNITY.)

MINUTES, School Board

See SCHOOL BOARDS, Meetings.

MISDEMEANOR

A misdemeanor is a crime less serious in nature than a FELONY. Conviction of a misdemeanor is generally punishable by a fine up to certain limits or imprisonment for less than one year or both.

---

[25]*Rhode Island Fed'n. of Teachers v. Employee Retirement System*, 542 A.2d 249 (R.I. 1988).

MITIGATION

See CONTRACTS; DAMAGES.

MONEY

See ACTIVITY FUNDS; BONDS; FEES; FUNDS.

MORAL TURPITUDE

Moral turpitude is conduct which violates the "accepted" moral standards of a community. Moral turpitude is a very imprecise concept which must be considered by judging the individual's conduct in relation to the surrounding facts and circumstances. Educators may generally be held to higher standards as exemplars to impressionable students.

See also COLLECTIVE BARGAINING; CONSTITUTIONAL LAW; CONTRACTS; DECERTIFICATION; DUE PROCESS; PRIVACY.

MUNICIPAL CORPORATIONS

A municipal corporation is a corporation in a particular place that is formed to carry out political purposes at a local level. A SCHOOL BOARD is a municipal corporation. Local boards are arms of the state government, and boards have certain delegated authority but no inherent power of their own. Local board power comes from the state, and school boards cannot exceed the authority which is granted.

MUSIC

Allocation of school FUNDS for music classes and instruments is within the power of the SCHOOL BOARD. Students may be required to deposit FEES for breakage, but generally not for sheet music and not unless the class is extracurricular in nature and not a part of the general CURRICULUM.

N

NEGLIGENCE

Negligence is the unintentional breach of the legal duty to protect others from unreasonable risks of harm. Negligence is not an intentional TORT. Negligence is the failure to use such care as a REASONABLE AND PRUDENT person would use under the same or similar circumstances. Negligence is the doing of some act which a person of ordinary prudence would not have done or the failure to do what a prudent person would have done under similar circumstances. Of all the lawsuits filed against teachers, administrators and SCHOOL BOARDS, negligence is the most prevalent. All educators should thoroughly understand the elements which constitute negligence as well as the defenses available to overcome a claim in negligence.

Schools and school employees are not automatically liable for every injury which may occur on school grounds or during school activities. In order to be liable, there are four elements of negligence which must be proved. If any one element is missing, there is no LIABILITY for negligence. Negligence equals:

1. Duty;

2. Breach of duty;

3. That the breach was the *proximate cause* of the injury; and

4. An actual injury.

1. All people owe all other people the *duty* of not subjecting others to an unreasonable risk of harm. School staff specifically have the duty to provide a safe environment for students. If a dangerous situation exists and a teacher or administrator is or should be aware of the condition, there is a

duty to eliminate the hazard before someone is injured. Furthermore, because of the special relationship between students and teachers and administrators, there exists a legal duty to come to one's aid in time of need. Accordingly, if a person walking down the street sees a stranger being beaten, there is no *legal duty* to come to the person's aid since there is no special relationship between the person being beaten and the witness. However, if the witness is a teacher and the person being beaten is a student and the event happens while the teacher is acting within the role of a teacher, even if not on school grounds, there is a legal duty on the part of the teacher to intervene on behalf of the student.

2. *Breach of duty* occurs whenever a person fails to act in the way a reasonable and prudent person would have acted in the same or similar circumstances. A breach of duty may be either an affirmative act or an act of OMISSION. Would a teacher or administrator consider it reasonable to leave a college-prep high school history class unsupervised for ten minutes? Probably yes. Would it be reasonable to leave a woodshop class unsupervised for five minutes? Probably not. Now, suppose the history class consisted of students with behavior problems who became un- manageable without constant SUPERVISION. Would it be reasonable to leave them for five minutes? Probably not. Suppose the woodshop class had finished working and all that the students were doing was cleaning the shop. Could the teacher leave them for five minutes now? Probably yes. As one can see, by changing the facts, we have changed the potential outcome. Therefore, whether or not a person has been negligent is a QUESTION OF FACT for the jury to decide on a case-by-case basis. The jury must consider all of the facts and all of the circumstances in order to reach a proper conclusion. (See ABSENCE FROM CLASS.) First, the jury must decide whether there was an established duty. Second, the jury must decide whether that duty was violated.

3. *Proximate cause* is present whenever there is a close causal connection between the breach of duty and the resulting injury. Causation itself involves two elements. First, for the injury to be proximately caused, there must be a closeness in the relationship between the breach of duty and the injury. Second, the injury must be a foreseeable consequence of the behavior. If an act or omission produces an event or if the event would not have occurred without the act or omission, that event is proximately caused by that act or omission. In other words, did the injury occur because of something the teacher or administrator did or did not do? If the injury would have occurred anyway, there is no liability for negligence. If the injury could have been prevented by an act or omission, then liability may be imposed as long as *all* other necessary elements are present.

As mentioned, the cause must be foreseeable. FORESEEABILITY means that the party who breached the duty could have or should have seen the probability of an injury occurring. That is, a reasonable and prudent person in the same or similar circumstances would have foreseen the danger. It is not necessary for the injury to be foreseen in the exact form in which the injury resulted, only that there be some form of probable injury.

Often, there may be more than one cause to an injury. If there are other acts or omissions which contributed in causing an injury, the question is whether those contributing causes supercede or intervene and take over the original cause. Suppose, for example, that while a first-grade teacher was absent from the classroom to make a personal phone call, a light fixture fell and injured a student. The teacher's conduct in leaving a class of first graders unsupervised for ten minutes may have been unreasonable. However, the accident still would have occurred even if the teacher were in the classroom. Therefore, the teacher is not liable for the student's injury. If, however, the teacher knew that the fixture was loose, the event is then foreseeable and the teacher would be liable for the injury for failing to act. In either case, school authorities may be found negligent since there is always the responsibility of maintaining the BUILDINGS in a safe condition.

If two or more causes occur simultaneously, the causes are considered "concurrent" causes; and one may escape liability by proving CONTRIBUTORY NEGLIGENCE, ASSUMPTION OF RISK, or COMPARATIVE NEGLIGENCE. For example, if the teacher had warned eighth-grade students not to sit under the loose light fixture but a student sat there anyway and was injured, the student's contributory negligence may overcome the teacher's negligence in not roping off or securing the area.

4. There must be an actual *injury to person or property*. Without an actual injury, there can be no liability. Even if one comes close to killing someone else by violating a duty, an injury must occur or there is no liability. The extent of the injuries determines the amount of DAMAGES which will have to be paid, and other defenses might include the expiration of the STATUTE OF LIMITATIONS, GOVERNMENTAL IMMUNITY, or both.

NEGOTIABLE ISSUES

See COLLECTIVE BARGAINING; SCOPE OF BARGAINING.

NEGOTIATIONS

See COLLECTIVE BARGAINING; MEET AND CONFER BARGAINING LAWS; SCOPE OF BARGAINING.

NEWSPAPERS

See ACADEMIC FREEDOM; CONSTITUTIONAL LAW; OBSCENITY; SCHOOL PUBLICATIONS.

NONPUBLIC SCHOOLS

See PRIVATE AND PAROCHIAL SCHOOL AID; PRIVATE SCHOOLS.

NONRENEWAL

Unlike a teacher dismissal, nonrenewal is a type of discharge "after" a CONTRACT has expired. The word *discharge* can be a bit misleading—legally, the person is not discharged; he or she is just not rehired. The outcome remains the same—the teacher or administrator is out of a job. Generally, nonrenewal applies either to those educators not on a CONTINUING CONTRACT or to those who do not have TENURE.

Unlike dismissals, NONRENEWALS can be based on any just cause and sometimes on no cause at all as long as the decision is not ARBITRARY, CAPRICIOUS, OR DISCRIMINATORY in nature. As one can readily see, there are not a great many protections against nonrenewal unless those protections are garnered through contract or COLLECTIVE BARGAINING agreements. Of course, the nonrenewal may not be in violation of the educator's constitutional rights, and strict nonrenewal procedures must be followed. Generally, notice of nonrenewal must be received on or before a certain date; the notice must sufficiently inform the teacher or administrator of the intent not to renew; and it must be delivered in the manner prescribed by STATUTE. Therefore, where a SCHOOL BOARD delayed the decision not to renew a probationary teacher's contract on recommendation of the SUPERINTENDENT, an Arizona court determined that this action did not coincide with the statutory requirements for nonrenewal and the teacher's job was not lost.[1] Because the teacher did not receive proper notification of the board's intention not to renew the contract, the teacher's contract was held to have been renewed automatically. On the other hand, where teachers are given notice before the statutory deadline defined by law, most COURTS have held that educators can be terminated without DUE PROCESS and without a showing of cause for termination.

If state laws specify that the notice must be sent by certified mail to the last known address, the notice would be insufficient and void if the notice was sent to the educator's mailbox at school. If the notice is sent late, the notice has no legal effect. If the statute says that the reasons for nonrenewal must be in the notice, the reasons must be there or the notice is inadequate. All aspects of nonrenewal must be followed exactly.

If improper notice is received, the teacher or administrator would be well advised to consult an attorney or his or her educational association. Quick and accurate steps must be taken, or there is a possibility that the courts will hold that proper notice has been waived.

See also DUE PROCESS; RENEWALS.

NOTICE

See DUE PROCESS; NONRENEWAL; RENEWALS.

NURSES

See MEDICAL SERVICES.

---

[1] *Peck v. Board of Education of Yuma Union High School*, 612 P.2d 1076 (Ariz. 1980).

OATHS

See LOYALTY OATHS.

OBSCENE LITERATURE

See ACADEMIC FREEDOM; CONSTITUTIONAL LAW; LIBRARY CENSOR-SHIP; OBSCENITY; SCHOOL PUBLICATIONS.

OBSCENITY

Case law, as well as statutory law, relating to obscene material is applicable in the school environment as well as in the community. The age, intelligence, and experience of the students are all relevant factors to be considered when trying to determine whether or not certain literature is obscene or is unsuitable for the student's instruction.

Over the years, various tests have been used in an effort to provide a uniform standard for making a determination of whether or not certain material is obscene. Prior to 1973, the test for obscenity was whether the material was "utterly without redeeming social value." Obscenity was defined as any material or conduct which was objectionable or offensive to accepted standards of decency. In making this determination, national standards were to be used.

In 1973, the Supreme Court of the United States rejected the prior test and applied a new test to be used in making a determination of obscenity. The Supreme Court ruled that:

1. Material may be declared obscene if "(a) ... 'the average person, applying contemporary community standards,' would find that the work taken as a whole, appeals to the prurient interest and ... (b) ... the work depicts or describes, in a patently offensive way, sexual conduct specifically defined by the applicable state law, and (c) ... the work, taken as a whole, lacks serious literary, artistic, political or scientific value."

2. The determination of "prurient interest" and "patently offensive" may be made in light of forum community standards rather than on the national standard.

3. Exhibiting obscene material in places open to the public is not protected as a constitutional right of PRIVACY.

4. States may find a nexus between antisocial behavior and obscene literature and may regulate its exhibition and commerce in public places.[1]

Through the United States Supreme Court rulings of 1973, the states are given much greater latitude and power to regulate literature. However, the state regulations must be specific and have a rational basis. As the court said:

> State statutes designed to regulate obscene materials must be carefully limited ... [W]e now confine the permissible scope of such regulation to works which depict or describe sexual conduct. That conduct must be specifically defined by the applicable state law, as written or authoritatively construed. A state offense must also be limited to works which portray sexual conduct in a patently offensive way, and which, taken as a whole, do not have serious literary, artistic, political or scientific value.[2]

The United States Supreme Court gave several examples of what could be defined for regulation:

(a) Patently offensive representations or descriptions of ultimate sexual acts, normal or perverted, actual or simulated.

---

[1] *Miller v. California*, 413 U.S. 15 (1973); *Paris Adult Theatre I v. Slaton*, 413 U.S. 49 (1973).

[2] *Miller v. California*, 413 U.S. 15 (1973).

(b) Patently offensive representations or descriptions of masturbation, excretory functions, and lewd exhibition of the genitals.

These examples are among the more obvious types of regulations which the states will make. It is possible that state STATUTES may tend to be far more restrictive with regard to obscenity than federal standards. However, it is not necessarily the state statutes themselves which will inhibit ACADEMIC FREEDOM. Reasonable apprehension on behalf of publishers from being punished or subjected to numerous lawsuits in different states and different cities over the same materials will necessarily force publishers to exercise some censorship over the materials which might be suitable for schools in one part of the country but not in another.

School administrators, teachers, and students, as well as publishers and book distributors, are left not knowing what constitutes obscenity. There are few clear guidelines for formulating policies concerning the kinds of materials and speech that may be used in the classroom. In case law determining what is obscene and thus excludable from a classroom, the court cautiously weighs such circumstances as age and sophistication of the students, the manner and context of presentation, and the relation between the technique used and valid educational objectives. School board regulations and SANCTIONS must reflect the community standards. While it is recognized that an educator cannot say, write, or exhibit whatever he or she feels like, academic freedom does protect the educator in the use of a "dirty" word if the word was conveyed for a demonstrated educational purpose.[3] In the case just mentioned, the school board was prevented from discharging a teacher who assigned an *Atlantic Monthly* article in which the vulgar term for an incestuous son was used. The court agreed with the teacher that the article was thought-provoking and in no way pornographic under the circumstances. Discussions of offensive or taboo words are relevant in some contexts.[4] There is no protection for conduct or language which is inappropriate and offensive to the accomplishment of educational objectives. For example, at least one teacher was not protected when that teacher was fired for showing an uncut *R*-rated film which contained nudity and violence.[5]

Vulgarity might not be defined as obscenity. Vulgarity is language used to express hostility or other emotion; and, sometimes, vulgarity is used to vent anti-established feeling or sometimes to describe people or states of mind. Unless vulgarity functions as "fighting words" or as tending to invite a breach of the peace, at least one court has said its usage will be

---

[3]*Keefe v. Glanakos*, 418 F.2d 359 (1st Cir. 1969).

[4]*Parducci v. Rutland*, 316 F. Supp. 352 (M.D. Ala. 1970).

[5]*Fowler v. Board of Education*, 819 F.2d 657 (6th Cir. 1987).

constitutionally protected.[6] This court's opinion may not be followed by other courts. We do know that, if the use of vulgarities causes material and substantial interference with school activities or encourages actions which endanger the health and safety of students, the language may be prohibited. This approach was espoused by the United States Supreme Court in 1972, stating that a school need not tolerate conduct that "substantially interferes with the opportunity of other students to obtain an education."[7]

State and local boards of education should establish rational guidelines about obscenity in the classroom, which guidelines do not demean academic freedom.

See also LIBRARY CENSORSHIP.

OFFER, Contract

Every bilateral CONTRACT, in order to be valid, must have the elements of offer and acceptance. The offer to enter into a contract must be clear and definite and with the present intent to have the offer accepted and to become binding. Generally, the offer should state the time to begin and the time to finish, the services to be rendered, and the consideration to be paid. The offer continues to exist for a reasonable time or for a stated period of time and must be accepted in order to be considered valid prior to the time the offer is extinguished. Prior to acceptance, the offer may be revoked.

See also CONTRACTS.

OFFICERS

See PRINCIPAL; SCHOOL BOARDS; SUPERINTENDENT; VICE PRINCIPAL.

OMISSION

An omission is simply failing to act when there is a legal duty to do so. For example, if a teacher was aware of a fight between two students and did not

---

[6]*Frasca v. Andrews*, 463 F. Supp. 1043 (E.D.N.Y. 1979).

[7]*Healy v. James*, 408 U.S. 169 (1972).

make any attempt to break up the fight, the teacher's failure to act is an omission. The teacher may be liable for injuries resulting from his or her omission.

See NEGLIGENCE.

OPEN HEARING

An open hearing generally becomes an issue in teacher or administrator dismissals. Whether a person has a right to an open hearing depends upon state STATUTES. Most statutes require that SCHOOL BOARD MEETINGS be open since school boards are public bodies which transact public business.[8] Apart from regular school board meetings, a teacher or administrator whose conduct is called into question generally has the right to ask for a closed hearing, particularly when discussing personal matters, even though an OPEN HEARING may be the party's right. For example, a wrongful morals charge could permanently damage an educator's reputation, and that educator may want to be heard privately. Of course, a teacher or administrator has the right to be heard before a decision is made, or else DUE PROCESS may be violated. If the teacher or administrator wants a public forum, he or she is exercising a valid right to a public hearing with publicly cast and recorded votes of each board member.

Administrative hearing regulations allow an educator to be represented by counsel, but the educator's constitutional rights do not necessarily require representation.[9] Again, fair notice must be given, and a termination hearing must be provided to an employee so that person has an opportunity to respond orally or in writing as to why the proposed action should be not taken.[10]

See also DUE PROCESS; NONRENEWAL; RENEWALS.

ORAL CONTRACTS

See CONTRACTS.

---

[8]*Blackford v. School Board*, 375 So. 2d 578 (Fla. 1979).

[9]*Wolfe v. Board of Education*, 524 N.E.2d 1177 (Ill. 1988).

[10]*Cleveland Board of Education v. Loudermill*, 470 U.S. 532 (1985).

OUTSIDE EMPLOYMENT

Assuring that public school employees devote their professional energies to the education of children, some COURTS have concluded that a SCHOOL BOARD's authority also allows prohibiting employees from engaging in outside employment during the school year. One school board employee's CONTRACT contained the phrase "shall not engage in any other business or profession directly or indirectly, for full time or part time, but shall devote his or her entire working time to the performance of ... duties under this contract" was reviewed and found constitutional in the Fifth Circuit. Under this case, a school board has exceptionally wide latitude in adopting policies necessary for effective administration of the schools, but such policies must be uniformly applied.[11] However, restricting outside employment that does not interfere with school responsibilities seems to have a chilling effect upon DUE PROCESS, CONSTITUTIONAL LAW, and one's right of ASSEMBLY. The better view is that one may not restrict outside employment that does not interfere with one's performance under the educational contract of employment.

---

[11]*Gosney v. Sonora Independent School District*, 603 F.2d 522 (5th Cir. 1979).

P

PARENTAL AUTHORITY

The parental right of control over a child's education is limited by the state's interest in preparing students to participate successfully in society. Therefore, the state may restrict parental control by requiring attendance at school and by mandating CURRICULUM. School districts, often by EXPRESS AUTHORITY, though sometimes by IMPLIED AUTHORITY, also may discipline students over parents' wishes with respect to matters related to a student's education.

Parents do have some rights involving the education of their children. Parents have the right to vote for school budgets and for members of the SCHOOL BOARD. Parents also have the right to review the student's record and to discuss problems with school personnel. Though generally parents have no right to control the curriculum, there are some instances where the parent has the right to determine whether or not his or her child will participate in certain classes or activities. If the objections are reasonable or are based upon the parent's or student's constitutional rights, the objections should be sustained. If the objections are not reasonable, those objections may be ignored without any remedy being available to the parent.

Parents, to some extent, can control what school their child attends. When the choice is between two public schools, the school district has the power to assign students to schools. (See ASSIGNMENT TO GRADE AND SCHOOL.) However, when the choice is between a public school and a PRIVATE SCHOOL, the district may not require students to attend the public school as long as the private school meets minimum education requirements as determined by the state. In one case, two teachers challenged a school district's RULE which prohibited employees from sending their children to private schools. The court found the policy impermissible because the policy interfered with the teacher/parents' right to control the education of their children.[1]

Parents of students with handicaps have additional rights which include participation in the planning of the students' individualized education programs. (See EDUCATION FOR ALL HANDICAPPED CHILDREN ACT OF 1975.)

See also CORPORAL PUNISHMENT; RELIGION; SEX EDUCATION.

PARENTAL LIABILITY

Parents are liable for their own TORTS but not for the torts of their children unless such LIABILITY is imposed by individual state laws. Most states have enacted legislation making parents vicariously liable for the conduct of children but have limited the liability to anywhere between $200 and $5,000. The child would be obligated to pay for any judgment over the statutory amount. Because the child is usually "judgment-proof," the injured party will either receive no compensation or will receive compensation through another source, such as personal injury or property insurance.

See also STUDENT LIABILITY; TEACHER AIDE.

PAROCHIAL SCHOOLS

See PRIVATE AND PAROCHIAL SCHOOL AID; PRIVATE SCHOOLS.

PATERNITY LEAVE

Paternity leave is a LEAVE OF ABSENCE granted to a father after the birth of his child. This type of leave has gained some momentum as recognition of the need for parental bonding and more DISCRIMINATION cases are decided.

---

[1]*Stough v. Crenshaw County Board of Educ.*, 744 F.2d 1479 (11th Cir. 1984).

In one case, the father of a new child applied for paternity leave for six months in order to care for the new infant in his family. Women had been allowed such leave, but the same right was denied to the male teacher. The teacher filed a complaint, and the court ruled that the teacher stated a valid cause of action.[2]

SICK LEAVE is not MATERNITY LEAVE or paternity leave. Sick leave can be used only by those disabled by child bearing. A nondisabled teacher would not be eligible for sick leave.[3]

PEACE CORPS LEAVES

Peace Corps leave is a LEAVE OF ABSENCE that is mandatory. In most cases, an educator who joins the Peace Corps is assured of his or her right to the educational position upon return. However, the educator must have worked in the district for a certain period of time, and the maximum allowable period of absence is generally two years.

See also LEAVES OF ABSENCE; MERIT PAY; SALARY SCHEDULES.

PERFORMANCE BONDS

See BUILDINGS.

PERMISSION SLIPS

See ASSUMPTION OF RISK; DETENTION; NEGLIGENCE; PARENTAL AUTHORITY; PARENTAL LIABILITY; SUPERVISION.

PERSONAL PROPERTY

See TRESPASS TO PERSONAL PROPERTY.

---

[2]*Danielson v. Board of Higher Education of the City University of New York,* 4 Employment Practice's Decision 7773, (N.Y. 1972).

[3]*In re Hackensack Board of Education,* 446 A.2d 170 (N.J. 1982).

PERSONNEL RECORDS

As a repository of "private" information, the personnel records of school district employees are generally protected by state laws and employment CONTRACTS governing access to and disclosure of information in those records. The public's right to know, legislated at both federal and state levels in Freedom of Information Acts, has been limited by the individual's right and expectation to PRIVACY promised in federal and state privacy laws and court decisions.

The COURTS require a weighing of interests between the public's right to know and an individual's right to PRIVACY.[4] A balancing test is used to consider four factors prior to any disclosure of information:

1. Would the nature of the particular information sought seriously invade the individual's privacy?
2. What is the purpose of the disclosure or access?
3. Is the particular seeker official or private?
4. Is the information available from other sources?[5]

The laws developed in each state control the content and disposition of personnel file information. The personal privacy interest must be substantial, and the contents of personnel records should not be disclosed if the disclosure would harm the individual by embarrassment or by loss of reputation or employment.[6]

Some states even go so far as to hold that a grand jury is not entitled to inspect personnel records. As stated by one court:

> [T]he personnel records of the district are maintained as confidential files; it is common knowledge that such matters are among the most confidential and sensitive records kept by a private or public employer, and their use remains effective only so long as the confidence of the records, and the confidences of those who contribute to those records, are maintained. It does not matter that here the employees themselves sought disclosure of the records; the records are the property of and are in the custody and control of the district, not of the employees."

---

[4]*Dept. of Air Force v. Rose,* 425 U.S. 352 (1976).

[5]*Wooster Republican Printing Co. v. City of Wooster,* 383 N.E.2d 124 (Ohio 1978).

[6]*Sims v. Central Intelligence Agency,* 642 F.2d 562 (D.C. Cir. 1980).

[7]*Board of Trustees of Calaveras Unified School District v. Leach,* 65 Cal. Rptr. 588, 593, 258 Cal. 2d 281 (1968).

Personnel records must be distinguished from the educator's permanent file, which is kept open for inspection by the employee or his or her agents. All evaluations are placed in this permanent file, and this file is kept separate from the personnel records kept by the educator's superior. Some states, such as Pennsylvania and Oregon, legislatively guarantee the employee's right to inspect and correct erroneous data (with exceptions) in this permanent personnel file.[8]

See also DEFAMATION.

PETITIONS

See GRIEVANCE.

PHYSICAL EDUCATION

See ATHLETICS; CURRICULUM; NEGLIGENCE.

PHYSICAL EXAMINATIONS

See COMPULSORY EDUCATION; MEDICAL SERVICES; VACCINATION.

PICKETING

See STRIKES.

PLAINTIFF

A plaintiff is a person who brings a lawsuit to obtain a remedy or the party who complains or sues for some injury or wrongs he or she has suffered due to the alleged wrongful acts of the DEFENDANT.

---

[8]Pa. C.S.A. 43 § 1321; *see also, Smith v. School District,* 666 P.2d 1345 (Or. 1983).

PLAYGROUNDS

Playgrounds are frequently the scene of injuries. LIABILITY arises in many situations, not the least of which is due to inadequate SUPERVISION and the existence of dangers from EQUIPMENT and the condition of the playground itself. NEGLIGENCE on the playground probably accounts for the vast majority of all injuries to students. Therefore, playgrounds and equipment should be checked on a regular basis; many injuries and accidents contain an element of FORESEEABILITY which, if recognized and corrected, will help prevent DAMAGES from being imposed.

See also BUILDINGS, Maintenance.

PLEDGE OF ALLEGIANCE

Neither an educator nor a student may be compelled to recite the Pledge of Allegiance to the flag. As long ago as 1943, the Supreme Court of the United States held that to compel a student to salute the flag or say the Pledge of Allegiance violates the FIRST AMENDMENT to the Unites States Constitution. The court explained its holding by saying:

> Words uttered under coercion are proof of loyalty to nothing but self-interest. Love of country must spring from willing hearts and free minds, inspired by a fair administration of wise laws enacted by the people's elected representatives within the bounds of express constitutional prohibitions. These laws must, to be consistent with the First Amendment, permit the widest toleration of conflicting viewpoints consistent with a society of free men.[9]

Subsequent to this case, several COURTS ruled that school employees also have the right to refuse to recite the Pledge of Allegiance, and educators may not be forced to lead their students in the recitation. One case involved a father-son situation (teacher and student) who refused to salute the flag or say the Pledge of Allegiance.[10]

School officials may require the teacher to instruct one of the students to lead the Pledge. In addition, the teacher can be expected to remain sitting or standing respectfully while the Pledge is recited. This is not to say that a teacher may thwart the pledge process. A teacher may be

---

[9]*West Virginia State Board of Education v. Barnette,* 319 U.S. 624, 644 (1943).

[10]*State v. Lundquist,* 278 A.2d 263 (Md. 1971).

dismissed for refusing to teach his or her school children about the FLAG SALUTE and other historical and patriotic subjects. A 1980 federal appeals court decided that a probationary kindergarten teacher who was a member of the Jehovah's Witnesses could rightfully be dismissed for failing to adhere to prescribed CURRICULUM. The teacher refused to recite the Pledge of Allegiance and to teach children patriotic songs and historical facts about national holidays.[11]

Some people object to the words "with liberty and justice for all." Others base their objections under freedom of RELIGION grounds. The phrase "under God" in the Pledge of Allegiance has been challenged as advancement of religion, but COURTS are reluctant to find First Amendment violations of such patriotic manifestations.

Persons within the school have the option of standing silently during the Pledge or leaving the classroom. In addition a student has the right to remain quietly seated since this is not disruptive or interfering with the rights of others.[12]

See also BIBLE READING; CONSTITUTIONAL LAW; FLAG SALUTE; PRAYERS.

POLICE

School officials have the right to cooperate with police regarding crimes or investigations of students and school personnel. However, school officials should consider such things as DEFAMATION and CONSTITUTIONAL LAW before throwing away the gown of an educator and taking up the cap of a police officer.

A student is not entitled to Miranda-type advice of rights when questioned by school authorities[13] as students might be if questioned by police. Although there may be no legal duty, it seems right that a student's parents should be called before allowing police to question a younger child. If parental notice is impractical, the teacher or administrator may have the ethical duty to inform the student that the student has the right to remain silent and that anything he or she says can be used against that person.

---

[11]*Palmer v. Board of Education of City of Chicago,* 603 F.2d 1271 (7th Cir. 1979), *cert. denied,* 444 U.S. 1026 (1980).

[12]*Goetz v. Ansell,* 477 F.2d 636 (2d Cir. 1973).

[13]*Boynton v. Casey,* 543 F. Supp. 995 (D. Me. 1982); *Keough v. Tate County Board of Educators,* 748 F.2d 1077 (5th Cir. 1984); *Brewer by Dreyfus v. Austin Independent School District,* 779 F.2d 260 (5th Cir. 1985).

A 1980 case found a student appealing his conviction of drug possession and carrying a concealed weapon subsequent to arrest for truancy. The court determined that, because the student was a minor and not in school, this gave the officers probable cause to arrest for truancy. The truancy STATUTE did not give probable cause for SEARCH AND SEIZURE. However, when the officers took the student to the detention center as prescribed by regulation, proper procedures were followed and the subsequent search was proper.[14]

State and federal COURTS consider the special need to provide a safe school environment conducive to education when they assess the legality of action such as detention or searches. The courts have generally upheld a standard less exacting than probable cause if there is a reasonable suspicion that the police will uncover a violation of the law or school RULES.[15]

POLICIES, School Board

See SCHOOL BOARDS, Policies.

POLITICAL ACTIVITIES

See ANTISUBVERSIVE LAWS; ASSOCIATION, Freedom of; CONSTITUTIONAL LAW.

PRAYERS

The New York Board of Regents recommended the reading of the following prayer in the public schools:

> Almighty God, we acknowledge our dependence upon Thee, and we beg Thy blessings upon us, our parents, our teachers, and our country.

---

[14]*Matter of Miguel G.,* 168 Cal. Rptr. 688 (Cal. App. 1980).

[15]*Tarter v. Raybuck,* 742 F.2d 977 (6th Cir. 1984); *Bilbrey v. Brown,* 738 F.2d 1462 (9th Cir. 1984).

The reading of this prayer was challenged on the grounds that it was contrary to the beliefs and RELIGION of some of the students and violated the FIRST AMENDMENT to the United States Constitution. In 1962, the United States Supreme Court ruled that this prayer was religious in nature and, therefore, violated the "establishment of religion" clause of the First Amendment. The court explained that:

> [I]n this country it is no part of the business of government to compose official prayers for any group of the American people to recite as a part of a religious program carried on by the government.[16]

A lower federal court reaffirmed this position in 1980, stating: "Only a ruthless, absolutist application of the principle (of separation of church and state) as it relates to officially composed prayers can insure the intended protection. No *de minimis* exception is tolerable.[17]

The United States Supreme Court's decision was written in such a manner that it seemed to apply only to prayers which constitute a religious exercise. As a result, some educators continued the practice of "prayer" recitation in a modified form. In one case, a kindergarten class was required to recite the following verse before "snack time":

> We thank you for the flowers so sweet;
> We thank you for the food we eat;
> We thank you for the birds that sing;
> We thank you for everything.

The word "God" had been eliminated from the original last line. This did not prevent a federal court of appeals from recognizing that this was in fact a prayer and, therefore, was unconstitutional.[18] Even when the prayer is unofficially prepared and presented by an instructor reading daily from the Bible on his or her own initiative, the courts have firmly held that such prayer and reading are impermissible.[19] Justice Frankfurter's statement still holds true in the courts: "Separation means separation, not something else. Jefferson's metaphor in describing the relation between Church and State speaks of a 'wall of separation,' not a fine line easily overstepped."[20]

---

[16]*Engle v. Vitale,* 370 U.S. 421, 425 (1962).

[17]*Hall v. Bradshaw,* 630 F.2d 1018 (4th Cir. 1980).

[18]*DeSpain v. DeKalb County Community School District,* 384 F.2d 836 (7th Cir. 1967).

[19]*Lynch v. Indiana State University Board of Trustees,* 378 N.E.2d 900, 903, *cert. denied,* 441 U.S. 946 (1978).

[20]*McCollum v. School District No. 71,* 333 U.S. 203 (1948).

The courts have developed a three-pronged test for church and state establishment cases. To pass the strictures of the separation requirements, an activity must (1) have a secular purpose, (2) neither advance nor inhibit religion, and (3) not foster excessive government entanglement with religion.[21]

To get prayer back into the schools, state legislatures passed STAT-UTES authorizing a "period of silence" for contemplation, meditation, or prayer. These statutes were also declared unconstitutional and self-serving as there was compelling evidence that there was no secular purpose sought to be achieved.[22] In 1985, the United States Supreme Court looked to the legislative history to show the motive behind silent meditation as an intent to impose prayer on students and found the Alabama statute unconstitutional.[23]

The Ninth Circuit Court of Appeals held in 1981 that, although attendance at school assemblies was voluntary, the concurring permission given to the student council by the high school PRINCIPAL and SUPERIN-TENDENT to recite prayers and Bible verses of their choosing, during school hours, was a violation of the establishment clause and was not saved from constitutional attack. Devotional activities with voluntarily spoken prayers are controversial because free speech rights as well as religious liberties are at issue.[24] Ignorance of the law regarding barred activities is no excuse, and one teacher obtained $300 for emotional distress from exposure to prayer led by the principal at an assembly.[25] In 1985, the Tenth Circuit awarded compensatory DAMAGES for the loss of the inherent value of the PLAINTIFF's rights even though the plaintiff was unable to demonstrate consequential injury.[26]

Another question presented to the courts regarding school prayer is whether religious student organizations may use school facilities to hold MEETINGS at which a central activity at many of the meetings is prayer. In a California case, the court held that high school students could not use school facilities to hold meetings of their Christian student organization.[27]

---

[21]*Lemon v. Kurtzman*, 403 U.S. 602 (1971).

[22]*Duffy v. Las Cruces Public Schools*, 557 F. Supp. 1013 (D.N.M. 1983); *May v. Cooperman*, 572 F. Supp. 1561 (D.N.J. 1983); *Beck v. McElrath*, 548 F. Supp. 1161 (M.D. Tenn. 1982).

[23]*Wallace v. Jaffee II*, 466 U.S. 924 (1985).

[24]*Collins v. Chandler Unified School District*, 644 F.2d 759 (9th Cir. 1981), *Cert. denied*, 453 U.S. 863 (1981).

[25]*Abramson v. Anderson*, No. 81-26 W. (Iowa 1982).

[26]*Bell v. Little Axe Independent School District No. 70*, 766 F.2d 1391 (10th Cir. 1985).

[27]*Johnson v. Huntington Beach Union High School District*, 137 Cal. Rptr. 43 (Cal. App. 1977).

However, on the college or university level, the courts seem to have a double standard. In 1982, the United States Supreme Court upheld the right of a university Christian student organization to have prayer meetings on state-supported campuses since the university campus was deemed an open forum. A compelling governmental interest must be demonstrated to bar access to expression of views—even religious views.[28]

Recognizing the states' compelling interest in removing any indication of public school sponsorship of religious activities, federal courts consistently rule that the Establishment Clause overrides rights to assemble and express religious views under the auspices of the public schools. However, the limited "open forum" concept *may* be applied to public high schools under the EQUAL ACCESS ACT of 1984 (EAA).[29] Schools receiving federal financial assistance must provide a fair opportunity for any non–curriculum-related student group to meet on school premises during non-instructional time.

The legal status of the EAA and whether this violates the Establishment Clause has yet to be clarified by the courts. Until the United States Supreme Court rules, the American Association of School Administrators (AASA) published Equal Access Interpretation and Implementation Guidelines in 1984 to address the "equal access" questions of whether to provide a limited forum to all student-initiated groups or to deny all access to groups that are not an extension of the CURRICULUM.

See also BIBLE READING; FLAG SALUTE; PLEDGE OF ALLEGIANCE.

PREGNANT STUDENTS

COURTS have held that MARRIED STUDENTS may not be prohibited from attending school. This rule holds true even though the student has a child; but, while a girl is carrying a child, some schools have RULES which prohibit her attendance at school. These rules require pregnant students to withdraw from school immediately upon becoming aware of the pregnancy or at a specified month during the pregnancy. Like similar rules involving pregnant teachers, these rules have been challenged in the COURTS. The main arguments against rules prohibiting pregnant girls are that these rules deny the student FOURTEENTH AMENDMENT rights of EQUAL PROTECTION and the rules are ARBITRARY AND CAPRICIOUS and, therefore, are in violation of the student's right to DUE PROCESS of the law.

---

[28]*Widmar v. Vincent*, 454 U.S. 263 (1981).

[29]*Title VIII of P.L. 98–377, 98 U.S.C. 1302, Section 801.*

The courts are increasingly willing to declare such rules invalid, indicating the judicial commitment to protect students from irrational classifications that violate their entitlement to educational opportunities. Although several of the earlier cases held that mandatory withdrawal from school during an advanced stage of pregnancy would be upheld, the trend of judicial reasoning is that such rules are unreasonable and unconstitutional. If rules are necessary for a student's health, safety, or welfare and if the rules are justified by an overriding educational objective, the courts will uphold them. However, rules that specify, for example, that a girl must withdraw from school after the fifth month of her pregnancy are arbitrary and capricious. If it is safety the schools are concerned about, the early stages of pregnancy have been shown to be the most hazardous and critical. It is also possible that absence from school would cause more serious harm to the girl than her attendance at school. For example, an unwed, pregnant high school girl was reinstated to her classes by a Massachusetts court. Several doctors testified that the girl's condition would not be an obstacle; yet, absence from school could cause depression and mental anguish. The court explained its decision in the following words:

> [N]o danger to ... [the student's] physical or mental health resultant from her attending classes during regular school hours has been shown; no likelihood that her presence will cause any disruption of or interference with school activities or pose a threat of harm to others has been shown; and no valid educational or other reason to justify her segregation and to require her to receive a type of education treatment which is not equal to that given to all others in her class has been shown.[30]

The fact that a pregnant student is unwed is not a sufficient reason to deny her attendance at a public school. However, one court has given judicial status to a seldom followed precedent that, if, after a fair and impartial due process hearing, it is found that such student is so lacking in moral character that her presence in school will "taint the education of the other students," she may be barred. This is a difficult test to comply with; but, unless such a finding is and can be made, it would clearly be unfair to forever brand such a person as a scarlet woman.[31]

Restrictions because of alleged lack of moral character or promiscuity that are not grounded in valid health or safety considerations will not

---

[30]*Ordway v. Hargraves*, 323 F. Supp. 1155 (D.C. Mass. 1971).

[31]*Perry v. Grenada Municipal Separate School District*, 300 F. Supp. 748 (N.D. Miss. 1969).

be tolerated by the courts. School officials were not allowed to expel an unwed pregnant student from the National Honor Society.[32]

In addition, rules necessary to implement the provisions of the CIVIL RIGHTS ACT OF 1964 have been adopted by the Department of Health, Education, and Welfare. These rules prohibit the denial of any benefits or participation in any programs administered by an agency receiving federal funds based on reasons which discriminate on the basis of race, sex, RELIGION, etc. Specifically, Section 86.40 of the Civil Rights Act of 1964, Marital or Parental Status, prescribes that a recipient of federal monies shall not discriminate against any student nor exclude any student from its education program or activity, including any class or EXTRACURRICULAR ACTIVITY, on the basis of such student's pregnancy, childbirth, false pregnancy, termination of pregnancy, or recovery therefrom, unless the student requests voluntarily to participate in a separate portion of the program or activity of the recipient. Pregnant students cannot be segregated into limited evening programs that require fees for TUITION and books.[33] This law not only reflects general public policy, but the law also provides an ample federal forum for violations. Suits brought under these rules, contending that denying a pregnant student the right to attend school is discriminatory, have a strong chance of success. Even though there is no inherent constitutional right to a public education, the vast majority of courts view exclusion of students, solely on the basis of pregnancy, as discrimination in violation of the Equal Protection Clause and as a punishment for exercising the fundamental right to beget children.

PREPONDERANCE OF EVIDENCE

A preponderance of evidence is the greater weight of evidence which is more credible and convincing to the mind. It is stronger proof that the facts on one side are more probable than not. If one proves that it is more likely than not that something did or did not occur (51 percent vs. 49 percent), then the BURDEN OF PROOF by a preponderance of the evidence has been met. However, if the scales are evenly balanced and one cannot say on which side the scales tilt, then the burden of proof by a preponderance of the evidence has not been met and the offered proof, therefore, fails.

See also CATEGORICAL INDEX; DUE PROCESS; EXPULSIONS; SUSPENSIONS.

---

[32]*Wort v. Vierline*, No. 82-3169 (Ill. 1984).
[33]*Houston v. Prosser*, 361 F. Supp. 295 (N.D. Ga. 1973).

PRESS, Freedom of

See ACADEMIC FREEDOM; CONSTITUTIONAL LAW; LIBRARY CENSOR-SHIP; SCHOOL PUBLICATIONS.

PRESUMPTION

A presumption is a rule of law that, if fact *A* exists, fact *B* is legally inferred to necessarily follow. A presumption may be either *conclusive* or *rebuttable*. If it is a conclusive presumption, the proof of fact *A* means that the court or jury must find that fact *B* exists; evidence to the contrary is inadmissible. On the other hand, if the presumption is a rebuttable presumption, the proof of fact *A* permits the jury to find fact *B*; but evidence is allowed to show that fact *B* does not, in fact, follow from fact *A*.

For example, at COMMON LAW, there was a conclusive presumption that a child under the age of seven could not be contributorily negligent. Therefore, evidence to show that a six-year-old child did, in fact, contribute to his or her own injury would be inadmissible. In contrast, there was a rebuttable presumption that a child from age seven to age fourteen was not capable of CONTRIBUTORY NEGLIGENCE. Therefore, evidence to show that a thirteen-year-old child did, in fact, understand a dangerous condition and, therefore, contributed to his or her own injury would be admissible.

Another example is that it is presumed that a school board decision is proper and within the scope of the board's authority. However, evidence would be admissible to prove otherwise, thereby rebutting the presumption.

PRINCIPAL

A principal is an employee of the school district, appointed to administer duties within a given school or schools. COURTS have consistently held that principals are not public officers of the SCHOOL BOARD. Boards possess the legal prerogative to transfer or reassign principals as with any other teacher or administrator, taking into consideration the CONTRACT or other rights granted under board policy or state law. The principal's property right is his or her position as a certified employee, not as an administrator.[34]

The principal is in charge of the day-to-day operation and management of the school; therefore, the chief administrator has a certain amount of discretion and authority to make and enforce reasonable RULES governing the school, educators, and students. Of course, the rules may not conflict with school board policy or with state law, and the rules must not violate CONTRACT rights or constitutional rights of the teachers or students.

Immunities or rights to indemnification that protect officers of the board or board members themselves generally do not protect principals. (See SCHOOL BOARDS, LIABILITY, and GOVERNMENTAL IMMUNITY.) The principal is personally liable just like any other adult in society for wrongful acts which may be committed.

However, the general rule is that a principal may not be held liable for the tortious acts of the teachers or for an injury unless it can be shown that there was personal NEGLIGENCE on the principal's part which contributed to the injury. The principal cannot, nor is he or she expected to, supervise every activity in which students are involved. Teachers have the duty to supervise. However, if a principal participates in the activity in a negligent manner or if the principal knows or should know that a teacher or employee is incompetent to fulfill the supervisory duties, the principal may then be liable for his or her own negligence. In such a case, both the teacher and the principal could be named as DEFENDANTS and could be jointly liable.

It should be noted that the principal's duty to ensure safety applies not only to students but to teachers as well. If the principal knows or should know that a certain student has dangerous propensities, it is the principal's duty to do something about it. If the principal does not and a teacher is injured as a result, it is quite possible that the principal could be liable for negligence in not having removed or properly disciplined the child for the protection of the teacher. The principal must be REASONABLE AND PRUDENT under the existing circumstances.

PRIVACY

The United States Supreme Court has lent support to the argument that an educator's private life may form the basis for his or her dismissal only when

---

[34]*Lane v. Board of Education,* 348 N.E.2d 470 (Ill. 1976).

it affects his or her fitness as a teacher. Prior to the 1960s, teachers' personal affairs were subject to close scrutiny by their employers and frequently were used as the basis for dismissal.

In 1936, Howard Beale described the restrictions placed on teachers. He explained that in North Carolina, in 1928, teachers were forced to sign CONTRACTS in which they promised "not to fall in love" and "not to go out with any young men except insofar as it may be necessary to stimulate Sunday-school work." This was quite liberal compared to several 1915 contracts in which teachers promised "not to loiter in ice cream stores," "not to go out with men," and "to be home between the hours of 8 P.M. and 6 A.M." The dismissal cases are even more enlightening. In one case, for example, a high school principal was dismissed for walking home from school every day with a high school teacher. In 1927, a science teacher found that going riding one afternoon with two of his girl students subjected him to removal from the public schools. As Mr. Beale related:

> Often petty social restrictions or offenses against them come up in combination, because the teacher who is a nonconformist is likely to get into trouble on several scores. A young South Carolina history teacher, now happier in a better school system, almost gave up teaching because of his first experience. He was not allowed to dance or to have "dates." He had to teach a Sunday school class. Then he got into trouble for saying that blacks had as much right to an education as whites. In a three-hour faculty meeting the superintendent dictated every detail of the teachers' lives. Even before he got into evolutionary difficulties, John Scopes was criticized in Dayton for smoking cigarettes and for dancing. In an Iowa town a woman was recently dismissed because she was known to smoke and to drink. One young teacher writes, "How I conduct my classes seems to be of no great interest to the school authorities, but what I do when school is not in session concerns them tremendously. My contract requires me to refrain from keeping company with young men in the community. Yet I must live in the school district and remain here three weekends out of four during the entire school year. I mustn't dance, play cards, or be out late on week-day nights; in fact, they want me to be an old maid."[35]

Historically, teachers' personal conduct has been expected to reflect an exemplary role-model standard. School officials' authority to restrict personal freedom rights without DUE PROCESS of law embodied in the FOURTEENTH AMENDMENT is frequently challenged in court by educators. An educator's implied constitutional right to live a life in privacy is often determined by the location of the conduct and the nature of the activity.[36] The SCHOOL BOARD's legitimate interest in safeguarding the

---

[35]H.K. Beale, *Are American Teachers Free?*, New York: Charles Scribner's Sons, 1936, pp. 394–395.

[36]*Lile v. Hancock Place School District,* 701 S.W.2d 500 (Mo. 1986).

welfare of the students and the management of the school must be weighed against the educator's privacy interests. The judicial balance has allowed school officials to restrict unconventional behavior if it is seen as harmful to students or detrimental to teaching effectiveness.

When the question of whether a teacher may be dismissed because of his or her lifestyle is asked, the following should be considered. There must exist some nexus between the conduct complained of and the teacher's ability to perform his or her necessary duties; the conduct must render the teacher unfit to teach.

One court explains the legislative intent and what may form the grounds for discipline as follows:

> In providing standards to guide school boards in placing restraints on conduct of teachers, the Legislature is concerned with the welfare of the school community. Its objective is the protection of students from corruption. This is a proper exercise of the power of state to abridge personal liberty to protect larger interests. But reasonableness must be the governing criterion. The board can only be concerned with "immoral conduct" to the extent that it is, in some ways, inimical to the welfare of the school community. ...
>
> The private conduct of a man, who is also a teacher, is proper concern to those who employ him only to the extent that it mars him as a teacher. ... Where his professional achievement is unaffected, where the school community is placed in no jeopardy, his private acts are his own business and may not be the basis of discipline.[37]

Under this "fitness as a teacher" standard, the detrimental effect on the teacher's services must be capable of being objectively ascertainable. The COURTS have developed two test questions:

1. Does the conduct directly affect the performance of the occupational responsibilities of the teacher?
2. Has the conduct become the subject of such notoriety as to significantly and reasonably impair the capability of the particular teacher to discharge the responsibilities of the teaching position?[38]

For example, a wrestling coach who instructed his wrestlers to lie, break rules, and in essence cheat fell within the meaning of statute provisions for termination of the teacher's CONTRACT for gross inefficiency or immorality, willful and persistent violations of reasonable regulations, or other good and just cause. The coach's effectiveness as a

---

[37] *Jarvella v. Willoughby-Eastlake City School District Board of Education*, 233 N.E.2d 143 (Ohio 1967).

[38] *Golden v. Board of Education of County of Harrison*, 285 S.E.2d 663 (W. Va. 1982).

teacher and guidance counselor had been substantially impacted and impaired. The board of education may not merely "rubber stamp" the referee's recommendations as to termination but must make an independent decision based on the needs and requirements of the students and community that it serves.[39]

A notice of dismissal should inform the educator of the logical connection between acts or omissions and the duties and responsibilities of the employee. The connection need not be specifically set out so long as it may reasonably be inferred.[40]

TENURE laws are designed to protect teachers who have acquired tenure from ARBITRARY OR CAPRICIOUS action by a school board, by providing teachers with an impartial and responsive process of administrative adjudication. Legislatures did not intend to subject educators to discipline or dismissal for private peccadillos or personal shortcomings that might come to the attention of the board of education, but have little or no relationship with students, teachers, or the school community. Dismissal for unwise actions under stressful emergency situations or singular misjudgments have been disfavored and overturned.[41] Personal grounds for dismissal that have been deemed to relate directly to the teacher's fitness to teach are, for example, immorality, physical and mental disability, incompetency, convinction of a FELONY, insubordination, and neglect of duty.

In 1988, a Colorado court ruled that the school board had the discretion to dismiss a tenured teacher for drinking beer with cheerleaders she was supervising on the grounds of "neglect of duty." A teacher's failure to carry out his or her obligations and responsibilities in connection with students, even outside the school setting, is neglect of duty which is directly related to the teacher's fitness to teach.[42]

The personal life of a teacher involving such matters as not attending church,[43] having a child out of wedlock,[44] or the location of one's home[45] are not, in themselves, grounds for discipline.

---

[39]*Florian v. Highland Local School District,* 493 N.E.2d 249 (Ohio 1983).

[40]*Shipley v. Salem School District,* 669 P.2d 1172 (Or. 1983). (Civil action/judgment against Shipley for molesting a minor under his charge in the Big Brother program was well known and need not be explicitly noted in his dismissal notice.)

[41]*Board of Education v. Wood,* 717 S.W.2d 837 (Ky. 1986).

[42]*Blaine v. Moffat County School District,* 748 P.2d 1280 (Colo. 1988). *See e.g., Woodard v. Professional Practices Council,* 388 So. 2d 343 (Fla. App. 1980).

[43]*Stoddard v. School District No. 1,* 590 F.2d 829 (10th Cir. 1979).

[44]*Avery v. Homewood City Board of Education,* 674 F.2d 337 (5th Cir. 1982). *See also, Ponton v. Newport News School Board,* 632 F. Supp. 1056 (E.D. Va. 1986) (pregnant unmarried teacher challenges board attempt to force her to take leave of absence during a pregnancy).

While regulations are progressively less restrictive than in the past, school authorities continue to justify constraints on educators' personal lives, attempting conformity with community norms. For example, growing fifty-two marijuana plants in a greenhouse cost two Florida teachers their certificates. The court determined that, since teachers are in special leadership positions, teachers have an obligation to maintain high moral standards in the community.[46]

Discharges for "immoral" dishonesty, in and out of school, were upheld for filing false tax returns,[47] shoplifting,[48] misappropriation of school funds,[49] welfare fraud,[50] and possession of $500 worth of stolen materials used to build a house.[51]

In one case, a teacher attended a school board conference after being denied paid personal leave from the district where she taught. When she returned, she filed a falsified request for excused absences due to illness. The court determined that questions of morality may also include lying and affirmed her dismissal.[52]

Most teachers' private lifestyle issues focus on domestic living arrangements at odds with community mores. These cases often involve nontraditional relationships with sexual connotations, including both heterosexual and HOMOSEXUAL relations, as well as extramarital affairs.

The modern judicial attitude toward removing a teacher from the classroom based merely on his or her private sex life was expressed by a 1969 court:

> Surely incidents of extramarital heterosexual conduct against a background of years of satisfactory teaching would not constitute "immoral conduct" sufficient to justify revocation of a life diploma without any showing of an adverse effect on fitness to teach.[53]

In a 1980 case, a United States district court jury awarded over $190,000 to a junior-senior high school principal whose employment contract was not renewed. The jury found the principal's right to privacy

---

[45]*Newborn v. Morrison,* 440 F. Supp. 623 (S.D. Ill. 1977).

[46]*Adams v. State Professional Practices Council,* 406 So. 2d 1170 (Fla. 1981).

[47]*Logan v. Warren County Board of Education,* 549 F. Supp. 145 (S.D. Ga. 1982).

[48]*Leslie v. Oxford Area School District,* 420 A.2d 764 (Pa. 1980).

[49]*Appeal of Flannery,* 178 A.2d 751 (Pa. 1962).

[50]*Perryman v. School Committee of Boston,* 458 N.E.2d 748 (Mass. 1983).

[51]*Covert v. Bensalem Township School District,* 522 A.2d 129 (Pa. 1987).

[52]*Bethel Park School District v. Krall,* 445 A.2d 1377 (Pa. 1982).

[53]*Morrison v. State Board of Education,* 461 P.2d 375, 385, (Cal. 1969); *See also, Erb v. Iowa State Board of Public Instruction,* 216 N.W.2d 339 (Iowa 1974).

had been violated when the school board refused to renew his contract because of his private social relationship with an assistant principal whom he later married.[54]

Many of the right-to-privacy cases also contain allegations of sex DISCRIMINATION. For example, in a federal court case, a female teacher who was discharged for her unmarried cohabitation with a man alleged both violations of her privacy rights and sex discrimination. To support the sex discrimination allegation, she claimed that male faculty members had adulterous affairs, some with female students, and those members had not been terminated although the administrators knew about them. The court awarded the teacher $45,000 in DAMAGES and ordered her records cleaned, but did not reinstate her.[55]

Regarding heterosexual conduct of a teacher, the court in a small rural town in South Dakota favored the school board's dismissal of a teacher cohabiting with her boyfriend in a mobile home close to the school, concluding that the state is entitled to maintain a "properly moral scholastic environment." The expectations, norms and negative community reactions have much to do with the acceptability of a teacher's conduct.[56] Eight years later, but in a small Florida town, the court held that consensual sexual conduct between a teacher and an adult of the opposite sex does not, in itself, constitute "good cause" for rejection of a teacher's nomination for reemployment.[57]

Courts have interpreted immorality in various ways, offering no clear-cut standards in most cases. However, there is no doubt in the court opinions as to the serious impropriety of any sexual involvement with students. There is an adequate basis in CHILD ABUSE reporting and in *in loco parentis* statutes, together with the broad duty owed to students by school officials, to conclude that there is a duty to provide affirmative protection to students.

A tenured teacher who made sexual remarks and touched female students was determined unfit to teach despite his reputation as a good teacher.[58] Testimony at a school board hearing that a student and teacher

---

[54]*Schreffler v. Board,* N. 79–217 (Del., Nov. 7, 1980).

[55]*Landshair v. Lynchburg,* No. 79-003-L (Va., June 1980).

[56]*Sullivan v. Meade Independent School District No. 101,* 530 F.2d 799 (D.S.D. 1976).

[57]*Sherburne v. School Board of Suwannee County,* 455 So. 2d 1057 (Fla. App. 1984).

[58]*Weissman v. Board of Education of Jefferson County School District,* 547 P.2d 1267 (Colo. 1976); *see also, Fadler v. Illinois State Board of Education,* 506 N.E.2d 640 (Ill. 1987); *Scott County School District 2 v. Dietrich,* 499 N.E.2d 1170 (Ind. 1986).

had engaged in sexual intercourse was sufficient to terminate the teacher's contract.[59] School districts may be held liable for their NEGLIGENCE arising out of a teacher's sexual assault of students.[60] Furthermore, school boards may be liable, under theory of *respondeat superior,* for a principal's homosexual assaults on a student.[61]

PRIVATE AND PAROCHIAL SCHOOL AID

This is an extremely complex area of the law, and one which has traditionally been subjected to a great deal of litigation. Over the years, many attempts have been made to directly or indirectly aid private and parochial schools. Some of these attempts have been successful, but a great many have not. The cases resulting from attempted aid to these schools have frequently been decided by the Supreme Court of the United States. This court has enunciated various tests which are to be used in judging the constitutionality of the state or federal government aid. These tests, though often difficult to understand and apply, are extremely important because the COURTS need a tool by which they can distinguish among the various kinds of attempted aid and break them into categories. Once this has been done, the courts can take a closer look at who or what is actually benefitting from the aid—the students, parents, schools, or state. This is crucial in helping the courts apply uniform standards.

The importance of categorizing aid and applying various tests to determine the aid's validity can best be demonstrated by mentioning just a few of the kinds of aid programs which have been established or attempted: free TEXTBOOKS, bus TRANSPORTATION, tax refunds, tax credits, tax deductions, VOUCHERS, school lunches, MEDICAL SERVICES, use of state-owned facilities by RELIGION instructors, teachers' salaries paid by the state, TUITION reimbursements, and a host of others. Many of these aid programs are new. The ingenuity of persons attempting to obtain government aid for private and parochial schools or for children attending those schools seems limitless, and there is no reason to expect that many new forms of possible aid will not be developed.

The following explanation of private and parochial school aid is intended to give the reader a general overview of legislative and court history in this complex area. A brief explanation will be made of some of

---

[59]*Libe v. Board of Education of Twin Cedars,* 350 N.W.2d 748 (Iowa 1984).

[60]*Doe v. Durtschi,* 716 P.2d 1238, 1243–44 (Id. 1986).

[61]*Galli v. Kirkeby,* 248 N.W.2d 149, 152 (Mich. 1976).

the tests the courts have used in determining the validity or invalidity of government aid. In this manner, the reader will be able to better understand the court rulings and, in many cases, will be able to judge for himself or herself the kinds of aid which are permissible under the United States Constitution. Keep in mind that some state constitutions may impose even greater restrictions on aid to nonpublic schools. The term "parochial schools" will be used in the subsequent parts of this section, and it is meant to mean both private and parochial schools.

The FIRST AMENDMENT to the United States Constitution established a two-pronged prohibition on government action with regard to RELIGION. In what has come to be known as the "establishment of religion" clause, the Constitution provides that "Congress shall make no law respecting an establishment of religion or prohibiting the free exercise thereof ..." Through the FOURTEENTH AMENDMENT of the Constitution, the United States Supreme Court holds that the states are also subject to the requirements of the establishment of religion clause.

The following three-pronged test (called the Lemon Test) explains the government's position regarding aid to religiously sponsored schools. In order to be constitutionally valid, aid to religious schools must:

1. Have a secular purpose;
2. Have a primary effect that neither advances nor inhibits religious activity; and
3. Not foster excessive governmental entanglement with religious activities.[62]

According to this test, the aim of the "establishment clause" is to promote a relationship of "benevolent neutrality"[63] between government and religious organizations. It should be noted that the difference between neutral accommodation and unconstitutional establishment is one of degree only. Therefore, in order to avoid "establishing a religion," a state must not sponsor or financially support or become actively involved in the operation of a parochial school.

> In the words of Jefferson, the cause against establishment of religion by law was intended to erect "a wall of separation between Church and State."[64]

The following cases should give an insight into the evolution of the courts' reasoning regarding the ban on aid to parochial schools. In 1925, it

---

[62]*Lemon v. Kurtzman,* 403 U.S. 602 (1971).

[63]*Walz v. Tax Commission,* 397 U.S. 664 (1970).

[64]*Everson v. Board of Education of the Township of Ewing,* 330 U.S. 1 (1947).

was firmly established by the United States Supreme Court that, although compulsory attendance laws obligate parents to send their children to school, the parents have a constitutional right to send children to private or parochial schools.[65] This case substantiated the legitimacy of parochial education. Since parochial education has been legitimized, supporters sought to justify government aid to such schools. For many years, the court's attitude was not *whether* the government should aid parochial schools but *how.*

Several state STATUTES provide that the state would supply free TEXTBOOKS to all students attending school. Students attending parochial schools were granted free secular textbooks under these laws. As early as 1929, this kind of law was challenged, but the court upheld the giving of textbooks.[66] In this case, the court applied what has become known as the CHILD-BENEFIT THEORY. Under this theory, the court explained that, where the state legislation is primarily for the benefit of the students themselves and the parochial school benefits only indirectly, the aid will be upheld. The state has the right to provide public aid to help all children learn about secular subjects; in doing so, school children and the state alone are the beneficiaries, not the parochial schools.

Thus, the courts had established one theory which could be used to validate aid even though the aid might indirectly benefit parochial schools. The child-benefit theory requires the court to examine two questions:

1. What is the legislative intent?
2. Who receives the aid, the parochial school or the parent and child?

In 1947, the Supreme Court of the United States reiterated some of the logic upholding indirect forms of aid. In this case, a New Jersey statute provided for reimbursement to all parents for money spent for bus TRANSPORTATION of students to their schools. The court explained that the establishment of religion clause prohibits the expenditure of any tax monies, large or small, in support of any religious activities or institutions. The court went on to say that: "The First Amendment has erected a wall between church and state. That wall must be kept high and impregnable. We could not approve the slightest breach."[67] This means that the state must remain neutral towards the church; it may not aid it nor oppose it. Therefore, the court upheld the bus transportation reimbursement and explained that this was public welfare legislation. By allowing public schools to provide transportation for all children, the court said that the

---

[65]*Pierce v. Society of Sisters,* 268 U.S. 501 (1925).

[66]*Borden v. Louisiana State Board of Education,* 123 So. 655 (La. 1929).

[67]*Everson v. Board of Education,* 330 U.S. 1 (1947).

transportation regulation "does no more than provide a general program to help parents get their children, regardless of their religion, safely and expeditiously to and from accredited schools." Therefore, the "benefit" is to the child and not to the parochial schools.

As a result of this line of cases, two legal principles evolved:

1. There can be no direct aid to church-related schools.
2. People may not be excluded from social welfare benefits because of their religion.

Therefore, it is clear that not all aid is impermissible. The test which the courts adopted was one of direct versus indirect aid. Direct forms of aid, such as providing facilities for religious instruction or paying the salaries of religion instructors, clearly are not permissible under this test.

Several additional theories were also used by the courts in trying to determine the validity or invalidity of various forms of aid. Among these theories were the external benefit theory and the FUNDAMENTAL INTEREST THEORY. The fundamental interest theory seemed to receive the most attention by the courts. Under this theory, in judging the validity of aid to parochial schools, education is perceived as being a fundamental interest. Aid to education is then perceived as aid granted in the furtherance of this interest. The court must then balance the benefit of furthering this interest against the requirements of the establishment of religion clause. If the main effect of the aid is furtherance of the fundamental interest in education, and the benefit to religion is incidental, the aid will be upheld. On the other hand, if there is a significant benefit to religion and there exists no overriding benefit to the fundamental interest, the aid will be judged as being impermissible.

Along the same line of reasoning as used in the fundamental interest theory, in the early 1960s, the United States Supreme Court explained that, in making a determination of whether state or federal laws aid religion in violation of the establishment clause, the courts must look at the legislation and try to see what the primary effect is and whether there exists a secular purpose. This test was explained in the United States Supreme Court ruling which declared that reading the Bible or saying PRAYERS in the school was unconstitutional:

> The test may be stated as follows: What are the purpose and primary effect of the enactment? If either is the advancement or inhibition of religion then the enactment exceeds the scope of legislative power as circumscribed by the Constitution. That is to say that *to withstand the strictures of the Establishment Clause there must be a secular legislative purpose and a primary effect that neither advances nor inhibits religion....* The Free Exercise Clause, likewise considered many times here, withdraws from legislative power, state and federal, the exertion

of any restraint on the free exercise of religion. Its purpose is to secure religious liberty in the individual by prohibiting any invasions thereof by civil authority....

... The place of religion in our society is an exalted one, achieved through a long tradition of reliance on the home, the church and the inviolable citadel of the individual heart and mind...In the relationship between man and religion, the State is firmly committed to a position of neutrality.[68] (Emphasis added.)

The child-benefit theory fits well into this kind of purpose and primary effect test. As a result, this theory was applied in a 1968 United States Supreme Court case which upheld the constitutionality of a New York statute requiring local SCHOOL BOARDS to lend textbooks free of charge to children attending public, private, and parochial schools. The court examined the statute and found that the purpose and the benefit were secular in nature.[69]

Then, in 1970, the United States Supreme Court was faced with the question of whether property tax exemptions for religiously owned and used PROPERTY were in violation of the Constitution. The court used the secular purpose and primary effect tests and then added a new test for consideration: "We must... be sure that the end result—the effect—is not an excessive government entanglement with religion. The test is inescapably one of degree."[70] The court upheld the tax exemptions because the court reasoned that taxation would increase the degree of government involvement with religion. This "entanglement test" may become the courts' new approach in judging the validity of state aid.

In 1971, the United States Supreme Court outlined how the courts should determine the constitutionality of state aid:

In order to determine whether the government entanglement with religion is excessive, we must examine the character and purposes of the institutions that are benefitted, the nature of the aid that the State provides, and the resulting relationship between the government and the religious authority.[71]

The secular purpose test was also added to the above outline. As a result, the courts must seek the answers to four questions:

1. Is there a secular legislative purpose?

---

[68]*Abington School District v. Schempp,* 374 U.S. 203 (1963).

[69]*Board of Education v. Allen,* 392 U.S. 236 (1968).

[70]*Walz v. Tax Commission,* 397 U.S. 664, 674 (1970).

[71]*Lemon v. Kurtzman,* 403 U.S. 602, 615, (1971).

2. Is the primary effect of the legislation a benefit or limitation on religion?

3. Does the legislation foster entanglement with religion?

4. Does the legislation prevent the free exercise of religion?

The United States Supreme Court's attitude has been to restrict the possible forms of government aid which are constitutionally permissible. However, certain forms of assistance which meet the requirements of secular purpose, primary effect, and government entanglement may be permissible. To withstand the test:

1. All children must benefit and be covered by the legislation;

2. No direct aid or payments may be granted to nonsecular schools;

3. Aid granted must be for a secular purpose; and

4. Aid granted must not require the nonsecular school to give up its religious instruction.

In applying the above tests, the United States Supreme Court has ruled that the state can provide parochial schools with secular, neutral, or nonideological services, facilities or materials. Students attending parochial schools may be provided such things as bus transportation, school lunches, public health services, secular textbooks, and drivers' education courses which are supplied to all students in the state. Aid practices are scrutinized for evidence of excessive entanglement and to assess the need for extensive state monitoring to ensure separation of state funds.

The United States Supreme Court has invalidated state laws which in essence provide direct financial aid to parochial schools. Such unconstitutional aid includes tuition reimbursements to low-income parents, direct aid to parochial schools for maintenance and repair of BUILDINGS, granting of state funds to parochial schools for testing and record keeping, use of school-owned or leased buildings for religious instruction, loan of instructional equipment which could be used for religious instruction, using public school buses for parochial school field trips, auxiliary services such as speech and hearing therapy (but diagnostic services have been sanctioned) and counseling, and scoring of teacher-prepared tests mandated by state testing programs.

In the past, the United States Supreme Court has suggested that, while the state may accept its obligation to see that children are educated, the state has no obligation to assure the survival of church-connected school systems which help the state meet its obligation of providing education. However, this is not a final shutting of the door. Many indirect forms of aid are permissible, but the extent of permissible aid often depends upon the tests and theories which the court uses.

In a 1980 case, the United States Supreme Court relaxed its policy regarding aid to parochial schools. In *Committee for Public Education v. Regan,*[72] the court held that a New York statute that allowed the use of public funds to reimburse church-sponsored schools for performing various testing and reporting services called for by law was constitutional. Although the court recognized that this expenditure had the secondary effect of benefitting the religious schools, the court reasoned that the primary effect was secular—providing equal testing for all children. Thus, under certain circumstances, the court will uphold direct cash disbursements to religious schools. In a 1983 case, the United States Supreme Court upheld tax deductions for tuition, transportation, and books for both public and private school children.[73]

In addition, in 1990 the United States Supreme Court ruled that the Equal Access Act, 20 USC 4071–4074, prohibited schools from discriminating against "noncurriculum related student groups" meeting on school premises during noninstructional time, even though this was a Bible study group engaging in religious activities.[74] The court ruled that the Equal Access Act did not violate the principle of separation of church and state. Therefore, this issue is probably best left to local control.

There are many different tests and theories; as the makeup and philosophy of the United States Supreme Court changes, the reasoning used in support of the case decisions changes. The court will likely continue to use the three-pronged "secular purpose, primary effect, and government entanglement Lemon test," to determine the outcome of any given case.

See also RELEASED TIME.

PRIVATE SCHOOLS

Private schools must provide students with an education that meets the minimum CERTIFICATION and CURRICULUM requirements as set forth in state STATUTES or State Board of Education regulations. However, in nearly all other aspects, private schools are regulated privately and not by the state. A private school may be a parochial school or simply a private business enterprise. Problems do arise in relation to how "private" the private school may be and to what extent the state does have authority over

---

[72]*Committee for Public Education and Religious Liberty v. Regan,* 444 U.S. 646 (1980).

[73]*Mueller v. Allen,* 463 U.S. 388 (1983).

[74]*Board of Education of the Westside Community Schools v. Mergens,* 58 L.W. 4720 (1990).

the private school's functions. Regulatory activity of states varies from no regulations to mere registration to mandatory institution and faculty regulations.

It is constitutional for a state to have COMPULSORY EDUCATION laws. However, even though a student may be compelled to go to school, he or she may not be forced into the public school system so long as a viable alternative is pursued. Children must obtain "equivalent or equal instruction" referring to the teachers' qualifications and teaching materials.[75]

There have been many constitutional challenges to the public school system based on religious grounds. Many parents have wanted to form their own schools or have their children attend "home school." The minimum state requirements are that there must be a qualified teacher; minimum prescribed CURRICULUM requirements must be met; pupil records must be maintained; health, safety, and zoning regulations must be followed; and there is some authority to the effect that students should have free association with other students, thereby enabling them to learn through social interaction. If these requirements are met, then a private "home school" could be formed and certified by the state. The state's interest in compliance to "reasonable" state educational requirements is not deemed by the COURTS as an encroachment on religious interests of private school operators and parents.[76]

Private schools may be held to the constitutional standards of public institutions if it can be shown that they are engaged in state action. Generally, this occurs when private school activities are closely involved with public function or purpose. However, because of the complexity of what actually constitutes state action, only a case-by-case examination can begin to provide an understanding of this issue. Different applications or exemptions of civil rights statutes are applied to nonpublic education. Race, RELIGION and sex DISCRIMINATION in employment may be applicable to programs that receive federal FUNDS and not to private schools in many operative areas.

In a case which drew a clear distinction between public and private functions within a private college, the dean suspended seven students. Four of the students attended the liberal arts college, and the others attended the ceramics college. The latter was supported almost totally by the state of New York. Thus, the court held that the dean was required to provide DUE PROCESS to the students of the ceramics college but was not obliged to do the same for the liberal arts students.[77]

---

[75]*Knox v. O'Brien,* 72 A.2d 389 (N.J. 1950).

[76]*State v. Calvary Academy,* 348 N.W.2d 898 (Neb. 1984); *McCurry v. Tesch,* 738 F.2d 271 (8th Cir. 1984).

[77]*Powe v. Miles,* 407 F.2d 73 (2d Cir. 1968).

Five factors which should be weighed when considering whether the requisite state action is involved in the acts of private institutions were set out by the Second Circuit in 1974. They are:

1. The degree that a private institution is dependent on government aid.
2. The extent and intrusiveness of government in regulating the activity or scheme.
3. Whether the scheme connotes government approval or whether assistance is provided to all without such connotation.
4. The extent to which the organization serves a public function or acts as a surrogate for the state.
5. Whether the organization has legitimate claims as a private organization in associational or other constitutional terms.[78]

The Supreme Court of Washington, in a 1978 case involving TENURE at a private college, stated that "private action is immune from the restrictions of the FOURTEENTH AMENDMENT"; and the court found nothing in the record to support a claim that the actions of this private institution include state action. The court did not foreclose the possibility that there may be sufficient intertwining of private institutional and government functions to constitute state action, but there was simply no proof of such in that case as the court held that the college had acted properly in dismissing a tenured teacher by adhering to its own faculty code governing such cases.[79]

To encourage viable educational choices for families, tax relief measures for tuition and educational VOUCHERS have been tried at state and federal levels.

The LIABILITY of private schools is different from that of public schools. In a private school, the protections of GOVERNMENTAL IMMUNITY do not apply. The private school is liable for its intentional TORTS and NEGLIGENCE just as any private individual would be. There is some authority to the effect that, if the private school is a charitable institution, it comes within the cloak of "charitable immunity." Charitable immunity is a dwindling legal concept meaning that a nonprofit charity cannot be sued and is immune from liability. This is thought to be an unfair law, and the better view is that this COMMON LAW immunity will be lifted.

See also PRIVATE AND PAROCHIAL SCHOOL AID.

---

[78]*Jackson v. Statler Foundation,* 496 F.2d 623 (2d Cir. 1974).

[79]*Lehmann v. Board of Trustees of Whitman College,* 578 P.2d 397 (Wash. 1978). *See also, Dayton Christian School, Inc. v. Ohio Civil Rights Commission,* 766 F.2d 932 (6th Cir. 1985) (commission did not have the authority to review the nonrenewal of a pregnant teacher's contract).

PROBATIONARY TEACHERS

A probationary teacher is one who is not yet tenured or entitled to a CONTINUING CONTRACT but is serving a specified probationary period prior to obtaining TENURE or greater contract rights. During the time of probation, the teacher is observed and evaluated for the purpose of determining whether the district wants to keep the teacher on a permanent basis. The probationary period is anywhere from one to five years, with most states requiring three years. The board has an absolute right to terminate a probationary teacher by timely notice of NONRENEWAL at the end of the contract.[80] If a teacher is renewed at the end of the probationary period, he or she becomes tenured at the board's discretion and is entitled to greater contract rights under most state laws.

The United States Supreme Court handed down two decisions which establish that, under federal law (not necessarily state law), probationary teachers have no right to a hearing on nonrenewals unless the teachers can demonstrate a deprivation of "property interests" (gained by direct or *de facto* legal obligations) or loss of liberty interests (stigma damaging good name and reputation).[81] A probationary teacher is only entitled to notice that his or her contract will not be renewed unless state STATUTES specify otherwise.[82]

Teachers do not possess legal entitlement to probationary employment. Service in a district does not automatically count as probationary time. For example, a teacher who had served six years in the school system under terminal contracts was not automatically given full-time tenure.[83] Some experienced tenured teachers may be required to serve a partial probationary period if they move from one district to another.

See also CONTRACTS; DUE PROCESS; NONRENEWAL; PRIVACY; RENEWAL.

PROFANITY

See ACADEMIC FREEDOM; CONSTITUTIONAL LAW; OBSCENITY; SCHOOL PUBLICATIONS.

---

[80]*Frasier v. Bd. of Educ.*, 530 N.Y.S.2d 79 (N.Y. 1988).

[81]*Bd. of Regents v. Roth*, 408 U.S. 564 (1972); *Perry v. Sindermann,* 408 U.S. 593 (1972).

[82]*Abbott v. Bd. of Educ.*, 558 P.2d 1307 (Utah 1976).

[83]*Sacchini v. Dickinson State College*, 338 N.W.2d 81 (N.D. 1983).

PROPERTY

Acquisition

State legislatures have the power to grant local school districts the power to acquire and hold property. Nevertheless, property acquired by a school district usually becomes the property of the state. As a result, if the legislature decides to reorganize school districts by consolidating some or abolishing others, the state is free to do so because the legislature is not allowed to relinquish complete control over state property to local districts. This also means that the state has the right to take school facilities in one school district and give them to another district or to a state agency. Compensation to the local school district or consent of the local residents is not required unless mandated by STATUTE.

SCHOOL BOARDS have the authority, either express or implied, to acquire property and construct buildings which are necessary to efficiently operate the public schools. This is not an unlimited power. Several cases have prescribed the rule that the school board may not purchase property as a means of speculation or with the intent to make a profit. While the board has the right to purchase land for building sites, playgrounds, and athletic events, the board may not purchase land for use as a farm unless this is connected to the school program. However, property purchased does not have to be adjacent to the school grounds.

The school board may acquire property by a direct purchase or, if authorized by STATUTE, through the use of eminent domain. The power of eminent domain allows the school board to condemn private property needed for school purposes. When private property is condemned, the school board must pay money to the landowner based upon the property's fair market value. The landowner *must* "sell" the property to the board. However, compliance with the state and federal constitutions is required. This means that the landowner has a right of DUE PROCESS. The public agency must give the landowner an opportunity to be heard, must demonstrate a public necessity for the property, and must pay a reasonable compensation.

Although most state laws allow local school boards to acquire property within the district for school purposes, the board has no right to condemn property outside the district in most states. The COURTS will look closely to determine the purpose of the property acquisition. Keep in mind that, in all cases, the property must be purchased in order to benefit the students' education and must be for the general public welfare. (See DONATIONS, Acceptance of.)

Selection of a school site is within the local school board's discretion, and the board's decision will not be overturned unless the decision is

ARBITRARY AND CAPRICIOUS. (See REORGANIZATION; SCHOOL BOARDS; Authority.)

Maintenance

Local school boards have the duty to maintain school property in a safe condition. In a Louisiana case, a six-year-old boy was injured while playing on property owned by the district when the boy ran into a broken chain link fence which was obscured by tall grass. The school district was held to have had notice of the condition since its AGENT, the groundskeeper, had mowed all the area around the broken fence. The court found that the school board had the duty to either maintain the premises in a safe condition or to provide adequate warning of the condition. The district breached the duty and was found negligent.[84]

School districts can be held liable for DAMAGES even in cases where the district does not know of the dangerous condition. In one case, a student was injured while playing a game of softball during a physical education class. The student was injured when he tripped over a piece of concrete imbedded in a base path. The court ruled that the school should have known about the field's condition and held the school liable for the injuries.[85]

Disposal

Disposal or sale of school property may be controlled by the state legislature because local school boards are deemed to be holding schools for the sole purpose of education of the state citizens. Therefore, even though a building might have been purchased and maintained solely by local FUNDS, if the legislature chooses, most legislatures can limit a local school board's discretion in the disposition of school property. When the school board does sell school property, the sale must be for an amount which is equivalent to the property's fair market value. The board cannot sell school property for a nominal sum. The board must receive the best price possible or the sale may be ENJOINED. School property must not be given away.

At times, questions arise regarding disposition of property which has been donated to the school district by a private party. Where such property has been donated to the district by a deed which conveys title in "fee simple absolute" (i.e., free and clear of all restrictions), the board may dispose of the property in the same manner as other school land. However,

---

[84]*Fusilier v. Northbrook Excess & Surplus Ins. Co.,* 471 So. 2d 761 (La. App. 1985).
[85]*Ardoin v. Evangeline Parish School Bd.,* 376 So. 2d 372 (La. App. 1979).

there are times when property is donated to the district "only so long as the property is used for school purposes." If this property ceases to be used for school purposes, the property can revert back to the original donor or his or her heirs.

See also BUILDINGS; CONSTRUCTION; REORGANIZATION.

PROTESTS

See ASSEMBLY, Right of; ASSOCIATION, Right of; CONSTITUTIONAL LAW.

PROVISIONAL CERTIFICATION

See CERTIFICATION; DECERTIFICATION.

PROXIMATE CAUSE

See NEGLIGENCE.

PUBLIC OFFICE

See CONFLICT OF INTEREST.

PUBLICATIONS

See CONSTITUTIONAL LAW; LIBRARY CENSORSHIP; OBSCENITY; SCHOOL PUBLICATIONS.

PUNISHMENT

See CATEGORICAL INDEX; DISCIPLINE.

Q

QUALIFIED PRIVILEGE

See DEFAMATION.

QUESTION OF FACT

A question of fact is a factual dispute issue which is decided by the jury, whereas a QUESTION OF LAW, requiring application or interpretation of the law, is decided by the judge. For example, if a person is on trial for illegal possession of drugs, it is up to the jury to decide from the evidence presented by both sides whether that person is guilty of all the elements of the crime. This is a question of fact. On the other hand, it is for the judge to decide whether the SEARCH AND SEIZURE procedure for such contraband was legal. This is a question of law.

As to questions of fact, the jury weighs all of the evidence, decides what is true, and then communicates that decision to the court. If, for example, the jury decided that a teacher was assaulted by a student, that determination would be final and the student could not generally appeal the decision unless as a matter of legal impossibility or other mistakes in the trial. Decisions as to questions of fact are final, and the court will not change such a decision without exceptional circumstances being prevalent.

QUESTION OF LAW

A question of law is an issue which involves the interpretation and application of the law to be decided by the court (judge) and not by the jury, which decides QUESTIONS OF FACT. For example, assume that the issue is whether a student's constitutional rights were violated when the student was suspended for wearing a black armband. It would be for a jury to decide as a question of fact whether the student wore the armband; but it would be for the court to decide whether, as a question of law, the wearing of the armband was a valid exercise of the student's constitutional right to free speech.

QUO WARRANTO

A quo warranto action is a suit brought to determine whether an officer has the right to exercise the duties of his or her office. This is an extraordinary proceeding to inquire "by what authority" one supports their claim to the position. It is intended to prevent exercise of unlawful power.

For example, if a SCHOOL BOARD member took a position on the local board and it was believed that the election was not proper or if the board member was not legally qualified, a quo warranto action could be brought. An injunction of writ of MANDAMUS would not be the proper remedy. As one court said:

> Quo Warranto is the Gibraltar of stability in government tenure. Once a person is duly elected or duly appointed to public office, the continuity of his services may not be interrupted and the uniform working of the governmental machinery disorganized or disturbed by any proceeding less than a formal challenge to the office by that action which is now venerable with age, reinforced by countless precedent, and proved to be protective of all parties involved in a given controversy, namely, quo warranto.[1]

The remedy of quo warranto belongs to the state in its sovereign capacity. It is for the state to bring suit against a person who is claiming a right to hold office in that state. If the state says that the officer has the

---

[1] *In re Vacancy in Board of School Directors of Carroll Township*, 180 A.2d 16 (Pa. 1962).

right to be in his or her position, a private citizen cannot complain through a quo warranto suit unless that citizen can show that he or she is being injured uniquely from the public at large.

QUORUM

A quorum is the number of persons needed to conduct the business of some official body. If a quorum is not present, any action taken or decision made is without legal effect. What constitutes a quorum can be set out by STATUTE or by enabling RULES of the official body. In the absence of statutes or rules in this area, a quorum generally constitutes a simple majority of the members needed to conduct business.

RACE RELATIONS

See DISCRIMINATION.

RATIFICATION

Ratification is the making good of something which is invalid due to some existing deficiency. For example, if a CONTRACT with a teacher is invalid because it was not properly adopted at a regular SCHOOL BOARD MEETING, the contract may be ratified and thus made good. If there are certain STATUTES or board RULES prescribing procedures to be followed in ratification, these must be closely adhered to. Once the contract is ratified, it becomes totally binding and may not be breached by any party. The entire contract must be ratified, not individual parts. The effect of ratification can be illustrated in the words of an early court decision:

> By the very nature of the act of ratification, the party ratifying becomes a party to the original contract. He that was not bound becomes bound by it, and entitled to all the proper benefits of it.[1]

There are many cases wherein SCHOOL BOARDS have needed to ratify otherwise invalid agreements. Ratification may be used, for example,

---

[1] *Hill v. City of Indianapolis,* 92 F. 467 (Ind. 1899).

where school BONDS have been issued without authority, where the lack of authority is simply procedural. However, if the incurrence of the indebtedness is in violation of state laws, ratification would be impossible. In addition to teacher or administrator contracts and bonds, the school board may ratify CONSTRUCTION contracts as long as the construction is within the constitutional or debt limits of the state. The ratification must be explicit and binding on both parties. It is difficult to ratify by silence; but, if the contractor is performing and nothing is said, there is a possibility a contract will be found, even if the original is not ratified, under the theory of unjust enrichment.

Of course, to be effective, ratification must not conflict with other statutory requirements. This was the case when a school board had delegated to the SUPERINTENDENT its statutory duty of notifying teachers of the board's intention not to renew their contracts. Although the school board ratified the superintendent's NONRENEWAL notifications to a number of teachers, the court held that the strict notification provisions proscribed to the school board could not be delegated away and the ratification was, therefore, invalid.[2]

RELEASED TIME

In the 1940s, it was a common practice in some school districts in the United States to allow nonsecular education teachers to come into the public schools and teach RELIGION classes to students who voluntarily chose to be released from secular education classes. All religious denominations were allowed to give such instruction, and the salaries of the nonsecular education teachers were not paid by the public school system. Nevertheless, in 1948, the Supreme Court of the United States held that this practice was, in fact, a utilization of the public school system to aid religious groups in spreading their faith. As a result, the court declared this system of released time to be a violation of the "establishment of religion" clause of the United States Constitution.[3]

In 1952, New York's released-time program permitting students to be excused from classes for one hour a week in order to obtain religious instruction off school premises was upheld by the United States Supreme Court. The court distinguished this program from the released time

---

[2]*Peck v. Board of Education of Yuma Union High School District,* 612 P.2d 1076 (Ariz. App. 1980).

[3]*McCollum v. Board of Education,* 333 U.S. 203 (1948).

program it had invalidated in 1948. The court explained that this was not an "aid" to religion; it was merely an "accommodation" to the religious interests of the people.[4]

The "establishment of religion" clause of the Constitution requires the state and federal governments to remain neutral where RELIGION is concerned. Releasing students to attend religious instruction does, of course, allow such classes to continue; but this is in no way an expenditure of government funds in aid of religion. Allowing instruction in BUILDINGS owned or leased by the school district is an impermissible aid. However, one school district allowed a mobile unit to park on the edge of school property for weekly, hour-long religious instruction, and this released-time program was upheld.[5] A Tenth Circuit Court, reasoning that allowing course credits for released-time programs would administratively entangle school officials with the church, stopped the school from awarding credits for daily instruction received at a Mormom seminary.[6]

It is also unconstitutional for the school district to pay the salaries of the religion instructors. In addition, if the school district were to pay the salaries of secular education to teachers who go to the nonsecular school to teach secular subjects, this would be an impermissible form of state aid.

See also PRIVATE AND PAROCHIAL SCHOOL AID.

REASONABLE AND PRUDENT

A teacher or administrator is required to be "reasonable and prudent" in school-related matters of instruction, SUPERVISION, and safety. Whether or not the teacher or administrator meets this standard is a QUESTION OF FACT for the jury to decide. The jury will look at all the facts and circumstances and then determine whether, under the facts and circumstances, the standard of care was met.

For example, if a teacher was supervising the playground and a student was injured, the jury will look at all the facts to determine if liability will be imposed. If the teacher was walking around the playground and looking after the children, that would be reasonable even though a child was injured in a different area on the school grounds. However, if the teacher sat in one place reading a book without circulating to see what the

---

[4]*Zorach v. Clauson,* 343 U.S. 306 (1952).

[5]*Smith v. Smith,* 523 F.2d 121 (4th Cir. 1975), *cert. denied,* 423 U.S. 1073 (1976).

[6]*Lanner v. Wimmer,* 662 F.2d 1349 (10th Cir. 1981).

children were doing, the failure to act would likely be considered unreasonable under the circumstances.

It should be noted that teachers and administrators are held to a higher standard of care than the ordinary man or woman on the street. The teacher or administrator is under the duty to possess more than the "ordinary" amount of intelligence in relation to students and their care. For example, it is the educator's duty to "foresee" an injury when students are left unsupervised for long periods of time or where large groups of students are gathered without adequate observation. The ordinary person does not have to foresee this, but the educator does.

An educator's standard of care is not that of the ordinary reasonable and prudent person. Instead, the educator's standard of care is that of the reasonable and prudent teacher or administrator in the same or similar circumstances.

RECORDS

See DEFAMATION; PERSONNEL RECORDS; STUDENT RECORDS.

REHABILITATION ACT OF 1973

The Rehabilitation Act of 1973, often referred to as Section 504, affects the way school districts educate handicapped students and also affects the way districts deal with prospective and current employees. This far-reaching legislation is but one sentence:

> No otherwise qualified individual with handicaps ... shall, solely by reason of her or his handicap, be excluded from participation in, be denied the benefits of, or be subjected to discrimination under any program or activity receiving federal financial assistance.

Under Section 504, a handicapped person is defined as one who:

1. Has a physical or mental impairment which substantially limits one or more major life activity (major life activities are functions such as caring for one's self, performing manual tasks, walking, seeing, hearing, speaking, breathing, learning, and working);

2. Has a record of such an impairment; and

3. Is regarded as having such an impairment.

Preschool, elementary, and secondary students are "otherwise qualified" when they are of the age during which nonhandicapped students are provided with educational services. Thus, it is illegal to exclude a student from a classroom or school activity due to a handicap. Section 504 does not spell out specific requirements for educating students with handicaps. However, COURTS generally hold that the requirements are identical to those imposed by the EDUCATION FOR ALL HANDI-CAPPED CHILDREN ACT OF 1975.

Postsecondary students are "otherwise qualified" when they meet the academic and technical standards requisite for admission in the educational program. The program may not use any test that has an adverse effect on handicapped persons or any class of handicapped persons unless the test has been validated as a predictor of success in the education program and alternative tests that have a less disproportionate, adverse effect are not available. Once a handicapped individual is admitted, postsecondary institutions must make reasonable modifications in their programs to accommodate handicapped students.

In making reasonable accommodations, an educational institution is not required to waive or modify program requirements or lower academic standards that are reasonable. For example, an optometry school was not required to waive its degree requirement that students demonstrate proficiency using certain instruments used to examine the pathology of the human eye.[7] The court, in this case, observed that it would be unreasonable to refuse to alter a physical education requirement for a history degree.

With respect to employment, the United States Supreme Court has defined "otherwise qualified person" as one who is able to meet all of a program's requirements in spite of the handicap after reasonable accommodations have been made.[8] The court held that the reasonable accommodations are those which do not place an undue financial or administrative burden on the employer. An administrative burden would be one which requires a fundamental alteration in the nature of the program.

The employment case involved a teacher who had tuberculosis. (See COMMUNICABLE DISEASES for a discussion of what constitutes "otherwise qualified" when a person's handicap is a disease.)

---

[7]*Doherty v. Southern College of Optometry,* 659 F. Supp. 662 (W.D. Tenn. 1987).

[8]*School Board of Nassau County v. Arline,* 480 U.S. 273 (1987).

REINSTATEMENT

A teacher or administrator should consider both the applicable statutory provisions and the court's discretion in seeking the appropriate relief when his or her substantive or procedural rights as an employee have been infringed. The most common forms of judicial remedies are reinstatement, back pay, DAMAGES, clearing the record, and attorney's fees and costs.

Damages are awarded for past injuries sustained; when reinstatement is not sought, damages are awarded for future losses where these losses are the necessary consequence of the breach of contract. Damages are generally for the purpose of "making one whole" again or, in other words, putting the person back into the same position he or she would have been in had the breach of CONTRACT not occurred.

Reinstatement is the usual relief sought by transferred or discharged school employees. If a tenured teacher or administrator is wrongfully dismissed or suspended, he or she would want the money lost during the dismissal or suspension, and that person may also have an expectation of reemployment. The COURTS have held that, if there is authority to dismiss a teacher, there is authority to reinstate the teacher. However, in some instances, reinstatement is not a proper remedy and may only be allowed where the party can show that, if there had been full procedural DUE PROCESS, there would have been a property right to continued employment.[9] For example, if a teacher was wrongfully dismissed and if that teacher had TENURE or was to obtain tenure, then reinstatement along with damages would be allowed. On the other hand, if the teacher was on a one-year contract that was subject to RENEWAL or NONRENEWAL at the board's discretion, the only remedy would be for the damages suffered under the broken agreement. However, reinstatement or at least a remand for a hearing will be granted to a nontenured teacher who has been dismissed or nonrenewed based on reasons which are in violation of his or her protected constitutional rights.

It might be noted that, even though a teacher or administrator has the right to be reinstated, that does not necessarily mean that the reinstatement will be to the exact position previously held. If the position is available and if there would be no hostile or adverse effect on the educational process, such a reinstatement is necessary. However, if such were not the case, reinstatement to the same type of position at a different school and not an unreasonable distance away would be proper under the circumstances.

---

[9]*McGhee v. Draper,* 639 F.2d 639 (10th Cir. 1981). *See also, State v. Bd. of Educ.,* 503 N.E.2d 748 (Ohio 1986).

RELATED SERVICES

Related services are the supportive services which assist students with handicaps to benefit from SPECIAL EDUCATION. Related services include TRANSPORTATION and developmental and corrective services. (See EDUCATION FOR ALL HANDICAPPED CHILDREN ACT OF 1975.)

RELIGION

The FIRST AMENDMENT to the Constitution of the United States provides in part that "Congress shall make no law respecting an establishment of religion or prohibiting the free exercise thereof ... " Note carefully that this is a two-pronged test. In essence, the language requires that the government must remain neutral towards religion. While it may not aid religion, neither may the government discriminate against or inhibit religion. The "establishment of religion" clause expressly refers to "Congress." However, through the FOURTEENTH AMENDMENT to the United States Constitution, the Supreme Court of the United States holds that the prohibitions on government action which are implicit in this clause are applicable to the states as well as to the federal government.

The meaning of the establishment of religion clause was clarified somewhat in 1947. At that time, the Supreme Court of the United States explained what the mandates of this clause are:

> The "establishment of religion" clause of the First Amendment means at least this: Neither a state nor the Federal Government can set up a church. Neither can pass laws which aid one religion, aid all religions, or prefer one religion over another. Neither can force nor influence a person to go to or to remain away from church against his will or force him to profess a belief or disbelief in any religion. No person can be punished for entertaining or professing religious beliefs or disbeliefs, for church attendance or non-attendance. No tax in any amount, large or small, can be levied to support any religious activities or institutions, whatever they may be called, or whatever form they may adopt to teach or practice religion. Neither a state nor the Federal Government can, openly or secretly, participate in the affairs of any religious organizations or groups and vice versa. In the words of Jefferson, the clause against establishment of religion by law was intended to erect "a wall of separation between Church and State."[10]

---

[10]*Everson v. Board of Education of the Township of Ewing,* 330 U.S. 1 (1947).

The establishment clause cases have developed a three-pronged test. To pass the strictures of the state-church separation requirements, an educational activity must:

1. Have a secular purpose;

2. Neither advance nor inhibit religion; and

3. Not foster excessive government entanglement with religion.[11]

As a result, the establishment of religion clause has wide implications with regard to the schools. Many cases and a great deal of publicity involve questions of state and federal aid for religious-oriented schools. (For an explanation of the issues and answers to many of these questions, see PRIVATE AND PAROCHIAL SCHOOL AID.) Attention has been devoted to the balance between an individual's right to freedom of religion and free speech versus the separation of church and state as expounded in the Constitution. BIBLE READING and PRAYERS in public schools were held to violate the no-aid principle of the Establishment Clause. It was also ruled that teachers and students could not be compelled to engage in a FLAG SALUTE or to recite the PLEDGE OF ALLEGIANCE.

In the late 1970s, the religion clauses again were invoked in school-related cases. With the emergence of many religious cults and controversial beliefs, the courts have been forced to determine the impact of the First Amendment's religious clauses on the practice and instruction of these beliefs in public schools. In order to determine whether a given group is "religious" for constitutional purposes, the courts may analogize the group with more established religious groups. Also, three fundamental aspects of religion that the First Amendment is designed to guard against are:

1. The belief proclaims the underlying theory of human nature;

2. The belief is the ultimate concern of the group; and

3. There are formal external signs, such as ceremonies or services, and attempts to proselytize those associated with the group are made.[12]

Groups such as Transcendental Meditation, Secular Humanism, Scientology, and Ethical Culture have been included by the court in the growing constitutional definition of religion. Such groups may not be sponsored nor encouraged by public schools.

A six-guideline brochure on "Religion in the Public School Curriculum" was compiled and disseminated by a coalition of fourteen organizations. They advance the following:

1. The school's approach is academic, not devotional.

2. The school may strive for student awareness of religion but should not press for student acceptance of any one religion.

---

[11]*Lemon v. Kurtzman,* 403 U.S. 602 (1971).

[12]*Malnak v. Yogi,* 592 F.2d 197 (3d Cir. 1979).

3. The school may sponsor study about religion but may not sponsor the practice of religion.

4. The school may expose students to a diversity of religious views but may not impose any particular view.

5. The school may educate about all religions but may not promote or denigrate any religion.

6. The school may inform the student about various beliefs but should not seek to conform the student to any particular belief.[13]

Court decisions have addressed the issue of whether exposure to religiously objectionable TEXTBOOK materials was an infringement on the right to freely exercise one's religion. One court rejected parents' complaints that forty-four textbooks were "anti-Christian" and advanced the religion of Secular Humanism.[14] The court held that the textbooks' omissions of religious influences in history did not convey a message that the government favored Secular Humanism over other religious views.

Another court upheld a SCHOOL BOARD's refusal to excuse students from required readings and discussions.[15] The court noted that students were not required to believe in the material but only to read and discuss the readings. One concurring judge found that the state's interest in having a uniform CURRICULUM and the administrative burdens inherent in exempting students from classes outweighed the possible free exercise violations.

Even though there are restrictions toward religion, the Untied States Supreme Court has shown more tolerance toward religious activities and has indicated that individual state constitutions may be more restrictive or more lenient depending on local interpretations. In 1990, the Court ruled that religious student groups may meet on school grounds during non-instructional time and that to deny access to the schools violated the Equal Access Act under 20 USC Sections 4071-4074.[16]

See also COMPULSORY EDUCATION; CONSTITUTIONAL LAW; SEX EDUCATION.

REMEDIES

See DAMAGES; REINSTATEMENT.

---

[13]*School Board News,* June 22, 1988.

[14]*Smith v. Board of School Com'rs.,* 827 F.2d 684 (11th Cir. 1987).

[15]*Mozert v. Hawkins County Board of Educ.,* 827 F.2d 1058 (6th Cir. 1987), *cert. denied,* 108 S. Ct. 1029 (1988).

[16]*Board of Education of the Westside Community Schools v. Mergens,* 58 L.W. 4720 (1990).

REMOVAL FROM OFFICE

Board Member

Once a person has been appointed or elected to office, he or she does not automatically remain in the office without some limitations being imposed. SCHOOL BOARD members may be removed for such things as a CONFLICT OF INTEREST, misappropriation of FUNDS, neglect of duty, and failure to perform the duties of his or her office. In some states, the grounds for removal are designated by STATUTE and certain procedures for removal are specified. In these instances, the statutory grounds must exist and the procedures must be followed or any attempted removal will be invalid.

In some instances, board members request or are asked to resign. Generally, a resignation cannot be implied by the conduct of the board member. That is, if a board member does not attend any meetings, his or her resignation will not be implied; but there will be grounds for legally removing the member. If a board member does resign, the resignation becomes effective when it is formally accepted. There is some authority to the effect that the resignation does not become effective until a replacement is elected and qualified, but such a situation exists in only a small minority of the states.

County Superintendent

A county superintendent may be removed for the same reasons as a school board member unless that county superintendent is protected by a CONTRACT with the local board. In addition, it has been held that a county superintendent may be removed for committing crimes involving MORAL TURPITUDE. Immorality has been ruled to be unconstitutionally vague in some cases, but it is clear that the commission of a FELONY constitutes grounds for removal. (See PRIVACY.)

If there are statutes listing the causes and procedures for removal, these statutes must be followed explicitly. Furthermore, there are statutes which prohibit certain types of conduct and prescribe that any violation means that the superintendent automatically vacates the position. In that case, once it has been proven that there is a violation, the position is vacated. The board of education, however, cannot make that determination. The issue must be decided by the COURTS, and the superintendent is entitled to DUE PROCESS and fundamental fairness.

State Superintendent

Whether a state superintendent is elected or appointed, the fact is clear that he or she can be removed for misconduct in office or failure to perform his or her duties. Generally, there is a QUO WARRANTO hearing, and the state is the PLAINTIFF or the party having proper standing to bring the cause of action. Of course, there is a right to due process, and a removal in this instance would be before a court and generally not before an ADMINISTRATIVE AGENCY.

RENEWALS, Contract

Teaching CONTRACTS are subject to renewal or NONRENEWAL when the initial term of the contract has expired. Employment contracts may be terminated for any reason other than constitutionally impermissible reasons such as DISCRIMINATION. Nonrenewal of a nontenured teacher does not require explanations or protection unless impairment of a protected "property" or "liberty" interest can be shown. The mere expectancy of being rehired does not create a property right.

The renewal procedure is to be followed strictly, especially when there is some question as to whether the teacher or administrator is to be rehired. Most state STATUTES set out notification requirements, and the local board and the teacher or administrator must adhere to DUE PROCESS procedures. In addition to the board having to follow statutory procedures and their own bylaws in delivering notice of RENEWAL or nonrenewal of a contract on or before a specified date prior to expiration, the teacher or administrator must follow proper procedures in accepting the new contract. The acceptance of the contract must be clear and unambiguous. If the statute says the educator must accept in writing, oral acceptance will not be binding. If the statute says the educator must accept by writing to the SUPERINTENDENT, then writing to the PRINCIPAL is not enough. The law assumes that the employee knows the proper procedures for acceptance. As a result, teachers and administrators have a duty to familiarize themselves with the proper procedures and act accordingly.

Established deadlines for notice and receipt are critical. Reemployment of a teacher for another year or even TENURE is granted if the timeliness of nonrenewal notices is missed.[17] Depending on the statute,

---

[17]*Matthiessen v. N. Chicago Comm. H.S. Dist.*, 857 F.2d 404 (7th Cir. 1988); *Lipka v. Brown City Community Schools*, 271 N.W.2d 771 (Mich. 1978).

nonrenewals mailed just before the deadline but not received by the set date were held insufficient notice by the COURTS.[18]

It is important for the educator to understand his or her employment status when each renewal period arrives. For example, in Ohio, statutory provisions dictated that a teacher who had a provisional certificate was not considered a substitute teacher. Rather, the teacher was entitled to automatic renewal for the succeeding school year when the board failed to notify the teacher prior to April 30 of the board's intention not to reemploy the teacher. However, because the teacher accepted a one-month teaching contract which stated clearly and unequivocally that the teaching position was to be eliminated at the end of the term by reason of lack of funding, the court held that the teacher waived his right to automatic renewal.[19]

Many people are concerned with so-called "letters of intent." These letters generally state that the district "intends" to rehire the teacher or administrator and then asks that he or she write a reply as to whether he or she will accept the position for another term. The letters of intent simply help the district project into the future. The letter says that the contract is forthcoming but is held up generally due to negotiations or budget approval. If the teacher or administrator replies that he or she intends to accept, the acceptance becomes binding on the board. That is, once the final contracts are issued, the contracts must be sent to those who have been accepted on the basis of the letters of intent.

Although the contracts must be issued by the board to the teachers and administrators pursuant to the letters of intent, final acceptance on the part of the teachers or administrators is not mandatory. Intent to accept based upon the letter of intent is tentative. The tentative acceptance is "subject to" the approval of final terms of the contract. If the budget is not approved and salaries are lowered as a result or if negotiations are not satisfactorily settled, the teacher or administrator may ignore his or her tentative acceptance and reject the contract offer.

Rather than send out letters of intent, some districts have the contracts signed prior to budget approval. If the budget fails, salaries as stated on the contract may have to be lowered. Generally, a party to a contract may not unilaterally change the terms of the contract after it has been signed. However, in this case, the courts imply that the board has the right to lower the salary stated on the contract, but the board may not lower the salary below what the teacher or administrator had received the previous year. If the contract has been negotiated pursuant to a COLLECTIVE BARGAINING law, the board may not act unilaterally in changing the contract terms. Such a law generally provides for a reopening of negotiations upon the request of either party where the legislative body or voters

---

[18]*Andrews v. Howard,* 291 S.E.2d 541 (Ga. 1982).

[19]*State v. Cincinnati Board of Educ.,* 411 N.E.2d 833 (Ohio App. 1979).

fail to provide sufficient funding to allow for compliance with the contract terms. Also, if, due to the budget rejection, the contract terms (salary) are changed, the teacher or administrator may choose to either accept or reject the new contract. This same option is not open to the board because the board is the party which is changing the contract terms. As soon as the teacher or administrator makes final acceptance, the contract becomes binding upon both parties.

Delays in issuing contracts are not unusual. There can be problems, however, when the contracts are not actually issued until school has finished for the preceding year and the summer session has begun. Many times, teachers and administrators are out of town during these months; it is quite possible that the educators would not discover the final issuance and, thus, would be unable to fulfill the teacher's or administrator's responsibility to accept within a stated or reasonable period of time. If this is the case, the teacher or administrator should notify the board of his or her final acceptance prior to leaving town. This protects the teacher or administrator and facilitates the local board's needs at the same time.

See also CONTINUING CONTRACTS; PROBATIONARY TEACHERS.

REORGANIZATION

School reorganization is synonymous with such terms as "consolidation," "annexation," and "merger." Reorganization basically means that the boundaries of a school district are changed or the organizational structure is altered in some manner. The extent of power to reorganize and the delegation of this authority has caused some difficulty in the past.

Although the STATE BOARD OF EDUCATION and local SCHOOL BOARDS share responsibilities in the management and operation of the schools, the ultimate authority to determine school district composition rests with the state legislature. This means that the state legislature may decide to create or abolish any school district without the consent of the citizens within that district.[20] The decision as to whether the boundaries of a school district should be changed is a DISCRETIONARY ACT, and the exercise of that discretion will be upheld by the COURTS as long as the decision is based on some rational purpose consistent with the best interests of the state in providing a sound education for its children.

Many difficulties can arise in the reorganization process. Although a district may be reorganized, the reorganization may not impair contractual obligations of the existing district. Article I, Section 10, of the United States

---

[20]*School Dist. No. 46 v. City of Bellevue,* 400 N.W.2d 229 (Neb. 1987).

Constitution provides that no law shall be enacted which impairs the rights of parties under preexisting contractual obligations. If a district is annexed to and becomes a part of a larger district, the first district does not totally disappear and become "one" with the second district. Even though the first district is no longer in existence per se, the district remains liable for the debts and contractual obligations previously owed. Therefore, educators' CONTRACTS would have to be honored; BONDS would have to be paid; and any obligations would continue. However, if all of the assets are delivered to the annexing district by the old district, there are no sources from which to draw. Therefore, state STATUTES have been enacted wherein the law provides that the second district incurs the debts of the former. These statutes are uniformly upheld unless there are state constitutional provisions stating that no indebtedness will be incurred by a school district without the vote of the people. In this type of situation, the district should not be annexed without first providing for paying all debts. If such payment is not made, the annexation would be unconstitutional in that it would impair preexisting contractual obligations.

The legislature may delegate administrative authority to the state board of education and to local school boards. However, when such authority is delegated, there must be some standards and guidelines defining the parameters or limits of the power given to the delegated authority. This means that the delegated authority should know what facts it should take into consideration, the purpose for its creation, and the policies it may adopt.

In addition to the need for standards and guidelines, problems arise with respect to such things as selection of the school site, PROPERTY valuation, computing indebtedness, and dissolution of school districts. First of all, the selection of the school site is discretionary unless the state statute says that the school site shall be within a central location or located on a public road, for example. If the statute is silent as to school site selection, only the legislative guidelines and standards must be followed, in addition to good faith.

With regard to property valuation and incurrence of indebtedness, there are basically two limitations. The first limitation is that the district shall not be indebted in excess of a certain statutory percentage when compared with the value of the property within the district. Except for tax-exempt property, all real property (land and buildings) will be included for valuation purposes. Some personal property is also includable, depending on state statutes with respect to taxation.

The second limitation is that a school district may not incur liabilities in excess of the revenue expected within the ensuing year. This means that the district cannot become indebted, using as collateral expected earnings within the distant future. If it does so, the debts would be void as to the district; but there is a possibility that individual board members could be personally liable. The expectation of earnings in the immediate future should be reasonable; and, if the revenue expected does not materialize,the indebtedness would be valid nevertheless. All districts are not bound by these limitations, but there may exist other limitations depending upon the state in which the district is located. If the limitation is reasonable, then, of course, it must be followed.

Once a district is dissolved and becomes part of another, questions might arise as to the extent of the authority of the district's officers to act and where the ownership of the district's assets goes. It is clear that the new district acquires title to the assets of the old, and the electorate in the old district automatically become voters in the new. The officers of the old district lose their authority to act, and the officers of the new district take over the responsibilities of managing and operating the new one.

RESCISSION

See CONTRACTS.

RESIDENCE, Students

Residence is the person's actual physical place of abode. Domicile, on the other hand, is where a person intends to remain indefinitely. A person may have many residences, but he or she may have only one domicile in most instances.

At COMMON LAW, a child's domicile followed that of his or her father. Even though the child might be living with his or her mother in New Jersey, if the father lived in California, the child would be domiciled in California. This has changed, and today a child's domicile follows that of his or her legal guardian. If the child is emancipated, domicile is where the child intends to remain indefinitely.

The basis of student residence requirements within the district's boundaries are within the state's legitimate objectives of preserving the school districts' financial integrity and not burdening taxpayers with the expense of educating nonresidents. When a child is physically living in a district with the intention of remaining, he or she is entitled to attend public schools TUITION-free.

With the increase in the population of homeless students, questions arise concerning the education of these students. The Homeless Assistance

Act of 1987[21] defines a homeless individual as one who does not have a regular or adequate nighttime residence or whose primary nighttime residence is a supervised public shelter. The Act directs each state to adopt a plan providing for the education of homeless children within its borders. The plan must include procedures for the resolution of disputes regarding the placement of homeless students.

Whether a school-age youth may attend a school in a district other than his place of residence depends on varying state STATUTES. Generally, the states say that this decision is DISCRETIONARY and that admission is mandatory only where a nonresident does not have proper facilities within his or her own school district.

School districts which receive federal "impact aid" to compensate districts for pupils associated with tax-exempt federal property (e.g., military bases) receive this aid on a factual condition to not change these nonresidents tuition.[22] Minors who live apart from their parents for the primary purpose of tuition-free admission to the school can be required to pay tuition for their education.

However, the Supreme Court of Arkansas has held that the district of residence school board must approve attendance in another district before payment of tuition or appointment of "school guardianships."[23] When families change their legal residence, students have no property right to attend public school tuition-free in their former district.[24]

In 1982, in a 5-4 vote, the United States Supreme Court ruled as unconstitutional a Texas law allowing undocumented, "illegal alien" children to attend public schools only if they paid tuition. The divided court extended many of the constitutional rights enjoyed by American citizens to families which live illegally in the United States by requiring that states must provide free public education to innocent children of illegal aliens.[25] Although the decision was hailed by some as a tremendous civil rights victory, it should be noted that some states were not affected by the decision as they already had laws requiring that school districts provide free education to anyone residing within their boundaries.

---

[21]42 U.S.C. Section 11302.

[22]*United States v. Onslow County Board of Education*, 728 F.2d 628 (4th Cir. 1984).

[23]*Delta Special School District No. 5 v. McGehee Special School District No. 17*, 659 S.W.2d 508 (Ark. 1983).

[24]*Daniels v. Morris*, 746 F.2d 271 (5th Cir. 1984).

[25]*Plyler v. Doe*, 457 U.S. 202 (1982).

RESIDENCE, Teachers

Claiming a violation of the EQUAL PROTECTION clause, many educators in the 1970s challenged the legitimacy of a residency requirement to live in the school district where one is employed. COURTS consistently uphold residency policies as constitutionally acceptable if residency restrictions pass the "rational interest test." Some studies have concluded that the state's compelling interests and purposes are supported with district residency of educators because the teachers and administrators have a better understanding of the community, tend to be more involved in community activities; and, therefore, tend to support increased tax levies in support of education.[26]

The United States Supreme Court's opinion of the residency issue upheld the constitutionality of a Philadelphia ordinance requiring city employees such as firemen to be residents of the city.[27] The court distinguished a requirement of residency "prior to employment" from a continuing residency requirement "after employment." The court decided that a continuing residency requirement, if appropriately defined and uniformly applied, does not violate an individual's constitutional rights.

On the other hand, the court has confirmed in several cases that "prior resident requirements" for conferring certain benefits or employment preference violate the equal protection clause and the constitutional right to travel.[28]

RULES

The state legislature delegates the responsibility of education to a state agency generally called the STATE BOARD OF EDUCATION. This agency is

---

[26]*Wardwell v. Board of Education of the City School District of Cincinnati*, 529 F.2d 625 (6th Cir. 1976). *See also, Meyers v. Newport Consolidated Joint School District*, 639 P.2d 853 (Wash. App. 1982). *But see, Angwin v. City of Manchester*, 386 A.2d 1272 (N.H. 1978) (Finding no "public interest which is important enough to justify the restriction on the private right," the court invalidated a school district's residency requirement.).

[27]*McCarthy v. Philadelphia Civil Service Commission*, 424 U.S. 645 (1976).

[28]*Attorney General of New York v. Soto-Lopez*, 476 U.S. 898 (1986); *Hooper v. Bernalillo County Assessor*, 472 U.S. 612 (1985); *Zobel v. Williams*, 457 U.S. 55 (1982).

directly responsible to the legislature but acts with a great deal of discretion. This agency, in turn, delegates some of its responsibilities to local SCHOOL BOARDS. Of course, the State Board of Education sets out minimum standards and RULES under which the local boards must operate. Generally, these standards are flexible and enable local boards to choose between a wide range of alternatives. The state board controls the local boards; that is, local boards cannot make any rule which contravenes rules set out by the state legislature or by the State Board of Education. As a rule, the State Board of Education retains authority (in a general way and sometimes specifically) over such things as TEXTBOOKS, basic CURRICULUM, and evaluation of local districts.

Just as the state may make up rules, local boards may do the same thing in relation to their delegated duties. Lawful local school board rules (those which are not in conflict with the state laws or state board rules) control the operation of the local schools, and school administrators and teachers are obligated to follow these rules. Generally, the rules of the local board must be clearly set out in a published handbook of school board policies. The rules must be reasonable and within the scope of the board's authority. The rules must be properly adopted and published and cannot conflict with constitutional or contractual rights of the people whom the rules are directed to govern.

As a general guide rule, the minimum standards of fairness in student disciplinary actions generally require the following:

1. School rules must be fair, not ambiguous, and must reasonably relate to the educational purposes of the school.
2. Students must be informed of rules affecting them and for which students may be disciplined.
3. Rules must be specific enough so students can understand what they may or may not do.
4. Where "serious disciplinary punishment" is involved, certain required minimum procedures must be complied with. (See EXPULSION; SUSPENSION.)

It must be recognized that a court determination of whether a school rule, infringing to some degree on an individual's liberty, violates the substantive requirements of DUE PROCESS will be determined in a narrow way. The COURTS will not rule on the wisdom or expediency of the rule: instead, the courts will question only two things:

1. Whether the rule deals with a matter of legitimate state interest; and
2. Whether the rule is reasonable.

Rules deal with a matter of legitimate state interest when rules are necessary to protect:

1. The *health* of the students;
2. The *safety* of the students;
3. The *welfare* of the students; or
4. The school from a material and substantial disruption of order and efficiency in the operation of the school.

Rules are reasonable if the rules have a rational basis and reasonable connection in fulfilling the legitimate state interest. Even though the rule may be harsh or inequitable, that does not necessarily make the rule invalid. However, if the rule is in violation of the students' constitutional rights, the school will have to meet a substantial burden of justifying that the rule is necessary to promote the efficient operation of the school. In addition, reasonableness of a rule must be considered in light of:

1. Possible alternatives (for example, to promote safety around shop class equipment, a hairnet may work as well as a haircut);
2. Seriousness of the punishment (for example, a rule denying an unmarried PREGNANT STUDENT the right to attend school could only be upheld where a very compelling state interest can be shown);
3. Consistency of application (for example, if the rule is only haphazardly enforced, it will be seen as arbitrary and unreasonable); and
4. EQUAL PROTECTION (that is, if the rule applies only to certain classes of individuals, the distinction must reasonably relate to the purpose for which the classification was made).

The question frequently is asked, "Does the student have a right to *notice* of existence of the rule, and must the rule be in *writing?*" Generally, the law is that a student must be notified that certain conduct is prohibited, at least when the rule infringes on the student's constitutional rights. However, the courts do not choose to bind school officials to take disciplinary action based only on written rules because the courts recognize that school officials cannot possibly anticipate all of the possible kinds of student action. As one court stated:

> [W]e would not wish to see school officials unable to take appropriate action in facing a problem of discipline or distraction simply because there was no pre-existing rule on the books.[29]

---

[29]*Richards v. Thurston*, 424 F.2d 1281 (1st Cir. 1970).

Of course, such authority is not limitless. The imposition of SANC-TIONS without a specific promulgated rule might be constitutionally deficient under certain circumstances as students are entitled to public education as a property interest protected by DUE PROCESS.[30]

Teachers and administrators have the authority to make up rules as long as the rules do not conflict with the rules of the state or the local school board. As one court has said:

> Among the things a student is supposed to learn at school…is a sense of discipline. Of course, rules cannot be made by authorities for the sake of making them but they should possess considerable leeway in promulgating regulations for the proper conduct of students. Courts should uphold them where there is any rational basis for the questioned rule. All that is necessary is a reasonable connection of the rule with the proper operation of the schools. By accepting an education at public expense pupils at the elementary or high school level subject themselves to considerable discretion on the part of school authorities as to the manner in which they depart themselves. Those who run public schools should be the judges in such matters, not the courts. The quicker judges get out of the business of running schools the better…Except in extreme cases the judgment of school officials should be final in applying a regulation to an individual case.[31]

As the court mentions, the rules of the teacher or administrator must be reasonable and within the scope of the educator's authority. The thing to remember is that not only must the rules be for an educational purpose, but the rules must be:

1. Communicated; and
2. Enforced.

The three main duties of a teacher involve INSTRUCTION, SUPERVISION, and safety. In order to carry out these duties, it is implied that the teacher may make up rules and may enforce the rules. Rules should be clear and concise and ones that the student can readily understand. The rules must be communicated to the student, and the rules must be enforced. There are certain areas wherein these guidelines are especially important. Many teachers are sued and held liable for simply not having enforced rules regarding the health and safety of their students. It has been held that a teacher should have safety rules in vocational classes, when the teacher is absent from the classroom, and when large crowds of students are gathered. Remember, the rules must be reasonable and lawful, and the rules cannot conflict with the student's constitutional rights.

---

[30]*Clements v. Board of Trustees of Sheridan City School District No. 2,* 585 P.2d 197 (Wyo. 1978).

[31]*Stevenson v. Wheeler County Board of Education,* 306 F. Supp. 97 (S.D. Ga. 1969).

S

SABBATICAL LEAVE

Sabbatical leave is a LEAVE OF ABSENCE granted to a teacher or administrator for rest, travel, or research without the leave affecting the teacher's or administrator's CONTRACT rights or TENURE status. There is a strong public policy in favor of granting sabbatical leave since teacher enrichment benefits the district. However, such leaves are granted at the discretion of local SCHOOL BOARDS. This DISCRETIONARY ACT is proper so long as arbitrary decisions are not made, and there are some standards or criteria used to determine when such a leave shall be granted. Generally, the person involved must have been with the district a number of years. Furthermore, the purpose of the leave normally must be related to the teacher's or administrator's function within the school. The leaves are limited in number; but, if one meets all the statutory requirements for mandatory leave, the rights to a sabbatical should be granted.[1] When the person returns, he or she should return to the same or a higher position depending on the credit authorization of each school district's salary schedule. There are time limitations during which appeals of the school board's reassignment must be brought or the claim is lost.[2]

SAFE PLACE STATUTES

So-called "safe place" STATUTES have been enacted in many states to partially combat the inequities of GOVERNMENTAL IMMUNITY. These

---

[1] *United School District v. Rushin*, 525 A.2d 868 (Pa. 1987).

[2] *Haynes v. Seattle School District No. 1*, 758 P.2d 7 (Wash. 1988).

statutes simply state that it is the duty of persons owning public BUILD-INGS to make those buildings safe to visit and to work in. The statutes require insurance to be carried so that, when an injury does occur due to an unsafe condition in the building, the injury will not go totally uncompensated.

SALARY SCHEDULES

Local SCHOOL BOARDS have the IMPLIED AUTHORITY to set the salaries of the educators they employ. Most districts have salary schedules. However, some states have state salary schedules which may be supplemented by local board enhancements. Salary schedules may be altered or amended within a narrow scope of school board discretion unless such action is prohibited within adopted school board policies, state STATUTES, or a part of the teachers' or administrators' CONTRACTS. Without an express provision in the contract, the salary schedules are not a part of the board's contractual obligations.

It is possible for a local school district to adopt a salary schedule that will incrementally raise the salaries of some employees and decrease the salaries of others. However, such a decision must be based on reasonable classifications and uniformity of treatment of those having like training and experience and performance of similar services.[3] Differentiations in salary must be reasonably specific and relevant. Increasing salaries for persons with postgraduate degrees from accredited schools is deemed a reasonable policy necessary to attract quality instructors.

Typically, school districts designate base salaries according to levels of experience and training. Disputes often center on the appropriate placement of the individual employee on the salary schedule. For example, a former teacher left the state of New York for a few years. Upon her return, she was reemployed by the same school district and placed at the same salary schedule she was at when she left. The district did not give her credit for experience gained elsewhere. She argued that there was no rational basis for the policy that placed her at the same point on the salary schedule. However, the court rejected her argument, stating that such policy served to attract qualified teachers and to discourage equally qualified teachers from leaving.[4]

See also MERIT PAY.

---

[3]*United Teachers of Ukiah v. Board of Education*, 251 Cal. Rptr. 499 (Cal. App. 1988).

[4]*Mandell v. Board of Education of the City of New York*, 411 N.Y.S.2d 827 (N.Y. 1978).

SANCTIONS

Sanctions, against a group or individual, are punitive acts intended to punish a party for a position or action taken or to get one's demands met. Penalties may include fines, dismissal, DECERTIFICATION, and loss of benefits and privileges.

See COLLECTIVE BARGAINING; MEET AND CONFER BARGAINING LAWS; STRIKES.

SAVE–HARMLESS STATUTES

Save-harmless statutes have been enacted in many states and will be enacted in more states as time passes. For those states which have waived GOVERNMENTAL IMMUNITY, save-harmless statutes simply say that, if a teacher or administrator is sued for acts done within the scope of his or her duty, the school district will "save" the teacher or administrator and will hold the teacher or administrator "harmless." Thus, the employee will not be held personally liable, though DAMAGES can still be recovered from the school district.

Some statutes state that school districts *must* save the teacher or administrator harmless. The laws of other states leave the decision to the discretion of the local school district. If such a decision is a DISCRETIONARY ACT, teachers and administrators should negotiate that the discretion be eliminated by adopted school board policies to that effect.

SCHOOL BOARDS

Structure

The local school board generally is made up of lay members of the community who are elected by the people within the school district. However, in some instances, members are appointed by the mayor or city council.

Education is a nonpartisan commitment, and school board elections are handled accordingly. Most state laws require that members of the school board must be able to read and write and must live in the community in which they are a member. No board member may have personal business dealings with the board without a full disclosure (some statutes say not at all), and no person may become a member if membership will create a CONFLICT OF INTEREST. (See ADMINISTRATIVE AGENCIES; REMOVAL FROM OFFICE; STRUCTURE OF THE SCHOOL SYSTEM.)

Code of Conduct

A typical code of conduct prescribing what a good school board member should do is as follows:

A CODE OF CONDUCT

A School Board Member Should:

Understand that his or her basic function is "policy making" and not "administrative."

Discourage subcommittees of the Board that tend to nullify the board's policy-making responsibility.

Refuse to "play politics" in either the traditional partisan sense, or in any petty sense.

Respect the rights of school patrons to be heard at official meetings.

Recognize that authority rests with the Board only in *official* meetings.

Recognize that he or she has no legal status to act for that Board outside of official meetings.

Refuse to participate in "secret" or "star chamber" meetings, or other irregular meetings which are not official and which all members do not have the opportunity to attend.

Refuse to make commitments on any matter which should properly come before the Board as a whole.

Make decisions only after all available facts bearing on a question have been presented and discussed.

Respect the opinion of others and graciously accept the principle of "majority rule" in board decisions.

Recognize that the superintendent should have full administrative authority for properly discharging his or her professional duties within limits of established board policy.

Act only after hearing the recommendations of the superintendent in matters of employment or dismissal of school personnel at an official meeting.

Recognize that the superintendent is the educational advisor to the board and should be present at all meetings of the board except when his or her contract and salary are under consideration.

Refer all complaints or problems to the proper administrative office and discuss them only at a regular meeting after failure of administrative solution.

Present personal criticisms of any school operation directly to the superintendent, rather than to school personnel.

Insist that all school business transactions be on an ethical and above board basis.

Refuse to use his or her position on a school board in any way, whatsoever, for personal gain or for personal prestige.

Refuse to bring personal problems into Board considerations.

Advocate honest and accurate evaluation of all past employees when such information is requested by another school district. (See DEFAMATION; PERSONNEL RECORDS.)

Give the staff the respect and consideration due to skilled, professional personnel.

Meetings

MEETINGS of the board are very important. During board meetings, policy is adopted and decisions for school operations are made. Only at a meeting does the school board exist or have power. If the meeting is convened improperly, if proper procedures are not adhered to, or if a decision is made outside of a meeting, any action taken is without legal authority or effect. Various states have specific laws regulating the manner of calling and conducting local board meetings. These laws must be strictly followed. In some places, board policy regulates the meetings, and these policies must also be followed. For example, if state law says that meetings shall take place within the school district, any meeting held outside the school district is invalid. However, there is a possibility that decisions made at an invalid meeting may be ratified at a later, properly convened meeting. (See RATIFICATION).

Meetings of the board are generally held on regularly scheduled dates. The meeting is public, and people have a right to hear most of the board's discussion and to discuss the public concerns with the board members. Generally, an agenda is prepared in advance of a regular meeting and should be available to school personnel and members of the public. The agenda should be followed closely and should provide for time in which to discuss old business, new business, and ordinary concerns of private individuals. Although members of the public have a right to express personal views, the public has no right to prohibit a school board's DISCRETIONARY ACTS.

Assuming that the agenda has been properly prepared, the meeting should follow ordinary parliamentary procedure. The meeting should be properly convened with a QUORUM present. Most states say that decisions may be made by a majority of the quorum present and do not require a majority of the board as a whole to be present. However, this could depend on the type of decision being voted upon. If the decision is to hire a new SUPERINTENDENT or to acquire PROPERTY, it is quite possible that the law will require a majority of the whole. Either way, each board member has the right to actual or constructive notice of all meetings and should also be given an opportunity to vote on all decisions.

After a meeting of the board, minutes should be made available to the schools and to the public. The minutes constitute the official record of the board and are the main channel of communication from the board to the school personnel and the public. Decisions, policies, RULES, and general opinions of the board should be clearly stated in the minutes and distributed to those who are interested or directly involved. These minutes are supposed to be public and open to public inspection at reasonable times. Because of their public nature, no secret decisions or policies should be adopted by the board. Such policies would have no legal effect and would be evidence that the action constituted ARBITRARY, CAPRICIOUS, OR DISCRIMINATORY ACTION.

In addition to "regular meetings" of the board, there are times when the board will have a "special meeting" or will call for an "executive session." A special meeting is simply a meeting that is not regularly scheduled and is generally held for a special purpose. A special meeting has all of the legal effect of a regular meeting; once convened, the meeting must follow the same adopted procedures of regular meetings. There must be notice of the meeting, and the meeting must be in public. The special meeting should also follow any other regulations required by statute or local board or state board policy.

A special meeting is not an "executive session." An executive session is a private conference between members of the board. This conference is not public and is restrictive in its purpose. Executive sessions are supposed to be for matters involving PROPERTY ACQUISITION and personnel hiring or dismissal. The public does not have a right to know what transpires in a properly convened executive session, but the public does have a right to know what the board members' opinions are in matters unrelated to property or personnel. These opinions should not be hidden under the cloak of an executive session. However, *decisions* made in an executive session have no legal effect until the decisions are adopted at a properly convened public meeting. This does not mean that the discussion leading up to a decision or even the facts relied upon in making that decision must be made public. Only the decision itself has to be made known.

Although the general rule is that the board can only bind itself when the board acts pursuant to a decision in a formal meeting, there are times when the COURTS will overlook the defect if overlooking the defect is necessary for justice and equity to result. Such action by the courts is rare, however, and such action only takes place when there is absolute good faith on the part of those involved or if an emergency absolutely requires the board to act without following necessary procedures properly.

Policies

School board policies are written statements indicating educational objectives and general methods by which these objectives are to be accomplished. Policies also include RULES for the management and control of schools. School board policies should be the primary concern of school board members. It is through their policy-making power that board members direct the educational accomplishments and goals for the children within the district. Therefore, school policy is the single most important duty of local school boards.

Since the purpose of school board policy is to give direction, it stands to reason that the board members alone should not define policy without considering the opinions of educators, students, and parents. The ultimate authority, of course, is with the board; but input from all interested groups should enhance communication and be conductive towards putting policies into practice.

Along with policy, the board makes up rules which govern the management and conduct of the schools. In adopting these rules, the local board must make certain that the rules are reasonable, are within the scope of the board's authority, are adopted according to required procedures, and are not in violation of constitutional or CONTRACT rights of those involved. If the rules violate any of these principles, they are not binding. However, in challenging an alleged unlawful rule, a person must follow appropriate GRIEVANCE procedures.

School board policies by their very nature must be communicated or made available to school personnel. It is advisable for each and every teacher and administrator to have access to a copy of school board policies. This is especially true in relation to those areas specifically directed at teachers' and administrators' duties, rights, and responsibilities. A copy of school board policies should be in the faculty lounge, in the school library, or in the main office of the school building. These written policies should not be hidden in the main administration building, nor should the policies be disorganized or difficult to read. Rules of the school board must be communicated, or they will have no binding effect.

School board policies adopted "after" a contract has been signed bind the teacher or administrator as do those adopted before the contract is signed. This is true unless the new policy goes to the very essence of the contract, thus substantially changing the contract terms, or unless it has been negotiated or adopted that the new policies will be binding only after a certain time has passed. (See CONTRACTS.)

All districts must follow the minimum standards set by the state board of education, but each district is allowed to adopt policies which are conducive to accomplishing the district's particular needs. The fact that policies differ from district to district is neither illegal nor controlling. In fact, state law may give certain districts the delegated authority to adopt policies which other districts within the state cannot adopt. For example, it is common for state laws to grant large districts more power than smaller districts in such areas as CURRICULUM, control, and management.

While the board creates school policies and steps for evaluating whether these policies are followed, the board itself does not go into the school or classroom to evaluate. This job is on the shoulders of the board's chief executive officer, the SUPERINTENDENT. The superintendent and his or her administrators carry out the executive requirements of the board and then report back to the board and make recommendations. The board then acts on these recommendations by developing policies and objectives.

All school boards should adopt policies to control action in the following areas:

1. Rules covering the procedures and conduct of school board meetings.
2. Guidelines for school personnel in relation to duties, rights, liabilities, curriculum requirements, EVALUATIONS, and grievance procedures.
3. Rules governing student conduct, rights and responsibilities, and grievance procedures.
4. Policies regarding school property, school services for the community, maintenance of school grounds, and general purchasing procedures.
5. Rules governing release of student records and PERSONNEL RECORDS (See DEFAMATION).

Authority

The authority of the local school board is delegated from the state. A local school board is a state agency and a type of quasi-MUNICIPAL CORPORATION with certain restricted duties and powers. In performing its functions, the local board has express and implied rights. Among these are the right to:

1. Enforce rules of the state and state board of education
2. Hire, dismiss, and determine the general duties of school personnel
3. Determine the curriculum of students so long as the curriculum does not fall below minimum state standards

4. Equip the district with the necessary materials for instruction

5. Adopt reasonable rules governing the operation of the schools

6. Adopt reasonable rules governing student and employee conduct

7. Enter into binding contracts

Local boards are not totally under rigid or inflexible controls of the state. The local board has the power to adopt certain TEXTBOOKS, to require certain courses of study, and to make reasonable rules in relation to instruction, SUPERVISION and safety. The local board may exercise these powers so long as (1) the state has not preempted the area, (2) the exercise of the power is reasonable and not ARBITRARY AND CAPRICIOUS, and (3) the exercise is not in violation of a person's contract or constitutional rights.

It would be nearly impossible to list each and every right or limitation of the local school board. Basically, the local board has the authority to manage and control the schools. To "manage and control" means that the local board has the authority to give direction, to define school policy, to list educational objectives, and to maintain an efficient educational system without *directly* participating in the transmission of knowledge. In other words, the local board has the power to adopt policies, but it does not have the power to implement those policies. For example, the board has the right to encourage the teaching of patriotism, but it does not have the power to enter a teacher's classroom to observe his or her methods and effectiveness. The local school board may adopt reasonable rules, but the administration and implementation of these rules is the responsibility of teachers and administrators.

Discretion

In exercising their EXPRESS or IMPLIED AUTHORITY, local boards have a great deal of discretion. So long as DISCRETIONARY ACTS are not abused, the board or its members will not be subject to LIABILITY nor will the board or its members be subject to judicial reversals of board decisions. It should be noted that the COURTS distinguish between the "power" of the board and the "discretionary" exercise of that power. If the board does not have the "power" to do something, that decision will automatically be reversed by the courts. However, if the local board does have the power, the court will only look to see if the power was abused by an arbitrary or unreasonable action. This would be a QUESTION OF LAW, not a QUESTION OF FACT. If it is not clear whether the board has the "power," there will be a rebuttable "PRESUMPTION" against such power. On the other hand, if the board does have the power, there is a presumption that the discretion has not been abused; the court will only look to see if the board's action was arbitrary or unreasonable. The problem lies in attempting to determine what constitutes an abuse of discretion. This can be partially solved by saying that, so long as the board acts in good faith, has afforded the parties involved fundamental fairness or DUE PROCESS, and has acted pursuant to relevant standards, the board's actions will not amount to an abuse of discretion.

The courts are generally reluctant to interfere with local school board decisions. Even if the court does look into a board decision, the court will seldom reverse that decision if the decision is based upon some reliable evidence and is not discriminatory in nature. However, if the decision is not within the scope of the local board's power, if the decision is unconsitutional, or if there is no evidence on which to base the decision, the court will not let the decision stand. Therefore, decisions must be analyzed objectively and should not be based on personal bias or opinion.

Liability

In talking about school board liability, it is necessary to talk about the possible liability of individual members of the board. The local board is liable for the contracts properly entered into and any other legal acts granted to the board by statute. Because the board is an entity created by the state, there may be restrictions on how much contractual liability the local board may incur. Furthermore, state STATUTES or local policies require that specific procedures must be followed if the board is to be bound by various contracts.

Many problems arise wherein a private party contracts with an individual member of the local board, thinking he or she is contracting with the board itself. The board may only act as a whole. Individual members cannot bind the board unless the board ratifies the actions taken. When one board member attempts to bind the board, there will generally be no remedy against the board itself. The general rule is that an individual contracting with the board has a COMMON LAW duty to inquire into the extent of the board's authority. This duty also requires that an individual must inquire into the extent of a board member's power to bind the board as a whole. Therefore, if inquiry is not made and the board or a board member exceeds proper authority, any contract made is voidable.

Individual board members seldom incur personal liability for actions done or not done by the board. The board member is fulfilling a public function and is shielded by the corporate veil of the board as a whole in addition to GOVERNMENTAL IMMUNITY statutes. Again, if a person is dealing with an individual board member, he or she is under the duty to inquire into that member's authority. As a result, even if a board member exceeds his or her authority, there will generally be no personal liability unless the acts are gross, indicate bad faith, or are fraudulent or misrepresentative in nature.

See also QUO WARRANTO; RATIFICATION; REMOVAL FROM OFFICE.

SCHOOL BUILDINGS

See BONDS; BUILDINGS; PROPERTY.

SCHOOL CALENDAR

The adoption of a school calendar is generally within the discretion of the local SCHOOL BOARD. However, if there are state STATUTES or state board of education RULES governing the school calendar, these rules must be followed. Minimum requirements relating to the required number of teaching days are often prescribed by statute or state board rules. These requirements must be met if the school district is going to be eligible for state funds. However, in emergency situations, the state board has the power to waive these requirements. These minimum requirements may be exceeded by local school districts.

Questions frequently arise when the ordinary termination date for school is extended to make up for class days which were missed during the year due to inclement weather or some other circumstance. Teachers and administrators may be compelled to remain for the extended period so long as that period is not unreasonable. This would depend upon the facts and circumstances. An extension of one or possibly two weeks is ordinarily not considered to be unreasonable. Beyond two weeks, authority to extend the year further seems questionable and may possibly be in breach of the teachers' or administrators' CONTRACTS. This problem can be solved before it ever comes into existence by spelling out the maximum termination date for school within the teachers' or administrators' contracts or within school board policies adopted by the local board. If class days have been missed due to teacher STRIKES, the school board may, in its discretion, choose to make up the lost days. However, the teachers could not force the board to do so in an effort to make up the wages lost for teaching days which were missed.

SCHOOL CLOSURES

Schools may temporarily be closed due to inclement weather, holidays, emergencies, and when there is a health or safety hazard. Generally, teachers and administrators do not have to attend school on these dates. They may, however, be expected to attend in inclement weather. If the teachers and administrators do attend, the day is counted as part of their contractual days under the SCHOOL CALENDAR. If educators do not attend, the day may be "made up" after the normal date for school closure would ordinarily expire. In fact, many states require a minimum number of school days which, if not completed, could result in the withholding of state funds to local districts.

Long-term closures due to declining enrollments, unsafe facilities, and excessive operational costs are sometimes governed by state STATUTE. A few states require voter approval while other states require public hearings. In states without specific school closure statutes, the decision to close a school rests with the SCHOOL BOARD.

SCHOOL FUNDS

See FUNDS.

SCHOOL PUBLICATIONS

A great many schools encourage and finance the publication of student newspapers or literary magazines. The United States Supreme Court in 1969 ruled for one of the first times that students are "persons"; therefore, students may be protected under the FIRST AMENDMENT freedoms of speech and press. Students are entitled to express student views in the context of public schools.[5] This major 1969 decision departed from the historical *parens patriae* power of guardianship of minors. However, school officials are not devoid of all authority to regulate student speech. Students' First Amendment rights "are not automatically co-extensive with the rights of adults in other settings" and must be "applied in light of the

---

[5]*Tinker v. Des Moines Indep. School Dist.*, 393 U.S. 503 (1969).

special characteristics of the school environment."[6] There are pragmatic concerns regarding the need to protect impressionable students from information harmful to their psychological and emotional development and the substantial state interest in controlling conduct in schools in order to provide an atmosphere conductive to learning.

The COURTS have been split with reference to student newspapers. The Seventh Circuit unequivocally has held that any student press censorship is unconstitutional.[7] On the other hand, the Fourth Circuit held that censorship and prior restraint of speech was justified if there might be substantial disruption, promotion of illegal activities, or material interference with control of school activities.

Against this backdrop of tangled precedent, the court granted CERTIORARI in the 1988 Eighth Circuit case of *Hazelwood School Dist. v. Kuhlmeier*.[8] In this case, the school principal, in his prepublication review of a school-sponsored newspaper, deleted pages containing two articles about pregnancy and divorce that the principal found objectionable.

The United States Supreme Court ruled that "school officials were entitled to regulate contents...in any reasonable manner" because a curricular newspaper was not a "public forum." With language resounding a return to *parens patriae*, this court retreated from a more liberal view chronicled in other court opinions and held that teachers and administrators can exercise editorial control over the style and content of student speech in school-sponsored expressive activities so long as the censoring actions are reasonably related to legitimate "pedagogical" concerns.

The *Hazelwood* decision does not give school officials total control over the content and style of "underground" publications which are student-initiated and which are not part of the CURRICULUM or school supported. However, administrators do have the power to establish reasonable regulations on the time, place, and manner of distribution of student publications. These restrictions are recognized as being "conditions" on freedom of press, not "prohibitions." School officials also have the power to prohibit the students from distributing clearly obscene or libelous materials. (See DEFAMATION; OBSCENITY.)

Many faculty advisors are charged with the duty to "censor" items to be printed in school publications. Ideally, the faculty advisor should serve as an advisor to the students with regard to matters of style, grammar, format, and suitability of materials. If the material is objectionable or disruptive, the student editor and the author should be held accountable. Faculty advisors may also be accountable for objectionable or disruptive

---

[6]*Bethel School Dist. No. 403 v. Fraser*, 478 U.S. 675 (1986).

[7]*Fujishimi v. Board of Education*, 460 F.2d 1355 (7th Cir. 1972).

[8]*Hazelwood School Dist. v. Kuhlmeier*, 484 U.S. 260 (1988).

material. However, a faculty advisor may not be dismissed, demoted, removed from the advisory position, or in any other way punished for allowing the printing of materials which are constitutionally protected.

The following guide rules should be observed when a school requires prior approval of a student publication:

1. The policy should specify that the policy is applicable only to distribution of materials on school property and at school-related functions.

2. The policy should spell out clearly what kind of materials are forbidden in order to allow the student to be able to ascertain what he or she may or may not write.

3. The policy should establish a procedure for submission of materials for approval. These essential elements should be included:

   a. "Distribution" must be defined in order to make it clear that the policy is directed at a substantial distribution and not at the passage of a note, paper, or magazine from one student to another.

   b. The policy must specify to whom the material should be submitted, how the submission is to be accomplished, and who is responsible for granting or denying approval.

   c. A definite period of time should be specified for approval or disapproval of what is submitted.

   d. The policy should state that, if school officials fail to act within the period of time set, the students have the right to distribute the materials.

   e. The policy should provide for an adequate and prompt appeal procedure.

SCOPE OF BARGAINING

In the early stages of teacher negotiations, the emerging agreements were limited to items of financial compensation for teachers (salaries, increments, dental insurance, for example) summer school work payment rates, and compensation for after-school coaching positions. These are "bread and butter" items. Teachers are still quite concerned about these issues, but many persons are also demanding a say in all items with which they, as professionals, are involved. Teachers want to negotiate items such as CURRICULUM, teaching aides and materials, work load, class size, GRIEV-ANCE procedures, calendar and school days, and a stream of other concerns. The issues or subjects that are negotiable fall into one of three categories: mandatory, permissive, or prohibited.

Legislatures throughout the country are granting teachers the right to COLLECTIVE BARGAINING. Some of these bargaining laws are in the form of MEET AND CONFER legislation, and many are general in nature. One of the main things which these laws tend to have in common is that most of the laws do not specify the mandatory scope of bargaining. As a result, most states are forced to take a case-by-case decision-making approach in trying to determine the scope of negotiable issues.

The mandatory scope of bargaining modeled after the National Labor Relations Act is frequently defined as "wages, hours, and terms and conditions of employment." This is rather broad, and phrases like "conditions of employment" are loosely interpreted by employee organiztions to mean that everything is negotiable.

SCHOOL BOARDS argue, and many bargaining laws provide, that specified matters of "inherent managerial policy" are prohibited and not bargainable. A reasonable limitation on the range of bargainable education problems and policies is necessary to preserve the school board's and administrators' discretion and to prevent compromises made in haste in the heat of a bargaining battle. For example, statutory procedural protections for the dismissal of a tenured teacher cannot be altered through a collective bargaining contract. Prohibited items are beyond the board's negotiating powers. This leads back, however, to what in essence is the same question: What items are within "inherent managerial policy," that is, what is bargainable? As previously stated, most COURTS and labor/employee-management boards are determining the scope of bargaining on a case-by-case basis. The mandatory scope of bargaining has not been definitely decided since most negotiable issues contain inseparable elements of employee and management interests. The mandatory scope will depend upon the wording of the state bargaining laws and case decisions.

However, permissible bargaining is whatever is agreed to by both parties. Permissive items cannot be pursued to the point of impasse; yet, if an agreement is reached, the parties are bound. Here, it is held that the school board may negotiate with employees over all terms and conditions of employment except those which are specifically prohibited by law. In other words, the school board is free to bargain over all terms and conditions of employment and related issued unless a specific state law prevents the board from negotiating on certain matters.

SEARCH AND SEIZURE, Unreasonable

Assertive efforts of government and school officials to deal with student drug use and violence on school grounds often require the search of students and their property. Practices such as physical body searches, canine sniffing, metal detectors, drug tests, two-way mirrors, and locker, desk, and car searches generate claims of FOURTH AMENDMENT violations.

The Fourth Amendment provides in part that people have a right "to be secure in their persons, houses, papers, and effects against unreasonable searches and seizures, and no warrants shall issue, but upon probable cause...." The reasons given for upholding such searches have been:

1. School officials are not acting as governmental or police agents in conducting the searches.
2. Searches are necessary to maintain discipline, health, safety, and welfare of the students in order to provide an atmosphere conducive to learning.
3. School personnel are acting IN LOCO PARENTIS to pupils under their charge.
4. School lockers and desks are not in the exclusive possession of the student, and the student, therefore, has no reasonable expectation of PRIVACY.
5. Parents have a right to expect safeguarding of their children, and school officials have a duty to search if necessary.

The standard test for reviewing searches of individual students by school personnel was adopted by the United States Supreme Court in a 1985 New Jersey case.[9] This case involved the search of a student's purse after the student's denial of a teacher's report of SMOKING in the restroom. The assistant principal found not only cigarettes but also drug paraphernalia and marijuana in the student's purse. The court held the search to be constitutional. The United States Supreme Court adopted the standard of "reasonableness under all the circumstances." A search will be deemed reasonable if the circumstances justify the search at the search's inception and if the scope of the search was reasonable in relation to the situation.

A search will be upheld if a teacher or other school official has "reasonable grounds for suspecting that the search will turn up evidence that the student has violated or is violating either the law or the rules of the

---

[9]*New Jersey v. T.L.O.*, 469 U.S. 325 (1985).

school." The search must not be excessively intrusive in relation to the age and sex of the student and the nature of the infraction.

The "reasonableness" balancing test must be considered in all school search and seizure cases. Most COURTS have required sufficient individualized suspicion. Students should not be subjected to dragnet-type mass searches, such as police dog sniff searches or luggage searches of band members, without a particularized suspicion that contraband would be found on each student searched. As one court stated, "the state may not constitutionally use its authority to fish for evidence of wrongdoing."[10]

A federal court ruled that a strip search of an entire fifth-grade class to recover a stolen three dollars was unreasonable and unconstitutional.[11] Even with enough particularized suspicion, school authorities' degrading searches of students' bodies have been ruled "not only unlawful but outrageous."[12] Searches for evidence that could result in criminal charges which require disrobing should be conducted by law enforcement officers who are held to the full probable cause and warrant requirements of the Fourth Amendment.

Inherent in school officials' authority to manage a school is the right and duty to inspect students' desks and lockers on a regular, publicized policy basis.[13] Students have no reasonable expectation of privacy, since schools exercise control over the lockers with master keys and procedures for inspection. The Fourth Amendment protects persons, not necessarily places. School officials can intervene and give law enforcement officers consent to search school property if there is reasonable suspicion. Any contraband found there may be admissible evidence in school discipline hearings or criminal prosecutions. School officials do not have to warn students of rights (such as Miranda warnings) before interrogations or searches.[14]

School policies and procedures for conducting searches should be publicized and based on reasonable standards to ensure a safe educational environment.

See also DRUG TESTING.

---

[10]*Jones v. Latexo Independent School Dist.*, 499 F. Supp. 223 (E.D. Tex. 1980).

[11]*Bellinier v. Lund*, 438 F. Supp. 47 (N.D.N.Y. 1977).

[12]*Doe v. Renfrow*, 631 F.2d 91 (7th Cir. 1980); *Also see Tarter v. Raybuck*, 742 F.2d 977 (6th Cir. 1984); *M. M. v. Anker*, 477 F. Supp. 837 (E.D.N.Y. 1979); *Horton v. Goose Creek Independent School Dist.*, 693 F.2d 524 (5th Cir. 1982).

[13]*State v. Brooks*, 718 P.2d 837 (Wash. App. 1986); *R.D.L. v. State*, 499 So. 2d 31 (Fla. App. 1986); *Zamora v. Pomeroy*, 639 F.2d 662 (10th Cir. 1981).

[14]*People v. Corey*, 250 Cal. Rptr. 359 (Cal. App. 1988).

SEARCH WARRANT

A search warrant is a written order issued by a judge or magistrate, in the name of the state, directing an officer to search a specified house or other premises for stolen or illegal property, contraband, or evidence of illegal acts. A valid search warrant is often required as a condition precedent to a legal search and seizure.

In keeping with the FOURTH AMENDMENT, in order to obtain a search warrant, the affirming officer must show that there is probable cause to believe a crime is being or has been committed and that the evidence of that crime is at or in a particular place. Furthermore, the specific items to be seized and places to be searched must be listed with particularity or else the search warrant will be held invalid and any evidence wrongfully obtained will be inadmissible at the time of trial.

SECRET SOCIETIES

Student-initiated social organizations or secret societies have not been afforded free expression and ASSOCIATION rights in school systems. COURTS have found it educationally necessary to prohibit organizations which create disruptive divisions among students and interfere with school morale as a whole.

Secret societies as used here is meant to refer to "exclusive" social clubs which derive their membership from students of a school. These clubs may take the form of fraternities, sororities, or other groups which are not open equally to all students.

Where statutory authority is given, schools may deny recognition and prohibit membership in fraternities, sororities, or secret societies. Expelling students or prohibiting them from participating in EXTRACURRICULAR ACTIVITIES because they belong to a secret society is within the lawful discretion of the SCHOOL BOARD's authority to protect the education environment from disruption and is neither discriminatory nor in violation of the students' EQUAL PROTECTION rights.[15]

In states which do not statutorily prohibit membership in such clubs or grant regulatory authority to local school boards, the school board has the IMPLIED AUTHORITY to regulate membership in such clubs. "Special" clubs tend to promote cliques and an undemocratic notion of castes.

---

[15]*Passel v. Fort Worth Independent School Dist.*, 453 S.W.2d 888 (Tex. App. 1970).

Although many clubs and societies are allowed and encouraged by school officials, RULES assuring that participation in certain clubs is not discriminatory (perpetuating its membership by the decision of its own members rather than a free choice of qualified students) and that the groups do not interfere with the other students' rights are advisable. If exclusive clubs do have an impact detrimental to the learning environment, public school officials can legitimately restrict students' out-of-class participation in these societies.[16]

See also DISCRIMINATION.

SEGREGATION

See DISCRIMINATION.

SELF–DEFENSE

Self-defense is the defense of one's person or property from an attempted injury by another person. The law of "self-defense" authorizes a person to act when he or she is acting under a reasonable belief of immediate danger without a convenient or reasonable mode of escape. The law will allow the person to protect himself or herself to the extent necessary to prevent an aggressor's imminent use of unlawful force. One cannot protect mere property with deadly force. Once the threatened injury is prevented, the law will not protect further action or acts of aggression. When acting in justifiable self-defense, a person may not be punished criminally nor be held responsible for civil DAMAGES.

See also BATTERY.

SELF–INCRIMINATION, Students

Freedom against self-incrimination comes from the FIFTH AMENDMENT of the United States Constitution. This right is not as all-encompassing as

---

[16]*Thomas v. Board of Education, Granville Central School Dist.*, 607 F.2d 1043 (2d Cir. 1979), *cert. denied*, 444 U.S. 1081 (1980).

many people believe. There is no right to "take the Fifth" where the answers would incriminate another person; and there is no right to take the Fifth when the questions and answers are of a civil nature and do not indicate that criminal activity is involved. Also, once "immunity" has been granted, there is no right to assert Fifth Amendment rights because there can be no criminal incrimination when such a cloak of immunity has been granted. Furthermore, even if there is a right to take the Fifth Amendment, that right can be waived by "opening the door" to questions and then trying to shut it again. In other words, once a witness starts answering questions that could be incriminating, he or she must continue answering the questions because the door has been opened and cannot be closed again.

Standing *IN LOCO PARENTIS*, a school official can compel the accused to testify or punish/expel the child for not cooperating. While all COURTS will not agree on this issue, some courts have indicated that students are denied the Fifth Amendment privilege against self-incrimination at school hearings because the Fifth Amendment applies only to criminal proceedings.[17] In addition, school officials do not have to give Miranda-type warnings of rights before interrogation.[18]

Since a student's testimony before a school tribunal can also be used against the student in a criminal prosecution, some commentators maintain that children should be able to "take the Fifth" without fear of reprisal. However, some courts have held that criminally trying the student for the same offense does not constitute double jeopardy, and what was said in the school hearing can be used again in court. This is a very controversial area of law, and although federal law interpretations of the United States Constitution may not protect students, individual state courts may differ in the interpretation of state constitutions. Therefore, one should obtain competent advice before plunging into this area.

See also SILENT, Right to Remain.

SEVERANCE PAYMENTS

Severance payments are CONTRACT provisions converting accumulated and unused SICK LEAVE into a cash payment upon retirement or death. The survivability of unused accumulated sick leave to the estate of a deceased teacher or administrator may depend on the union contract

---

[17]*Nzuve v. Castleton State College*, 335 A.2d 321 (Vt. 1975).

[18]*People v. Corey*, 250 Cal. Rptr. 359 (Cal. App. 1988).

construction or state-based STATUTES, or both.[19] The formula used to compute the lump sum of these payments is to multiply the per diem rate by the number of accumulated sick-leave days.

Where severance payments have been established as a negotiable part of a contract or COLLECTIVE BARGAINING agreement for wages, hours, etc., these are not considered gifts; therefore, the board is not giving away school PROPERTY in violation of the law. Sick-leave conversion plans are of benefit to the school district because they help to:

1. Reduce employee absences;
2. Curb or eliminate abuses of sick leave;
3. Reward faithful employees; and
4. Assure school administrators of sufficient teachers on the job.

Severance payments are fringe benefits which are negotiable items under most collective bargaining laws. Agreement to pay retiring educators for unused sick leave is generally upheld as a retirement allowance.[20] School boards should be careful to provide that severance payments are available only to employees who have worked a specified number of years in the district. Contingencies such as death and dismissal should be covered. In addition, the policy should specify the maximum number of sick-leave days which may be accumulated and at what rate. Failure to do so might lead to an open-ended liability, and the COURTS might be forced to set it aside as being vague or unreasonable.

See also MEET AND CONFER BARGAINING LAWS; SCOPE OF BARGAINING.

SEX, Discrimination Based on

See ATHLETICS; CIVIL RIGHTS ACT OF 1964; CONSTITUTIONAL LAW; DISCRIMINATION; EQUAL PROTECTION; MATERNITY LEAVE; PATERNITY LEAVE; PREGNANCY DISCRIMINATION ACT; PREGNANT STUDENTS.

---

[19]*Carpenter v. School Dist. of the City of Flint*, 321 N.W.2d 772 (Mich. App. 1982).

[20]*Pa. State Educ. Ass'n. v. Baldwin Whitehall School Dist.*, 372 A.2d 960 (Pa. 1977).

SEX EDUCATION

No uniform legal rules or state policies have been adopted with regard to the controversial matter of sex education in the public schools. COURTS have consistently found that family life/human sexuality "sex education" courses present public health information that furthers legitimate educational objectives. Some legislatures have enacted legislation providing for comprehensive sex education instruction, but a few states expressly prohibit the teaching of birth control. However, for the most part, the decision of whether sex education shall be taught in the public schools rests with the state and local SCHOOL BOARDS.

Parents have objected to sex education on many grounds. Among the objections raised are that sex education:

1. Violates DUE PROCESS;
2. Prohibits parents from having a voice in selection of CURRICULUM;
3. Violates a right of PRIVACY and encroaches on RELIGION;
4. Is an unlawful assumption of power by the school board;
5. Is an abuse of board discretion; and
6. Teaches the students more about sex than their parents know and, therefore, makes it difficult for parents to "scare" their children into being "virtuous."

Other than the last assertion, the validity of these arguments is doubtful. Parents do not have any right to prohibit the teaching of sex education in the public schools. Nevertheless, parents generally do have the right to prohibit children from being compelled to take such a course. If the subject matter is a legitimate, though controversial, area of study, individuals cannot prohibit its teaching because that would constitute "an unwarranted intrusion into the authority of the public school system to control the academic curriculum."[21]

Because parents have the right to prohibit their children from being forced to take sex education, the school board and the school administrators should provide for two essential safeguards:

1. Explicit procedures for obtaining parental consent for students enrolled in sex education courses should be established with

---

[21]*Wright v. Houston I.S.D.*, 487 F.2d 1401 (5th Cir. 1973).

excusable arrangements for all or specific portions which the student or parent finds objectionable.[22]

2. Only qualified instructors who have been adequately trained in the teaching of sex education should be allowed to instruct students on this controversial subject.

If the above safeguards are provided, school boards may offer sex education instruction to the public schools. Teachers of sex education should be careful to treat this subject in an objective manner. Teachers should not try to "frighten" students, nor should teachers try to "encourage" students. When asked about his or her feelings with regard to various sexual activities, the teacher should not act as an advocate one way or the other but should present objectively both the pros and cons of controversial sex topics. Sex should not be discussed in an oppressive or degrading manner; but, when sex is relevant to the subject being taught, the teacher's constitutional right of free speech allows for him or her to discuss the necessary topics relating to sex education.

See also ACADEMIC FREEDOM; CONSTITUTIONAL LAW.

SEXUAL ABUSE

Schools may not be protected under GOVERNMENTAL IMMUNITY statutes for sexual abuse that takes place within the school. If teachers or school administrators know or should know of sexual abuse, then affirmative action must be taken or the district or educator may be found liable for NEGLIGENCE or even under Section 1983 of the CIVIL RIGHTS ACT OF 1871. In a 1989 Pennsylvania case, a district was held liable to a high school girl who had been molested by the school band director.[23] In this case, the administrators knew of prior complaints of sexual abuse and not only ignored those complaints but sought to keep the activity concealed. Obviously, the educators owed a duty of SUPERVISION, and the cloak of immunity could not protect the administrators from DAMAGES that were rightfully forthcoming.

See also CHILD ABUSE.

---

[22]*Smith v. Ricci*, 446 A.2d 501 (N.J. 1982).

[23]*Stoneking v. Bradford Area School District*, 882 F.2d 720 (3d Cir. 1989).

SHARED TIME

Shared time is often called "dual enrollment." Under the usual shared-time arrangement, a child regularly attends a parochial school for part of the school day and also attends a public school for courses not offered or available in the parochial school. The courses taken are generally those which involve expensive equipment which the parochial schools cannot afford. Also, since parochial schools tend to be academically oriented, vocational education courses are often taken in the public schools.

Shared-time arrangements have become increasingly popular and necessary in some areas of the country, because many parochial schools no longer have the financial resources to provide their students with a complete educational program. In addition, many United States Supreme Court decisions have drastically limited the kinds of public aid which may be granted to help students enrolled in religiously oriented schools. (See PRIVATE AND PAROCHIAL SCHOOL AID.)

A majority of state COURTS have held that typical shared-time arrangements are constitutionally permissible as long as the subjects the student wishes to enroll in are not available in the parochial school and as long as these arrangements are not in violation of the state constitution or STATUTES. Whether to implement them is at the local board's discretion. Although the parochial school student may be allowed to attend classes at the public school, such a student may only take classes which are available; he or she may not demand that certain courses be offered at a specific time of the day. It is the prerogative of the public school board whether to establish a shared-time program. To deny shared-time programs is not an EQUAL PROTECTION violation.[24] The PLAINTIFF's only remedy is "to elect a school board which will change the district's policy."[25]

The theory behind shared-time arrangements is that a parochial school student would normally have every right to attend the public school. Therefore, why should he or she be denied the right to attend classes which are not offered at the parochial school? However, by freeing the parochial schools from having to provide expensive classes in science, vocational education, and the like, it can be argued that the state is helping such schools remain in existence. The state has an obligation to remain neutral, and aid to or entanglement between church schools and the state is unconstitutional. When shared-time arrangements are challenged before the United States Supreme Court, the main question is: "Do these arrange-

---

[24]*Luetkemeyer v. Kaufmann*, 419 U.S. 888 (1974); *Cook v. Griffin*, 364 N.Y.S.2d 632 (N.Y. App. 1975).

[25]*Snyder v. Charlotte Public School District*, 333 N.W.2d 542 (Mich. App. 1983).

ments foster an excessive government appearance of endorsement or entanglement with religion?" If so, they are unconstitutional. If not, they are permissible. The three-pronged Lemon test is applied to this established question. In a 1985 Iowa case, the Iowa Supreme Court struck down a shared-time program on private property where the district hired private school teachers.[26] The Supreme Court's ruling in this case clearly delineated the court's position that shared time on campuses of religion-affiliated schools are unconstitutional because the programs have the effect of advancing religion and create excessive entanglement.

See also RELEASED TIME; RELIGION.

SHOP CLASSES

See VOCATIONAL PROGRAMS.

SICK LEAVE

Sick leave is a LEAVE OF ABSENCE from school which is granted with pay and without loss of position or other employment rights for a certain period of time. Sick leaves are generally made mandatory by state STATUTE or specified in COLLECTIVE BARGAINING agreements. Under most sick-leave provisions, a person is allowed a certain number of days' absence each year, but most states and local school districts allow sick-leave days to accumulate over the years by up to a certain maximum number.

Whether sick-leave days are transferrable from one district to another depends upon state statute or local board policies. Also, whether a person has a right to be paid for unused days depends again on state statute and local policies. (See SEVERANCE PAYMENTS.)

Sick-leave days are to be used when the person is sick. However, a few states have statutes which are broad enough to allow for sick leave when an immediate member of the family is sick and in need of attention. "Not feeling good," headaches, physical injuries, cramps, and colds are all valid reasons for sick leave. The school board cannot require a teacher or administrator to present a doctor's certificate as proof of each and every illness, but a doctor's certificate can be required if the absence is for an

---

[26]*Grand Rapids School District v. Ball*, 473 U.S. 373 (1985).

extended period of time or if there is a detrimental effect on the classroom.

RULES governing sick leave must be reasonable. It is unreasonable to require that a teacher or administrator be bedridden or at home in order to receive sick-leave benefits. If a teacher or administrator is seen at the grocery store during the day, that does not prove that he or she was not sick. However, if a pattern of behavior is developed, there is a possibility that it could be proved that the person was not really ill; and, if the person was not ill, he or she should not be paid for the time absent.

Under certain circumstances, should a teacher misuse his or her sick leave, it is possible that he or she could be disciplined or dismissed. In a 1980 case, a teacher was found to have twice misused her sick leave.[27] The decision, however, focused primarily on the fact that the teacher had been warned of the consequences of repeated misuse following the first violation.

If the teacher or administrator is absent due to a prolonged illness beyond the sick-leave time which he or she has accumulated, the CONTRACT between the teacher or administrator and the school district may be terminated. However, the length of time of the absence beyond the accumulated leave time must be substantial, and it is often prescribed by statute.

SILENT, Right to Remain

The FIFTH AMENDMENT to the Constitution of the United States provides in part that "no person...shall be compelled in any criminal case to be a witness against himself..." Through the Fifth and the FOURTEENTH AMENDMENTS to the Constitution, a person has the right to refuse to make statements which may be used as evidence in a criminal proceeding against himself or herself. In other words, in regards to incriminating statements, people have a right to remain silent.

The COURTS have not only recognized that teachers and administrators have a right of free speech, the courts have indicated that such persons also have a right to remain silent. Generally, it would appear that a teacher or administrator may not be dismissed, refused employment, or threatened with discharge for refusing to divulge incriminating evidence. However, the history of the law in this area is sometimes to the contrary. (See SELF–INCRIMINATION.)

In a 1957 case, the Supreme Court of the United States held that a university professor could not be compelled to answer questions relating

---

[27]*Anderson v. Independent School District No. 623*, 292 N.W.2d 562 (Minn. 1980).

to the content of his classroom lectures or his knowledge of alleged subversive activities.[28] However, decisions of this nature were apparently limited by several subsequent decisions of the Supreme Court. In 1958, the Supreme Court ruled that it was not an infringement on a teacher's rights to dismiss the teacher for INSUBORDINATION for refusing to answer a school superintendent's questions concerning his membership in the Communist Party.[29] However, the 1960s witnessed a dramatic change in public school law. The courts accepted the view that teachers do not shed their constitutional rights at the schoolhouse gates. The Supreme Court made reference to teachers when it was called upon to decide whether a lawyer could be disbarred for invoking the privilege against self-incrimination. In holding that the lawyer could not be disbarred for exercising this right, the court said:

> Lawyers are not excepted from the words "no person…shall be compelled in any criminal case to be a witness against himself"; and we can imply no exception. Like the school teacher…and the police-man…lawyers also enjoy first-class citizenship.[30]

This suggests that the teacher's and administrator's rights to remain silent does in fact still exist. As a result, he or she cannot be dismissed for invoking the privilege against self-incrimination.

See also ACADEMIC FREEDOM; ANTI-SUBVERSIVE LAWS; CONSTITUTIONAL LAW.

SLANDER

See DEFAMATION.

SMOKING

Most states prohibit the sale of tobacco to minors, but only a few states make it unlawful for minors to smoke. As a result, local SCHOOL BOARDS have the authority to make their own RULES regarding the use and

---

[28]*Sweezy v. New Hampshire*, 354 U.S. 234 (1957).

[29]*Beilan v. Board of Public Education School District of Philadelphia*, 357 U.S. 399 (1958).

possession of tobacco in the schools. In some instances, local fire ordinances prohibit smoking in public buildings such as schools. If that is the case, the school board must respect these prohibitions.

There is no doubt that smoking is a health and safety hazard. As such, rules relating to smoking are reasonable and will be upheld. There are only a few court cases involving schools' anti-smoking rules. Nevertheless, the anti-smoking rules have been upheld by implication.[31] So long as procedural DUE PROCESS is properly administered, dismissals are upheld.[32]

Since many states have lowered the age of majority to 18, the necessity of having a uniform school policy becomes increasingly clear. If the school board chooses to permit faculty members to smoke, students could argue that the board should not prohibit eighteen-year-olds from smoking if there is a safe place to do so.

Many school boards have enacted clear rules on the smoking issue, explaining that, since smoking is a health hazard, it is prohibited on school buses, in school BUILDINGS, on school grounds, and at school-sponsored, off-campus activities. These rules are valid and may be enforced. Some schools have established smoking areas, some of which are on school grounds but not in school buildings. If smoking lounges are provided in school buildings, the school should be careful to supervise the area and make certain that it is safe.

School officials have no authority to regulate student conduct which is outside of the school's jurisdiction. As a result, if a teacher or administrator sees a student smoking several blocks away from the school grounds, he or she would have no right to punish the student.

See also EXPULSION OF STUDENTS.

SORORITIES

See SECRET SOCIETIES.

SOVEREIGN IMMUNITY

See GOVERNMENTAL IMMUNITY.

---

[30]*Spevack v. Klein*, 385 U.S. 511 (1967).

[31]*Davis v. Ann Arbor Public Schools*, 313 F. Supp. 1217 (E.D. Mich. 1970).

[32]*Wood v. Strickland*, 420 U.S. 308 (1975).

SPECIAL EDUCATION

Special education is specially–designed instruction, at no cost to parents, which meets the unique needs of a student with handicaps. Special education includes whatever instruction and RELATED SERVICES are necessary to meet the individual needs of the student. Special education can include classroom instruction, instruction in physical education, home instruction, and instruction in hospitals and institutions.

See also EDUCATION FOR ALL HANDICAPPED CHILDREN ACT OF 1975; REHABILITATION ACT OF 1973.

SPECIAL MEETINGS, School Board

See SCHOOL BOARDS, Meetings.

SPEECH, Freedom of

See ACADEMIC FREEDOM; CONSTITUTIONAL LAW; PLEDGE OF ALLEGIANCE; SELF-INCRIMINATION; SILENT, Right to Remain.

SPORTS

See ATHLETICS; CURRICULUM; MARRIED STUDENTS; NEGLIGENCE; SPORTS-RELATED INJURIES; SUPERVISION.

SPORTS–RELATED INJURIES

Schools are obligated to instruct and supervise students who are engaged in activities during physical education class and athletic events. Schools also must insure that proper EQUIPMENT is used. Furthermore, supervisors are obligated to take appropriate measures following an injury to prevent additional injuries. For example, an eleven-year-old student recovered a judgment of $2.5 million for the school district's delay in procuring medical assistance.[33] The delay caused a blood clot in the student's head to enlarge from the size of a walnut to that of an orange, causing catastrophic and severe permanent injuries.

Claims involving spectators usually involve injuries caused by equipment striking spectators, players injuring spectators who are located near the sidelines, and injuries caused by the condition of the premises (see BUILDINGS, Maintenance).

See also ASSUMPTION OF RISK; INSTRUCTION; NEGLIGENCE; SUPERVISION.

SPRING NOTIFICATION

See ANNUAL OR LONG-TERM CONTRACTS; CONTRACTS; RENEWAL; TENURE.

STARE DECISIS

Stare decisis is a legal doctrine in which the COURTS tend to follow precedent. Under this doctrine, when a court has once laid down a principle of law as applicable to a certain set of facts, other courts will adhere to that principle and will apply it to future cases if the facts are substantially the same. The "higher" the court, the more influence the decision will have.

Stare decisis is an extremely important legal doctrine. Through this doctrine, uniformity and EQUAL PROTECTION are assured. It is this doctrine which allows people to predict with some degree of certainty what a court's decision will or should be with regard to a given set of facts. Although courts will generally not disturb a settled legal point, the courts are not forced to follow precedent and will change if public policy influences the courts to give a different consideration to the facts and circumstances.

---

[33]*Barth v. Bd. of Educ.*, 490 N.E.2d 77 (Ill. App. 1986).

STATE BOARD OF EDUCATION

See STRUCTURE OF THE SCHOOL SYSTEM.

STATE COMMISSIONER OF PUBLIC INSTRUCTION

See CHIEF STATE SCHOOL OFFICER.

STATE SUPERINTENDENT OF PUBLIC INSTRUCTION

See CHIEF STATE SCHOOL OFFICER.

STATUTE OF LIMITATIONS

The statute of limitations limits the time within which a cause of action can be brought. For example, if a contract is breached, there is a right of action; any lawsuit filed must be brought within the specified statutory time limit. If a claim is not made within the time allowed, then the right to bring a suit is expired and there is no legal remedy available. Generally, for personal or property injury cases, the statute of limitations is two years. It can be as little as one year as in California and many other states, or it can be extended to three years as in Washington. For contract cases, the limit is often six years.

Special statutes of limitations are not uncommon when there is a potential cause of action against a governmental agency. For example, in many states, if a party in a personal or property injury suit intends to sue a city or state agency, *notice* of the pending suit *must be filed within 180 days* of the injury. If the notice is not sent within the time limit, the lawsuit cannot be filed and would, therefore, be dismissed.

STATUTES

Statutes are the written state laws. The written law should be distinguished from the "unwritten" laws of case law and the COMMON LAW. Whenever the state legislature enacts a new law, the law is written down and known as a state statute. Statutes may not conflict with state or federal constitution. If a conflict does exist, the law, as set forth in the state or federal constitution and as interpreted by the COURTS, supersedes the state statute.

STRIKES

A strike is defined under most state STATUTES to mean a public employee's willful absence, in concerted action with others, from the full, faithful, and proper performance of his or her duties of employment for the purpose of inducing, influencing or coercing a change in employment relations. A public employee may have the right to express a complaint or opinion on any matter related to employment relations. However, this right is generally not within the meaning of a strike.

In essence, a strike is any concerted refusal to work. A strike involves a group of persons and not just one individual. The refusal to work must be for the purpose of coercing the employer to accede to the employees' demands in regards to wages, hours, or terms and conditions of employment. A valid resignation amounts to a severance of the employer-employee relationship—a strike does not. However, in some cases, MASS RESIGNATIONS are equivalent to strikes. It should also be noted that mass sick calls will also be considered as a concerted work stoppage or sanction rather than a mere coincidence of a large number of employees becoming "emotionally upset" at the same time and for the same duration.[34]

Social and economic changes in America have contributed to strikes. Persistent low salaries during periods of economic prosperity and inflation have forced many educators to take on a more "militant" attitude. During 1960, there were only three teacher strikes; during the 1970s and 1980s, there were hundreds.

In an effort to minimize the problems caused by strikes, several different approaches have been tried. At one extreme, several states rely on severe anti-strike laws which include the imposition of monetary penalties

---

[34]*In re Forestville Transportation Association*, 4 PERB No. 8020 (1971).

on strikers, removal of civil service status or other job rights, withdrawal of DUES CHECKOFF privileges from employee organizations, application of court INJUNCTIONS, and criminal CONTEMPT sanctions (jail sentences and fines) when court injunctions are defied. Such laws do discourage some strikes, but these laws are just as likely to produce labor martyrs and headline seekers in addition to hindering harmonious labor relations. COURTS use contempt punishments sparingly for only the most unequivocal proofs of willful misconduct.

At the other extreme, public employees could be treated like private employees and, therefore, would have an unlimited right to strike. In the early 1970s, several states adopted laws which authorized public sector strikes for certain classes of employees under specified statutory conditions and restrictions such as:

1. The parties have first followed an elaborate procedure of bargaining, including MEDIATION and FACTFINDING.
2. Strikes which present a clear and present danger to the public health, safety and, in some states, welfare may be enjoined. For example, a strike which would cause failure to comply with the required minimum instructional day and result in loss of state funds was considered a clear and present danger.[35]

A growing minority of states have adopted "limited right to strike enabling statutes." For example, Alaska, Hawaii, Oregon, Pennsylvania, and Montana were forerunners in this concept as early as 1973. The right to strike is generally limited to CONTRACT negotiation impasses. Unfair labor complaints or GRIEVANCE disputes on existing contracts are not allowable as a legal strike basis because there are mandated procedures to resolve these impasses.

A majority of the states approach public employee bargaining by combining a strike prohibition with an emphasis on COLLECTIVE BARGAINING, mediation, and factfinding. Also, a great deal of well-deserved attention has been focused upon the benefits of ARBITRATION.

Strikes remain illegal in this majority of "in-between" states, and the SCHOOL BOARD may seek injunctive relief from the courts as the standard strike termination method. There are several legal bases for allowing injunctions to issue against public employee strikes:

1. Such strikes are in direct contravention of statutes.
2. Public employee strikes are against public policy and public welfare.

---

[35]*Jersey Shore Education Association v. Jersey Shore Area School District*, 512 A.2d 805 (Pa. 1986).

3. Public employee strikes interfere with and render the government incapable of performing its necessary duties and essential services (police protection, firefighting, etc.).

4. Such strikes present a clear and present danger or substantial harm to the public health, safety, or welfare in many instances.

Educators have occasionally argued that injunctive relief gives the school board the power to compel involuntary servitude. Legislative or judicial rulings against public employees' right to strike have not been found to constitute involuntary servitude or an unwarranted impingement of constitutional rights such as ASSEMBLY, DUE PROCESS, speech, or EQUAL PROTECTION.[35] Educators have contracts with the state. Teachers and administrators cannot lay claim to their positions and at the same time refuse to perform contractual obligations. New York has its Taylor Law, which provides for the loss of two days' pay for each day on strike.

Occasionally, a few courts have suggested that educators may have a de facto right to strike. Several judges have recognized that one of the main purposes of a labor organization is to force management to bargain fairly. If the employee organization is denied an effective bargaining weapon, such as arbitration, or the right to strike, freedom of ASSOCIATION amounts to little or nothing because the employee organization is incapable of fulfilling its functions. Labor's position is that one cannot negotiate without the ability to reject the proffered terms. Effective bargaining can hardly exist without preserving the right to strike/withhold services. As explained by one judge:

> [T]he right to strike is, at least, within constitutional concern and should not be discriminatorily abridged without substantial or "compelling" justification.[46]

Statutes give judicial discretion to delay, grant, modify, or deny injunctive decrees, depending on the circumstances.

Generally, strikes by school district employees are not protected, lawful activities. Some states specifically list strike activity as a prohibited practice. In addition to such prohibition, some state legislatures empower the officer or body generally having disciplinary authority over an employee to terminate the employment or impose other disciplinary action, such as fines or suspension of benefits, on an employee who strikes in violation of the statute.

---

[35]*Wolkenstein v. Reville*, 694 F.2d 35 (2d Cir. 1982), *cert. denied*, 462 U.S. 1105 (1983).

[46]*United Federation of Postal Clerks v. Blount*, 325 F. Supp. 879, 885 (D.C. 1971), Wright, J., concurring, *aff'd.* 404 U.S. 802 (1971).

However, if it is found that the school district engaged in an unfair labor practice, the appropriate employment agency may order reinstatement despite the illegality of the public employee strike. Thus, oftentimes whether an employee will be reinstated is determined by the gravity of the employee's misconduct in light of the district's unfair labor practices and discriminatory charges. Public interest has voiced the principle that, if a public employee strikes and is automatically denied reinstatement, this penalty should be relaxed when fault on both sides comes into play.

Two factors should be considered before holding that employee misconduct automatically precludes reinstatement:

1. The employer's unfair labor practices may have been so offensive that they provoked the employees to resort to unprotected activity; and

2. Reinstatement may be the only remedy that prevents an employer from benefitting from his or her unfair labor practice of discharge, thereby resulting in the weakening or destruction of a union.[37]

It should be remembered that the school board is under the duty to continue to bargain during a strike in those states where a strike is legal. An employer's interference with a lawful strike constitutes an unfair labor practice.[38]

Although a board cannot dismiss a teacher or administrator solely for engaging in union activity per se, as evidenced by judicial decisions, an employer is permitted a wide latitude in discipline for unprotected activities. Specifically, it has been held that an employer may pick and choose in discharging or refusing to rehire employees who have engaged in unprotected activities. For example, a 1978 case held that a public employee, who resigned during the term of the employee's contract as part of a strike action, engaged in unprotected activity and the employer did not commit an unfair labor practice in failing to reinstate the employee back to the position although the employer took back a number of employees who had also joined the strike.[39] Due process procedures for dismissal of striking public employees is satisfied by a hearing before the school board.

An employer may also impose fines, decertification of representa-

---

[37]*Rockwell v. Board of Education of School District of Crestwood*, 227 N.W.2d 736 (Mich. 1975).

[38]*Board of Trustees of Billings School Dist. v. Montana*, 604 P.2d 778 (Mont. 1979).

[39]*Pennsylvania Labor Relations Board v. Pleasant Valley School District*, 66 D&C 2d 637 (Pa. 1978).

tives, and suspension of union security privileges, such as dues checkoff or facility access.[40]

In light of the discrepancy of state statutes and judicial discretion in their interpretation, there exists a certain amount of uncertainty as to when an injunction will be ordered. However, it can be argued that, by not absolutely knowing that an injunction will terminate a public employee strike, management may be compelled to stay at the bargaining table in an effort to resolve a dispute rather than risk a strike which cannot be enjoined. Evading the legislature's intent, the Michigan Supreme Court seemingly embraced this theory and concerned itself more with the benefits of people resolving disputes through collective bargaining than by following the letter of the law and imposing an injunction on a per se illegal strike.[41]

Displaying similar irreverence to its legislature's intent that all public employee strikes be enjoined, the Wisconsin Supreme Court held that courts should not enjoin unlawful work stoppages by public employees merely because the stoppages are illegal but should determine in each case whether irreparable harm could result if the particular strike were not enjoined. However, the petitioning school district's burden of showing such harm was so slight that the injunction was imposed; and, undoubtedly, in most cases, the legislature's intent will ultimately be followed.[42]

The courts and public attitudes toward public sector employee strike situations are becoming more moderate, especially when means to assert the employees' perceived rights have not been ensured through legislation.

STRUCTURE OF SCHOOL SYSTEM

Many of the laws which govern the operation of the schools are found in state STATUTES, the COMMON LAW, and in case law handed down by the COURTS. However, these laws are mainly general standards or apply only to specific kinds of situations. The RULES and policies which govern the operation of the schools on a day-to-day basis are enacted within the school system itself. The laws as provided by the constitutions, statutes, and courts are reflected in the policies of the school system.

---

[40]*Independent School District v. Oklahoma City Fed. of Teachers*, 612 P.2d 719 (Okla. 1980).

[41]*Holland School District v. Holland Education Association*, 157 N.W.2d 206 (Mich. 1968).

[42]*Joint School Dist. No. 1 v. Wisconsin Rapids Education Association*, 234 N.W.2d 289 (Wis. 1975).

Much like the courts, the school system has a hierarchy of authority. The structure of the school system is important to recognize because, as a general rule, the "lower" bodies in the school system may not enact rules or policies which are contrary to those specified by a "higher" body.

State Board of Education

The State Board of Education is the policy-making body for the public schools within the state. The power, authority, and duties of this board vary somewhat among the states. Generally, the state board prescribes rules which are consistent with state law for the operation of the public schools. The authority of the state board is just below that of the state legislature.

State Superintendent or Commissioner of Education

In many states, the State Superintendent of Education or the State Commissioner of Education, whichever he or she is called, is selected by the state board of education. In other states, this person is popularly elected by the voters. In a few states, appointment is made by the governor.

The authority and responsibilities of this CHIEF STATE SCHOOL OFFICER vary among the states. As a general rule, he or she carries out the duties specifically designated for the State Superintendent or Commissioner of Education in the state constitution and statutes, as well as the plans and policies of the state board. This person is the executive head of the State Department of Education. In some states, most notably New York and New Jersey, the state commissioner is given the power and duty to render opinions on certain types of local education employee relation controversies and disputes.

State Department of Education

The State Department of Education consists of professional workers and education specialists who carry out the administrative, educational functions required to be performed on the state level. These persons must see to it that the laws relating to the schools are complied with. The State Department of Education frequently advises and consults with local SCHOOL BOARDS. In nearly all states, the state department handles CERTIFICATION and DECERTIFICATION of teachers and teacher education programs and institutions.

An intermediate administrative unit which functions between the State Department of Education and local school boards exists in the majority of states. These units are frequently formed to serve individual counties. They often process reports and check to see if local school districts are complying with state laws and requirements. In many states, these intermediate units are used to provide specialized services which would be either too expensive for local school districts to perform or which could be more effectively and efficiently handled through these units. Such programs frequently include specialized education programs for teaching gifted, handicapped, or retarded students; trade and industrial arts; testing and counseling; and film and record services and libraries.

Local School Districts

The state legislature can create, reorganize, or dissolve local school districts in the manner it deems most beneficial to the educational interests of the state. Consolidation frequently occurs when school districts are too small to afford the kind of educational programs required to meet the needs of modern times. However, decentralization of extremely large school districts is also an option. (See REORGANIZATION.)

Local School Boards

With the exception of Hawaii which is run by one statewide school district board, public schools are operated by local school boards. Although local school board members are elected or appointed on a local level, legally, school board members are deemed to be acting as state officials.

Most state statutes prescribe minimum qualifications for local school board members, but these are not very restrictive. For a detailed explanation of the powers and duties of local school boards, see SCHOOL BOARDS.

STUDENT LIABILITY

A student is liable for his or her own TORTS. However, most students are "judgment-proof." Although a person may be able to obtain a judgment against a minor who wrongfully injures another person, the minor will generally have no money from which to pay. Because minors commit torts and because they are generally judgment-proof, most states have enacted legislation making the minors' parents liable for children's conduct. In one case, a student received injuries when a second student wrapped his legs around the first student's body as the first student was hanging from a set of horizontal monkey bars, causing them both to fall. The court found the second student negligent, and DAMAGES were recovered from his parents.[43] This type of vicarious LIABILITY is limited, however.

---

[43]*Collins v. Bossier Parish School Bd.*, 480 So. 2d 846 (La. App. 1985).

Parental liability generally is limited to an amount less than $500 in many states but as high as $5,000 in a few states. Anything over the statutory amount remains as the sole obligation of the minor. An injured party may take a minor and his parents to small claims court for injuries that are not too serious. For those which are more serious in nature, a higher court is necessary.

See also FELONY; MISDEMEANOR; and CATEGORICAL INDEX regarding Discipline and Control of Students.

STUDENT RECORDS

The school has a clear right to collect and maintain student records. However, problems frequently arise in two areas: (1) *use* of the records and (2) persons having *access* to the records.

A student's record generally contains information on his or her family background and relationships, health reports, attendance records, achievement and standardized test scores, and personality and behavior evaluations and observations made by teachers, counselors, and other school officials. The need for protection of the student's right to PRIVACY must be weighed against the school officials' and the public's need to know certain information. Many states have made an effort to specify guidelines and policies governing the kinds of information which may be collected and who may have access to the records under prescribed conditions. Such established record-keeping guidelines are necessary to curb abuses, to prevent needless resulting harm, and to protect teachers and school districts from LIABILITY. The necessary guidelines should:

1. Specify the types of information to be collected and the reasons for collection.
2. Designate a procedure for obtaining consent of the student and his or her parent for collection of certain personal information.
3. Establish a procedure for destruction of outdated, useless, and inaccurate information.
4. Establish reasonable rules as to who may have access to certain kinds of information and under what conditions the information may be released.

In establishing the necessary guidelines, the following cases and legal principles should be considered.

Legally, student records are considered to be "quasi-public" and, as such, are available for inspection only by "real parties in interest." Parents have the right to inspect student records. This right of inspection is related to the right of citizens to inspect public documents of many kinds. Parents should be granted access to the records, but the school should have established guidelines for release. During inspection of the records, appropriate personnel should be present to prevent misinterpretation of these records. This is particularly true of student behavior records, because certain statements may not be properly evaluated or understood by parents.

Students also have a sufficient interest to entitle them to inspect certain information in their own records. By STATUTE, states give the power of release of student records to older students. Delaware, for example, grants this power to students who are 14 years of age or older. Note that, although students may have this right of inspection, guidelines for release may be lawfully established which provide for release of only certain kinds of information under proper conditions.

In one case, a Pennsylvania court held that student records relating to nonacademic matters could be released to higher education institutions. The court upheld the right of school officials to record a student's infractions of school RULES in his or her permanent file:

> School officials have the right and, we think, a duty to record and to communicate true factual information about their students to institutions of higher learning, for the purpose of giving to the latter an accurate and complete picture of applicants for admission.[44]

However, if the school releases student records in violation of a state statute, the student can recover DAMAGES. Promiscuous circulation of information about which the public has no right to know will subject school officials to liability.

Where there exists a professional justifiable reason, school district officials and professional employees, (PRINCIPALS, teachers, counselors, and health personnel) have a right to inspect certain information contained in student records. In addition, some general information *may*, at times, be obtained by SCHOOL BOARD members. For example, a 1960 case held that a school board member could compel the SUPERINTENDENT to give him the names and addresses of students enrolled in certain schools. This information was needed for a particular purpose.[45]

There have even been times when the COURTS have held that, if a sufficient interest or need for inspection can be shown, an "outsider" may have a right to inspect certain school records. For example, in one case, a person who was not a student, parent, college admissions officer, or

---

[44]*Einhorn v. Maus*, 300 F. Supp. 1169 (E.D. Pa. 1969).

[45]*Wagner v. Redmond*, 127 So. 2d 275 (La. App. 1960).

member of the school faculty sought to be allowed to inspect certain records. The court granted him this right and explained that:

> Where the defense of a person accused of a crime requires access to public records or even to records sealed from general examination, the right of inspection has a greater sanction and must be enforced.[46]

In view of the fact that many persons are entitled to inspect student records, the school district should try to protect itself from making improper disclosures. In order to do so, behavior records should be kept separate from academic records. Guidelines for release should be set forth in a clear and specific policy statement.

Student behavior records should contain information about disciplinary and counseling actions. This information should only be released:

1. To school personnel;
2. To persons outside of the school system who have the express consent of the student and his or her parents; or
3. Under court order.

The school should provide that this information shall be released only in the presence of someone who is qualified to interpret it.

Congress has established a policy regulating the keeping and release of school records called the Family Educational Rights and Privacy Act of 1974.[47] If a school district fails to comply with this law, it is subject to forfeiture of federal funds which it receives. Among the requirements of this federal law is a provision mandating release of the records to parents who request to see them. The school district is given a short period of time to establish procedures for release of the records. This law also applies to colleges; students, therefore, are allowed to inspect many of their records, including perhaps placement files and recommendations.

Teachers and administrators must be careful not to libel the student in the records. However, a carefully worded professional opinion made as a part of his or her duty as a teacher or administrator, made in good faith and made as a part of the education process and with regard to the student, will be held privileged against any libel suit.

See also DEFAMATION; EDUCATION FOR ALL HANDICAPPED CHILDREN ACT OF 1975.

---

[46]*Werfel v. Fitzgerald*, 260 N.Y.S.2d 791 (N.Y. App. 1965).

[47]P.L. 93-380, § 438.

STUDENT RIGHTS

See CATEGORICAL INDEX regarding Constitutional Rights of Students and Discipline and Control of Students.

SUBPOENA

A subpoena is a legal process which compels a person to appear at a certain time and place to give testimony before a COURT or hearing body on a specified matter. A "subpoena duces tecum" is a process by which the court or authorized hearing body commands a person to produce certain documents or records pertinent to the issues in controversy. There is a penalty for failure to appear or produce the designated evidence at the trial.

SUBSTANTIVE LAW

Substantive law is the portion of basic law which creates, defines, and regulates an individual's duties, rights, and obligations. On the other hand, adjective or remedial law provides procedural methods of enforcement of rights or obtaining redress for their invasion.
See also DUE PROCESS.

SUBVERSIVE ORGANIZATIONS

See ANTISUBVERSIVE LAWS; ASSEMBLY; CONSTITUTIONAL LAW; LOYALTY OATHS.

SUMMER SCHOOL

Summer school sessions may be conducted, and TUITION may be charged because summer school is in excess of the state requirements of providing students with a free education. Tuition cannot be charged when the program is offered as part of an individualized education program for a student with handicaps.

See also EDUCATION FOR ALL HANDICAPPED CHILDREN ACT OF 1975.

SUPERINTENDENT

Both the state constitution and STATUTES delineate the powers and duties of the superintendent's position. The local school district superintendent has the responsibility of advising the local board about the operation and management of the schools. He or she also must make certain that state law, state board regulations, and local SCHOOL BOARD policy are implemented and educational objectives are achieved.

On the one hand, the superintendent is practically a member of the board. At least, he or she is the board's chief administrator and educational advisor with the delegated responsibility of evaluating whether or not the educational objectives are being met. The local board relies on the superintendent's judgment and recommendations in making many of the board's major decisions as long as those decisions are not ARBITRARY OR CAPRICIOUS. On the other hand, the superintendent is an employee without TENURE but with the delegated responsibility of exercising independent professional judgment in the everyday operation of the schools and supervision of school staff. Superintendents are contracted (usually for a term fixed by state law) by the school board. Even though superintendents have great latitude and discretion in professional decisions, these administrators are accountable to the board and subject to dismissal like any other employee. Many states require superintendents to have substantial training in administration and supervision.

There are always judgments by various groups as to just what should be taught and how it should be done, who should be hired, and what methods and materials should be used. Because these judgments sometimes conflict, it is necessary for the board to clearly set forth the superintendent's rights, duties, and responsibilities in relation to the board, to subordinates, and to students. Policies should state specifically which duties and responsibilities the superintendent may delegate to other administrators and, in turn, which of those duties and responsibilities should be delegated to teachers and to students. Formal, concise, and clear procedures should be established in order to ensure that these functions are properly executed. Many state statutes now require complete staffing charts and job descriptions for each position.

It is clear that included within the superintendent's authority are the following:

1. He or she is in charge of the day-to-day administrative operation of the schools and staff.

2. He or she is in charge of evaluating whether the educational objectives of the board are being carried out, often recommending TEXTBOOKS and instructional materials.

3. The superintendent must make certain that teachers and others are evaluated pursuant to the law or to local school board policies.

4. The superintendent is in charge of investigating whether an educator is competent or should be dismissed. This should be done through the administrative staff. (See also DUE PROCESS.)

5. The superintendent must advise the board which applicants should be hired to fill vacant positions.

6. It is the superintendent's duty to attend all school board meetings and to advise and give his or her opinion on all educational development issues.

7. Superintendents serve as chief budget officers, managing and protecting school FUNDS. As the guardian of funds, the superintendent may be held personally liable for misappropriations or improper expenditures.

8. The superintendent must provide safety checks for school BUILD-INGS and EQUIPMENT.

The superintendent is not charged with the responsibility of knowing the individual needs of every student nor should he or she be expected to know which teaching methods best fit a particular classroom situation. Those duties should be left with classroom teachers and administrators.

As far as legal risks are concerned, much depends upon whether the superintendent is considered an "officer" of the board or an "employee." Generally, the superintendent is considered a state or county school board officer. The legal status of superintendents was analyzed in depth by a 1982 court in Virginia in a TORTS case. That court held that the superintendent was a supervisory official entrusted with independent decision-making authority and, therefore, entitled to sovereign immunity.[48] This means that he or she enjoys the same immunities as local board members and will be indemnified or immune for acts done within the scope of his or her authority. (See GOVERNMENTAL IMMUNITY; SCHOOL BOARD, Liability.)

---

[48]*Banks v. Sellers*, 294 S.E.2d 862 (Va. 1982).

Of course, if the superintendent is outside of the scope of his or her duty, there will be personal liability regardless of whether he or she is considered an employee or an officer.

Sometimes the question will arise as to whether the superintendent is liable for the tortious acts of subordinates. The general rule is that there is no liability, unless the superintendent somehow participated in the wrongful conduct or had reason to know that such conduct was probable. If that were the case, the superintendent might be considered negligent for not foreseeing certain injuries and enacting rules for their prevention. In such an instance, he or she would be liable for his or her own NEGLIGENCE but not for the negligence of a subordinate.

SUPERINTENDENT OF PUBLIC INSTRUCTION

See CHIEF STATE SCHOOL OFFICER; SUPERINTENDENT.

SUPERVISION

One of the primary responsibilities of all educators is to provide adequate supervision of students. The extent of this duty depends on the facts and circumstances surrounding the activities. What constitutes adequate supervision will depend upon many factors, including age, experience, maturity of the students involved, the activity in which the students are engaged, and the FORESEEABILITY of harm. The ultimate test is whether or not the educator acted in a REASONABLE AND PRUDENT manner under the existing circumstances. Whether the educator has fulfilled his or her duty of supervision is a QUESTION OF FACT for a jury to decide. A few cases will help illustrate what the COURTS say regarding the duty to supervise.

In a case involving a thirteen-year-old student who was hit by a car while crossing a street during a school field trip, the court found that the student had no vision or hearing problems and that the student was a smart boy who understood the safety precautions involved. Even though teachers had given permission to the student to cross the street, the court found that the teachers were not negligent in their supervisory duties.[49] In a

---

[49]*King v. Kartanson*, 720 S.W.2d 65 (Tenn. App. 1986).

second case, a nine-year-old student died after he was injured during a lunchtime recess which was supervised by a teacher. A group of third graders independently organized a softball game. The boy was injured while trying to pick up his baseball glove, which was located on home plate. As the boy went to retrieve the glove, approaching the area from behind the plate, the batter swung and hit the boy in the temple, causing an injury which resulted in death. At the time of the injury, the teacher was forty-five feet from the field helping a kindergarten student. The court found that the teacher was reasonable in her supervision and that the act which resulted in the injury was not foreseeable.[50]

There is a heightened need for supervision when students are in dangerous situations. NEGLIGENCE is often found by COURTS when teachers do not supervise students using power-driven EQUIPMENT. In one case, a student operating a drill press while the teacher was ABSENT FROM CLASS received head injuries resulting in a five percent disability to the student's body. The court found that the teacher who gave the student the drill bit and then left the room, knowing that the boy wanted to finish his project, was negligent.[51]

One court has found that running does not present a dangerous condition which would ordinarily impose a duty upon teachers to stop students from running or to issue warnings about the risks of running.[52] This ruling came as the result of a suit involving injuries a seven-year-old student suffered in a collision with another student. Both students were running at the time of the collision. However, in another case, a school district was held liable when a student wrestler was injured during a running drill "in the school's hallway." The wrestler suffered severe injuries to the student's arm and hand when a plate glass window shattered as the student turned into the hallway door in the furtherance of the exercise drill. The claim was not protected under Pennsylvania's GOVERNMENTAL IMMUNITY laws in part because the district permitted the regular use of the hallway for wrestling practice and such injuries could foreseeably have been prevented.[53]

There may be a heightened need for supervision when the students have handicaps. In a case where a twelve-year-old boy received injuries while running through the playground, the court found that there was a failure to supervise. The court found that the teacher was well aware of the

---

[50]*Ferguson v. DeSoto Parish School Bd.*, 467 So. 2d 1257 (La. App. 1985).

[51]*Roberts v. Robertson County Bd. of Educ.*, 692 S.W.2d 863 (Tenn. App. 1985).

[52]*Norman v. Turkey Run Comm. School Corp.*, 411 N.E.2d 614 (Ind. 1980).

[53]*Gump v. Chartiers-Houston School Dist.*, 558 A.2d 589 (Pa. 1989).

student's physical and mental limitations and had the opportunity either to shout at the student or to physically stop him as he ran past the teacher.[54]

It should be mentioned that supervisory duties may be imposed upon teachers if the duties are not arbitrary and are not unreasonable. (See CONTRACTS.) Supervisory duties should either relate directly to the teacher's classroom duties or be equally assigned to all teachers. For example, an English teacher could be expected to direct a play, or a music director could be expected to supervise a "pep" band. Physical education teachers could be expected to coach, and shop teachers could be expected to put on demonstrations of how to construct whatever the students are building. The supervisory duty may, at times, extend into the evening or even on weekends. The only limitation is that the duty must be reasonable and not arbitrary.

Many of these "extra" supervisory duties are the subject of school negotiations. Generally, there is no legal requirement that a teacher should be entitled to extra pay for each extra duty. In order to solve these problems, the local board could adopt a policy whereby teachers are given compensation to supervise extracurricular activities. (See ASSIGNMENTS, Nonclassroom.)

SUPPLEMENTAL CONTRACTS

See CONTRACTS.

SUSPENSION OF STUDENTS

See EXPULSION OF STUDENTS.

SUSPENSION OF TEACHERS

See CATEGORICAL INDEX regarding Dismissals, Grievances, and Tenure.

---

[54]*Rodriguez v. Board of Educ.*, 480 N.Y.S.2d 901 (N.Y. 1984).

T

TALENTED AND GIFTED STUDENTS

The Talented and Gifted Children's Education Act was passed in 1978 and repealed in 1982. Currently, there is no federal right to special education programs for talented and gifted students. However, some state STATUTES require special education programs for these students.

TEACHER AIDE

Most states have regulations concerning the requirements for teacher aides. These requirements sometimes include the number of training hours required and the extent of the aide's responsibilities.

A teacher's aide must meet the standard of care of the ordinary teacher in the same or similar circumstances. Teachers have a higher standard of care for the SUPERVISION and safety of their students than the ordinary man or woman on the street. If this care is entrusted to a teacher's aide, the aide must be instructed in how to supervise and how to maintain safety just like the ordinary teacher. If the aide does not meet this standard, the aide will be personally liable. Whether the teacher or administrator will be held liable along with the aide depends on the circumstances. If the aide was properly instructed and given proper directions, there would generally be no vicarious LIABILITY. However, if the teacher or administrator knew or should have known that the aide was incapable of meeting the necessary standard but ignored this fact and assigned the aide supervisory duties anyway, that in itself constitutes NEGLIGENCE and both could be held liable.

In addition to adequate instruction of the aide, there is a duty on the part of the teacher or administrator to supervise the aide and make certain that he or she is properly performing the assigned duties. This does not mean that the teacher or administrator must constantly be with the aide. It does mean, however, that the aide must be watched in a REASONABLE AND PRUDENT manner.

All of this holds true for parent volunteers and student tutors. Everyone is liable for his or her own TORTS. It does not matter that the parent is a volunteer or that an older student is tutoring another. These persons should be covered with insurance, either on their own or paid by the district. All supervisory duties within the school or at school-sponsored activities, such as field trips, must meet the standard of care of the reasonable and prudent teacher. RULES of safety should be communicated and should then be enforced.

TENURE

Tenure or CONTINUING CONTRACT law is a privileged status given to teachers and some administrators by their state legislature. Statutory tenure rights may not be arbitrarily removed by school authorities.[1] Tenure does not guarantee continued employment, but tenure does provide a tenured teacher or administrator with job security. A tenured employee may not be removed from his or her position without substantial just cause and in compliance with procedural safeguards and DUE PROCESS. Tenured teacher dismissals cannot be for ARBITRARY OR CAPRICIOUS reasons.[2] Tenure rights vary dramatically from state to state.

The concept of tenure was developed in the late 1800s in an effort to guarantee that good educators would not be subjected to arbitrary, capricious, or discriminatory dismissals. By the early 1970s, nearly forty states had statewide tenure laws. There are differences in the amount of protections granted under these laws, but all tenure laws are aimed at trying to protect good educators while at the same time allowing for dismissal of incompetent ones. In addition, some states have what are known as continuing contract laws or ANNUAL OR LONG-TERM CONTRACTS.

---

[1]*Bernland v. Special School Dist. No. 1*, 314 N.W.2d 809 (Minn. 1981).

[2]*Detroit Board of Education v. Parks*, 296 N.W.2d 815 (Mich. App. 1980); *Simmons v. Drew*, 716 F.2d 1160 (7th Cir. 1983).

Tenure is an effective means of preventing personal affiliations from entering into appointments or removals. This was noted and explained in one of the reports in the American Historical Association's investigation of the social studies in the schools:

> Although teachers in Colonial times had no legal claim to permanent tenure, in practice they often held office for life. Then, at about the same time the schools fell under public control, and Jacksonian democracy came into power with its sense of popular "possession" of public offices, its spoils system, its theory of rotation in office. Teachers' tenure became precarious. All too often the position was handed about as a petty favor to friends of those in power. After all, anyone could teach school. Towards the end of the century, training for teachers had become so common that "anyone" could not always satisfy requirements. Demands for the merit system in politics were accompanied by a new attitude toward teaching and a realization that good teachers could not be procured and kept under the old methods of filling positions. In 1875, President Eliot of Harvard wrote, "Permanence of tenure and security of income are essential to give dignity and independence to the teacher's position." In 1885, a committee of the National Education Association rendered an exhaustive report on tenure. It urged reform because "The public school system should be independent of personal or partisan influence and free from the malignant power of patronage and spoils." (Footnotes omitted.)[3]

Tenure law protection, upon satisfactorily serving a probationary period over the years, has been uniformly sustained as constitutional. Frequently, the COURTS have explained the intended purpose of tenure laws:

> While tenure provisions...protect teachers in their positions from political or arbitrary interference, they are not intended to preclude dismissal where the conduct is detrimental to the efficient operation and administration of schools of the district...Its object is to improve the school system by assuring teachers of experience and ability a continuous service based upon merit, and by protecting them against dismissal for reasons that are political, partisan or capricious.[4]

By protecting teachers and administrators, tenure acts to free educators from special interest and pressure groups and allows them to exercise

---

[3]H. K. Beale, *Are American Teachers Free?* (New York: Charles Scribner's Sons, 1936).

[4]*Pickering v. Board of Education*, 225 N.E.2d 1, 6 (Ill. 1967), *rev.* 391 U.S. 563 (1968).

initiative. In effect, the ultimate purpose of tenure laws is to improve the educational system and to benefit students.

Coaching positions, extra-duty positions, and temporary teachers are generally hired under supplemental service contracts and are often not protected positions under tenure laws. The courts are split as to whether SUPERINTENDENTS, PRINCIPALS, certain administrative personnel, and substitutes are covered under certain tenure STATUTES. Only those positions enumerated in the tenure statute are encompassed by its provisions.[5]

To qualify for the benefits of a tenure statute, one must show that he or she has complied with the precise conditions articulated in the applicable statute. Thus, if the statute says benefits are limited to "teachers," one must establish that he or she is within the contemplation of that term used in the particular statute. For example, if a statute defines a teacher as a professional employee who spends 120 days a year teaching, then one must show not only that one has the requisite certificate to qualify as a professional employee, but one must also show that he or she spends the required amount of time teaching.[6]

In most states, tenure can only be attained after successful completion of a probationary period during which the board assesses ability and competence. The most common requirement is satisfactory, regular, and continuous service for three years plus RENEWAL for a fourth. Substitute, intern, and student teaching are usually not counted as being a part of the probationary period. At the end of the probationary period, tenure is automatic by default or acquisition in some states; but, in many others, recommendation by the superintendent plus affirmative action by the SCHOOL BOARD is required.

It has been held that the school board has broad, personnel management discretion in determining whether to grant tenure to a probationary teacher. Furthermore, this discretion is unfettered unless the teacher establishes that the board acted for an unconstitutionally impermissible reason or acted in violation of the statutory procedures.[7] In a few states, the probationary period may be extended in order to give an employee whose work had not met the district's tenure standards an additional opportunity to improve the quality of his or her work.

During the probationary period, most state laws provide that an employee may be nonrenewed without cause at the end of the school year or with cause if the dismissal is during the school year. In many states, the

---

[5]*Burns v. Dept. of Educ.*, 529 So. 2d 398 (La. 1988); *Thrash v. School District 189*, 435 N.E.2d 866 (Ill. App. 1982).

[6]*Selmeyer v. Southeastern Indiana Vocational School*, 509 N.E.2d 1150 (Ind. App. 1987).

[7]*Merhige v. Copiague School District*, 429 N.Y.S.2d 456 (1980).

reasons for NONRENEWAL of a contract at the end of the year are not required to be given. In a New York case, third-year nontenured teachers were given notice before the statutory deadline that the teachers would not be offered contracts for the fourth year. The court ruled that, since the teachers had not completed three years of teaching when notified of nonrenewal, the teachers were neither entitled to DUE PROCESS nor the showing of cause for termination upon this notice.

Once a teacher has attained tenure, he or she may be dismissed only for what is often termed "just cause." Causes which are required to lawfully dismiss a tenured teacher may include incompetence, immorality, insubordination, incapacity, neglect of duty, unprofessionalism on duty, and conviction of a FELONY. (See PRIVACY.) In determining whether the required cause does in fact exist, the school board is required to strictly comply with certain designated dismissal procedures.[8] Failure to comply will generally result in the teacher having a right to REINSTATEMENT plus DAMAGES.

Tenure status does not give an employee a vested right to a particular position or to a particular school.[9] SCHOOL BOARDS have the discretionary power to reassign or transfer teachers or administrators when such action is made in good faith and with proper motives. The transfer must be to a position of equal pay and status and within a reasonable distance of the other position, or the transfer may be considered tantamount to a DEMOTION. (See also TRANSFERS.) In addition, ABOLITION OF POSITIONS for financial reasons may be valid grounds for terminating a tenured teacher's or administrator's contract.

Tenure obtained in a particular district may or may not be honored by another school system.[10] Although the constitutionality of such laws has been challenged on the grounds of DISCRIMINATION and EQUAL PROTECTION, these have been upheld. However, if the exclusion of some counties from a tenure law was, in effect, intended as a means of racial discrimination, the law has been found unconstitutional.[11]

With the advent of COLLECTIVE BARGAINING, tenure laws are subjected to renewed challenges. Some people feel that job security should be a negotiable item and there is no longer any necessity for the state to grant this "fringe benefit" by statute. Through collective bargaining, many of the tenure protections could be provided for in contract agreements.

---

[8]*Rhodes v. Laurel Highlands School Dist.*, 544 A.2d 562 (Pa. 1988).

[9]*Connell v. Bd. of Educ.*, 465 N.Y.S.2d 106, (N.Y. 1983).

[10]*Imbrunone v. Inkster Public Schools*, 410 N.W.2d 300 (Mich. App. 1987). *See also, Carpenter v. Bd. of Educ.*, 514 N.Y.S.2d 264 (N.Y. App. 1987).

[11]*Alabama State Teachers Association v. Lowndes County Board of Education*, 289 F. Supp. 300 (N.D. Ala. 1968).

Nevertheless, it is doubtful that the tenure laws will be repealed. Tenure laws provide too great a benefit for the students and the school system—as well as for the teachers and administrators themselves. However, to remain viable in modern times, tenure laws should require:

1. A probationary period;

2. A method of evaluating teachers;

3. That tenured teachers who are unable to adequately perform their teaching duties be dismissed;

4. That review of the school board's decision on whether cause for dismissal exists be limited to checking to see if the required due process procedures were followed and if substantial reliable evidence existed to support the decision; and

5. That other penalties besides complete dismissal be examined and allowed as alternatives.

Rising costs, declining enrollments, and shrinking endowments are beginning to characterize some areas of the academic marketplace. As a result, faculty members are pressing for greater job security by either liberalizing standards needed to acquire tenure, applying classic review when tenure is denied, or seeking greater procedural safeguards against faculty dismissals. Of course, all of the factors that are pressuring the teachers are imposing no less a burden on the administrators. It must be remembered that tenure is not a guarantee of employment for life. Rather, tenure only limits the institution's ability to dismiss educators in situations where their performance levels drop below *minimum* standards. A tenured educator is guaranteed certain due process safeguards with reference to grounds for dismissal and the proof required to substantiate the charges.

TESTING, Student

There are several types of student testing:

1. As a placement tool, see INTELLIGENCE TESTING;

2. As an admission guideline, see DISCRIMINATION;

3. As a requirement to advance to the next grade or graduate from high school, see COMPETENCY TESTING.

TESTING, Teacher

See MENTAL AND PHYSICAL EXAMINATIONS; MERIT PAY.

TEXTBOOKS, Adoption of

See ANTI-EVOLUTION STATUTES; CURRICULUM; RELIGION; SCHOOL BOARDS.

TEXTBOOKS, Free

Many state laws require school districts to provide free textbooks for students attending public schools. This is a proper expenditure of school FUNDS. The more controversial question arises in connection with state laws which require school districts to provide free textbooks for all students attending school, including those attending a private or parochial school. As a general rule, this kind of law is constitutional and is held not to be in violation of the Establishment of RELIGION clause. For example, in 1968, the Supreme Court of the United States upheld a New York program of providing free textbooks to students attending private and parochial, as well as public, elementary, and secondary schools. The court recognized this "aid" as being secular in nature and the benefit to the private and parochial schools as being indirect.[12]

The constitutionality of this form of aid may be challenged if DISCRIMINATION is involved. In 1973, the United States Supreme Court was faced with a Mississippi textbook program in which the state purchased textbooks and loaned them to students attending both public and private schools without regard to the fact that some of the PRIVATE SCHOOLS had racially discriminatory admission policies. The court found the law unconstitutional because the law aided the establishment of schools which might discriminate. The court explained that the granting of textbooks to sectarian schools for secular subjects does not significantly advance the religious functions such as to make the law unconstitutional,

---

[12]*Board of Education v. Allen*, 392 U.S. 236 (1968).

but this must be distinguished from aid to schools which are discriminatory.[13] COURTS are split as to whether districts can assess textbook fees where STATUTES do not specify that textbooks are to be provided at no cost to students. (See FEES.)

See also PRIVATE AND PAROCHIAL SCHOOL AID.

THREATS

See ASSAULT; BATTERY.

TORT

A tort is a civil wrong committed against someone's person or property, resulting in an injury, which gives rise to a right to collect money DAMAGES. A crime is a criminal wrong or violation against society. Punishment may be a monetary fine, imprisonment, or both. Tort actions for school purposes can be grouped into two major categories: NEGLIGENCE and intentional TORTS. The most common form for a lawsuit in the field of education is negligence.

See also ASSAULT; BATTERY; DEFAMATION; FALSE IMPRISONMENT; INTENTIONAL INFLICTION OF EMOTIONAL DISTRESS; INTENTIONAL TORTS; TRESPASS TO PERSONAL PROPERTY.

TRACKING OF STUDENTS

See ABILITY GROUPING.

TRANSFERS OF STUDENTS

Some school districts use the involuntary transfer of students as a discipline method. COURTS have usually equated transfers with EXPUL-

---

[13]*Norwood v. Harrison*, 413 U.S. 455 (1973).

SIONS and have held that, before transfers for disciplinary reasons can be made, students must be afforded the same DUE PROCESS rights which are afforded before expulsion.

Schools wishing to transfer students with handicaps must follow specific change in placement procedures spelled out in the EDUCATION FOR ALL HANDICAPPED CHILDREN ACT OF 1975.

See also ASSIGNMENT TO GRADE AND SCHOOL.

TRANSFERS OF TEACHERS

Transfers of teachers and administrator are not always challenged as punitive acts. As a result, good-faith transfers do not require a formal DUE PROCESS hearing. As one court explained:

> It is conceivable that many teachers are transferred by county boards of education, not because of inefficiency, misconduct or unfitness, but rather because of the mere fact that they are competent, effective teachers, and that, therefore, a proper administration of the county public school system dictates the basis of transfers to places and positions where the teachers' special qualifications will better promote the entire public school program of the county.[14]

Some teachers or administrators are transferred because of personality conflicts or because of unsatisfactory service. SCHOOL BOARDS cannot generally initiate disciplinary transfers unless the individual was informed in prior EVALUATIONS that the conduct could result in a transfer and the educator had time to improve.[15] Most transfers are upheld by the COURTS because transfers which are not intended to punish the employee are of administrative necessity.

Reassignments due to financial constraints or good-faith REORGANIZATION do not require a hearing, but generally the transfer must be to a position of equal pay and status and in the same general location. In addition, the transfer must be to a position within the educator's area of certified qualification or the area specified in his or her contract. Assignments to teach different subjects in the same school grade would not be a transfer calling for a hearing.[16]

---

[14]*State ex rel Withers v. Board of Education of Mason County*, 172 S.E.2d 796 (W. Va. App. 1970).

[15]*Holland v. Bd. of Educ. of Raleigh County*, 327 S.E.2d 155 (W. Va. App. 1985).

[16]*Robertson v. Alabama State Tenure Comm'n.*, 513 So. 2d 636 (Ala. App. 1987).

Agency regulations and statutory procedures established for transfer must be strictly followed. In addition, TENURE status may not be affected by transfer to a new position. As a result, a teacher or administrator cannot be forced to go through another probationary period in order to obtain tenure. However, if one is tenured as a teacher and is transferred to an administrative position, the person can be forced to undergo a new probationary period before tenure is acquired as an administrator.

See also ABOLITION OF POSITIONS; DEMOTIONS; DESEGREGATION.

TRANSPORTATION

COURTS have clearly held that it is constitutional to authorize the expenditure of public FUNDS for the transportation of students. As a result, school districts may own and operate their own school buses, may contract with private operators, or may even reimburse parents for providing students the necessary transportation. In one case where the state STATUTE required that districts "provide or furnish transportation," a court held that districts could pay parents residing in out-of-the-way places a mileage rate in lieu of providing transportation.[17]

Some states require school districts to provide transportation while others either make it optional or make it mandatory only under certain conditions. Districts may also be required to provide transportation for the purposes of racial integration or as a RELATED SERVICE to students with handicaps. (See BUSING; EDUCATION FOR ALL HANDICAPPED CHILDREN ACT OF 1975.)

If state law makes it mandatory for districts to provide transportation, all students must be treated equally. The fact that a road is not safe to travel will not relieve a district of its responsibility. For example, one court heard a case involving elementary school children who lived on a two-mile dirt road that crossed a creek four or five times. The court reasoned that the children had the right under state constitution to a "thorough and efficient" education and held that to deny the students their right because they live on an inconvenient road would be to deny them EQUAL PROTECTION of the law.[18]

State law may, however, mandate the free transportation of students in one district and mandate that students in other districts pay a fee for

---

[17]*State v. Board of Educ. of Unified School Dist. /428*, 647 P.2d 329 (Kan. 1982).

[18]*Collins v. Ritchie*, 351 S.E.2d 416 (W. Va. 1986).

transportation if there is no constitutional right to transportation. For example, in a case heard by the Supreme Court of the United States, the state statute required that only certain districts provide free transportation services. Other districts were required to assess a tranportation FEE. Parents of students residing in a district assessing a fee filed suit claiming that their children's equal protection rights were being violated. The United States Supreme Court held that, where there is no statutory right to free transportation, the district was not required to provide it.[19]

Some statutes mandate transportation only for students who live within various designated distance limitations. These limitations are easily susceptible to varying interpretations and, therefore, lawsuits in which distances not within the designated limitations are called "unreasonable," "remote," or "inaccessible." In these instances, by questioning the reasonableness of the board ruling, the courts will determine whether the SCHOOL BOARD has abused its discretion. The result will depend on the individual facts and circumstances, and the court will consider such things as age of the pupils, weather conditions in the area, traffic hazards and conditions, and width and surface of the road required to be traveled.

In cases of transportation of private and parochial school students, the legal issues generally center on the constitutionality of spending public funds in support of RELIGION. Although furnishing transportation to private and parochial school students benefits their schools to some extent, such expenditures have been upheld on the bases of the CHILD-BENEFIT THEORY. This theory holds that, when the main benefit inures to the child, the secondary benefit to the school can be disregarded and such an expenditure will be upheld. It should be noted that, unless the state statutes explicitly require it to do so, the school board cannot be compelled to furnish transportation to private or parochial school students. In addition, some state laws forbid school boards to provide such transportation. (See PRIVATE AND PAROCHIAL SCHOOL AID.)

In certain instances, districts are responsible for the safety of the students the districts transport. For example, one court held that a district was liable for injuries suffered when the district placed a bus stop in an area where students were exposed to unnecessary dangers.[20] In this case, the district created a bus stop on a grassy area near a 55-mph highway. There were no signs or traffic signals indicating either a bus stop or an intersection even though there was an uncontrolled intersection 200 feet from the bus stop. A twelve-year-old boy was killed when a vehicle attempting to pass the slowing bus swerved widely to avoid being hit by a vehicle turning onto the highway from the cross-street.

---

[19]*Kadrmas v. Dickenson Public Schools*, 108 S. Ct. 2481 (1988).

[20]*Duval County School Board v. Dutko*, 483 So. 2d 492 (Fla. App. 1986).

Districts may suspend students from riding a bus for a violation of RULES. In one case, a court upheld the suspension of an entire bus route even though the suspension deprived students who did not take part in the vandalism.[21] However, caution needs to be exercised when suspending bus transportation. In one case, a BUS DRIVER, in contravention of district policy, suspended a student without notifying the school or the student's parents. The boy did not tell his parents and instead the following day rode his bike to school. On the way, he was involved in an accident. A court held the bus driver 99 percent liable for the boy's injuries and the district 1 percent liable.[22]

TRESPASS TO PERSONAL PROPERTY

Trespass to personal property is the intentional taking or interfering with the use, possession, or physical condition of the personal property of another without authority to do so. This is an intentional TORT. There are seldom any suits brought for this TORT as the result of school activities. Nevertheless, it is one of the most common torts committed by teachers, administrators, and students. At the end of every school year, teachers can be seen emptying various articles from their desks and closets. These articles—squirt guns, comic books, and slingshots—all have been confiscated from students and all are wrongfully detained. The personal property of a student is his or her own to keep. A teacher or administrator cannot interfere with that possession unless the property in question is interfering with the educational process. Even when the property is interfering with the educational process, the teacher or administrator only has the authority to retain temporary possession. Thereafter, the property must be returned to its rightful owner.

Trespass to personal property is not usually particularly serious. The articles involved are often of little value, and no one complains over the confiscation. However, it is still wrong to keep what is not one's own. The teacher or administrator, therefore may not detain the property for an unreasonable period of time nor may he or she damage the student's property. Usually, at the end of the school day, it is proper to return the goods to their owners. The educator may instruct the students not to return the articles in question to school; but, if the articles are returned, there is still no right to keep them. If the students bring the squirt guns or

---

[21]*Rose v. Nashua Board of Educ.*, 679 F.2d 279 (1st Cir. 1982).

[22]*Toeller v. Mutual Service Casualty Ins. Co.*, 340 N.W.2d 923 (Wis. App. 1983).

other "banned" articles back again, the remedy is not to keep the property but to resort to other disciplinary measures.

In referring to the wrongful detention of personal property, we are talking about personal property which is legal to possess. If a student brings contraband (property which is illegal to possess) to school, the teacher or administrator has the legal right and duty to take the property and may turn it over to the proper authorities. This type of property should not be given back to the student because he or she has no right to possess what is illegal. Cigarettes, pocketknives, lighters, and things of that nature are not necessarily illegal to possess. It may be illegal to sell cigarettes to minors; but, in nearly all states, it is not illegal for a minor to possess them. Lighters and certain pocketknives can be lawfully possessed.

There are times when, although a teacher knows that he or she has no right to deprive a student of his or her property, the teacher considers it to be dangerous or wrong to return the confiscated articles to the student. Under these circumstances, it is reasonable to inform the child's parents that the school does not allow students to carry knives, cigarettes, etc., at school. School officials could also ask the parents to come to discuss the matter and return the "banned" articles at that time. If the student continues to bring the "banned" but legal articles to school, harsher disciplinary measures should be taken. However, keep in mind that there is no right to permanently deprive the owner of possession of legal items.

See also SEARCH AND SEIZURE.

TUITION

Tuition is a payment charged for instruction. The legal residence of a student is the RESIDENCE of his or her parents or legal guardian. A student is entitled to attend school in the district of his or her legal residence without paying tuition.

Nonresident Tuition

Here, the issue is whether a child living in one school district may attend school in another district without paying tuition. Some state STATUTES cover this problem; but, if no such statutes exist, the local SCHOOL BOARD has the discretion to do as it wishes. The board does not have to allow a nonresident to attend the district's schools in the absence of statutes to the contrary and, therefore, may condition admittance upon payment of a reasonable tuition.

Summer School Tuition

Summer school, as used in this context, is meant to refer to a session of school which is offered in excess of the minimum school program. The constitutions of most states require their state legislatures to provide free and uniform systems of public schools. However, no provision is made in state constitutions for summer schools; therefore, most districts charge tuition for summer sessions. One court upheld summer session tuition, reasoning that, since summer school was in addition to the mandated 185-day school term, there was no duty to make it available free of charge.[23]

Tuition Reimbursements

Tuition reimbursements and tax credits to parents of PRIVATE SCHOOL students have been found unconstitutional by the United States Supreme Court. However, in 1983, the Supreme Court upheld the constitutionality of a Minnesota statute that provided for deductions in state income tax of actual expenses incurred for tuition.[24] In upholding the program, the United States Supreme Court observed that the deductions were available to all parents of school-age children, not just parents whose children attended private religious schools. The court declined to attach significance to the fact that Minnesota's public schools do not charge tuition and that 96 percent of the children attending private schools attended religiously-affiliated institutions. (See PRIVATE AND PAROCHIAL SCHOOL AID.)

College Tuition

The state may charge tuition for students attending state colleges. One of the more controversial issues has been that of charging a higher tuition to out-of-state students than resident students are charged. Such a difference in the amounts payable has been upheld by the COURTS. However, once a student establishes a residence in the state, the out-of-state tuition fee may no longer be charged. A state may not permanently classify a student as being out-of-state merely because his or her residence was not within the state at the time of admission. As the Supreme Court of the United States said when it struck down Connecticut's regulations which permanently classified students as "out-of-state" if their residence was not in Connecticut when they applied for admission:

---

[23]*Washington v. Salisbury*, 306 S.E.2d 600 (S.C. 1983).

[24]*Mueller v. Allen*, 463 U.S. 388 (1983).

...permanent irrebuttable presumption of nonresidence...is violative of the Due Process Clause, because it provides no opportunity for students who applied from out of State to demonstrate that they have become bona fide Connecticut residents.[25]

In making a determination of whether or not a previously out-of-state student has become a bona fide resident, the state may consider all relevant factors, such as voter registration, state in which tax returns are filed, property ownership, whether the student remained in the state year-round, driver's license, marital status, vacation employment, car registration, and so forth.

See also EDUCATION FOR ALL HANDICAPPED CHILDREN ACT OF 1975 for a discussion of districts' responsibility to pay tuition, including summer school tuition, for handicapped students in certain situations; FEES.

---

[25]*Vlandis v. Kline*, 412 U.S. 441 (1973).

U

UNDERGROUND NEWSPAPERS

See ACADEMIC FREEDOM; CONSTITUTIONAL LAW; LIBRARY CENSORSHIP; OBSCENITY; SCHOOL PUBLICATIONS.

UNIFORMS

See APPEARANCE; CURRICULUM; RULES.

UNION SECURITY

Union security in the public schools really should be termed organizational security. Organizational security is the protection of the employee organization's status by provisions in an agreement establishing a closed shop, AGENCY SHOP, or maintenance-of-membership. Depending on state law, SCHOOL BOARDS can grant exclusive privileges to the certified bargaining unit that is denied to rival unions or individual employees. Some of these union security rights are: access to school facilities, DUES CHECK-OFF, internal school mailings, and allowance of paid time off for representational activities. Whether exclusive rights grants are discriminatory depends on the circumstances of the grant and the subject matter.
See also COLLECTIVE BARGAINING.

UNIONS

See ASSEMBLY; COLLECTIVE BARGAINING; UNION SECURITY; and CATEGORICAL INDEX regarding Collective Bargaining and School Negotiations.

V

VACCINATION

Vaccinations necessary for the health and welfare of all students may be required as a condition of school attendance. If the parent objects, he or she would be in violation of COMPULSORY EDUCATION laws. The right to require vaccinations extends to private and parochial schools. In other words, if the state STATUTE requires vaccinations for smallpox or diphtheria, all schools must follow that directive, including the private or religious institutions.

In the absence of state statutes, a vaccination may be required in emergency situations such as an epidemic. Even without an emergency situation, it has been held in some states that schools may give vaccinations and may require students to be immunized against certain COMMUNICABLE DISEASES. In Pennsylvania, the courts held that mandatory tetanus shots as a condition to play interscholastic baseball did not impermissibly burden a student who opposed vaccinations on religious grounds.[1]

Generally, (1) each state legislature has the power to enact a law providing for vaccination which carries a penalty for noncompliance; (2) without complying with the statutory requirement of vaccination, a child does not have a constitutional right to schooling; and (3) religious objections have not, for the most part, prevented the enforcement of compulsory vaccination.

Without federal legislation, the state COURTS will determine how to enforce vaccination laws. Therefore, one should not expect complete uniformity, as exemplified by two decisions elicited by the New York and Mississippi courts.

---

[1] *Calandra v. State College Area School District*, 512 A.2d 809 (Pa. 1986).

The New York court upheld the New York statute which allowed as an exemption to inoculation (as a prerequisite of attendance in public school) those children whose parents were bona fide members of a religious organization and were able to substantiate the allegation that the parents had a genuine and sincere religious belief that was actively practiced and followed, which forbade such inoculation.[2] However, the Mississippi Supreme Court upheld the trial court's dismissal of a suit, reasoning that the statute which required that children be immunized against certain diseases before admission to school was constitutional as a reasonable exercise of the state's police power and that the provision which provided an exemption to the vaccination requirement on the basis of religious beliefs was an unconstitutional denial of EQUAL PROTECTION.[3] Again, a parent cannot rely on the statutory religious[4] exemption merely because the parent is "philosophically opposed" to immunization.[5]

See also MEDICAL SERVICES.

VICE-PRINCIPALS

The vice-principal is part of the administration and is not a part of the teaching staff while carrying out his or her administrative functions. He or she is considered an employee and not an officer of the SCHOOL BOARD. The vice-principal reports directly to the PRINCIPAL and is generally in charge of specific areas, such as student discipline. The vice-principal is liable for his or her own acts but not the acts of teachers unless the vice-principal knew or should have known of the potential tortious conduct.

See also GOVERNMENTAL IMMUNITY; NEGLIGENCE.

VOCATIONAL PROGRAMS

Money may be allocated to vocational programs without violating any constitutional provisions. Vocational education is a proper educational endeavor; but it is, by its very nature, one of the more hazardous activities

---

[2]*Maier v. Besser*, 341 N.Y.S.2d 411 (N.Y. 1972).

[3]*Brown v. Stone*, 378 So. 2d 218 (Miss. 1979).

[4]*Avard v. Dupuis*, 376 F. Supp. 479 (D.N.H. 1974).

[5]*Kleid v. Board of Education of Fulton*, 406 F. Supp. 902 (W.D. Ky. 1976).

carried on within the school system. Because of this, vocational education teachers need to be very cognizant of safety RULES. Before any student is allowed to use a machine, proper INSTRUCTION concerning the use of the machine must be given. These instructions must include rules of safety. Students not only should be required to pass an examination regarding each machine or activity to be pursued, but rules of safety must be impressed upon students; and, if a student later violates rules of safety, the student should be disciplined immediately.

Many vocational classes are overcrowded, and the students, lacking proper SUPERVISION, are inclined to present disciplinary problems. In addition, many machines, torches, and other instruments are present which can cause serious damage to students. As with all teachers, the vocational education teacher has a duty of supervision. Due to the nature of the class, this duty of supervision is even higher than that of the ordinary teacher. If the classroom is overcrowded, the duty cannot be properly fulfilled. Therefore, if this situation exists, it is recommended that the teacher notify the administration of the hazardous condition. The teacher should keep accurate records of incidents relative to safety; if he or she properly documents the situation, the classload should be lowered without difficulty. If the classload is not lowered and the teacher has acted in a REASONABLE AND PRUDENT manner under the circumstances, LIABILITY for any injuries would shift to the ones responsible for letting the hazardous condition exist.

In many places, the machines or instruments used are hazardous in themselves in that they do not meet the minimum standards of safety as set forth in state STATUTES or state administrative standards. If a student is injured in this situation, he or she would have two causes of action. One would be for NEGLIGENCE, and the second would be for violation of state law. Realistically, this would almost impose strict liability automatically; the school district and the teacher would have few, if any, defenses. Therefore, in such a situation, these machines must be replaced or the class should be cancelled.

See also GOVERNMENTAL IMMUNITY.

VOUCHERS

Although the idea of a voucher system to fund education has been proposed in Congress and many state legislatures, to date no extensive experiment with the system has been implemented.

The basic form of a voucher plan is to provide each student's parent or parents with a voucher for a designated amount which could be redeemed for admission into any school which is accredited and is participating in the voucher system. The schools would then present their vouchers to the state board of education for reimbursement. Public, private, parochial, and experimental alternative schools would all be eligible for possible accreditation and participation in the voucher system.

Proponents of educational voucher plans believe that decisions regarding education are better made by parents than by bureaucrats. Proponents of these plans also believe that capitalistic competition amongst a variety of public and private educational institutions is healthy. Supporters of vouchers believe that providing the consumer of education with a choice in the type of education his or her child receives satisfies the demands of accountability and quality. Opponents of the voucher system feel that vouchers would facilitate segregation and DISCRIMINATION, constitute a violation of the constitutional requirement of separation of church and state, and pose a threat to the stability of public school systems (which do not have complete control over resources, funding, and personnel).

Parochial schools would be allowed to participate in the voucher system because failure to include them would perhaps be an unconstitutional discrimination against RELIGION since the state is required to remain neutral. However, from a realistic standpoint, parochial schools might be allowed to participate not because of the Constitution but because of pressure to increase the forms of aid to alleviate the financial problems being faced by parochial schools. If parochial schools are forced to close, many states and local school districts would face a serious financial crisis by being required to absorb the thousands of parochial school students into an already crowded public school system. Whether or not a voucher system would violate the FIRST AMENDMENT's establishment of religion clause by being viewed as an impermissible state aid in support of religion was addressed by the United States Supreme Court in 1986. The court ruled that vocational rehabilitation aid given to visually handicapped persons could be used to provide ministry education at a Christian school of their choice. Since the aid went directly to the student, the aid was not considered government subsidy to religious schools.[6]

The state cannot levy taxes to support religious activities or institutions. However, the United States Supreme Court has ruled that state tax deductions for educational expenses does not violate the establishment clause.[7] Various theories have been used to uphold certain other forms of

---

[6]*Witters v. Washington Dept. of Services for the Blind*, 474 U.S. 481 (1986).

[7]*Mueller v. Allen*, 463 U.S. 388 (1983).

indirect state aid to parochial schools. (See CHILD-BENEFIT THEORY; FUNDAMENTAL INTEREST THEORY). These theories could perhaps be used to validate a voucher system since the vouchers go directly to the family to encourage educational choices.

WAIVER

Legally, waiver is the voluntary intentional relinquishment of a known legal right, claim or privilege. Once there is a clear decisive waiver of that right, the party is not permitted to repudiate or recapture what was waived. Many cases turn on this important point. For example, in contract RENEWAL cases, the local board must give the teacher notice of NON-RENEWAL on or before a certain date. If notice is not given, the teacher or administrator must properly accept the CONTRACT on or before a certain date and the right of nonrenewal is waived by the board.

WITNESSES

Witnesses are people who testify under oath (or affirmation) at an administrative hearing or COURT trial to what the witness saw or heard, or testify as to personal knowledge of certain facts and issues. Generally, the fundamental rights of DUE PROCESS allow the opposing party to confront the witnesses against him or her and CROSS-EXAMINE witnesses with questions.

See also BURDEN OF PROOF; SELF-INCRIMINATION; SILENT, Right to Remain.

WORKSHOPS

Workshops are "in-service" type programs specifically designed to help educators become more aware of certain areas within education and to keep their knowledge up to date. Teachers and administrators may be required to attend a certain number of workshops or earn credits through college courses or in other prescribed ways. The number of required workshops must be reasonable and may be at the educator's expense.[1] Continuing education requirements adopted by the local SCHOOL BOARD are based on the reasonable belief that, if a teacher or administrator refreshes or broadens his or her knowledge, then the quality of performance will improve.

Finding no constitutional flaw in the continuing education requirement, the United States Supreme Court unanimously upheld the dismissal of a tenured teacher who refused to comply with the completion of in-service courses.[2]

See also CERTIFICATION; SCHOOL BOARDS.

---

[1] *Guthrie v. Taylor*, 185 S.E.2d 193 (N.C. 1971).

[2] *Harrah Independent School District v. Martin*, 440 U.S. 194 (1979).

Index

A

Ability grouping, *1*, 188, 189
Abolition of positions, *1–3*, 341, 346
Abortion, *3–4*
Absence. *See* Compulsory education; Leaves of absence
Absence from class, liability, *5*
Absence from class, teacher, 334
Academic freedom, *6–9*, 16, 30, 92, 176, 198, 227
Academic penalties, students, *9–10*, 122
Accidents. *See* Negligence, torts
Achievement testing. *See* Competency testing, students
Accountability, *10–11*, 96
Acquisition of property. *See* Buildings; Property
Activity funds, 11, 41
Administrative agencies, *11–13*, 108, 279
Administrators. *See* Constitutional law; Principal; Superintendent; Vice Principal
Age Discrimination in Employment Act. *See* Discrimination
Agency fees. *See* Dues checkoff
Agency shop, *13*
Agent, 14, 152, 262
Aides, teacher. *See* Teacher aides
AIDS. *See* Communicable diseases
Amendments. *See* Constitutional amendments
Annual or long-term contracts, *14–15*, 338
Anti-evolution statutes, *15–16*
Antisubversive laws, *16–17*
Appearance, administrators and teachers, *17–19*
Appearance, students, *19–22*, 92
Arbitrary, capricious or discriminatory action, *22–25*, 33, 63, 68, 69, 92, 145, 208, 214, 222, 241, 248, 259, 262, 279, 294, 331, 338

Arbitration, *25–26*, 72, 73, 151, 176, 209, 321
Assault, *26–27*, 47, 66, 104, 191
Assembly, student right of, *28–31*, 36, 306, 322
Assignment to grade and schools, students, *32–33*, 345
Assignments, nonclassroom, *33–35*, 243, 335
Association, Freedom of, *35–40*, 74, 92, 123, 230, 322, *See also* Antisubversive laws; Assembly; Constitutional law; Loyalty oaths)
Assumption of risk, 40, 221
Athletics, funds. *See* Activity funds; Funds
Athletics, participation requirements, *41–42*
Athletics, required participation in. *See* Curriculum
Athletics, sex discrimination in, *42–45*, 70
Attendance of pupils. *See* Compulsory education
Attrition. *See* Abolition of positions; Tenure
Authority, parents. *See* Parental authority
Authority, school board. *See* School boards
Authority, teachers. *See* In loco parentis; Rules
Automobiles, *45–46*

B

Bargaining. *See* Collective bargaining; Meet and confer bargaining laws
Battery, 27, *47–49*, 66, 104, 191
Beards. *See* Appearance; Constitutional law
Bible reading, *49–51*, 110, 276
Bids. *See* Buildings; Construction
Bilingual/bicultural, *51–52*
Boards of education, *52*
Bonds, *53–54*, 209, 270
Borrowing. *See* Bonds
Boundaries. *See* Reorganization
Budgets. *See* Funds
Buildings, 36, *54–58*, 170, 196, 221, 256, 270, 271, 290, 316, 332

Burden of proof, 20, *58*, 116, 120, 130, 243
Bus drivers, *59*, 348
Busing, *59–60*

C

Capacity, *61–62*, 96
Censorship. *See* Academic freedom;
    Constitutional law; Obscenity; Library
    censorship; School publications
Certification, 10, 34, *62–64*, 83, 95, 96, 214,
    258, 325
Certiorari, writ of, *64*, 105, 301
Chief state school officer, *65*, 325
Child abuse, *65–66*, 250
Child benefit theory, *66–67*, 253, 347
Church-state relations. *See* Bible reading;
    Prayers; Private and parochial school Aid;
    Religion; Shared-time
Civil Rights Act of 1871, 4, *68–69*, 114, 311
Civil Rights Act of 1964, *69–71*, 122, 145, 207,
    243. *See also* Maternity leave
Closed shop. *See* Agency shop; Union security
Collective bargaining, 3, 10, 13, 26, 35, *71–76*,
    94, 126, 195, 209, 212, 213, 222, 280, 303,
    308, 313, 321, 341
Commencement exercises, 74, 121
Commissioner of education, 77
Common law, *78*, 91, 96, 121, 244, 260, 283,
    298, 320, 324
Common schools, *78*
Communicable diseases, *79–80*, 210, 355
Comparative negligence, *80–81*, 103, 221
Competency testing, students, *81*, 121
Compulsory education, 4, *82–84*, 187, 193,
    203, 204, 258, 355
Condemnation. *See* Property
Conflicts of interest, 39, *84*, 124, 278, 292
Consolidation *See* Reorganization
Constitutional amendments of the United
    States, 2–4, 15, 20, 23, 28, *85–88*, 153, 163
Constitutional law - teachers and
    administrators, *91–93*, 100, 230, 237
Constitutional law - students, 3, 4, *88–90*, 163,
    237
Construction. *See* Buildings
Contempt of court, *93*, 321
Continuing contracts, *93–94*, 128, 222, 257,
    338
Continuing education. *See* Workshops
Contracts, 13, 26, 34, 35, 61, 62, *94–102*, 113,
    118, 126, 151, 152, 176, 202, 206, 209, 222,
    228, 230, 244, 245, 247, 274, 278, 279,

Contracts (*cont.*)
    289, 295, 299, 308, 314, 321, 335, 361
Contracts, construction. *See* Buildings
Contibutory negligence, 80, *103*, 221, 244
Controversial matters, right to teach. *See*
    Academic freedom; Constitutional law;
    Curriculum
Corporal punishment, 27, 48, 66, *104–105*,
    122, 153
Court organization—federal, 20, *105*
Court organization–state, *105–108*
Cross-examination, *108*, 361
Curriculum, 24, 28, 51, *108–111*, 161, 164, 188,
    197, 217, 231, 237, 258, 259, 277, 286,
    296, 297, 301, 303, 310, 332

D

Damages, contracts, 5, 68, 98, 101, *113–114*,
    119, 126, 173, 202, 221, 240, 274, 291, 311,
    326, 328, 341
Debts, authority of school to incur. *See* Bonds
Decertification, *115–116*, 291, 325
Defamation, *116–117*, 191, 237, 329
Defendant, 58, 81, 103, 115, *118*, 166, 172, 235,
    245
Demonstrations. *See* Assembly, student right of
Demotions, *119–120*, 126, 150, 341, 346
Desegregation, 146, 346
Detention, *120*, 122, 141, 153, 160.*See also* False
    imprisonment
Diplomas, 77, *120–121*, 188,
Discharge of teachers. *See* Contracts; Due
    process; Tenure
Discipline, students, *121–122*. *See* Academic
    penalties; Authority; Due process;
    Expulsion; Negligence; Rules
Discretion, school board. *See* School boards
Discretionary act/authority, 52, 121, *122–123*,
    169, 214, 281, 289, 341, 343, 358, 291, 293,
    297
Discrimination. *See also* Arbitrary, capricious
    or discriminatory action
Dismissals. *See* Arbitrary, capricious or
    discriminatory action; Contracts; Due
    process; Privacy
District reorganization. *See* Reorganization
Donations, acceptance of, *124*
Dress, manner of. *See* Appearance;
    Constitutional law
Drug testing, *124–125*
Drugs. *See* Search and seizure
Dual enrollment. *See* Shared-time

Due process, 3, 13, 69, 92, 96, 104, 108, 119, *125–132*, 146, 153, 204, 207, 223, 229, 230, 241, 246, 259, 261, 274, 278, 288, 298, 310, 316, 322, 332, 338, 341, 345, 361

Dues checkoff, 13, *132*, 321

Duties of teachers. *See* Contracts; Negligence

E

Education for All Handicappd Children Act of 1975, 80, *133–143*, 153, 189, 202, 209, 273, 329, 345, 346

Educational Amendment Act of 1972. *See* Athletics, sex discrimination in

Eighth amendmnent. *See* Constitutional amendments

Elementary and Secondary Education Act of 1965, 70, *143*

Emancipated students, *143–144*

Eminent domain. *See* Property

Emotional distress. *See* Intentional infliction of emotional distress

Employee organizations, right to join. *See* Assembly; Collective bargaining; Constitutional law

Enjoin, *144*, 262

Equal Access Act of 1984. *See* Buildings, use; Prayer; Bible reading

Equal Employment Opportunity Commission, (EEOC). *See* Civil rights act of 1964; Discrimination; Equal protection

Equal Pay Act, 119, 122, *145*

Equal protection, 63, 70, 122, *146–149*, 204, 207, 241, 285, 306, 312, 322, 341, 346, 356

Equipment, 24, *149–150*, 176, 317, 332, *150–152*, 296, 334, 345

Evaluation. *See also* Accountability

Evolution. *See* Anti-evolution statutes; Religion

Executive sessions, school board. *See* School boards

Exhibits, *152*

Express authority, 53, 54, *152*, 185, 231, 297

Expulsion of students, 4, 110, 122, 126, 141, *152–156*

Extracurricular activities. *See* Assignments, nonclassroom; Athletics; Constitutional law; Fees; Negligence

F

Factfinding, 25, 73, *159*, 321

Fair-share expenses. *See* Dues checkoff

False imprisonment, *159–160*, 191

Federal aid to education. *See* Civil Rights Act of 1964; Constitutional law; Education for all Handicapped Children Act of 1975; Elementary and Secondary Education Act of 1965; Private and parochial school aid

Federal courts. *See* Courts

Fees, *161–162*, 217

Felony, *162*, 216, 248, 278, 327, 341

Field trips. *See* Governmental immunity; Negligence; Rules

Fifth amendment. *See* Constitutional amendments; Constitutional law; Self-incrimination; Silent, right to remain

First aid. *See* Medical services

First amendment. *See* Assembly; Association, freedom of; Constitutional amendments; Constitutional law; Religion

Flag salute, 8, 110, *163–164*, 237, 276

Foreseeability, 27, *165–166*, 221, 333

Fourteenth amendment. *See* Constitutional amendments; Constitutional law; Due process; Equal protection; Expulsion of students

Fourth amendment. *See* Constitutional amendments

Fraternities. *See* Assembly, student right of; Association, freedom of; Constitutional law; Religion; Secret societies

Free speech. *See* Academic freedom; Assembly, student right of; Bible reading; Constitutional amendments; Constitutional law; Obscenity; Prayers; School publications

Freedom of association, students, *35–40*

Fundamental interest theory, 146, *167*, 254

Funds, *167–170*, 196, 217, 259, 262, 278, 332

G

Gifts, acceptance of. *See* Donations

God, act of, *171*

Governmental immunity, 78, *172–175*, 196, 197, 260, 289, 291, 298, 311, 334

Graduate records examination. *See* Certification

Graduation requirements. *See* Curriculum; Diplomas

Grievances, 13, 24, 25, 95, 108, *175–177*, 295, 303, 321

H

Handicapped students. *See* Education for All
  Handicapped Children Act of 1975;
  Rehabilitation Act of 1973
Health programs. *See* Abortion; Athletics;
  Funds; Medical services; Sex education;
  Vaccination
Hearings. *See* Constitutional law; Due process;
  Expulsion of students; Open hearings;
  School boards
Hearsay, *179–180*
Home instruction. *See* Compulsory education;
  Private schools
Homeless students. *See* Residence, Students
Homework, *180*
Homosexuality, 29, *180–183*, 249

I

Immorality. *See* Constitutional law; Contracts;
  Due Process; Homosexuality; Privacy
Immunity. *See* Governmental Immunity
Immunizations. *See* Vaccination
Implied authority, 54, 77, 168, *185–186*, 231,
  290, 297, 306
Implied contract, *186*
Incompetency. *See* Categorical index,
  dismissals, grievances and tenure
Indebtedness. *See* Bonds
Individualized education programs. *See*
  Education for All Handicapped Children
  Act of 1975
Injunction, 28, 142, 144, *186*, 321
Injuries. *See* Corporal punishment;
  Governmental immunity; Intentional torts;
  Negligence. *Also see* Catgorical Index
In loco parentis, 66, 78, 104, 121, *187*, 197,
  304, 308
Inoculation. *See* Vaccination
In-Service. *See* Workshops
Instruction, *187–188*, 357
Insubordination. *See* Arbitrary, capicious or
  discriminatory action; Contracts; Due
  process; Privacy; Tenure
Insurance. *See* Funds; Governmental immunity
Integration. *See* Busing; Desegregation;
  Discimination
Intelligence testing, 1, *188–189*
Intentional infliction of emotional distress,
  190–191
Intentional tort, 26, 47, *191*

K

Kindergartens, 78, *193*

L

Labor unions. *See* Agency shops; Association,
  freedom of; Collective bargaining;
  Constitutional law; Union security
Lease of school property. *See* Buildings;
  Property
Leaves of absence, 39, *195–196*, 206, 232, 233,
  289,313
Lemon test. *See* Private and parochial school
  aid
Letters of intent. *See* Contracts; Nonrenewal;
  Renewals
Liability, 48, 171, 172, *196–197*, 202, 219, 232,
  260, 297, 326, 327, 337, 357
Libel. *See* Academic freedom; Constitutional
  law; Defamation; Records; School
  publications
Library censorship, *197–198*
Local school boards. *See* School boards
Lockers, searches. *See* Constitutional law;
  Search and seizure, unreasonable
Loyalty oaths, 16, *199–200*

M

Maintenance of property. *See* Buildings,
  maintenance
Malice, *201*
Malpractice, *201–202*. *See also* Accountability
Mandamus, 94, *202–203*, 266
Mandatory education. *See* Compulsory
  education
Marriage. *See* Married students; Maternity leave
Married students, 82, 146, *203–205*
Mass resignation, *206*, 320
Maternity leave, 123, 147, 195, *206–208*, 233
Mechanic's lien, *208–209*
Mediation, 25, 73, *209*, 321
Medical services, 168, *209–211*, 251
Medication, *211–212*
Meet and confer bargaining laws, *212–213*,
  303. *See also* Collective bargaining
Meetings, 61, 117, 213, 293
Mental and physical examinations, *213–214*
Mental distress, infliction of. *See* Intentional
  infliction of emotional distress
Mergers. *See* Reorganization

Merit pay, *214–215*. *See* Accountability
Methods, *215*
Military leave, 195, *215–216*
Ministerial acts, 121, *216*
Minutes, school board. *See* School boards, meetings
Misdemeanor, *216*, 327
Mitigation. See Contracts; Damages
Money. *See* Activity funds; Bonds; Fees; Funds
Moral turpitude, 116, *217*, 278
Municipal corporations, *217*
Music, *217*

N

Negligence, 5, 40, 48, 78, 80, 103, 114, 115, 117, 149, 160, 165, 168, 171, 172, 176, 187, 191, 197, 201, 207, 210, *219–221*, 245, 251, 260, 311, 333, 334, 338, 341
Negotiable issues. *See* Collective bargaining; Meet and confer bargaining laws; Scope of bargaining
Newspapers. *See* Academic freedom; Constitutional law; Obcenity; School publications
Ninth amendment. *See* Constitutional amendments
Non-public schools. *See* Private and parochial school aid; Private schools
Nonrenewal, 93, 96, 118, 126, 151, *222–223*, 257, 270, 279, 341, 361
Notice. *See* Contracts; Due process; Nonrenewal; Renewals; Tenure
Nurses. *See* Medical services

O

Oaths. *See* Loyalty oaths
Obscene literature. *See* Academic freedom; Constitutional law; Library censorship; Censorship; Obscenity; School publications
Obscenity, 8, *225–228*
Offer, contract, *228*
Officers. *See* Principal; School boards; Superintendent; Teachers; Vice principal
Omission, 220, *228–229*
Open hearing, 95, *229*
Oral contracts. *See* Contracts
Outside employment, *230*

P

Parental authority, 4, 197, *231–232*
Parental liability, 197, *232*
Parent volunteers. *See* Teacher aide
Parochial schools. *See* Private and parochial school aid; Private schools
Paternity leave, 70, 195, *232–233*
Peace corps leaves, 195, *233*
Performance bonds. *See* Buildings
Permission slips. *See* Assumption of risk; Detention; Negligence; Parental authority; Parental liability; Supervision
Personal property. *See* Trespass to personal property
Personnel records, 118, *234–235*
Petitions. *See* Grievance
Physical education. *See* Athletics; Curriculum; Negligence
Physical examinations. *See* Compulsory education; Medical services; Vaccination
Picketing. *See* Strikes
Plaintiff, 40, 50, 58, 81, 103, 201, 203, *235*, 240, 279, 312
Playgrounds, *236*
Pledge of allegiance, 8, 110, 163, *236–237*, 276
Police, *237–238*
Policies, school board. *See* School board, policies
Political activities. *See* Antisubversive laws; Association, freedom of; Constitutional law; Public office
Prayers, 50, *238–241*, 276
Pregnancy discrimination act. *See* Civil Rights Act of 1964; Maternity leave
Pregnant students, 146, *241–243*, 287
Preponderance of evidence, 58, 130, 139, 156, *243*
Press, freedom of. *See* Academic freedom; Constitutional law; Library censorship; School publications
Presumption, *244*, 297
Principal, 3, 24, 197, 240, *244–245*, 279, 328, 340, 356
Privacy, 20, 92, 124, 226, 234, *245–251*, 304, 310, 327
Private and parochial school aid, *251–257*, 347
Private schools, 67, 83, 141, 231, *257–260*, 341, 350
Probable cause. *See* Search and seizure
Probationary teachers, *260*
Profanity. *See* Academic freedom; Constitutional law; Obscenity; School publications

Property, acquisition, use, maintenance, disposal, 30, 55, 96, 255, *261–263*, 293, 294
Proprietary Acts, 173
Protests. *See* Assembly, student right of; Association, freedom of; Constitutional law; Strikes
Provisional certification. *See* Certification; Decertification
Proximate cause. *See* Negligence
Psychological injuries. *See* Intentional infliction of emotional distress; Intentional torts; Negligence
Public law 94-142. *See* Education for All Handicapped Children Act of 1975
Public office. *See* Conflict of interest
Publications. *See* Academic freedom; Constitutional law; Library censorship; Obscenity; School publications
Punishment. *See* Discipline; Rules

Q

Qualified privilege. *See* Defamation
Question of fact, 5, 165, 220, *265*, 266, 271, 297, 333
Question of law, 265, *266*, 297
Quo warranto, 266–267, 279
Quorum, *267*, 293

R

Race relations. *See* Desegragation; Discrimination
Ratification, *269–270*
Reasonable and prudent, 5, 41, 103, 165, 191, 219, 245, *271–272*, 333, 338, 357
Records. *See* Defamation; Education for All Handicapped Children Act of 1975; Personnel records; Student records
Reduction in force (RIF). *See* Abolition of positions
Regulations. *See* Expulsion of students; Rules
Rehabilitation Act of 1973, 42, 79, 133, *272–273*
Reinstatement, 126, *274*, 341
Related services, *275*, 317, 346
Released time, *270–271*
Religion, 4, 50, 82–83, 92, 122, 146, 167, 169, 237, 239, 251, 252, 259, 270, 271, *275–277*, 310, 343, 347, 358
Remedies. *See* Damages; Reinstatement

Removal from office, *278–279*
Renewals, contract, 94, 202, 274, *279–281*, 340, 361
Reorganization, 3, 120, 280, *281–283*, 345
Rescission. *See* Contracts
Residence - students, 143, *283–284*, 349
Residence - teachers, 285
Rules, 28, 45, 74, 92, 95, 110, 123, 124, 165, 186, 187, 196, 208, 213, 232, 241, 267, 269, *285–288*, 286, 294, 295, 299, 307, 314, 315, 324, 328, 338, 357

S

Sabbatical leave, 195, *289*
Safe place statutes, *289–290*
Salary schedules, *290*
Sanctions, 291. *See also* Collective bargaining; Meet and confer bargaining laws; Strikes
Sanctions, 74, 160, 181, 227, 288
Save-harmless statutes, 175, *291*
School boards, 2, 9, 18, 23–24, 26, 52–53, 54, 61, 63, 66, 73, 74, 79, 84, 92, 94, 95, 110, 113, 117, 121, 123, 124, 151, 153, 164, 166, 174, 176, 182, 195, 198, 199, 202, 203, 206, 210, 212, 213, 216, 217, 219, 222, 229, 231, 244, 246, 261, 266, 269, 277, 278, 281, 286, 289, 290, *291–299*, 300, 303, 306, 310, 315, 325, 326, 328, 331, 332, 340, 341, 345, 347, 349, 356, 362
School buildings. *See* Bonds; Buildings; Property
School calendar, *299*, 300
School closures, *300*
School district organization. *See* Bonds; Buildings; Reorganization
School funds. *See* Funds
School publications, *300–302*
Scope of bargaining, 73, *302–303*
Search and seizure, unreasonable, 125, 238, 265, *304–305*
Search warrant, *306*
Second amendment. *See* Constitutional amendments
Secret societies, 36, *306–307*
Segregation. *See* Desegregation; Discrimination
Self-Defense, *307*
Self-Incrimination, students, *307–308*
Seventh amendment. *See* Constitutional amendments
Severance payments, *308–309*

Sex, discrimination based on. *See* Athletics; Civil Rights Act of 1964; Constitutional law; Discrimination; Equal protection; Maternity leave; Paternity leave; Pregnancy discrimination; Pregnant students

Sex education, 111, *310–311*

Sexual abuse, *311*

Shared time, *312*

Shop classes. *See* Vocational programs

Sick leave, 195, 233, 308, *313–315*

Silent, right to remain, *314–315*

Sixth amendment. *See* Constitutional amendments

Slander. *See* Defamation

Smoking, 304, *135–316*

Sororities. *See* Secret societies

Sovereign immunity. *See* Governmental immunity

Special education, 275, *317*

Special meetings, school board. *See* School boards, meetings

Speech, freedom of. *See* Academic freedom; Assembly, student right of; Constitutional amendments; Constitutional law; Defamation; Flag salute; Pledge of Allegiance; School publications; Self-incrimination; silent, right to remain

Sports. *See* Athletics; Curriculum; Married students; Negligence; Sports-related injuries; Supervision

Sports-related Injuries, *317–318*

Spring notification. *See* Annual or long-term contracts; Contracts; Renewal; Tenure

Standford-Binet IQ test. *See* Intelligence testing

Stare Decisis, 318

State board of education. *See* Structure of the school system

State commissioner of public instruction. *See* Chief state school officer

State superintendent of public instruction. *See* Chief state school officer

Statute of limitations, 221, *319*

Statutes, 2, 36, 53, 54, 63, 65, 66, 91, 96, 116, 122, 126, 145, 150, 152, 162, 167, 181, 196, 206, 209, 212, 215, 222, 227, 229, 238, 253, 258, 261, 267, 269, 278, 279, 284, 290, 298, 299, 300, 308, 312, 313, *320*, 324, 328, 331, 337, 340, 344, 346, 349, 355, 357,

Strikes, 71, 73, 101, 206, 299, *320–324*

Structure of school system, 281, 285, *324–326*

Student liability, 197, *326–327*

Student records, *327–329*

Student rights. *See* Categorical index

Subpoena, *330*

Substantive law, *330*

Substitutes. *See* Teachers, substitutes

Subversive organizations. *See* Antisubversive laws; Assembly; Constitutional law; Loyalty oaths

Summer school, *330–331*

Superintendent, 24, 197, 216, 223, 240, 270, 279, 293, 296, 328, *331–333*, 340

Superintendent of public instruction. *See* Chief state school officer

Supervision, 5, 48, 96, 165, 219, 297, 311, *333–335*, 337, 357

Supplemental contracts. *See* Contracts

Suspension of students. *See* Expulsion of students

Suspension of teachers. *See* Contracts; Due process; Protection from arbitrary, capricious or discriminatory action; tenure

T

Talented and gifted students, *337*

Teacher aide, 14, 197, *337–338*

Tenth amendment. *See* Constitutional amendments

Tenure, 3, 10, 78, 95, 119, 126, 206, 208, 222, 248, 257, 274, 279, 289, 331, *338–342*, 346

Termination, teachers. *See* Contracts; Due process

Testing, student, *342*

Testing, teacher. *See* Mental and physical examinations; Merit pay

Textbooks, adoption of. *See* Anti-evolution statutes; Curriculum; Religion; School boards

Textbooks, free, 66, 161, 251, 253, *343–344*

Third amendment. *See* Constitutional amendments

Threats. *See* Assault; Battery

Title VII. *See* Civil Rights Act of 1964

Title IX. *See* Athletics, Sex discrimination in; Elementary and Secondary Education Act of 1965

Tort, 27, 48, 114, 115, 116, 159, 190, 197, 219, 232, 260, 326, 332, *344*, 348

Tracking of students. *See* Ability grouping; Assignment to grade and school

Transfers of students, 122, *344–345*